W9-AWI-303

———————— **Fifth Edition** ————————

THREE GENRES
The Writing of Poetry, Fiction, and Drama

STEPHEN MINOT
University of California, Riverside

PRENTICE HALL   Englewood Cliffs, New Jersey   07632

Library of Congress Cataloging-in-Publication Data

MINOT, STEPHEN.
  Three genres : the writing of poetry, fiction, and drama / Stephen
Minot.—5th ed.
      p.   cm.
  Includes index.
  ISBN 0-13-918467-8
  1. Creative writing. I. Title.
PN145.M5 1993
808'.02—dc20
                                                        92-20807
                                                            CIP

Acquisition editor: Phil Miller
*Editorial/production supervision and
  interior design:* Hilda Tauber
Prepress buyer: Herb Klein
Manufacturing buyers: Patrice Fraccio, Bob Anderson
Cover design: Barbara Clay

Copyright acknowledgments appear on pages 381–382,
which constitute an extension of the copyright page.

 © 1993, 1988, 1982, 1972, 1965 by Prentice-Hall, Inc.
A Paramount Communications Company
Englewood Cliffs, New Jersey 07632

Printed in the United States of America

10 9 8 7 6 5 4 3 2

ISBN 0-13-918467-8

Prentice-Hall International (UK) Limited, *London*
Prentice-Hall of Australia Pty. Limited, *Sydney*
Prentice-Hall Canada Inc., *Toronto*
Prentice-Hall Hispanoamericana, S.A., *Mexico*
Prentice-Hall of India Private Limited, *New Delhi*
Prentice-Hall of Japan, Inc., *Tokyo*
Prentice-Hall of Southeast Asia Pte. Ltd., *Singapore*
Editora Prentice-Hall do Brasil, Ltda., *Rio de Janeiro*

To Ginny—
who has patiently proofread more
drafts of this text than either of
us can remember

CONTENTS

Preface for Students   *ix*

Preface for Teachers   *xi*

Part One

The Writing of Poetry   *1*

  1 What Makes a Poem a Poem? *1*

  2 The Sources of Poetry *12*

  3 The Language of Poetry *23*

  4 Images *33*

  5 The Sound of Words *46*

  6 Traditional Rhythms *58*

  7 Unique Rhythms *70*

  8 Tone *80*

  9 From Units to Unity *91*

10 Writing Poetry on Your Own *104*

11 Poems for Study *111*

Part Two
The Writing of Fiction   *133*

12   The Creative Process *133*
13   The Sources of Fiction *141*
14   A Story by Melissa Pritchard:
      "Phoenix" *151*
15   Viewpoint: Strategies of Presentation *158*
16   A Story by Stephen Minot:
      "Sausage and Beer" *169*
17   Structure: From Scenes to Plot *177*
18   A Story by Deborah Joy Cory: "Three Hearts" *185*
19   Narrative Tension *192*
20   A Story by John Updike: "Man and
      Daughter in the Cold" *201*
21   Characterization *207*
22   Setting *219*
23   Implication: Metaphor, Symbol, and Theme *228*
24   Style and Tone *236*
25   Writing Fiction on Your Own *246*

Part Three
The Writing of Drama   *253*

26   Theater: A Live Performance *253*
27   A Play by William Saroyan:
      "Hello Out There" *259*
28   The Dramatic Plot *272*
29   Conflict *281*
30   Dramatic Characterization *288*
31   A Play by Louis Phillips:
      "Goin' West" *295*
32   Realistic and Nonrealistic Approaches *308*
33   Visual Impact *318*
34   Dramatic Themes *329*
35   The Voices of Comedy *338*
36   Writing Plays on Your Own *345*

Appendices *349*

A Submission of Material for Publication *349*
B Resources for Writers *358*

Glossary–Index *367*
Index of Authors and Titles *383*

PREFACE FOR STUDENTS

People write poetry, fiction, and drama for a number of different reasons. For some it is one of the best ways of understanding literary writing. Just as those who have played a particular sport become better spectators and those who play an instrument listen to music with greater awareness and pleasure, those who have written poems, short stories, or plays know what to look for in published work. They see more and as a result enjoy reading more. It is a resource that stays with them for life.

Others write because they hope it will become an avocation. They don't expect that it will ever become their true vocation, but they want to continue writing and perhaps to publish from time to time. They are like those who take up musical instruments seriously but without any intention of becoming professional musicians. Such individuals may have to set aside their creative work for long periods, but many return to writing whenever their schedules permit.

Then there is that small group of writers who are deeply committed to a particular genre and are determined to make it their central concern. They may have to enter other fields to earn income—especially at first. But they identify themselves as *poets, writers*, or *dramatists*. They have to fashion an individual lifestyle that will allow time for writing. They must also allot a portion of each day to reading contemporary fiction, poetry, or drama in a close, professional way. Once out of school, they attend readings and conferences. In short, they are immersed in their art—not just their own work but the best of what is being published as well.

Which group do you fall into? If you are just beginning, you may well be in a fourth group—those who aren't sure just how important writing will become in their lives. If so, stay open to what may develop. It may be that you will begin with high expectations and will discover after graduation that you are really a reader rather than a writer. If that happens you will have lost nothing because you will have become a far more perceptive reader than you were before. Or perhaps you will begin with a commitment to one genre and find that your real talent and interest lie in another. Writers, unlike ballet dancers, don't have to start at an early age. Anything is possible at any stage and at any age. There is no way of predicting how much talent and commitment will develop until you make an initial effort.

This book is designed for people in all four of these categories. And it should serve equally well whether you are in a creative writing class, informal writers' group, or working on your own.

I do, however, have one word of warning: You will not make full use of this book if you simply read it the way you might a history text. It is very important to keep applying the analysis of writing to literary samples and to your own work as well. Here are some specific suggestions that will help you draw the most from this text:

- In the poetry section, I frequently refer to poems that are printed in Chapter 11, "Poems for Study." Since these poems are used repeatedly to illustrate different aspects of verse, they are conveniently grouped in that chapter. *Take the time to turn to the poem in question each time.* Read it over carefully and see how the analysis applies. In this way you will come to understand the concepts much better and in the process will acquire an increasingly deep understanding of what that poem has to offer.

- Although I have limited the literary terms to those that are really useful in the practical business of analyzing and discussing poetry, there are a number which may be unfamiliar to those who have not studied verse. *Try to use these terms in your discussions.* If you need a quick review at some later point, *use the Glossary-Index* at the back of the book. These terms will help you to keep your analysis precise, and they will soon become a useful part of your active vocabulary.

- There are four stories in the fiction section and two complete plays in the drama section. Read them carefully as you come to them, but *don't hesitate to reread specific scenes whenever they are analyzed in detail.* As with poems, you will come to know these works well if you make the effort to review them regularly.

- In all three sections, try to *apply concepts and specific terms to literary samples not printed in this text.* Remember that your goal is not merely to acquire terms but to gain and understand literary concepts and to apply them to other work—including your own.

All this will take you a little more time than it would simply to read a textbook from beginning to end. But creative writing is not a skill that can be mastered in ten easy lessons. It is a slow process of growth—growth both in your understanding of what literature has to offer and in your ability to create new work with your own individual stamp.

PREFACE FOR TEACHERS

A student recently informed me that her father had used *Three Genres* as an undergraduate. Startled, I realized that this college sophomore was not yet born in 1965 when the first edition appeared. The text has clearly come of age.

In one sense, this fifth edition is essentially an outgrowth of the course I taught at Trinity College for many years. Two basic goals have remained the same: first, to help students appreciate and truly enjoy poetry, fiction, and drama in ways not often possible without actually experiencing the creative process; and second, to speed the development of those relatively rare students who will go on to make writing a true vocation.

In another sense, however, this edition of *Three Genres* is a new text, distinct from the previous editions with its own stamp. Although contemporary literature is not subject to the rapid fluctuations in style that dominate painting and popular music, it is nonetheless never static. This new edition keeps pace with the literary and pedagogical values of today to meet the needs of its users in the 1990s.

How does a writing text stay young? The answer lies partially with the author and partially with the response from readers. I have been fortunate in being able to alternate full- and part-time teaching, remaining active as a free-lance writer on the one hand and involved in classroom experience on the other. My present position as Chair of the Creative Writing Department at the University of California, Riverside gives me a valuable window into student response. In addition to teaching my own classes in creative writing regularly, I visit every class given in our program at least three times each year. I talk with students and colleagues daily about writing and about the teaching of writing.

Every institution attracts a slightly different type of student, so it is important not to tailor a text too closely to a specific type of student. My present experience in a mid-sized western university is balanced by more than two decades at two small liberal arts institutions in the East. This exposure to the varieties of student needs and abilities is augmented by written responses from teachers across the country. Now that the text has been used in 49 states and a few Canadian provinces as well, it has been tested in every conceivable sort of institution. Fellow teachers, students, and readers outside the academic world write and advise—many with specific suggestions. Their views are reflected in each new edition.

What's New in This Edition

In revising the poetry section, I relied heavily on a full and comprehensive review prepared by Steven Bauer of Miami University, Ohio, a distinguished poet with solid teaching credentials. Thanks in part to his suggestions, I have expanded the "Poems for Study" chapter, retaining most of those poems that readers have found helpful as illustrations of various poetic techniques and adding 14 new poems to provide greater variety. In addition, you will find a description of new formalism, a movement that has recently come into prominence.

A number of you have pointed out that having a chapter entitled "Rhythms of Free Verse" tended to exaggerate the separation between free and metered rhythms. This is particularly true in the 1990s, when a number of poets have been improvising freely with older verse forms, blurring the distinction between metered and so-called free verse. For this reason, Chapter 7 is now called "Unique Rhythms," a title that provides a helpful contrast with Chapter 6, "Traditional Rhythms."

As a pedagogic device, I include examples of what I have found helpful in class: composing inferior versions of lines from published poems as if they were early drafts. By adding marginal suggestions, I point out weaknesses and then provide the poet's actual version. This approach simulates the process of revision and encourages students to rework their own poems line by line.

In the fiction section, I have added stories by two young and highly talented authors—Melissa Pritchard and Deborah Joy Cory. Their language is contemporary and their subject matter is close to the experiences of many young writers. I have also included a longer story by John Updike, "Man and Daughter in the Cold." It is an excellent example of plotting, characterization, and the use of setting. In addition it serves both as an example for younger writers who may want to write from the point of view of a parent, and as an encouragement to mature writers who may have a rich background of parenting on which to draw.

Another improvement in Part Two is that a separate chapter has been devoted to figurative language, symbol, and theme (Chapter 23), whereas style and tone are now discussed in Chapter 24.

The most dramatic change in Part Three is the inclusion of the play *Goin' West* by Louis Phillips. This drama is a rare example of the use of farce to develop a complex and serious theme. Students accustomed to the vacuous satires often shown on television may be surprised to learn how comedy can be used to present serious issues.

In this connection, I have added an entirely new chapter on the technique of comedy and comic relief (Chapter 35). Comedy that is sophisticated in treatment and theme is a vastly underrated subject and sadly under-represented in undergraduate writing.

Another significant change is the use of boldface type in the text to highlight the literary terms that are defined in the Glossary-Index. Students should be encouraged to make use of this signal, refreshing their memories whenever they are uncertain about the meaning of a literary term.

The Instructor's Manual, available upon adoption of the text, contains suggestions for syllabuses as well as exercises for individual topics. I urge teachers to contact the publisher for a copy of this helpful resource which has been prepared especially for them.

I owe special thanks to my production editor, Hilda Tauber. Her skill, patience, and good humor are admirable and much appreciated.

My thanks also to all those who wrote and made suggestions—both positive and negative. Now, looking ahead, I invite teachers, students, and individuals working on their own to write to me care of Prentice Hall, Englewood Cliffs, NJ 07632. Let me know what is helpful in this fifth edition and, equally important, what is not. Because of the time involved in forwarding, my reply may take months, but I do answer every correspondent. In a very real sense, this text is a collaboration between the author and you, the readers.

1
WHAT MAKES
A POEM A POEM?

The four distinguishing characteristics of poetry: emphasis on the poetic line, heightened use of sound, poetic rhythms, and density. Simple versus sophisticated poetry. Using poetic conventions to achieve true originality.

Yes, but is it really a poem? This question keeps coming up whenever we discuss poetry—particularly contemporary work. But we rarely take the time to answer it. Defining poetry seems difficult because the genre includes such an astonishing variety of forms and approaches—from lengthy Greek epics to three-line haikus, from complex metrical schemes to the apparent formlessness of some free verse. And the definitions offered by poets themselves tend to reflect their own work.

In spite of all this variation, however, there are certain basic characteristics shared by poetry of all ages. These not only help to distinguish poetry from prose, they suggest special assets which have drawn men and women to this **genre** in almost every culture since before there were written languages. As readers, we have come to expect these qualities unconsciously. When they are missing, we may sense the lack without knowing exactly what is wrong. As writers of poetry, we depend on them.

The four fundamental qualities of **poetry** that distinguish it from **prose** are: concern for the **line** as opposed to the sentence, greater attention to the

sound of language, development of **rhythms,** and a tendency to create **density** by compressing both meaning and emotions.

As we shift from writing prose to writing poetry, the creative process itself shifts, dominated by these new concerns. When we evaluate a poem, either our own or someone else's, these aspects are what we examine. And when we revise, most of our efforts focus on one or more of these areas. Because they are central to both the creative process and to revision, each deserves a close look, both here and in subsequent chapters.

The Poetic Line

When you write prose, the length of the line is determined simply by the size of the paper you are using. If your work is published, the length of the line will be changed to fit the magazine column or book page, and you won't feel inclined to complain. Line length is not a part of the prose art form.

Not so with poetry. The length of the line is an essential part of the art form. For a printer to change it would be as outrageous as revising the wording itself. This first characteristic of poetry, then, is embedded in the very definition of the genre.

The importance of the **poetic** line is more than just a matter of definition. The line is for most poets the basic unit of composition. When we write prose, we naturally think in terms of sentences; but when we turn to poetry, we usually move line by line. Sentences still exist, but their importance is muted.

Every poem differs in its formation, but most move from one visual image to the next. As we write, we are guided more by association than by a logical sequence, particularly in early drafts. Lines tend to migrate through successive drafts. The final version will have a structure of some sort, but what was once the first line may end up as the fifth or the last, and the original ending may now be buried in the middle.

This does not mean that lines always end with a period. Both the sentence structure and the idea or feeling expressed frequently continue smoothly into the next line in what is called **enjambment,** or **run-on lines.** But the poet tends to compose line by line nonetheless.

The importance of the line in poetry actually preceded the written word. Epics like the *Iliad* and the *Odyssey* were apparently memorized and recited before they were written, and the rhythms of spoken lines were an essential aid to memorization. So was rhyme. This theory has been further supported by the discovery of lengthy Yugoslavian epics that even today have been memorized by individuals who can neither read nor write.

As soon as poetry was recorded on the page, there was less need for memory aids. But it has never lost its roots in the spoken language nor its reliance on the line. This is why most poets keep reading their work aloud as they compose so that they can hear as well as see the lines as they develop. It also accounts for the increasing popularity of poetry readings in which an audience can respond to the auditory aspect of the genre.

In the case of metered verse, the length of the line is determined at an early stage. **Meter** is based on a recurring pattern of stressed and unstressed syllables in each line, so the length of the line is determined in advance by the poet's choice of a metrical scheme. Writing a metered poem does not mean giving up control; it merely means that the choice is made at the outset rather than line by line. Meter is a structuring of natural speech rhythms, just as formal dance steps are agreed-upon patterns drawn from improvised dancing.

Free verse, like free-style dancing, has no such overall or preset structure, so the length and nature of each line is determined as the poem develops. But, again like free-style dancing, those variations can be extremely important. They can be used to control the pace of reading, to emphasize a key image, to establish rhythms, and sometimes even to give the printed poem as a whole a significant shape on the page.

Metered or free poems are organized by lines. For many poets, the patterning of lines becomes a kind of signature, an identifiable style by which his or her work becomes distinct from all others. In addition, a poet's control over the line provides control over white space—an element similar to what artists call negative space. White space consists of the areas where there are no printed words. It includes vertical space (margins) and horizontal space between lines. White space is important both in metered verse (as in the visual distinction between couplets and quatrains) and in free verse (as seen dramatically in E. E. Cummings' "Buffalo Bill's," which appears on p. 117).

Control over the line is one of the special attributes of poetry. It is also an absolute distinction that differentiates all verse from all prose. The degree to which the line becomes a unit of thought in the creation of poetry is highly significant.

The remaining three characteristics of poetry are not as absolute. One can find poems that may not make use of them all. But they are the qualities that we associate with the genre and that give us that seemingly intuitive sense that a particular work is indeed a poem.

Heightened Use of Sound

When we think of how poetry makes use of the sound of language, we are apt to think of **rhyme**. This is natural enough, since ending two lines with matching sounds is an unmistakable device. Jingles, nursery rhymes, and simple ballads almost always rhyme in an obvious way. But as we will see, rhyme can be muted to keep it from becoming obtrusive. In addition, there are two other ways to link words by sound: By matching the initial letter ("*g*reen as *g*rass") or through internal syllables which echo each other ("tr*ees* and leaves"). The paired sounds, of course, must appear in words that are close enough together so that the reader can hear the linkage.

"Fern Hill" by Dylan Thomas is a good example of an unrhymed poem that nonetheless ripples with sound linkages. The poet is describing with dreamlike phrasing his memories of his childhood on a beautiful farm. Here are three of the 54 lines. I have circled several of the linkages in sound.

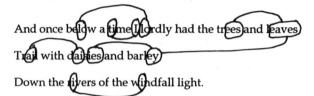

And once below a time I lordly had the trees and leaves

Trail with daisies and barley

Down the rivers of the windfall light.

The poem is printed in its entirety on page 125. You may wish to turn to it now and discover for yourself how intricate sound linkages can be, even in poetry that is not rhymed.

Prose can also appeal to the ear. We hear the effect of sound occasionally in oratory and sermons where repetition of initial sounds and repeated phrases create effects similar to those in the sample from "Fern Hill." Significant pauses sometimes provide an effect resembling that of a poem's white space on the page. But these techniques are rare in prose. The conscious, regular use of the sound of language is a characteristic that is far more common in verse.

Poetic Rhythms

Rhythm is clearly an aspect of sound, but it is more specifically defined as the beat. It is that aspect of sound we can imitate with clapping hands.

Because words—especially in English—are made up of **stressed** and unstressed syllables, it is a fairly simple matter to create regular patterns of these stresses. Some of those systems have become regularized as metrical schemes. Here are two lines taken from Richard Wilbur's "The Pardon":

In my kind world the dead were out of range

And I could not forgive the sad or strange

There are five stressed syllables (') in each line and five unstressed (ᴜ). If we group them in pairs of unstressed and stressed syllables, the rhythm sounds like ta-*tum*, ta-*tum*, ta-*tum*, ta-*tum*, ta-*tum*. Traditional patterns like this are called meter, and I will return to metrics in Chapter 6. Although these lines are unusual in their regularity, I use them here simply as an example of how language can be infused with a regular rhythmical system without making it sound artificial.

Although metrics dominated British and American poetry for some five hundred years, looser systems referred to as **free verse** have dominated the work of our own century. Now, starting in the 1980s and into the 1990s, there is a renewed interest in metrical schemes; this revival of metrics is generally referred to as the **new formalism**. Poets disagree, often vehemently, on whether or not this is a good development, but behind the debate is the fact that both approaches are ways of infusing language with rhythms not generally found in prose.

Nonmetrical rhythms are not unique to our own century. Samples of what we now call free verse can be found as far back as the Song of Songs, one of the books of the Old Testament.

Nonmetrical rhythms can be created in many ways. Some poets develop a recurring pattern based on the number of syllables in each line. The **haiku** is about the shortest form of this, with five syllables in the first line, seven in the second, and five in the third. "Fern Hill" by Dylan Thomas is a much more complex example, and I will return to both it and the haiku in Chapter 7. Other poets arrange long and short lines on the page in such a way as to highlight certain phrases or even trip the reader. The poems by Denise Levertov and E. E. Cummings in Chapter 11 are good examples. I will be analyzing these techniques in greater detail in Chapter 7, "Unique Rhythms." I mention them here simply as an overview of the range of rhythmical techniques available to the poet.

Density

The fourth and most subtle characteristic of poetry is **density**. Fiction is loose and wordy by comparison. One reason we read poetry more slowly and often repeatedly is that it usually implies much more than the immediate, surface meaning. Both the statement and the emotions are frequently layered with overtones. In fact, the resistance some feel to reading a new poem comes from the realization that it will probably take more work than does a short story or an article. With practice, however—and it does take practice—this more densely packed genre offers the reader special pleasures which make it well worth the effort.

When we turn to writing poetry, we may have to spend hours, often spaced over several days, going through draft after draft to achieve this density. The process may seem slow, but the reward comes when we have the feeling that we have said more in a few lines than a prose writer could have said in pages.

The fact that poems are concentrated does not mean they necessarily have to be short. Long epic poems like the *Iliad* and *Beowulf* deal with the mythic and historical events that unify a culture. In spite of their length, however, they still have greater density than prose. One cannot read them at the same rapid pace as a novel.

We still produce "epics" today—works that deal with major historical events and help to define our culture; but they are more likely to be produced as novels or films. Perhaps as a result, poets have turned increasingly to personal experience and the subtleties of private emotions. Even when they are making blunt social or political statements, they frequently draw on their own lives, creating impact through language charged with overtones.

One way poetry achieves density is by selecting words and phrases that are evocative. All words have a **denotative** meaning—their literal definition; but most also have **connotative** meanings as well—their associations. *Waking*, for example, denotes literally the end of sleep, but it can also imply (or connote) awareness, as in "I suddenly woke to the idea that...." *Sleep* has, in addition to its literal meaning, the connotation of death. So when Theodore Roethke begins "The Waking" (p. 117) with the statement, "I wake to sleep," we recognize, at least on second reading, the connotations and understand that he is describing how he plunges abruptly into life's experiences knowing full well that he is mortal and will ultimately die. Notice, however, that it took me 17 words to explain rather clumsily in prose what he communicated in four.

Poetry also achieves density through comparisons known as **similes** and **metaphors**, and through symbolic language—all of which will be discussed in Chapter 4. What concerns us here is the fact that what all these devices have in common is the capacity to make language suggest far more than its literal meaning.

As you start out to write poetry, the most fertile sources to consider will be your own feelings and experiences. What is important to you can be shared with others if you are truly honest. But poetry isn't simply a collection of feelings spilled out on the page like journal entries. Useful as journals are, their entries are more like grocery lists than a carefully prepared meal. A poem is an art form in itself, as is a painting or a musical composition. It is a verbal and auditory art which makes special use of the line, the sound of words, the rhythms of language, and the impact of genuine insight. These are not only the recurring characteristics of poetry, they are the special assets of the genre which poets keep working to develop. They form the core of the chapters that follow.

Simple versus Sophisticated Poetry

What is a *good* poem? This question invites a second: good for what? If a poem is intended for a mass market—as greeting cards are—it should have a positive message and be phrased in unvaried metrical lines with a regular rhyme scheme. Both the sentiments and phrasing should be familiar, not fresh or startling. To be "good," a mass-market poem should soothe, not probe.

Poems that are literary, however, are intended for readers who ask for an entirely different set of characteristics. These poems attempt to share personal experience and feelings honestly, to comment in a fresh manner on what it is to be human. They often probe deeply and can contain disturbing insights. The language is fresh and sometimes demanding. They may create unusual rhythms. Some such poems emphasize language itself, playing with words in complicated ways; others are more concerned with image and statement. Many assume that the reader has some previous familiarity with the genre and is willing to work a little.

There are problems with calling this kind of work literary. For one thing, the term seems a bit pretentious when applied to contemporary work. Besides, we then face the problem of defining *literary*. Our problems are compounded when we call it "good" poetry. This seems like a value judgment and implies that popular, mass-market poetry is "bad." It is as subjective as calling classical music "good" and popular music "bad." Too often, the terms lead to lengthy and pointless arguments.

The best solution is to borrow two terms from the language of science. To a biologist, simple forms of life are *simple* and complex forms are *sophisticated*. Thus, the bird is not better in any objective sense than the jellyfish, but it is far more sophisticated in that its potential as a living creature is greater.

In writing—as in nature—**simple** and **sophisticated** represent a scale with an infinite number of points between. The clever, comic verse of someone like Ogden Nash is certainly more sophisticated than most nursery rhymes, but less sophisticated than the poems of, say, Dylan Thomas. The works of an individual poet will also vary. Just because someone is able to write highly sophisticated work that is dense in meaning and complex in treatment does not mean that he or she can't also write comic verse or light, satiric pieces as well.

Should all poetry be sophisticated? Of course not. Millions enjoy not only greeting cards but volumes of simple verse. Others take pleasure in relatively simple ballads and inspirational poetry. Mass-market magazines publish simple verse as "fillers." Writing verse like that is an honest craft which requires practice. There are books to help those who want to succeed at it, but this is not one of them.

Sophisticated writing—poetry, fiction, and drama—is the subject of this text. Such work is by definition complex, but it is not necessarily cluttered or obscure. There are technically complex poems in which the intricacies of meter or repeated refrains become a kind of game; but these may end up being less sophisticated as poetry than a three-line haiku which manages to convey a wide range of suggestion. Complexity of meaning is not always achieved by complex language or metrical schemes.

Joyce Kilmer's "Trees" has been used many times in battles over what is and what is not "good" poetry. Let's sidestep that argument and take an objective look at what makes it a good example of highly popular simple verse. Here are the first three of its six stanzas:

> I think that I shall never see
> A poem lovely as a tree.
>
> A tree whose hungry mouth is pressed
> Against the earth's sweet flowing breast;
>
> A tree that looks at God all day
> And lifts her leafy arms to pray;...

What can we say objectively about these six lines? First, they clearly come from a poem. The length of the lines has been set by the writer, and some kind of regular rhythm can be heard simply by reading it aloud. In addition, the intentional use of sound is unmistakable: the lines are grouped in pairs which end with the same sounds to form rhyming couplets.

We can also say objectively that it is relatively simple verse. As with nursery rhymes, there is great regularity to the rhythm and to the rhyme. Without knowing anything about meter, one can detect four distinct beats to each line, and every rhyme is an exact matching of sound landing on a stressed syllable. This regularity creates a singsong effect.

As for the element of suggestion, that too is on a fairly simple level. Since trees are generally regarded as beautiful, the poet is repeating a commonly held view, a **truism**, rather than presenting a fresh concept or experience. Seeing the tree as a praying figure is somewhat **hackneyed**. We can't say that the poem is "bad" since it has given pleasure to millions of readers. But we can say that both the poetic techniques and the assertion it makes are on a simple level.

By way of contrast, here in its entirety is a two-line poem by Ezra Pound:

In a Station of the Metro

> The apparition of these faces in the crowd;
> Petals on a wet, black bough.

If this were printed in a solid line like prose, we would probably assume that it was merely a fragment—perhaps from a journal—and skip over it quickly. But because it is presented with a title and in two lines, we are assured at the outset that this is a poem and that it is intended to be read with some care. As with "Trees," its very shape on the page has influenced the way we will read it.

How seriously should we take it? After a single reading it is clear that this is not a comic jingle, nor is it a conventional statement about the beauty of nature. Something more sophisticated is going on. Perhaps, though, it is just a descriptive poem. Saying "just" suggests that such poems are not as sophisticated as those that have some kind of contrast or conflicting emotion. If this poem were, as it seems at first, merely a quick verbal snapshot of faces in the Metro (the Paris subway), then it would be more sophisticated than a jingle but not the kind of poem we need to spend much time on.

But what is being suggested with that word "apparition"? These faces have appeared suddenly, almost like ghosts. In what way might they resemble "petals on a wet, black bough"? Faces seen in the windows of a dark subway car come to mind. The car has abruptly arrived at the station and the faces inside remind the poet of petals.

Are there any more overtones? Petals that have been torn from blossoms by a rainstorm and plastered on the limb of a branch are being swept along by events over which they have no control. Does this apply to the passengers? The wording of the poem suggests that it does. This is how they appeared to the poet.

It would be a mistake to push the poem beyond this. There is nothing here to suggest forces of evil against good; the poet isn't calling on the passengers to rebel. Nor are we told that this is beautiful or pitiful. It is more as if the poet has seized our arm and said, "Hey, look at that!"

Except for this: The poet has not only caught our attention the way one might in conversation; he has created the scene as well. The suddenness of the "apparition," the fragile quality of those petals torn loose by the rainstorm, and the impact of the subway car highlighted by those three stressed syllables at the end—"wet, black bough"—all these help us to share both the visual impression and his reaction to it.

There is no rhyme in this poem, but like the lines from "Fern Hill" quoted earlier, it has a number of linkages in sound. "Crowd" and "bough" echo the same vowel sound in what is known as a **slant rhyme**. The second line has two linked pairs: the *e* sound in "petals" and "wet" and that heavy *b* in "black" and "bough." Unlike most prose passages, these lines are linked together not only with meaning but with sound.

The essential difference between these two poems is that Kilmer makes a conventional or commonplace assertion about trees in general, while Pound gives us a unique insight drawn from a very specific scene. In addition, the two poems represent a difference in technique which often distinguishes simple from sophisticated work: Kilmer employs rigid metrical and rhyme schemes, while Pound mutes both the rhythms and the sound linkages so that they do not become obtrusive. Even with the sonnet, a metered and rhymed form I will turn to in Chapter 9, rhythm and sound can be kept in the background.

Simple verse has its function. It soothes. Often it marks an occasion like an anniversary or a birthday in a simple, positive way. Who wants to be told he or she is impossible to live with at fifteen or getting cranky at 60? Sophisticated poetry, the subject of this text, has more complex and intricate rewards:

It gives pleasure through fresh insights and subtle use of form. When it speaks to us, we don't throw it away after the first reading. We savor it.

Conventions versus Individuality

Anyone who hopes to write sophisticated poetry wants to be fresh and original. Is there a danger, then, that studying the works of others and the long tradition of the genre will stifle our individuality? Actually, the opposite is true. Those who are not familiar with what the genre has to offer are apt to settle on just one approach and begin repeating themselves. Finding one's own unique voice requires being familiar with a wide range of poetic conventions.

An artistic **convention** is any pattern or device that is used in a large number of works. In popular music, for example, it is helpful to distinguish blues from bluegrass and rock from jazz. Artists distinguish realists from impressionists, surrealists, and minimalists. Within each category there are usually subdivisions. Being familiar with basic terms makes conversation about music or art more precise and enjoyable, even for the casual listener. Those who compose music or who paint, however, need to know a few more terms.

It is the same with poetry. Some terms describe the form. We will be examining the characteristics of the sonnet, the villanelle, and a technique called **syllabics**, among others. Other terms refer to type—narrative, lyric, and the like. Basic classifications like these are valuable for anyone who wants to read poetry with enjoyment. When we turn to *writing* poetry, however, we have to go a bit further. It helps to know how to use meter and the free-verse technique of spacing lines on the page, for example. Rhyme is an important technique even if you later decide not to use it, and so are those more muted effects achieved by linking words through similar-sounding syllables.

When poetry (some would prefer the term **verse**) is rigidly bound by conventions such as unvaried meter and blatant rhyme, stock themes, and overly familiar metaphors, we say it is conventional and simple. By **conventional** we mean that the conventions have become too rigidly used, too obvious. But all poetry—even the most sophisticated—is based on conventions. They are for the poet what notes, measures, and phrases are for the musician.

Our first task as poets, then, is to master the basic conventions of the genre. Only in this way can we achieve freedom as writers, for only when we are at ease with a particular technique are we free to decide whether to use it.

Take, for example, the various methods of creating rhythm. Which is "best"—to adopt strict meter or to work with a looser, improvised approach? The choice is ultimately yours. Practicing poets base their decisions partly on personal preference and partly on the needs of a particular poem. They can do this only when they are at home with various techniques.

The following nine chapters deal not only with the conventions of the craft but also with the ways in which you can mute those conventions and use them subtly. These chapters will also help you to learn directly from the limitless body of published poetry.

As you study the various options open to you and apply them to your own creative work, you will find yourself developing your own individual "voice" as a poet. This will reflect what is unique in you—your specific feelings and insights.

2
THE SOURCES OF POETRY

Four sources to avoid. Positive sources: personal experience, ambivalent feelings, speaking in other voices. Utilizing the five senses. The pleasures of language. Getting started.

Poems spring from every aspect of our daily lives and from our dreams as well. They are conceived in what we have seen, felt, and read about. Many reflect our innermost thoughts and emotions; others explore the lives of others. Most make use of language as language.

Before we turn to the vast array of positive sources, we should take a brief look at areas that should be avoided. A poem drawn from one of these infertile sources will probably end up stillborn no matter how much time and effort went into its composition and revision. Like the black holes in outer space, these sources consume everything around them—the poet's energies, class discussion time, and the good will of editors.

Here, then, are four sources that you should guard against. Avoid them and you will save yourself and your readers both time and effort.

• **Life-and-Truth-in-a-Nutshell.** Poems that begin with "Life is…," "Truth is…," or "Beauty is…" are in deep trouble from the start. There are three problems with these kinds of poems—and none of the three can be solved by revision. First, the subject is too large for most of us to handle in less than 400 pages of philosophical prose. Second, you are apt to start using **truisms**—conventional statements that repeat generally held convictions ("Life is tough," "Life is full of paradoxes"). Third, you may find yourself borrowing from nineteenth-century poets who did occasionally handle such topics but did it with considerable skill and insight. You run the risk of being imitative.

To put it more positively, poems are relatively small vessels and lend themselves to specific rather than general topics. Far better to work with something immediate and personal and let it *suggest* aspects of life rather than to begin with an unmanageably broad and abstract topic.

• **The-Blind-Puppy-on-the-Freeway**. No, it rarely gets this bad. But sentimentality can be a problem. The phrase that best explains why sentimentality undermines attempts at sophisticated poetry is *unearned emotions*. That is, the poem has taken shortcuts to generate our sympathy. It has not built a genuine situation. It has not earned the right to move us. Sentimentality is acceptable in greeting card verse (as long as it is bland) because such verse is not intended to be read twice. Like cotton candy, its effect vanishes almost instantly.

• **I-Bleed-I-Die-For-You!** How many times is this kind of sentiment, or something close to it, repeated in song lyrics? And are we moved? We hardly hear it.

But what if you really feel deep anguish at the moment of writing? The best tactic is to wait a year or so before trying to express it in verse. Self-pity is often unavoidable, but it makes pitiful poetry. Truly deep feelings of anguish can be woven into poetry, but you need time to gain some objectivity and perspective.

• **The-Impenetrable-Muddle**. Although this is not a problem for those fortunate enough to be encouraged to write poetry in the fourth and fifth grades, it is a frequent cause of difficulty for those in their twenties. The reader can barely penetrate the haze, trying to pick out an image here or a phrase there. The theme remains hopelessly hidden even after extensive and conscientious effort. In worst-case situations, the poet adopts an unassailable defense: "It means whatever you want it to mean." This is another way of saying that it has no meaning.

Ironically, one of the most common causes for obscurity comes from studying good but difficult poetry. We have all read poems by respected poets that we do not understand. It is easy to draw the conclusion that filling the page with vivid but indecipherable phrases is acceptable.

But put yourself in the place of your readers. If they are conscientious, they are willing to put more time and effort into your work than they would into a passage of fiction, but they expect something in return. They want you to meet them halfway. To leave a poem in indecipherable form is to relinquish one's role as a creative artist.

In other cases, obscurity in poetry is a form of shyness. Since poems often spring from our most personal feelings, we are occasionally reluctant to make them explicit. The solution, however, is not to hide the poem behind veils of obscurity but to alter the setting, the events, or the characters, so that you as poet are no longer personally identified with the poem. Frequently this can be done by presenting the poem through the words of a **persona**, a speaker who is clearly not the poet.

The third cause for obscurity is the most indefensible. It can be a conscious or unconscious cloak covering lack of insight or genuine feeling. To guard against this, ask yourself exactly what it is that you want to communicate. If it sounds banal or insincere in prose, it won't get any better dressed up in figurative language.

Personal Experience

One of the best ways to avoid all four of those problem areas is to draw on personal experience with courage and honesty. Consider, for example, those moments in which you have had an intense visual experience. Think of these as private visions. Something happened to you alone that has stayed in your memory, lodged there like a tune that keeps playing over and over in your mind.

Ezra Pound's "In a Station of the Metro" (p. 118) is such a poem. Vivid, provocative, precise, it is a way of sharing an instantaneous experience.

You don't have to have traveled abroad for such a visual impression. Maya Angelou clearly had such a flash of insight right in her own kitchen. Her poem "This Winter Day" (p. 124) describes an intense image that struck her while slicing vegetables for soup. Here is the first stanza:

> The kitchen in its readiness
> white green and orange things
> leak their blood selves in the soup.

Notice that she is not writing about kitchens or cooking in general. She doesn't begin with "Life is…" or even "Kitchens are places where.…" She places us in a particular place at a particular time in that opening line.

The idea that these vegetables were bleeding may have been the first impression, but that alone is not quite enough for a poem. At some point it occurred to her that the whole act of preparing a meal involves a "ritual sacrifice." The poem developed from there.

The language is fresh, the statement clear and brief. The writing may have taken many drafts over a long period, but the original insight, like Pound's "apparition," is the sort that comes as quickly as a camera's click.

Walt Whitman's "The Dalliance of the Eagles" (p. 115) is a similar kind of vision. The speaker looks up and sees two eagles "clinching" with "interlocking claws"—an astonishing moment of sexual union. Then they move on, each in separate ways. The poet observes this without comment, as if saying, Hey, look at that!

Sometimes personal experiences are not sudden flashes but more prolonged events. When a poem has a sequence of actions, a kind of plot, we call it **narrative poetry**. Maxine Kumin, for example, uses such an experience in "Morning Swim" (p. 113). There is not enough of a plot or interaction between characters to make a story in the fictional sense, but there is a sequence of events: In a dreamlike fantasy she walks out on a dock on a foggy morning, hangs up her bathrobe, and goes swimming. Once in the water she begins singing an old hymn, "Abide with Me," in time with her strokes. This sequence is more than a single visual image, but her sensation of a union with all of nature is clearly a kind of vision.

When you turn to that poem, notice that neither the word *nature* nor the word *God* is used anywhere. Yet both are implied through the specifics of the experience.

Ambivalent Feelings

Poems, like stories, often spring from relationships with other people: parents, brothers, sisters, cousins, best friends, lovers, strangers on the street, even enemies. What differentiates sophisticated treatment of these relationships from simple greeting card verse is the element of **ambivalence**. Ambivalence is a crucial concept both in fiction and in poetry. It comes from *ambi-*, meaning *both* (as in *ambidextrous*) and *valence*, meaning *value*. It describes a combining of two emotions—love and hate, fear and desire, courage and cowardice. In its true sense, it does not refer to alternating emotions but to that most common and often disturbing capacity to experience opposite emotions at the same time.

A simple poem usually reflects a single, simple emotion. It is often unadulterated love or unquestioning admiration. Joyce Kilmer, for example, expresses no reservations in "Trees." They are simply wonderful. Most sophisticated poems, on the other hand, contain at least two different emotions or attitudes that create what is referred to as poetic **tension**. Ezra Pound's petals on that wet, black bough are both beautiful and, as one thinks about their having been plastered there by a storm, subtly tragic.

Poems about human relationships usually have this same kind of mixed emotions. And in many cases the ambivalence is more dramatic. Robert Hayden's "Those Winter Sundays" (p. 113) is a good illustration. It recalls in harsh and realistic phrasing his hard-working and taciturn father on the family farm, a man who would never express his feelings. The narrator as a boy would "rise and dress / fearing the chronic angers of that house"—not exactly sentiments for a Father's Day card! Yet looking back, the persona recognizes his father's "austere" expression of love. The poem is charged with the contrast between his father's apparent severity and a hidden layer of warmth not recognized by the son until years later.

A similar ambivalence is implied in Michael Ryan's "Milk the Mouse" (p. 115). Here the speaker feels an even greater hostility toward his father, a man who would pinch his son's finger until the boy squeaked like a mouse. "Be strong Be tough!" is what the father kept saying. Only at the end of the poem does the narrator, now an adult, recognize that the father was not speaking to his son but trying to reassure himself. The bitter hostility the narrator expresses toward his father (and which most readers will share) is contrasted with an insightful sense of pity in the last stanza.

When you read these poems in their entirety, notice how the emotions I have been analyzing here in abstract terms are presented in the poems primarily through visual **images**. An image is in essence any specific piece of sense data—something seen, felt, heard, or smelled. By far the most common are visual images. And as Ezra Pound has pointed out, the poetic image usually has both an intellectual and an emotional element.

An important visual image in "Those Winter Sundays," for example, is the banked fire his father brought to blaze each morning. Intellectually this tells us something about life on a farm in those days; emotionally it reflects both the cold (in the weather and in the father's personality as well) on those winter mornings, and the warming not only of the house but of the narrator's own feelings about his father through this recollection. The ambivalence of the narrator toward this father is embedded in that single image of making those "banked fires blaze."

This is not an isolated example. When a poem develops mixed feelings about a character, it almost always does it through images that carry both thought and feeling. When abstract analysis is offered, it is usually brief and is often delayed until after we have met the characters. This reliance on the visual helps to dramatize the relationship and keeps the poem from becoming over-analytical.

Few student poets make the mistake of attempting love poems that are simple expressions of unalloyed affection. They can use Hallmark cards for that. But the inverse—the expression of unalloyed hostility—is not at all unusual. Parents are a frequent target. Such poems are more effective when there is a range or mix of emotions, since only then do readers have the feeling that they have met a real person. If you find this impossible, it may be that you are too close to the subject matter.

Writing sophisticated poetry that shares genuine feelings with readers is sometimes embarrassing, even painful. Remember, though, that your readers expect honesty. A poem written on the page or read aloud rises above the level of casual conversation. If well done, the poem takes on a life separate from that of the poet.

Here are three questions that can help you keep your poetry genuine, honest, and insightful:

1. Did I really feel that?
2. Was that all I felt?
3. Have I found the specific details that will help my reader to share the same feelings?

Emotions that most naturally generate poetry do not have to be intense, but they do have to be honest and fairly complex.

Speaking in Other Voices

When writing poems about other people, remember that you can present them through the voice of someone distinctly different from yourself. A **monologue** poem takes the form of someone speaking, and a **dialogue** poem adds a second speaker. T. R. Hummer's "The Rural Carrier Stops to Kill a Nine-Foot Cottonmouth" (p. 114) is an excellent example of a monologue. You can tell from the title that it is probably going to be in the voice of a rural letter carrier. And you know for certain when you read the first three lines:

> Lord God, I saw the son-of-a-bitch uncoil
> In the road ahead of me, uncoil and squirm
> For the ditch, squirm a hell of a long time.

That's not T. R. Hummer speaking. Nor is it a speaker even close to him. The poem is presented as a monologue, and it echoes the speech of a rural man telling a story.

At first, the poem seems to be just a simple anecdote—a dramatic monologue in verse. But when you read the poem in its entirety, you will see some extraordinary insights develop.

Hummer's poem may have been based on someone he knew, but you can also make use of historical figures or characters of pure invention. What might Napoleon have said to his son after the disastrous battle of Waterloo? What if Hamlet had played it safe, married Ophelia, and become a successful banker in London? Would he feel twinges of guilt? Would he still write his mother? Such poems sometimes edge their way toward satire, but there is no reason why they cannot develop serious themes that probe aspects of our own lives.

Utilizing the Five Senses

Regardless of whether you draw material from your own life or from the lives of others, it is important to make use of your five senses: seeing, hearing, touching, smelling, and tasting. Some people do remarkably well with one or more of their senses impaired. Many more have been graced with all five but don't use them fully. Such people don't stop to look at a scene carefully, don't linger to listen, say, to the sound of cars on a highway. They avoid the feel of a cat's tongue and ignore a subway's rocking motion, and they may try to stay clear of unfamiliar smells and tastes. Poets, on the other hand, draw heavily on all five senses.

Sight is by far the most frequently used sense in poetry. While writers of fiction look for a sequence of events, poets more often start with a visual impression. The poems we keep returning to in Chapter 11 provide excellent examples. Even before you study them in detail, you can see how many of them present a clear visual image in the title or within the first three lines. Of the three we have been using as examples in this chapter, Robert Hayden shows us the father's "cracked hands that ached," T. R. Hummer introduces his "nine-foot cottonmouth" in the title, and Maxine Kumin grounds her poem with a "cotton beach" (in the mist) and a dock. Simply by thumbing through the poems in Chapter 11 you can come across other examples—one by Anthony Hecht that presents "lizards and snakes" both in the title and in the second line; one by Robley Wilson that gives us images of rock pools on the beach and of "worn change" and barnacles; and one by Richard Wilbur that hits us hard with the image of a dead dog in the very first line.

Not all poems, of course, adopt this tactic. There are no absolute rules in the writing of poetry. But the fact that so many poems begin with a visual image of central importance suggests that there are real advantages to starting with a specific, concrete detail and letting the abstract implication develop through the course of the poem.

Sometimes the visual scene is an entire landscape, as in Dylan Thomas' "Fern Hill" (p. 125). The scene is the farm on which he was raised, and although the phrasing is dreamlike ("About the lilting house and happy as the grass was green"), it is clear that we are being introduced to a landscape seen through the delighted eyes of a child. The poem is filled with precise visual details—wagons, apple trees, daisies, barns, foxes, horses, owls, and the like.

More often, poets avoid such a wide focus, preferring instead more specific places that have lingered in their memories for some reason. In Robley Wilson's "On a Maine Beach" (p. 118), it is clear that the initial image presents a whole setting:

> Look, in these pools, how rocks are like worn change
> Keeping the ocean's mint-mark; barnacles
> Miser on them...

Written in Iowa, the poem draws on an earlier summer. It doesn't indulge in generalities about the Maine coastline the way travel ads usually do; instead it focuses on specific details, drawing a pattern from them. Almost every line contains a precise visual image that the poet eventually uses to link this scene with broader, more abstract suggestions. I will return to this poem in a later chapter on images, but it would be useful to read it now as an example of how a relatively simple experience can serve as the genesis for a highly sophisticated poem.

Occasionally, sounds may also serve as sources for the poet. In "Fern Hill," for example, the boy imagines that calves "sang" to his horn like a pack of hunting dogs, and he hears the foxes bark "clear and cold," and the sound of distant church bells mingled with that of the brook is described with the phrase, "the sabbath rang slowly"—all this in one stanza!

In using sounds, the poet has to go further than generalities. "The roar of traffic" doesn't give the reader enough to work with; besides, the metaphor is worn out from overuse. The poet tries to recall those specific elements that created the general effect—the sounds of pneumatic drills, police whistles, car and truck horns, and the like. Or if the scene is in the country, he or she may try to isolate exactly how the wind sounds in a pine grove or through wheat fields.

It is annoying when the sound that actually initiated a poetic sequence is sufficiently overused to be considered a cliché. Brooks babbling, gulls crying, and wind whistling in the rigging have all reached the level of song lyrics. That is the end of the line. If the sound is truly an individual experience, one can include it in the early drafts and decide later whether to delete the image altogether or to revitalize it, as Howard Moss does in "Local Places," where what might have been a babbling brook becomes "the stream's small talk at dark."

The other senses—touch, smell, and taste—serve less frequently as sources for the poet, but they are worth considering. They may come as mild reactions like the feel of grit on a cafeteria table, the coarse lick of a cow, the smell of a pine grove in August, the taste of potato chips combined with the smell of sweat or the exhaust of a diesel bus.

Often, taste and smell are linked with visual images, as in Maya Angelou's "This Winter Day" (p. 124). Right there in her kitchen she describes "green and orange things" which "leak their blood selves in the soup," creating "an odor at my nose" which "starts my tongue to march...." Read that poem when you're hungry!

In addition to simple sensations, there are heavy ones to consider: the sharp pain of a knife wound or of childbirth; or the sounds an injured man makes.

All these examples of sense data are **images**—details that can be seen, heard, felt, smelled, and tasted. Images can be used directly or as similes, metaphors, or symbols. More about that in Chapter 4. I am concerned here with how you as a poet must not only keep your eyes open but keep your other senses alert and receptive to every stimulus about you.

The Pleasures of Language

This final source of poetry is in some ways the most significant. All writers have to be aware of how they use words, but poets often take a special pleasure in fresh and ingenious phrasing. Because poems are read more deliberately than prose, poets can push language into new configurations.

Returning to Wilson's poem "On a Maine Beach," we see barnacles that "miser" on the rocks and, later, snails that spend their lives "pinwheeling." Here he has made new verbs of familiar nouns—a liberty that would be confusing in prose. In the context of the poem, however, we understand what they mean. His verbal ingenuity is similar to the liberties Dylan Thomas takes in "Fern Hill." Out of context, it is hard to imagine a "lilting house" or a fire "green as grass." This is phrasing we rarely see in prose. But as we read the poem over carefully in its entirety, the lines themselves teach us to make sense of such language: His childhood home lingers in his memory like a lilting tune, and the fire in the fireplace was as lively as youth which, we are informed elsewhere, is like green shoots of new growth.

Wit, ingenuity, fresh phrasing are to poetry what yeast is to bread. Without them, you are apt to serve up something heavy and inedible. Take a quick look at E. E. Cummings' "Buffalo Bill's," a semicomic poem which points out how even a man who can shoot pigeons "onetwothreefourfive...just like that" is himself subject to death. The theme is ultimately serious, but the phrasing and the lively use of the line produce a kind of linguistic comedy.

Nonfiction prose is apt to be utilitarian. We have to do this kind of writing so much we sometimes forget that language can also be fun to write. One of the special pleasures of writing poetry comes from the fact that your readers will move through your work more slowly and more deliberately than they would prose. As a poet, you can be more ingenious, more inventive. There is, of course, an obligation in this too: It is hardly fair to give readers a jumble, hoping they will discover a meaning that is not really there. But if you honestly want to share your work with a reader, writing poetry gives you a chance to play around with language, give it a twist, look for the unexpected.

Getting Started

Resist the temptation to start with rhyming couplets! In later chapters I'll discuss the ways metrical and nonmetrical rhythms can be developed with subtlety. Instead, start by exploring the verbal associations we all share. It may surprise you how many words have overtones that have little connection with their denotative meaning.

Here is an exercise that will start you thinking about language in a nonintellectual way—that is, in a poetic way. Buy a journal, a separate note-book for poetic "sketching," and carefully draw at the top of a fresh page the two shapes you see on page 21.

If each shape had a name, which one would be Kepick and which Oona? Write the name you have selected under each figure and then record these choices: If they are a couple, which is the man? If one is a brand of gasoline and the other a type of oil, which is which?

Suppose one is a melon and the other a lemon? And now listen to them: one is a drum and the other a violin. Too easy? One is a saxophone and the other a trumpet; one is the wind and the other a dog's bark. It is an odd and significant fact that nineteen out of twenty people will give identical answers. This is the "language" of association, of connotation, which is the special concern of the poet both consciously and subconsciously.

Thinking of them once again as a couple, give each of them four more nonsense names. Now try a few lines of very free verse describing Oona and Kepick, using their other names as adjectives or verbs. (Surely you think of Oona looking feenly in the shane, but what happens when Kepick kacks his bip and zabots all the lovely leems?)

There is no end to this. It won't lead directly to sophisticated poetry, but it does help to link language with music. The two should not be confused, but poems often have as much to do with sound, rhythm, and overtones as they do with making a pronouncement.

All that is intended to get you in a poetic mood. As you turn to material that might generate a poem, stay with your journal. There's something intimidating about a fresh sheet of paper. A journal, on the other hand, reassures you that you are still casting about for ideas and feelings. Here are some suggestions to stimulate your creative energies.

Recall briefly some of the most vivid experiences you have had in the past year. Why do they stick in your mind? Can you remember and record specific details that no one else would have noticed?

What were the three most memorable experiences of your childhood? Did they change your attitude? Did they help you to see things in a different light? Read Richard Wilbur's "The Pardon" (p. 122). Did you experience anything like this?

What about your feelings toward members of your family? Any mixed emotions there? (Remember that this is a *private* journal!) How about relatives? Friends? Look closely and be honest. Which of these people have influenced you? Can you recall any special insight into the lives of any of these people?

Turning to the five senses, list very briefly a few of the objects you saw today that you might remember twenty years from now. What aspect seems memorable? Try the same for last summer. Reach back to visual impressions from childhood.

Now turn to sound. Music may come to mind first, but don't forget the voice or laugh of a particular person; the sounds of mechanical objects like a car, truck, or old refrigerator; or natural sounds like wind or rain. Describe these with fresh language—no babbling brooks or howling gales.

Now try the same for memorable sensations of touch, taste, and smell. If memories flood back, make lists. If they come slowly, describe them in greater detail.

When a topic strikes you as having poetic potential, consider what **voice** you will use. Voice reflects your relationship with the speaker or assumed speaker of a poem. In some cases the poem appears to be autobiographical, perhaps even confessional. In other cases the apparent speaker in a poem is clearly far removed from the poet.

We have already taken a preliminary look at two good examples—Maxine Kumin's "Morning Swim" and Dylan Thomas' "Fern Hill." If you would prefer more objectivity, try the third person. This is called **distancing** a poem— placing more distance between you and your subject. Donald Hall's "Names of Horses" (p. 112) is a good example. The most extreme form of distancing is achieved when you present the poem through the voice of a persona who is clearly far removed from you as poet. T. R. Hummer's "The Rural Carrier..." (p. 114) is a particularly good example. There is, of course, no "right way" in making these choices. You have to judge which way feels right—a subjective factor—and which will be the most effective—a literary judgment.

The essential first step in writing poetry is getting phrases and lines down on paper. Since you never know what you may eventually use, a journal is almost a necessity. It is for a poet what a sketch pad is for an artist. You don't have to write a lot at any one time. Twenty minutes a day will give you plenty to look over at the end of each week. Stay loose, stay open. Don't confuse your journal explorations with the careful, concentrated effort that goes into the writing and rewriting of a poem.

3
THE LANGUAGE
OF POETRY

Levels of usage from colloquial through degrees of formality. The four primary dangers in poetic diction: clichés, hackneyed language, sweeping generalities, and archaic diction. When and what to revise. Achieving vitality through original phrasing, concrete nouns, forceful verbs, contemporary language, and compression.

There is no such thing as a good poem poorly expressed. No matter how insightful or compelling the theme may be, the poem itself will fail if the language is dull or inappropriate.

To some degree, this applies to all types of writing, but in a poem the manner of expression is inseparable from what is being expressed. We can analyze the language of a poem as if it were a separate entity, but remember that as you write, the questions of how you express yourself and what you wish to say become merged.

Levels of Usage

When we speak, we automatically adopt different levels of usage. While giving a prepared address before an audience, for example, our **diction** (word choice) tends to be more precise and our phrasing more formal than it will be ten minutes later when we are chatting with friends in the cafeteria. This isn't dishonest; it is merely a matter of using the type of language that meets the occasion.

As we have seen, poetry often deals with personal feelings and insights, but there are two quite different ways of expressing this. One is to present the work through a **persona**—a fictional character—so that it echoes the speech patterns of a speaker. The other is to make the language denser—more packed with meaning and with overtones—than daily speech. There are infinite gradations between the extremes of the as-if-spoken level of usage and what is sometimes referred to as elevated language.

A poet's task is to find the appropriate words and phrases. What is appropriate for one poem may not be for another. Ask yourself these three questions: who is speaking in this poem, what is his or her mood, and who is the implied audience?

As I pointed out in the last chapter, the persona or implied speaker of a poem may in some cases be clearly defined through the language that is used. The voice in T. R. Hummer's "The Rural Carrier..." (p. 114) is an excellent example. Turn to it now and note the words and phrases that give us the illusion of a man speaking.

From the very first line we realize that we are listening to the rural letter carrier identified in the title. We assume that this is going to be a **narrative poem**—that is, one that tells a story—and that it will be in the form of a **monologue**.

Once Hummer establishes this through the profanity and mild obscenity in the opening, the language he uses is fairly straightforward. It is not inappropriately formal, but he has not studded his poem with further examples of profanity, obscenity, or phonetically spelled words. He doesn't have to. Yet we never lose the sense of listening to a speaker. He reminds us with phrases like "Don't ask me why." At the end, when the speaker stumbles onto a discovery about the relationship between those who kill and their victims, it is presented as though it might be actual conversation.

Gwendolyn Brooks' "We Real Cool" (p. 124) is also colloquial, though the pronoun used is "we" rather than "I." Read it now once for pleasure and then again for analysis. Pick out the diction and phrasing that echo the language of the fictional speaker.

Phrases like "real cool" and "strike straight" might be heard from speakers on the street. "Lurk late" and "Jazz June" are not as close to common speech, but they seem appropriate. They adopt the *flavor* of street language just as rap songs often do.

One word of warning, however: Don't try colloquial speech or street language unless it comes from your own personal experience. Attempts to echo other people's speech often sound patronizing and unconvincing. But if street language is a part of your own life, it may well be a rich source.

Now contrast the level of usage in the Brooks poem with that in this opening stanza from "The Bay at West Falmouth" by Barbara Howes (p. 120):

Serenity of mind poises
Like a gull swinging in air,
At ease, sculptured, held there
For a moment so long-drawn-out all time pauses.

The heart's serenity is like the gold
Geometry of sunlight...

Phrases like "serenity of mind," a gull "sculptured," and "the heart's serenity" are selected with more care than we usually put into a casual conversation. The individual words—the diction—are not the sort that would send you to the dictionary, but the total effect is of elevated language.

The same is true with Theodore Roethke's "The Waking" (p. 117). Even though the poem is cast in the first person, the voice is closer to what we might imagine as being the poet's. Here are the opening three lines:

I wake to sleep, and take my waking slow.
I feel my fate in what I cannot fear.
I learn by going where I have to go.

As in the Howes poem, the diction is simple enough. There are no long or unfamiliar words. But the phrasing is deliberate, not colloquial.

Which approach you prefer is a personal matter; what concerns us as poets is how the level of usage reflects an unidentified persona and a particular mood. Effective language is that which is appropriate to the tone of the poem and to the persona.

Does this mean that anything goes? Hardly! The most sincerely felt theme can be lost if the phrasing is not fresh. Let's look at four areas that seem to give the most trouble: clichés, hackneyed language, sweeping generalities, and archaic words.

The Cliché

We have all been warned against clichés since grade school. Yet they remain a temptation—particularly when we are tired and careless. It is important to understand what a cliché is and why it is so damaging to any kind of writing, especially a poem.

The **cliché**, as George Orwell points out in his essay "Politics and the English Language," is actually a dying metaphor—that is, an expression that was once fresh enough to create a clear picture in the reader's mind but has now lost its vitality through constant use. The normal function of both metaphors and similes (discussed in greater detail in the next chapter) is to clarify an abstract word (*serenity*, for example) by linking it with a concrete one (like *gull*). But when comparisons like this are used over and over, they lose all visual impact. Thus, "sharp as a tack" has become dull; "free as a bird" no longer takes flight; "clean as a whistle" sets readers wondering whether they are to picture one of those bright, shiny referee's whistles or the sound of someone whistling. And as Orwell points out, "to toe the line" (literally to place one's toe on a line) has strayed so far from the original metaphor that it is now often seen in print as "to *tow* the line."

When a metaphor or simile finally "dies," it often becomes a part of the language as a single word that no longer appeals to a visual comparison. For example, to be baited like a badger has created a new verb, to *badger*, but most of us have forgotten that the badger was originally the victim, not the tormentor. The meaning is the same as to *hound* someone into doing something, but the original image was just the opposite. We accept these new verbs, *badger* and *hound*, without seeing them as metaphors. The same applies to *cliché* itself and to *stereotype*, both of which were originally printers' terms for metal plates of print. They are now useful nouns. No harm in this. What does the damage to poetry are those phrases that are both wordy and too familiar to provide a mental picture. They are excess baggage.

There are three different ways of dealing with clichés that appear in a first draft. First, one can work hard to find a fresh simile or metaphor which will force the reader to see (hear, taste, and so on) the object being used in the comparison. One can drop the comparison completely and deal with the subject directly. Finally, one can twist the cliché around so that it is reborn in some slightly altered form. This technique is often seen in comic verse, but it can be highly effective in serious poetry as well.

For example, if you discover that you have allowed "blood red" to slide into your verse, you can avoid this ancient cliché with such alternatives as "balloon red," "hot red," or "shouting red," depending on the overtones you wish to establish. If none of these will do, go back to just "red."

A good way to improve your skill in dealing with clichés is to apply these techniques to "mother nature," "strong as an ox," "wise as an owl," and "where there's smoke, there's fire."

Hackneyed Language

This is a general term which includes not only the cliché but the far broader areas of phrases that have simply been overused. Whereas clichés usually consist only of conventionalized similes and are easily identified, **hackneyed language** also includes direct description that has been seen in print too often to provide impact. A seventh-grader can compile a list of clichés as readily as names of common birds; but only someone who has read literature extensively can identify that which is literarily hackneyed. This is one reason why vocabulary lists are no substitute for wide and varied reading.

Certain subjects tend to generate hackneyed language. Take, for example, sunsets. The "dying day" is a true cliché, but perfectly respectable words like "golden," "resplendent," "magnificent," and even "richly scarlet" all become hackneyed when used to describe a sunset. It is not the word itself that should be avoided—one cannot make lists; it is the particular combination which is limp from overuse.

In the same way, smiles are too often "radiant," "infectious," or "glowing." Trees tend to have "arms" and frequently "reach heavenward." The seasons are particularly dangerous: Spring is "young" or "youthful," suggesting virginity, vitality, or both; summer is "full blown"; and by autumn many poets slide into a "September Song" with only slight variations on the popular lyrics. Winter, of course, leads the poet to sterility and death, terms that too often describe the quality of the poem as well.

Our judgment of what is hackneyed depends somewhat on the age we live in. That which was fresh and vivid in an earlier period may have become shop-worn for us. Protesting "But Pope used it" does not make a metaphor acceptable for our own use. Standards of fresh language, however, are far less tied to period than many believe. It is difficult to find lines in, say, Shakespeare's sonnets which would even today be considered hackneyed. Conversely, many of the conventions he attacked as stale and useless have continued in popular use and reappear like tenacious weeds in mass-market poetry.

In "Sonnet 130," for example, he protests that

> My mistress' eyes are nothing like the sun;
> Coral is far more red than her lips' red....
> And in some perfumes is there more delight
> Than in the breath that from my mistress reeks.

The poem is directed not so much at his mistress as at those poets of his day who were content to root their work in conventions which were even then thoroughly stale. Yet more than 300 years later poetry is produced (more often by the greeting card industry than by students) in which eyes sparkle like the sun, lips are either ruby or coral red, and breath is either honeyed or perfumed.

Remember that your task as a poet is to find fresh insights. If you are dealing with seasons, don't announce that spring is a time for growth. We know that. There are other aspects of spring, however, that are worth considering. Here is what T.S. Eliot saw in that season and described in the opening of "The Waste Land":

> April is the cruellest month, breeding
> Lilacs out of the dead land, mixing
> Memory and desire....

Winter kept us warm, covering
Earth in forgetful snow, feeding
A little life with dried tubers

Not only is he telling us that in some ways winter is "kinder" by keeping the ground covered; he is suggesting that sometimes memory and desire awaken aspects of ourselves which we would rather forget. Both are reversals of the simple sentiments we see so often in simple verse.

Abstractions and Sweeping Generalities

In the chapter on the sources of poems, I warned against beginning with a broad, abstract principle like love, death, nature, and the like. It is equally dangerous to allow a poem that was originally inspired by some genuine experience or personal reaction to slide into generalities. Last stanzas are particularly vulnerable. There is a temptation to "explain" one's poem in a concluding stanza that too easily turns into a truism.

If the origin of a poem is a specific love, try to deal with the details as precisely as possible. There will be, of course, aspects that would mean nothing to another reader without a great deal of background explanation, and these should be avoided. But if the relationship is dealt with honestly, the reader will be able to draw universals from the specifics you provide.

The same is true of death. Treating the subject in the abstract almost always seems empty, devoid of genuine feelings. Before the concept becomes poetically effective, we have to find a set of images that will make the familiar abstraction fresh and convincing.

Several poems in this volume have death as a central theme, yet each is unique. In fact, they approach the subject in entirely different ways.

Robley Wilson is concerned with death in his poem "On a Maine Beach" (p. 118). Read it now and notice how what appears to be a simple description of tidal pools ends with an observation that helps us to deal with death.

The poem is deceptive. All those details about the rock pool take on a far deeper meaning with those concluding lines: "Beach rhythms flow / In circles. Perfections teach us to die."

Richard Wilbur deals with death even more directly in his poem "The Pardon" (p. 122). Here are the first two of six stanzas:

My dog lay dead five days without a grave
In the thick of summer, hid in a clump of pine
And a jungle of grass and honeysuckle-vine.
I who had loved him while he kept alive

Went only close enough to where he was
To sniff the heavy honeysuckle-smell

Twined with another odour heavier still
And hear the flies' intolerable buzz.

That opening line announces the topic unmistakably. But there is nothing abstract about it. We are thrust into a personal experience and are given concrete details—sight, sound, and smells. If you turn to it now and read the poem in its entirety you will see how Wilbur develops important abstract concerns toward the end. But the poem remains rooted in specifics.

Dylan Thomas' "Fern Hill" (p. 125) and Ann Leventhal's "Pilot Error" (p. 127) provide two more examples of poems dealing with death. They also are unique in treatment. The first contrasts the joys of a carefree youth with the harsh reality of our mortality, and the second focuses on how survivors cling to familiar routines when faced with the death of someone close. All four of these poems are rooted in what appear to be vivid personal experiences. We are introduced to aspects of death, the abstract concept, through highly concrete images we can see.

Other abstractions like patriotism, liberty, and peace are also dangerous; in addition, they have a special tendency to attract clichés. It is hard not to be influenced by unimaginative political orators. The best solution is to select a single specific example of the abstraction and concentrate on that. If it is social injustice that concerns you, pick one person you know and one incident that occurred to that individual. If you help readers to share your feelings about that event, you will have done more than any generalized statement about Truth and Justice could possibly have done.

If you begin a poem with a line about "life" or "love," *stop!* Ask yourself what made you feel like that? What event or experience brought that to your mind? Is there a particular person involved? Develop those specifics and you will reach your readers.

Archaic Diction

This is the last in the list of four threats to fresh language. Quite often, **archaic diction** takes the form of time-honored but dated contractions such as "o'er" and "oft" as substitutions for "over" and "often." But there are other words that now have the same musty quality: "lo!" "hark!" "ere," and even "O!" are the most frequently used.

The majority of poets writing today need no such warning, and some may be surprised that it must be included here. Yet the practice is still seen in writing classes and in some of the less distinguished poetry journals.

Sometimes the temptation to use archaic words comes from a determination to write perfectly metered poetry. Meter is the subject of Chapter 6, but I should point out here that the rhythms one creates from a metrical line should never be so regular as to dominate the choice of words. Mature use of meter allows substitutions and variations. There is no need to use "lo!" "hark!" and "ere" just to make the line go "ta-*tum*, ta-*tum*, ta-*tum*" like a toy drum.

More often, archaisms slip in because the writer understandably admires poets from former centuries. There is nothing wrong with studying poetry of earlier periods; indeed, for every hour of work on your own compositions you really should spend an hour reading the poetry of others. But remember that language changes. You will benefit richly from studying the sonnets of Shakespeare, the ballad as refined by Coleridge, the lyrics of Wordsworth; but don't forget that they were writing with the language of their day, just as you should be doing. You can learn a great deal about the *use* of language without imitating the words themselves.

When and What to Revise

At first, the major effort in writing poetry seems to be finding the right subject matter. But as you gain experience you will find yourself spending much more time on the revision process. This is because the more you study poetry, the more concerned you become with the language itself. Finding just the right word, the most effective phrasing becomes almost a compulsion.

To encourage this process, here are some lines that cry out for revision. Each has marginal comments of the sort a conscientious but kindly critic might offer. Although the revised lines are borrowed directly from poems in this volume, the unsuccessful versions are invented and should not be blamed on the poet.

EXAMPLE 1

Too impersonal

(Children) do not think of (death) or dying.

A solution from Richard Wilbur's "The Pardon":

In my kind world the dead were out of range

EXAMPLE 2

Not the true subject of poem

watch out for these abstractions.

(The mind) is never sure of (truth) and so

(It) turns to (feelings) for what we think we know   *whose feelings?*

A solution from Theodore Roethke's "The Waking":

We think by feeling. What is there to know?

EXAMPLE 3

Be more specific

avoid sentimentality

For many years the poor dead horse lay in his grave,
while weeds and trees grew to cover the spot

Focus rather on the horse

A solution from Donald Hall's "Names of Horses":

For a hundred and fifty years, in the pasture of dead horses,
roots of pine trees pushed through the pale curves of your ribs

EXAMPLE 4

Sentimental

In childlike joy I played in wagons and orchards
Pretending to be the king of my realm

Seems formal for a kid's view

A solution from Dylan Thomas' "Fern Hill":

And honoured among wagons I was prince of the apple towns

Achieving Vitality in Language

Vitality, freshness, energy—these are the goals. There is no simple set of rules that will generate them in your work. But here are five areas of special concern to poets. They are essential if you are going to make the best possible use of language.

• *Look for phrasing that will catch your readers' attention.* Give them fresh insights and new ways of looking at the familiar. Remind yourself of how tired your readers probably are of the utilitarian prose in newspapers, magazines, and, yes, even textbooks. Try to give them something interesting to savor in every line. It doesn't have to be sensational. Just a new metaphor or an original phrase.

• *Find nouns that are solid, specific, and visual.* Don't write about "life" and "mortality" if you can suggest something about these abstractions through a rock pool with barnacles and snails. Avoid "women" if "Aunt Martha" is your true subject. Don't even settle for "bird" if "gull" is what hovers in your mind's eye. Take a second look at every adjective in your first draft and see if selecting a different noun will do the job alone. Replace "big hills" with "mountains" if that's what you see. Scratch out "howling wind" if "gale" will do.

- *Find verbs that are specific.* The right verb rarely needs to be modified. Birds that "fly suddenly" are not as memorable as those that "scatter." Vegetables that "add their colors to the soup" are bland compared with those that "leak their blood selves in the soup." Move slowly through the poems printed in Chapter 11 and circle the verbs. Notice how many of them provide a kind of impact we rarely achieve in the rush of daily speech or even in utilitarian prose writing.

- *Use the language of your own age.* Adapt it to your persona, the implied narrator of your poem. There is no such thing as "poetic language"; there is only language that is appropriate for a particular poem.

- *Compress, compress, compress.* Occasionally you will find wordy poems in print, and you will even find poems that read like prose in short lines. But one of the special attributes of the genre is its capacity to say more and imply more in each line than prose can in a paragraph. The only way to achieve this is to weed out those do-nothing phrases and lines. What is left will have impact and vitality.

Sophisticated poetry stimulates the reader in some way—intellectually, spiritually, or emotionally. To achieve this goal, the language must be fresh, and every line should work toward that end.

4
IMAGES

The image defined. Using all five senses. Images as figures of speech. The image as symbol. Building image clusters. Playing with images in journal writing. Shifting to serious work.

An **image** in poetry is any **concrete** detail. Unlike an **abstraction**, it can be perceived with one of our five senses. Although we tend to think of images as visual details, the term also includes sounds heard, textures felt, odors smelled, and objects tasted.

As I pointed out in Chapter 2, most poetry is rooted in concrete details. This is one of its distinguishing characteristics. In contrast, philosophy, mathematics, and literary criticism often deal directly with abstractions like truth, meaning, infinity, symbol, and structure. This text also discusses abstract terms like image, language, and literary sophistication. Poetry may deal with abstract concepts, but it usually does so by means of specific concrete nouns such as Ezra Pound's metro, Dylan Thomas' apple towns, and T. R. Hummer's nine-foot cottonmouth.

An image can be used as a simple, descriptive detail or, as we will see, it can serve as the central element in similes, metaphors, and symbols. It's no wonder that the image is a major concern at every stage of writing poetry.

Because the term **imagery** is so closely associated with similes and metaphors, it is sometimes used interchangeably with these terms. Keep in mind, however, that an image is any detail seen or perceived by the senses regardless of whether it is used literally or as a part of a figure of speech or symbol.

Images, then, tend to be concrete nouns. If you are in doubt about whether a word is concrete or not, ask yourself how much the object weighs and where you would find it. But, oddly, there is no sharp line between words that are clearly concrete and those that are totally abstract. It all depends on how vividly we can perceive the object with our senses.

"Serenity," for example, is not an image. It is an abstraction that, like all abstractions, cannot be seen or heard. You can't weigh it or put it in a closet. "Bird" is more concrete, though it is still rather general. It includes many different creatures, from a sparrow to an ostrich. "A gull" is more specific, and "a gull swinging in air, / At ease, sculptured, held there..." is a fully developed image. We not only see the bird, we see it in motion. This image is taken from Barbara Howes' poem "The Bay at West Falmouth" (p. 120). Turn to it now and see how this first image—the gull in flight suggesting "serenity of mind"—is followed by a second image in which the poet compares "the heart's serenity" with "the gold geometry of sunlight."

Another good example of imagery is found in Anthony Hecht's poem "Lizards and Snakes" (p. 111). The idea of evil is highly abstract, so the image of a devil has been used for centuries to suggest it. The trouble with the "devil" image is that through overuse it has become a visual cliché and so has lost impact. When Hecht wants us to see what Aunt Martha sees, he has her describe a terrible vision without using the word "devil" at all: "Look how he grins / And swings the scaly horror of his folded tail."

Images of Sound, Touch, Smell, and Taste

When we think of images, visual details come to mind first. Poets depend heavily on what they see. But don't neglect the other four senses. Sounds, for example, can be highly effective. Chase Twichell begins her poem "Rhymes for Old Age" (p. 122) with a vivid auditory image:

> The wind's untiring saxophone
> keens at the glass.

The verb to keen is not widely used, so if you are not familiar with it, take the time to look it up. Its overtones contribute to the mournful sound of the wind. This is, incidentally, a good illustration of why one has to spend a little extra time in the first reading of a sophisticated poem.

Sometimes auditory images like this one are repeated several times in the same poem. We are so used to eliminating redundancies in prose that we forget how effective repetition can be in poetry. When used with care, a repeated word or phrase can have the effect of a recurring phrase in music.

Here are six lines from Robert Frost's "Mowing" that make use of a scythe's "whispering." I have circled the occurrences:

There was never a sound beside the wood but one,

And that was my long scythe (whispering) to the ground.

What was it it (whispered?) I know not well myself;

Perhaps it was something about the heat of the sun,

Something, perhaps about the lack of sound—

And that was why it (whispered) and did not speak.

In the next seven lines, not one reference is made to sound—either directly or metaphorically. But the image returns again with this final line:

My long scythe (whispered) and left the hay to make.

You have to be careful about the word *sound*, of course. Song lyrics and popular verse have long made use of "sounds in the night," "sounds of the street," and "sounds of the sea." But if you can link the word "sound" with something specific which we can hear—like Frost's "scythe whispering to the ground"— the image will have vitality.

Images of touch, smell, and taste are often used in conjunction with one another and with visual details. The poem "Local Places" by Howard Moss provides a fine example. The following stanza is the first of five, and I have identified some of the images.

(The song you sang) you will not sing again,	*auditory*
Floating in the spring to all your local places,	
Lured by archaic sense to the wood	
To watch the (frog jump from the mossy rock,)	*visual*
To listen to the (stream's small talk) at dark,	*auditory*
Or to feel the (springy pine-floor) where you walk—	*touch*
If your green secrecies were such as these,	
The mystery is now (in other trees.)	*visual*

Three of the five senses are used in this single stanza. Only taste and smell are missing, and one of these appears in the next stanza with the phrase, "To perfume aridness." These images of sight, sound, touch, and smell are not mere decorations. They are the basic materials from which the poem is constructed.

Images as Figures of Speech

To this point, I have been describing images used simply as descriptive details—things seen, heard, felt, smelled, and tasted. Images also serve as the concrete element in almost any figure of speech.

Figurative language most commonly takes the form of the **simile** and the **metaphor**. These are both comparisons, the simile linking the two elements explicitly with "like" or "as" and the metaphor implying a relationship. Here are three similes from three different poems included in Chapter 11. I have circled the image that completes the simile.

1. From Barbara Howes' "The Bay at West Falmouth":

    Serenity of mind poises

    Like a gull swinging in air

2. From Robley Wilson's "On a Maine Beach":

    ...rocks are like worn change

3. From Dylan Thomas' "Fern Hill":

    Now as I was young and easy under the apple boughs

    About the lilting house and happy as the grass was green

It should be clear from these examples that similes are not simple comparisons. When we compare, for example, a starling with a grackle, we imply that *in most respects* the two objects are similar. But when Barbara Howes describes serenity as being like a gull, she certainly does not want us to picture the emotions as having a sharp bill or a raucous cry. Serenity is like a gull *only in certain respects*—in this case, the way it seems to float effortlessly in the air. As with most similes, the area of similarity is far narrower than the area of differences. Its impact depends on how sharply it can make the reader see a new relationship.

A metaphor is often described as a simile that doesn't use "like" or "as." But the true difference is much deeper than that. Similes are a special kind of comparison, but they are nonetheless phrased like comparisons. A metaphor, on the other hand, is a statement that is literally untrue. We understand its meaning only by implication.

It doesn't make literal sense, for example, to refer to a house as "lilting." Lilting is normally applied to melodies, not objects. You won't get far telling a builder to construct a lilting house. Yet this is the word Dylan Thomas uses in the lines quoted earlier, and we understand his meaning through the context of the poem.

To analyze how a metaphor works, convert it to a simile. The result may be awkward, but it is a good technique to use with your own work as well as with published poems. In the case of Thomas' metaphor, the conversion comes out something like this: "A house as cheerful and merry as a lilting tune."

Notice how compressed the metaphor is compared with the corresponding simile. This is a case where a metaphor is far more than just a simile with "as" left out. Its compression makes it a kind of shorthand that provides greater impact. More than that, it's a true transformation. Because it is literally untrue, it seizes the reader's attention in ways a simile rarely can.

There are two more terms that are extremely helpful in analyzing any figure of speech—including those in your own work. The critic I. A. Richards has suggested **tenor** to describe the poet's actual subject of concern (often an abstraction) and **vehicle** as the image associated with it. Take, for example, the simile in the lines from "Fern Hill" quoted earlier: "Happy as the grass was green." The tenor or true subject here is "happy," and "green grass" is the vehicle—with overtones of spring growth, vividness, intensity.

One advantage of being familiar with these terms is that they can help you identify and get rid of **mixed metaphors**. A mixed metaphor is one with two contradictory vehicles. For example:

> The wind's untiring saxophone
> hammers at the glass

The wind here is the tenor, and there are two vehicles that suggest characteristics of that tenor: the sound of a saxophone and the pounding of a hammer. Individually, each vehicle is effective in its own way, but together they are "mixed" badly since saxophones are rarely used as hammers.

One solution is the wording we saw in Chase Twichell's "Rhymes for Old Age":

> The wind's untiring saxophone
> keens at the glass.

This version also uses a double metaphor (that is, two vehicles applied to one tenor), but the vehicles are harmonious. A saxophone often produces a wailing sound, and the verb *to keen* means to wail for the dead. The two tenors work together, and that wail is appropriate to the theme of the poem, which is a lament for a woman close to death.

The term **figurative language** is used primarily to describe similes and metaphors. Most other figures of speech are specialized forms of the metaphor and are of more value to critics analyzing literature than writers in the process of composition. Three, however, concern us here. They are techniques you may wish to use.

Hyperbole is usually defined as extreme exaggeration, but in most cases it is a metaphorical exaggeration as well. The persona in Lucille Clifton's "What the Mirror Said" (p. 126), for example, looks at herself and says, "Listen, …you a city of a woman." This cheerful bit of self-affirmation is not only an exaggeration, it is a metaphor. Converting it back to a simile, we end up with something like, "You're so complex and interesting, you're like an entire city."

Even the **pun** can be seen as a form of metaphor when one is able to separate the tenor from the vehicle. In Thomas' "A Refusal to Mourn…" he uses a play on "grave":

> I shall not murder
> The mankind of her going with a grave truth.…

The tenor here is "solemn truth," and he has, in effect, added "*as if* spoken at the grave-side." He uses essentially the same device in "Do Not Go Gentle Into That Good Night" with the line, "Grave men, near death, who see with blinding sight.…" Once again, we have only to convert the pun to a simile in order to see it as a part of a metaphorical construction.

Unfortunately, the pun is in low repute in the twentieth century and is apt to be greeted with groans rather than laughter. But as Dylan Thomas has shown, it can be used seriously if you select your phrasing with care and restraint.

Synecdoche is the third of these helpful terms. It is a figure of speech in which a part is used for the whole. When we say "bread for the starving" we're not just appealing to the baking companies. Bread represents food in general. Sometimes an individual is used for a group. When we say "the plight of the blue-collar worker" it's understood that we are referring to a whole class, not just an individual wearing a work shirt.

These examples are taken from common speech; poetic use of synecdoche is fresher and as a result has more impact. Compare the prosaic phrase "All day long" with Dylan Thomas' version, "All the sun long." The sun is only one aspect of the day, but by allowing it to stand for the day he is able to catch the overtones of summer warmth and, in context, childhood.

Synecdoche occasionally reverses the process, using the general to represent the specific, although this is far less common in poetry. In the phrase "deceit won the election," the abstraction defines the individual. Notice that here too the figure of speech can be translated into a simile: "The candidate, as if the embodiment of deceit, won the election."

Figures of speech are important in poetry because they help to increase the degree of compression. That is, they allow you to suggest more without being wordy. Be careful, however, not to "dress up" a poem by using figurative language merely for adornment. Sometimes straightforward language is more appropriate. A fine example of this is Donald Hall's "Names of Horses" (p. 112). There are almost no figures of speech in that 29-line poem, yet it generates true strength and resonance. The decision on when and how much to use figurative language should be based on the poem itself and on your own inclination.

Image as Symbol

Symbols also add density of meaning to a poem, but the way they function is the opposite of figures of speech. As we have seen, a figure of speech introduces an image simply for comparison. A **symbol**, on the other hand, uses an image that exists as a part of the poem and adds to it a greater range of meaning. If that strikes you as confusing in the abstract, consider these examples.

First, a metaphor from "Morning Swim" by Maxine Kumin:

> ...I was the well
> that fed the lake...

A simile based on that metaphor:

> ...I was like a well
> that fed a lake...

A symbol making use of the same material:

> Behind my house is an open well
> That, overflowing, feeds the lake...

The well in this last case is not a figure of speech introduced merely for comparison, it is a literal part of the poem that will, through implication, be given additional meanings as the poem develops.

Here is a second example, this one a metaphor taken from Dylan Thomas' "Fern Hill." He is describing how he felt in those ideal childhood days:

> I was huntsman and herdsman...

As a simile it would be spelled out:

> I, like a huntsman one day, a herdsman another...

But if we used this image as a symbol, we would have to add actual hunters and herders to the poem, perhaps in this way:

> I befriended huntsmen and herdsmen
> Who came my way.

The distinctions between a simple comparison, a simile, a metaphor, and a symbol are subtle, but they are enormously important for anyone who writes poetry. You can rely on your intuition in the first draft, but you will have difficulty revising effectively if you do not understand the logic behind these techniques.

For some, a diagrammatic presentation is more helpful than a description in words. The schematic drawing on page 41 is simply a different way of explaining how these literary devices work. Remember that the *tenor* is the principal subject and the *vehicle* is the word or phrase used to convey the subject to the reader. I have cited examples from "Fern Hill," but the diagram will be more helpful if you select an image in another poem and in a similar manner analyze the figurative techniques the poet has relied on to express it.

The term **public symbol** refers to symbols that are widely recognized and are almost a part of the language. Madison Avenue, for example, suggests commercial values; the flag represents the country; the cross stands for the Christian church. These are so common that they can be used in cartoons.

Because public symbols are hackneyed from overuse, poets usually construct their own **private symbols**. Devised for a particular poem, a private symbol has to be introduced in such a way that its meaning is made clear through the context of the poem.

As we have seen, Anthony Hecht carefully avoids the word *devil* in "Lizards and Snakes"; through overuse this public symbol has become almost comic. Instead, he introduces the aunt's terrifying vision of the devil through her description of him.

Notice how that symbolic image of the devil is sprung on us. We are introduced to the lizard at the outset of a poem that appears to be an almost cute little anecdote. Not until the end of the poem do we realize that for Aunt Martha the lizard suggests (symbolizes) the devil and, by extension, death itself.

Wilson's "On a Maine Beach" provides another good example of a symbol. We have already seen how frequently Wilson uses similes: rocks "like worn change," the "small thoughts" of snails that eventually "rust like a mainspring." But when we come down to "snails think they bleed / In their trapped

The image used literally.	Grass	Green grass
Comparison of two items. The area of agreement (shaded) is broad.	Grass Wheat	Grass is like wheat
Simile: A linking of essentially dissimilar items (using "like," "as," etc.) to highlight certain similarities (shaded).	Happiness (tenor) Green grass (vehicle)	"Happy as the grass was green" **Paraphrase:** *Happy* in a vital, vibrant way like the green grass of early spring.
Metaphor: An implied simile (without "like" or "as") that is not literally true.	I (tenor) Prince (vehicle)	"I was prince of the apple towns" **Paraphrase:** I was like a prince in the apple orchards.
Symbol: An item presented as if for its own sake which then takes on a broader, implied meaning.	The farm (vehicle) Aspects of life and death (tenor)	"Fern Hill" The entire farm becomes a vehicle suggesting aspects of life itself: birth, rapid growth; the certainty of death at the end of the "season"—an endless cycle.

Use of the image in comparisons, similes, metaphors, and symbols.

world," we begin to see that these short-lived sea colonies are in a sense like our own lives. Nowhere does he say, "Our lives, like those of snails and barnacles...." The poem implies it instead. Why not state it directly? One good reason is that it would deprive readers of the pleasure of discovering it on their own—as if they themselves were on the beach.

Poems like this are in some ways like detective stories: A series of clues is given early in the work, sometimes in a fairly light tone; the full implication is not revealed until the end. A sophisticated version of this same pattern appears in several of the poems we have been discussing. If it were not for the unfolding of a unifying and serious symbol at the end, "Lizards and Snakes" would be nothing but a humorous anecdote. In the same way, "On a Maine Beach" would be a simple nature piece, and "Fern Hill" would be a highly sentimental and romanticized description of childhood. In each case, however, the full impact of the poem is revealed through the force of a concluding symbol that gives a new range of meaning to everything that came before.

Important as symbols often are, however, don't feel that they are essential. Donald Hall's "Names of Horses" (p. 112) is a moving tribute to farm horses who served patiently and willingly over the years, and it may remind the reader of loyal servants, but the central image is never developed into a symbol. It is a mistake to tack on a symbol to a poem that has power and strength without it.

Examine your subject carefully and determine what it has meant to you. Try to get beyond the simple observation that you liked it or hated it. If at that point, a symbol comes to mind, let it develop naturally. Revise the poem so that you can share the symbolic suggestion with your readers, being careful in the process not to make it so obvious that it becomes obtrusive. When symbols are shaped this way, they will be an organic part of the poem.

Building Image Clusters

Regardless of whether images are used figuratively, symbolically, or simply as enriching details, they are often more effective if presented in clusters. That is, a group of images that have the same source (a farm, a beach) or are linked visually gain a certain strength as compared with those that are used once and then dropped. When you read a new poem, look for such **image clusters** or groups of related details even before you are entirely clear about the theme. If the book is your own, it is well worth the time to circle these clusters and identify them. If it is not, photocopy the poem and mark the copy. This kind of visual analysis is not only helpful in the process of understanding new work, it will help you to adopt the same techniques in your own work.

Here is a copy of "On a Maine Beach" by Robley Wilson annotated with marginal notes indicating image clusters. An unmarked copy appears on page 118, and you may wish to read that first.

money
images
Look, in these pools, how rocks are like worn change

Keeping the ocean's mint-mark; barnacles

Miser on them; societies of snails

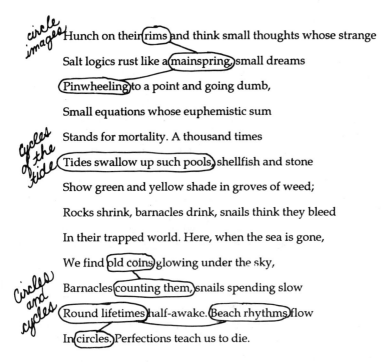

Hunch on their rims and think small thoughts whose strange

Salt logics rust like a mainspring, small dreams

Pinwheeling to a point and going dumb,

Small equations whose euphemistic sum

Stands for mortality. A thousand times

Tides swallow up such pools, shellfish and stone

Show green and yellow shade in groves of weed;

Rocks shrink, barnacles drink, snails think they bleed

In their trapped world. Here, when the sea is gone,

We find old coins glowing under the sky,

Barnacles counting them, snails spending slow

Round lifetimes half-awake. Beach rhythms flow

In circles. Perfections teach us to die.

The first of these image clusters is coins. The second has to do with circles and spirals. As the last line suggests, watching these cycles of living and dying within the rock pool helps us to see our own mortality in perspective. In this way, the life and death of the reader is included in the dominant image cluster of circles and cycles.

Playing Games with Images

When you first start working with similes and metaphors and their components, tenors and vehicles, the subject is apt to seem rather forbidding. It's hard to imagine playing games with them. But remember that although writing poetry is ultimately a serious and complex art, practicing in your own journal can be just plain fun—as well as valuable.

Here, for a start, is a list of five images. Two of them are visual, one olfactory, one auditory, and one tactile.

1. An old cat
2. A tree bending in the wind
3. The smell of incense on a summer night
4. A child's shriek
5. The feel of rough concrete

The simplest sort of conversion is to make each one into a vehicle for a simile. For example: "After an enormous meal, they reclined like two old cats." Then devise a metaphor (use the image as the subject).

Now that you have used two lethargic people as tenor, try using the image to describe a section of a city or a segment of society. Be careful to avoid clichés like "fat cats."

Next, work with the other four images. What would have the qualities of a tree bending in the wind or incense on a summer night? Consider people, animals, songs, your mood on certain occasions. Recall moments with other people—contented, discontented, anguished.

Now reverse the process, using each item as the tenor. Try, first, to find an image that would serve as a vivid simile to describe an old cat. Not just any cat—perhaps a street cat, lean and battered; perhaps an aging, well-fed house cat. How would you make those trees bending in the wind memorable for your reader? Picture a scene involving incense on a summer night (inside? outside?) and find a simile that would intensify the scene for someone else.

Projects like these are for poets what finger exercises are for pianists. As you work toward material that might eventually become the nucleus of a developed poem, consider people and places that are or were close to you. Remember that most of these will, if examined honestly, elicit mixed or **ambivalent** feelings. Your old home, your high school, your best friend in the eighth grade, your first love, a parent, your sister or brother, a hated uncle. How can you best communicate the unique quality of your feelings? What kinds of metaphors can you find that would successfully communicate your feelings to a reader?

Before you commit yourself to a long poem, you may find it helpful to try a three-line form known as a **haiku**. This is a traditional Japanese verse form that contains no rhyme or meter but is based entirely on line length. Traditionally the poem is three lines long, with five syllables in the first line, seven in the second, and five in the third. Occasionally this pattern varies when the poems are translated from the Japanese, but you will find it relatively easy to maintain the form. The great advantage of writing haiku is that you usually focus intensely on one or two images. They may be used metaphorically, but often they are presented simply for their visual impact—more like a quick photograph or sketch. Here are two anonymous samples of the sort you might try in your journal; five more haiku appear on pp. 120, 121, and 128.

> Her song seizes me,
> Takes me on a secret trip
> Through lands without time.

> Small town of my birth
> Nurtures its sons and daughters,
> Smothers those who stay.

From Games to Serious Work

Poets never stop playing with language. But there is a difference between random experimentation in a journal and the concentrated effort required for a poem you take seriously. Journal writing is for your own benefit, but a poem you ask others to read is on another level. Presumably it has been carefully revised. It is your best work.

In general, the more poetry you read, the more time you will spend revising your own work. I will have more to say about this at the end of the poetry section, but for now consider this: A textbook like this can suggest what to look for in a poem, but it cannot substitute for careful reading of specific examples. This chapter has focused on various types of images and the ways in which they can serve to create similes, metaphors, and symbols. Before you go on to the next chapter, take some time to study the poems in Chapter 11 and perhaps others from an anthology. Circle the images you consider effective and determine for yourself whether they are used directly or as vehicles for similes or metaphors. Link image clusters. Identify those that have symbolic overtones. No good poem is ever spoiled by analysis.

Then apply the same objective view to your own work. Have you made the best possible use of images? No matter how penetrating or insightful your theme may be, your poem will depend on the effectiveness of your images.

5
THE SOUND OF WORDS

The oral tradition in poetry. Nonrhyming devices of sound including
alliteration, assonance, consonance, and onomatopoeia. True rhyme; its
use in rhyme schemes. Achieving subtlety in sound. Sound as meaning.
Training your ear.

Poetry was recited aloud long before it was written down to be read on the
page. We are fortunate today to have such an enormous body of work available
in print, but the genre has never lost its roots in the oral tradition. The growing
popularity of readings and recordings and the introduction of poetry video
cassettes are good indications of how poetry, far more than prose, continues
to appeal to the ear.

There are two approaches to developing the musical aspect of poetry,
and while there is no sharp division between them it is helpful to consider
them separately. One makes use of **rhyme schemes**—traditional patterns of
regularly recurring rhyme endings. The other, generally known as **free verse**,
relies instead on more irregular patterns. It also shifts the emphasis from
word endings to similarities of sound at the beginnings of words and within
words.

When we consider the sound of language we are apt to think of rhyme
schemes first because this particular device dominated the genre for so many
centuries. And some of the major poets of our own century have preferred
rhymed to unrhymed verse. Anthony Hecht, Elizabeth Bishop, Richard Wilbur, and Maxine Kumin are good examples. They are all represented in
Chapter 11.

The term **new formalists** (also called *neoformalists*) refers to contemporary poets who are making innovative use of traditional verse forms. Although few poets like to be classified in this or any way, the term is useful in describing an interest that has risen sharply in the 1990s.

It is important to remember, however, that varieties of free verse still dominate the poetry scene, as they have for most of this century. Although they do not draw on systems of regularly recurring rhyme endings, they can and often do make "music" with words. Sometimes the techniques are so subtle that the casual reader is only aware that the poem "sounds nice." For those who write, however, it is important to examine these devices closely in order to make good use of them.

Nonrhyming Devices of Sound

Nonrhyming sound techniques are found both in rhymed and unrhymed poems. Because they are the least technical, they are a good introduction to sound in language. They also serve as a reminder that there is less difference between traditional, metered work and free verse than many people think.

Significantly, these devices can be found in prose and oratory as well. The following passage, for example, is actually prose in spite of its *lyrical* or "musical" quality. It comes from Dylan Thomas' "August Bank Holiday" and describes a summer day at the beach not through plot but, in the manner of poetry, through a succession of vivid images. The first paragraph is typical. I have made annotations to point out some of the linking sounds.

> August Bank Holiday.—A tune on an ice-cream cornet. A
>
> slap of sea and a tickle of sand. A fanfare of sunshades opening.
>
> A wince and whinny of bathers dancing into deceptive water. A
>
> tuck of dresses. A rolling of trousers. A compromise of
>
> paddlers. A sunburn of girls and a lark of boys. A silent
>
> hullabaloo of balloons.

What makes this prose passage sound "poetic"? Primarily it is all those linkages of sounds—vowels, consonants, and combination clusters—some occurring at the beginning of words and others within words. Notice also how some words themselves echo an action or evoke an object or sensation.

Anyone interested in poetry should be familiar with the following four techniques for using sounds.

- **Alliteration** is the repetition of consonants, particularly those at the beginning of words. There are three groups of these in the Thomas paragraph:

> slap—sea—sand
> wince—whinny (a similarity, not an identity of sound)
> dancing—deceptive

- **Assonance** is the repetition of similar vowel sounds regardless of where they are located in the word. Some good examples in the passage are:

> wince—whinny
> sunburn—girls (similarity of sound, not spelling)
> hullabaloo—balloons

- **Consonance** is the repetition of consonantal sounds. Since *alliteration* is used to describe similarity in initial sounds, *consonance* usually refers to sounds within the words. Often the two are used in conjunction. There are three sets of consonance in this passage:

> wince—whinny
> girls—lark
> silent—hullabaloo—balloons

- **Onomatopoeia** is often defined as a word that sounds like the object or action it describes; but actually most onomatopoetic words suggest a sound only to those who already know what the meaning is. That is, we are not dealing with language that mimics life directly; it is usually just an echo. There are three good examples in Thomas' paragraph:

> slap of sea (the sound of a wave on the beach)
> whinny (an approximation of a horse's cry)
> hullabaloo (derived from "hullo" and "hello" with an
> echo of "babble")

Analyses like these tend to remain abstract and theoretical until one tries the technique in actual composition. Stop now and think of a scene, a friend, or a piece of music that comes to you with the soft, gentle contours you associated with the Oona figure in Chapter 2. Now try a paragraph of descriptive prose in which you make use of as many sound devices as possible. Remember that this is prose, so there is no need to worry about rhythm or a regular rhyme scheme. It might help to circle the linkages in sound. The point of this exercise is merely to help you find and use sound clusters.

Now, by way of contrast, think of a place, a person, or a piece of music that more closely resembles the sharp characteristics of the Kepick figure. Again, work out one or two prose paragraphs. This is to poetry what preliminary sketches are to a finished painting.

The Sound of Rhyme

A rhyme scheme is one device that is the exclusive property of poets. Prose may contain scattered rhymes, but only when the writer controls the length of the line is a rhyme scheme or system possible.

True rhyme can be defined in three short sentences: (1) It is an *identity in sound in accented syllables.* (2) The identity begins with the *accented vowel and continues to the end.* (3) The sounds preceding the accented vowel must be *unlike.*

Here are three examples of true rhymes:

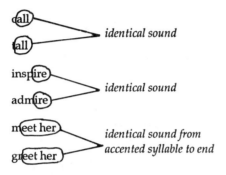

In the three-sentence definition above, I have italicized the key concepts that seem to give the most trouble. First, we are describing true rhyme as opposed to the slant rhymes or off rhymes that will be discussed shortly. True rhyme is not a general similarity in sound like assonance and consonance, it is an actual identity. Thus "ru*n*" and "co*me*" are not true rhymes because of the subtle difference in sound; nor are "seen" and "cream."

Second, rhyme is a matter of sound, not spelling. "Girl" and "furl" rhyme, but "to read" and "having read" obviously do not. They are called **eye rhymes**. It is often necessary to repeat the final syllable aloud several times before one is sure whether the rhyme is true or not—as do composers when testing the relationship between chords.

Next, there is the matter of continuing identity which must begin with the accented vowel and run through to the end of each word. This is only a problem with two-syllable rhymes (known as **feminine rhymes**). In "running," for example, the accented vowel is *u* and the only words that rhyme with it end with *unning*, as in "sunning." The word "jumping" has the *u* sound, but the *mp* keeps it from rhyming with "running."

Finally, the sound that comes before that accented vowel must differ from its rhyming partner. Thus, "night" and "fight" rhyme since the accented vowel (*i*) is preceded by *n* in one case and *f* in the other. But "night" and "knight" do not. These are technically known as *identities*.

Since rhyme is based on the sound of syllables and has nothing to do with the division of words, the same principles apply when more than one word is involved in each rhyming end. "Bind me" and "find me" rhyme (the accented vowel is *i* in each case, and the rhyming sound is *ind me*), but neither rhymes with "kindly" because of the *l*.

Rules like these seem artificial when you first meet them; but like the rules of any new game, they become second nature once you get used to working with them.

If you have the mechanics of rhyme clearly in mind, study the following table. To test yourself, cover the explanations and judge whether the pair of related words on the left is a true rhyme or not, and what makes it so.

RELATED WORDS	ACCENTED VOWEL SOUND	ACTUAL RELATIONSHIP AND EXPLANATION
1. night / fight	*i*	True rhyme (meets all three requirements)
2. night / knight	*i*	An identity (preceding consonant sounds are identical)
3. ocean / motion	*o*	True rhyme (*cean* and *tion* sound the same); also known as *double* or *feminine rhyme* (two syllables)
4. warring / wearing	*or* and *air*	Consonance or off rhyme (accented vowel sounds do not match)
5. track to me back to me	*a*	True rhyme (a triple rhyme)
6. dies / remedies	*i* and *em*	Eye rhyme (*dies* is similar only in spelling)
7. then you see us; when you flee us	*e*	Quadruple rhyme—true rhyme (rare and usually appears forced— often comic)

For a less mechanical examination of rhyme, turn to the Anthony Hecht poem, "Lizards and Snakes," on page 111. You have already studied this poem for its use of image and symbol, but you may not have noticed that it is perfectly rhymed. The rhyme endings don't stand out because they occur on alternate lines—a rhyme scheme referred to as *abab*—and also because the poet has adopted an almost conversational tone. But every line is rhymed and all but two are true rhymes. Can you spot the exceptions? When looking for them, identify the accented syllable in each rhyming word.

Varieties of Rhyme Schemes

Most poets who use rhyme use it regularly in a recurring pattern—a rhyme scheme. And the basic unit of that scheme is the **stanza**. Sometimes a stanza is indicated with an extra space and sometimes not. In either case, the stanza begins where the cycle starts again.

Stanzas in poetry are like paragraphs in prose. But in metered verse, each stanza usually has the same number of lines. I will have more to say about stanzas and how they relate to meter in Chapter 9, but our concern here is limited to systems of sound.

The rhyming **couplet** is the shortest possible stanza and consists of two rhymed lines. Those pairs of rhymed lines are designated as *aa, bb, cc*. This pattern was popular in the eighteenth century, but it is used less often today, partly because the paired rhymed endings are apt to be so obvious. Unless skillfully done, they have all the auditory subtlety of a suitcase dragged down a long flight of stairs.

Maxine Kumin's "Morning Swim" (p. 113) is proof that couplets don't have to sound that way. I'll turn to ways of muting the impact of rhyme later in this chapter, but you may wish to study the poem now since it is an unusual sample of this verse form.

Triplets (also known as tercets) are more popular than couplets, partly because it is easier to complete an idea in three lines than in two, but also because the rhyme can be made far less pronounced by connecting every other line. Rather than having the *aa, bb, cc* of couplets, you can work with the muted pattern of *aba, cdc, efe*. As you can see, this pattern gives you one "free" line—one for which you don't have to find a rhyme.

If, however, you are feeling ambitious, you can also use the triplet in a pattern that links each stanza with the next by rhyming the center lines this way: *aba, bcb, cdc*, and so on. It is a somewhat demanding form in English because the language doesn't have as many rhyme endings as does Italian or Spanish, but using what is known as **terza rima** puts you in good company. Dante invented it, and Browning, Auden, and Eliot all used it.

Quatrains, stanzas of four lines, give an even wider range of rhyming options. Patterns of *abab* and *abba* are the most common. Or one can leave the third line unrhymed to make a less demanding rhyme scheme of *abcb*.

Richard Wilbur uses quatrains in "The Pardon" (p. 122), and he rhymes every line in a system that is essentially *abba*. I say "essentially" since he occasionally uses slant rhymes that I will turn to shortly. The third stanza is one of those that use true rhymes consistently and is the clearest example of the pattern used throughout:

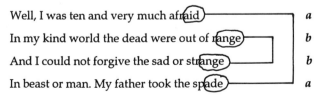

Well, I was ten and very much afraid	*a*
In my kind world the dead were out of range	*b*
And I could not forgive the sad or strange	*b*
In beast or man. My father took the spade	*a*

Anthony Hecht uses the rhyme scheme *abab* in "Lizards and Snakes." The stanzas appear to be eight lines long, but if you examine them closely you will see that the rhyme scheme starts fresh every four lines—the quatrains are visually run together.

Longer stanzas and more complex rhyme schemes were popular in earlier centuries and are well worth careful study. But the trend today is toward relatively simple systems. The poems in Chapter 11 provide a wide range of options.

Achieving Subtlety in Sound

When the sound of language becomes obvious and draws attention to itself, it dominates the entire poem—even the theme. This is no problem with nursery rhymes where rhyme and rhythm are half the fun, mass-appeal poems like Kilmer's "Trees," and **occasional verse**—light pieces written for special occasions like anniversaries or birthdays. Comic verse also uses blatant rhymes, often as part of the comedy. But if you are working with a serious and complex set of themes, obtrusive rhymes can reduce all your efforts, to a jingle. Even a free-verse poem can be made to sound trivial if you use techniques like alliteration without restraint, but the most common problem is the sing-song effect in rhyming poetry.

One way to mute rhyme is to use **enjambment** or run-on lines occasionally. An enjambed line is one in which the grammatical construction or the meaning continues to the next line. It is distinguished from the **end-stopped** lines, which are usually concluded with a period or a semicolon. Rhyme is less noticeable when the reader is drawn without a pause to the next line.

As I have pointed out earlier, maintaining subtlety of sound in rhyming couplets is a real challenge. One of the best examples of the use of enjambment to accomplish this is Maxine Kumin's "Morning Swim." In this poem there are twelve stanzas rhyming *aa, bb, cc,* and so on. Ten out of the twelve stanzas are enjambed. Some are fully enjambed, like this one:

> Invaded and invader,   *No pause here*
> I went overhand on that flat sky.

There is no way you can stop or even pause at the end of that first line. Other lines are partially enjambed, like this couplet:

> that fed the lake that met my sea || *slight pause*
> in which I sang *Abide with Me.*

You could stop at "sea" without being confused, but the sentence does continue into the second line.

Only two out of the twelve stanzas are truly end-stopped. Here is one:

> Fish twitched beneath me, quick and tame. ‖ *Full pause*
>
> In their green zone they sang my name

End-stopped lines are usually concluded with a period or a semicolon, but not always. The deciding factor is whether the reader must continue to the next line to make grammatical sense.

A more radical method of muting rhyme is simply to separate the rhyming lines. As I have already pointed out, triplets, quatrains, and longer stanza forms allow you to alternate the rhyme endings, as in *abab, cdcd*. More radical still, you can leave a line regularly unrhymed—triplets with *aba, cdc* or quatrains with *abcd, efgf*.

A third method of muting the sound relationships is by using a few **slant rhymes** instead of true rhymes. Slant rhymes (also called **off rhymes**) are similar but not identical in sound, as in *account* and *about*. Often they are simply a form of assonance placed at the end of two lines.

Slant rhymes are frequently used in combination with other muting techniques to keep the rhyme from taking over like a drumbeat. Here, for example, is a drumbeat revision of the second stanza of Richard Wilbur's "The Pardon." Remember, this is *not* how Wilbur wrote it.

> I went in close to where the poor dog was.
> I heard the flies' intolerable buzz.
> The air was heavy with honeysuckle-smell.
> It was twined with another whose source I could not tell.

Notice how every line ends with a true rhyme and how the scheme has been converted to *aa, bb* as if it were two couplets. More important, each line is end-stopped, with the rhyme landing heavily at the end: was–buzz, smell–tell.

Here is the actual stanza as written by Richard Wilbur:

> Went only close enough to where he was
> To sniff the heavy honeysuckle-smell
> Twined with another odour heavier still
> And hear the flies' intolerable buzz.

You can hear the difference even from a casual reading of these two versions, but you have to look more closely to see how it is achieved. The rhyme is there, but *smell* and *still* are slant rhymes. In addition, the scheme is, like the rest of the poem, *abba*. No line in this stanza is a complete sentence ending with a period, so there is no tendency to place a heavy emphasis on the rhyming words.

Wilbur uses slant rhymes sparingly—only three pairs out of twelve—and he distributes them through the poem. If you find that your slant rhymes are bunched toward the end, it probably means you were tired and quit too soon!

Robley Wilson's "On a Maine Beach" (p. 118) makes such extensive and consistent use of slant rhymes that you may have assumed it was free verse on first reading. As with some recurring phrases in music, the effect of the rhymes is almost subliminal. But the pattern is unmistakable if you look closely.

To see the rhyme scheme, it helps to divide the poem into four groups of four lines each. These "stanzas" are for analysis only. Here is a list of the last words in each line, with marginal identifications:

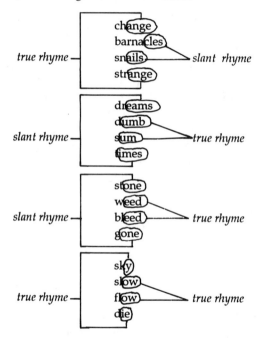

The rhyme scheme is partially hidden by the fact that the poet has not used stanza divisions. And even after we divide the lines for purposes of analysis, the true rhyme endings are separated by two apparently nonrhyming lines. The last "stanza," however, is made up of true rhymes in a pattern of *abba*, and when we look closely at the other lines we see that the scheme is completed with slant rhymes.

In addition to this somewhat hidden rhyme scheme, Wilson has used alliteration (initial sounds), assonance (vowel sounds) and consonance (consonantal sounds) on almost every line. There are three pairs of these nonrhyming devices in the first two lines:

Look, in these pools, how rocks are like worn change

Keeping the ocean's mint-mark;...

And later there is a triple assonance:

Rocks shrink, barnacles drink, snails think they bleed

Many poets avoid rhyme altogether, but this does not mean that they necessarily ignore the sound of language. Dylan Thomas in "Fern Hill," for example, relies almost entirely on alliteration, assonance, and consonance in much the same way he did in the prose passage quoted at the beginning of this chapter. The only trace of a rhyme is seen (if you look hard) linking the third and the eighth lines in all but one stanza. These are slant rhymes, and the gap is far too great to hear on first reading, but when they are added to the heavy use of other sound devices, they contribute to what we sense as the "musical tone" of the poem as a whole.

The number of sound connections is astonishing. Almost every line contains two or more words that are linked by sound. Yet the connections are muted enough so that we sense the general effect long before we see the mechanics of how he achieves it.

Some contemporary poets rely more heavily on images than on the sound of language. Donald Hall's "Names of Horses" (p. 112), for example, is not only unrhymed but contains very few examples of assonance or consonance. The effect he achieves comes through a succession of highly visual, fresh, and memorable images. But a significant number of poets continue to draw on the auditory aspect of the genre in one form or another.

Sound as Meaning

When working with rhyme, guard against the tendency to treat it like a mechanical game, filling in the appropriate blanks. Sound devices are most effective when they become a part of the meaning. The best rhymes are those that draw together two images and produce a heightened or expanded meaning. In Maxine Kumin's "Morning Swim," for example, one of the most effective rhyming couplets links the act of swimming with that of singing a hymn of praise:

and in the rhythm of the swim
I hummed a two-four-time slow hymn

This is more than a simple link. The act of swimming *becomes* a hymn, and the rhyme is a part of that fusion.

In the same way, assonance can be used to unify and intensify an image. Robley Wilson's simile "rocks are like worn change" is essentially a visual association, but the similarity of those *o* sounds help to fuse the vehicle and tenor. Dylan Thomas uses both assonance and consonance in the auditory metaphor "the sabbath rang slowly" from "Fern Hill." The *s* sounds and the repeated *a* sounds and the pacing of the those three stressed words all add to the illusion of church bells ringing. In the same poem his vision of fields marked with "rivers of the windfall light" is almost more auditory than it is visual as those *i, i, i* sounds ripple through the reader's mind. And what finer way is there to bid farewell to childhood than through an image fused by alliteration in "the farm forever fled from the childless land"?

Other examples of sound as meaning appear in Walt Whitman's un-rhymed poem "The Dalliance of the Eagles" (p. 115). Turn to it now and read it through for pleasure. Then study it analytically with special attention to linkages in sound.

As the eagles come together, listen again to the clash in the hard *c* sounds linking this visual image: "The clinching interlocking claws." And as they fall, locked together, listen to their revolving motion in the *u-ing* sounds in "tum-bling turning clustering loops." More subtle and yet doubtless intentional, the two birds fly off, their images separate now and growing small as the poem itself fades away in that truncated last line: "She hers, he his, pursuing."

These are not simple examples of onomatopoeia like Dylan Thomas' "slap of sea" quoted at the beginning of this chapter. They are relatively subtle ways of using the **overtones** or associations connected with certain sounds to establish meaning in poetry. If you recall the word games you played with those abstract forms named Kepick and Oona back in Chapter 2, you will understand how the sound itself of "clinching interlocking claws" communi-cates a different set of signals than does the sound of, say, "the sun born over and over."

Training Your Ear

It is hard to imagine a musical composer who doesn't spend a good deal of time listening to music. Yet some beginning poets are reluctant to read too much published poetry for fear of being influenced. Actually there is no danger of becoming imitative if one reads a wide variety of works; and only by reading—preferably aloud—can one begin to appreciate the ways in which poetry is written for the ear.

The best way to hear poetry is to read it slowly and aloud. But you can also "hear" a poem by mouthing the lines—a necessity if you are working in the library.

The analysis of the sound devices in Robley Wilson's "On a Maine Beach" is only a first step. Now that you know what to look for, turn to the complete poem on page 118 and read it through without stopping—preferably aloud. Then mark as many of the rhyme endings and the nonrhyming sound devices as you can find. After you have done this, read the poem aloud again. This sequence of reading, analyzing, and reading again is a good way to combine close study with general appreciation.

Next, turn to Chase Twichell's "Rhymes for Old Age" on page 122. It is similar to the Wilson poem in that it has a rhyme scheme highly muted with slant rhymes. In fact, there are only two pure rhymes. Although some of the connections are difficult to hear, the basic pattern for each stanza is *aba cbc*. Look closely and sound out the linked words. You can teach yourself how to identify the sound in poetry if you use the same sequence with this poem as you did with the Wilson poem: Read for pleasure, analyze carefully, and read again.

In training your ear to hear the sound of language, be careful not to stress rhyme at the expense of other devices. Alliteration, assonance, consonance, and onomatopoeia are equally important. For many poets they are more important.

A textbook analysis such as this is only a first step. It suggests what to look for. The next step is to go over and over a poem like "Fern Hill" or "The Dalliance of Eagles," marking the great variety of sound linkages and indicating in the margin where they have become a part of the meaning of the poem.

Another method of training your ear is to listen to recordings of poets reading their own work. Most libraries have collections of tapes and video cassettes. Dylan Thomas' readings are particularly effective. Consider buying tapes for your own personal use. Repeated listening is valuable as well as pleasurable.

Listening to a good reading is entertaining, but if you want to develop your own abilities as a poet, don't be a passive listener. Whenever possible, listen with a copy of the poem in front of you. Make marginal comments and then play the tape again. You will actually hear more as you become increasingly familiar with the work.

Finally, practice sound combinations in your poetry journal. Don't limit yourself to those lines that might develop into finished poems. Let yourself go. Experiment with assonance, with alliterative runs, with light verse in rhyme. Try a few imitations of poets with pronounced styles.

Sound in poetry is partly a matter of knowing what you are doing—technique. But it is also a matter of hearing what you are writing—a sensitivity to spoken language. Good poetry requires both.

6
TRADITIONAL RHYTHMS

Rhythms of daily life. Rhythm of stressed words. Syllabics. Metrics—the rhythm of stressed syllables. Keeping meter subtle. The appeal of meter.

Rhythmical patterns are buried deep in the human psyche. This is not surprising when one takes stock of the rhythms all about us. We record our cultural history in centuries and decades and our biographies by birth, youth, age, and death. We celebrate each passing year—even the bad ones; and we divide the years by seasons, which in turn alter the way we live. Within each season the moon waxes and wanes, affecting our emotions and our bodies in mysterious ways; tides rise and fall, and periods of light and dark determine our behavior. Within each waking day we are guided by cycles of hunger and energy, and at night our levels of sleep rise and fall like the tides, dipping regularly into crucial periods of REM. Beneath all this we sense the drumbeat of our hearts, and within each ebb and flow of blood the brain records a crucial rat-a-tat-tat of electric beats.

It's not surprising that some babies thump their cribs with rhythmic precision long before they are introduced to language. Young people throughout the world learn and enjoy schoolyard chants taught to them not by teachers but by older children, generation after generation. And in almost every culture people of all ages take pleasure in rhythmical music and dance. No luxury, music and dance are valued even when we are poor or oppressed. In fact, when we are forcibly deprived of rhythmical variation through solitary confinement, our very sanity is threatened.

The rhythms of poetry, then, are not mere adornment. They are not frills to be added. The rhythms of poetry are echoes of the rhythms of life.

If you look again at the previous three sentences, you will see two overlapping prose rhythms repeated: *not...not; rhythms...rhythms...rhythms.* This is a simple pattern compared to what one finds in poetry and is easily missed. But it contains the prime element found in every rhythmical system: a pattern of repetitions. It also illustrates how rhythmical patterns can become a part of the meaning—in this case by emphasizing two key words as effectively as if I had added, "and this is really important."

Poetry is not music, but it is a first cousin. We can sing poems or read song lyrics as if they were poetry. And it seems natural to use the word **verse** to designate both poetry in general and lyrics to be sung. Most important, it's hard to imagine either without some sense of rhythm.

There are two different approaches to creating rhythm in poetry. Although they are not absolutely separate, they provide a helpful way of looking at the subject.

Traditional rhythms, the subject of this chapter, are patterns that have been shared by poets over a period of centuries. They are familiar to those who enjoy reading poetry, and although each poet uses a traditional pattern in a slightly different way, part of the pleasure for the reader is the interplay between the basic pattern and the variation developed in a specific work.

Unique rhythms, on the other hand, refers to patterns that are devised exclusively for a particular poem. They are unique to that work. Although they are associated with what in our own century has been called **free verse**, unique rhythms as an approach goes back to Biblical verse. Creating unique rhythms is the subject of the next chapter.

Rhythm of Stressed Words

The simplest traditional rhythm in use today is based on the fact that when we speak we naturally place greater emphasis on some words than we do on others. We may not be consciously aware of it, but this is a part of how we use the language. Take, for example, this straightforward sentence:

> I went to town to buy some bread.

Written on the page it looks like eight one-syllable words of even weight. But imagine how that same sentence might sound to someone who doesn't understand English.

> i-WENT t'TOWN t'BUY s'mBREAD

The stressed words have muscled out the unstressed. This is why you can study a foreign language from textbooks for years and still be baffled when you first hear it spoken. But the frustrations of a language student become an asset for the poet. It is easy enough to construct lines in which there are, say, four stressed words—especially in English, which from the beginning has relied heavily on stress. In fact, this is exactly the system used in *Beowulf*, the Old English epic.

Here is a passage (translated into modern English) in which Beowulf, the hero, pursues a sea monster (the "brine-wolf") to her underwater lair. Read the selection a couple of times and underline the stressed words.

> Then bore this brine-wolf, when bottom she touched,
> the lord of rings to the lair she haunted,
> whiles vainly he strove, though his valor held,
> weapon to wield against wondrous monster
> that sore beset him; sea-beasts many
> tried with fierce tusks to tear his mail

It is obvious that poets in this tradition never counted syllables. They were concerned only with having two stresses, a pause known as a **caesura** and two more stresses in each line. They concentrated on this simple beat, and in *Beowulf* it is so clear that one can pound on the table while the song is chanted or sung—which is probably just what the ancients did in the mead hall over a thousand years ago.

The version above is a translation of a manuscript that dates from the eighth century, so one might think that its rhythmical systems would be of interest only to scholars. But poets can and do recycle anything that seems appropriate. In the 1970s the poet and playwright George Keithley turned to writing a book-length poetic account of the ill-fated Donner party, a group of pioneers most of whom perished trying to cross the Sierra Nevada range in the 1840s. Like the unknown bard who composed *Beowulf*, Keithley was working with a lengthy epic account that had already become a part of our cultural heritage. It seemed appropriate to him to use a traditional rhythmical system, but he wanted it strong, flexible, and highly accessible. He adopted a modification of the *Beowulf* pattern—generally two stressed words in each line or, occasionally, as in the following example, two pairs of stressed words. Also in the tradition of *Beowulf*, he frequently uses alliteration. Here is a brief sample from *The Donner Party*, one of the few narrative poems that became a Book Of The Month Club selection, and perhaps the only one that was later adapted as an opera, a radio play, and a stage play.

> The tongues of our flames licked at the dark.
> In time, our talking floated up like smoke
> and mingled with the chatter of the leaves.
> But the night unnerved us even as we spoke.

Syllabics: The Counting of Syllables

Rhythm that relies on stressed words in each line lends itself to long narrative poems—especially those with echoes of the spoken language. But its weakness is that it is not very subtle. Another approach is to count syllables rather than stressed words.

Syllabic verse establishes a pattern based not on stresses but on the number of syllables in each line. In some cases, every line has the same number of syllables. In others, line length varies, but the first stanza sets the pattern. The number of syllables in the first line of each stanza is the same; the number in each second line matches the other second lines, and so forth.

Syllabic poems are usually unrhymed, and no effort is made to have a consistent number of stresses in a line. The pattern may not be immediately apparent when the poem is read aloud. But it does constitute a rhythmical system since the structure is apparent on the page, and that in turn cues a reader when reading it aloud.

The **haiku**, discussed briefly in Chapter 4, is one traditional form of syllabics. It is an unrhymed and unmetered poem in which the first line has five syllables, the second has seven, and the third has five. Two contemporary haiku are printed on page 44. Here are two more samples, both of them translated from the Japanese:

> After spring sunset
> Mist rises from the river
> Spreading like a flood
>
> Even with insects...
> Some are hatched out musical...
> Some, alas, tone-deaf

Like all types of syllabics, this form is partially visual and only faintly auditory. When we look at a haiku we recognize the shape even before we count syllables—just as we do the fourteen-line form of the sonnet. The shape creates certain expectations if we have read other haiku. We assume that probably there will be a single image (often from nature) and that the central concern may be merely a visual impression rather than a philosophical statement.

This traditional rhythmical pattern is simple, yet the variety of treatment is infinite. In Japan, where many nonpoets enjoy writing and reading haiku, it has been estimated that a million new haiku are published each year.

Syllabics for the practiced poet can become a far more complex form of expression. Dylan Thomas' "Fern Hill" is a fine example. It is clear that the poem is not metered. The lines do not scan and they are far too varied in length to fit any traditional stanza pattern. But you can read the poem many times (as I did) without realizing that it is meticulously composed in stanzas that repeat the same pattern of syllables.

To be specific, the first line of every stanza has fourteen syllables and so do all the second lines. The third line of every stanza has nine syllables, the fourth line regularly has six syllables, and the fifth line always has nine. Up to this point the system is absolutely regular.

The sixth line has fourteen syllables in every stanza but the first (which has fifteen); the seventh line also has fourteen in every stanza but—you guessed it—the last (which again has fifteen). The eighth lines are either seven or nine syllables, and the final lines are either nine or six. Even his variations take on a certain order.

This is an astonishingly complex system. Why on earth should he bother when a majority of his readers will enjoy the poem as if it were an essentially formless work? There are three possible answers, all speculative. First, one might argue that this hidden structure beneath apparent formlessness echoes the portion of the theme that deals with the rhythms of life: "young and easy" in youth, yet mortal and already heading toward aging and eventual death— as sure as the tides, another rhythm. Thus, the line "I sang in my chains like the sea" reflects the rhythmical patterns of the poem itself, the "chains" being the limits set by line length.

A second and less academic explanation is his obvious delight in working with form for its own sake. Here, after all, is a poet who in another poem adopted the bizarre rhyme scheme *abcdefggfedcba*. One can read that poem a hundred times and not be aware of more than the central and apparently accidental couplet. But Thomas, like many other poets, seems to have enjoyed working with ingenious systems.

Finally—and most significantly—hidden form has its effect even on read- ers who have not analyzed the system precisely. There is a certain sense of control in these stanzas that one senses even without counting syllables. This is probably the best reason for considering some type of rhythmical system even in an apparently free work.

From Syllabics to Meter

Syllabic poetry has been the norm in Japan for centuries and has traditionally been popular in France and Italy as well. It has never, however, been as widely adopted by British and American poets. This is partly due to the fact that in English we stress certain syllables and glide over others. We pronounce *animal* with a heavy accent on the first syllable, for example, but the French pro- nounce *l'animal* with equal stress on each syllable. These natural stresses in English are like a rhythmical system waiting for development. All one has to do is to go one step beyond syllabics and establish identifiable patterns of stressed and unstressed syllables. This produces a rhythmical system that is far more subtle than merely counting the stressed words in the tradition of

Beowulf and is much more readily discerned by the ear than any system of syllabics. As a result, it has become the basis of all **meter** in English.

Historically, meter came to English verse when the French language was imposed on the Anglo-Saxons after the Norman invasion. It has been in use ever since. Although it has gone through considerable refinement over the centuries, remember that meter is basically a way of structuring the natural rhythms of the spoken language. It is similar in this respect to the way an established dance step creates rhythms from the motions we go through in daily living. The poet selects a metrical system that reflects the mood and tone of the poem that is developing and then adds to it his or her own style and variations.

Before we turn to the terminology, here is how a metrical rhythm is created. First, look at a slightly extended version of our simple prose statement:

> I went to town today to buy some bread.

If you pound out the rhythm in the tradition of an Anglo-Saxon poetry reading, it comes out like this:

> 1   2   3   4   5   6 7   8   9   10
> I *went* | to *town* | to*day* | to *buy* | some *bread*. |

This looks very much like our Anglo-Saxon line of stressed words, but in the case of "to*day*" we counted syllables rather than words. There are, in fact, ten syllables—five stressed and five unstressed. Since we are dealing with pairs of syllables, the pattern can bridge words as in the following line:

> My fa|ther can|not gam|ble with | his health. |

Notice that we are not forcing anything on the language; we are only arranging the words so as to emphasize a natural spoken rhythm.

If we want to describe this particular rhythmical effect without using technical terms, we might say that it goes ta-*tum*, ta-*tum*, ta-*tum*, ta-*tum*, ta-*tum*. There are five pairs of unstressed and stressed syllables here.

How might we convert that to a line which reverses the pattern? That is, how can we arrange the syllables to go *tum*-ta, *tum*-ta? Here is one possible version:

> Father | can not | gamble | with his | illness. |

I made two changes: dropping the initial unstressed syllable, *my*, and adding a syllable at the end by replacing *health* with *illness*. There are still ten syllables, but the pattern has changed to *tum*-ta.

This conversion shows how much depends on how we begin a line of metered verse. The pattern you start with is frequently (though not always) the scheme used throughout the line. None of this applies in prose, of course. In metrical poetry you have to control where each line begins and ends.

Referring to metrical patterns as "ta-*tum*" and "*tum*-ta" begins to get cumbersome; time to learn a few terms. Each unit of stressed and unstressed syllables is called a **foot**. The foot with the pattern ta-*tum* is called an **iamb**. The **iambic foot** is by far the most popular in English.

A line with five feet is called **pentameter** (from the Greek word *penta* for *five*). Iambic pentameter has been a favorite metrical scheme from Shakespeare to Robert Frost and Richard Wilbur.

Now that we have a basic metrical line and some terms for describing it, let's apply them to the following pair of lines from Richard Wilbur's "The Pardon" (p. 122).

> And death | was breed|ing in |his live|ly eyes. | *5 iambs*
>
> I start|ed in |to cry |and call |his name | *5 iambs*

Such perfectly regular iambic pentameter is actually unusual. More often verse contains minor variations in the pattern—an important aspect I will return to shortly. Other examples of iambic pentameter in Chapter 11 are Robley Wilson's "On a Maine Beach" and T. R. Hummer's "The Rural Carrier."

One reason for the popularity of the iamb is that so many two-syllable words fall naturally into this pattern: ex*cept*, al*low*, dis*rupt*, a*dore*, and the like. In addition, there is a natural tendency for sentences to begin with an unstressed syllable—often with words like *a, the, but, he, she, I.* But there are three other types of feet that are also used as the basis for metered poems, and two that serve as useful substitutions.

The **trochee** is the reverse pattern that we achieved by beginning our line with a stressed syllable: "*Father can* not *gamble*..." Trochees can be used as the basic foot for an entire poem, but more often they are used as a substitution for an iambic foot in an iambic poem. As we shall see, this can give a special emphasis to a word or phrase, particularly if it is done at the beginning of a line.

The **anapest** consists of three syllables—two unstressed followed by one stressed: ta-ta-*tum*. It has a lively, cheerful beat, as in this anonymous couplet:

> With a swoop | and a glide | the swift | in delight,   *Each line has*
>
> Arous|es our en|vy, our long|ing for flight.   *3 anapests and*
>   *1 iamb*

Notice how naturally the two iambic substitutions blend in and mute what might have been a singsong effect. Conversely, anapests serve well as substitutions in a basically iambic poem. The anapest is not used as the basic meter in many poems, but it has real potential for work that is light and lyrical.

The **dactyl** is the reverse of the anapest: *tum*-ta-ta, as in "*heav*ier," "*follow*ing," and "*talk* to me." It's a weighty foot.

Almost every metered poem in English uses one of these four feet as a basic pattern, and probably more than half take the iambic pattern. There are, however, two more feet that are useful when you **scan** a poem—that is, analyze it metrically. You will find yourself using them as substitutions as well.

The **spondee** is two heavy stresses, as in the word "spondee" itself, and in "heartbreak." The **pyrrhic** is two equally unstressed syllables, as in "in the" or "and the."

As a review, the following table shows the six metrical feet, with the stress pattern and examples of each.

FOOT	ADJECTIVE	STRESS PATTERN	EXAMPLES
iamb	iambic	ta-*tum*	except; the deer
trochee	trochaic	*tum*-ta	asking; lost it
anapest	anapestic	ta-ta-*tum*	understand; in delight
dactyl	dactylic	*tum*-ta-ta	heavily; talk to me
spondee	spondaic	*tum-tum*	heartbreak; faithful
pyrrhic	pyrrhic	ta-ta	in the; on a

In addition to the types of feet, there is the matter of how many feet are used in each line. By far the most popular length in English is five feet—pentameter. Unrhymed iambic pentameter, known as **blank verse**, was used by Shakespeare in his plays; pentameter is also the line used in the sonnet, described in the next chapter. In our own century such poets as Robert Frost, Richard Wilbur, and Anthony Hecht have made extensive use of this line.

The four-footed line, **tetrameter**, is a close second. And **trimeter** is also used widely. Lines that are longer than pentameter and shorter than trimeter are used far less frequently, but for the purpose of clarity, here is a list of types:

Two feet to each line (rare and usually comic)	*dimeter*
Three feet to each line (fairly common)	*trimeter*
Four feet (sometimes combined with trimeter)	*tetrameter*
Five feet (most common in English)	*pentameter*
Six feet (less used in this century)	*hexameter*
Seven feet (rare)	*heptameter*
Eight feet (a heavy, very rare line)	*octometer*

Don't let these traditional terms, collectively known as **scansion,** put you off. They are intended for your use both in reading metered verse and in composing. At this point, it would be helpful to try writing three lines of iambic tetrameter. Take some simple topic as if you were about to write a haiku and follow the iambic pattern: ta-*tum,* ta-*tum,* ta-*tum.* Don't worry about rhyme and don't feel you have to be profound. This is just to help you feel the rhythm.

Now try shifting your lines so that they are trochaic; *tum*-ta, *tum*-ta, and so on. Once you get the line started, the rest should follow somewhat more easily.

Next, shift the topic to something lighter and try a few lines of anapests: ta-ta-*tum,* ta-ta-*tum.* For example: "In a leap and a bound, the gazelle in delight welcomes spring!"

Iambs and anapests end on a stressed syllable, creating what is called **rising** (or *ascending*) **meter.** Trochees and dactyls end on unstressed syllables and therefore are called **falling** (or *descending*) **meters.** This distinction becomes important when one begins to use substitutions for variety and special effects.

Keeping Meter Subtle

Until now, I have been working only with skeletal outlines. They may appear to be as far from the actual creation of lyrical poetry as the study of notes and clefs appears to be from musical composition. But the process of absorption is similar in these two cases. What appears at first to be a set of arbitrary rules eventually becomes—even for those who may then depart from them—an internalized influence.

When you first begin working with meter, there is a natural tendency to make it as perfect and obvious as possible. The result is apt to be like the dancer who is still counting out each step. As soon as possible, try to mute your meter—not by careless construction but by adopting the methods of poets you admire.

There are four ways of keeping your metrical rhythm from taking over a poem, and often you will find three or even all four of them used in a single work.

The first and most commonly used method is to make sure that at least some of your words bridge two metrical feet. Contrast, for example, these two versions:

Tides drown | such pools | each day |

Tides swal|low up | such pools |

There is nothing wrong with the first version, but each beat is a separate word. It may have been to avoid such regularity that Robley Wilson chose the second version for his poem "On a Maine Beach." The word "swallow" bridges the first and second feet, muting the impact of the meter.

A second method of muting meter is to use **enjambment**, also known as the **run-on line**. An enjambed line, described briefly in the previous chapter, is one in which both the grammatical construction and the sense are continued into the next line. It is opposed to the **end-stopped line**, in which there is a natural pause—usually with a comma or a period. Some enjambed lines are more abrupt than others, of course; and the more pronounced such a pause is, the more it will emphasize the meter.

Enjambment helps to soften the impact of meter just as it mutes rhyme endings. At the conclusion of Wilson's "On a Maine Beach," for example, the run-on line appropriately echoes the "beach rhythms" he is describing:

> Round lifetimes half-awake. Beach rhythms flow
> In circles. Perfections teach us to die.

Another technique of softening the impact of meter is rarely used but well illustrated in Anthony Hecht's "Lizards and Snakes." Instead of writing consistently in lines of pentameter or tetrameter, he alternates between these two. The first line has five feet and the next has four. A few of his lines even have six feet.

This is a risky approach, since the reader is apt—at least unconsciously—to expect greater regularity. One reason it seems natural here is that the poet has consciously adopted an informal, conversational tone.

The fourth and by far the most frequently used method is called **substitution**. That is, the poet occasionally substitutes a different foot from the one that has been adopted for the poem as a whole.

We have already looked at Richard Wilbur's "The Pardon" for examples of how to mute the sound of rhyme. It is also a good illustration of how to keep iambic pentameter meter from becoming monotonous. Here, for instance, is how he uses a trochaic substitution with the phrase "twined with."

> ⏑ ´ ⏑ ´ ⏑ ´ ⏑ ´ ⏑ ´
> To sniff | the heav|y hon|eysuck|le-smell |
>
> ´ ⏑ ⏑ ´ ⏑ ´ ⏑ ´ ⏑ ´
> Twined with | anoth|er o|dour heav|ier still |

The substitution not only offers variation, it also highlights the metaphor that links the way smells mix and the way vines twist about each other. The substitution, then, is not arbitrary—not simply a matter of the poet getting tired. It adds to the emotional impact of the line.

Later in the same poem he has a line that has two substitutions, the first an anapest and the second a trochee. I have left it unmarked so that you can scan it yourself.

In the carnal sun, clothed in a hymn of flies

How much substitution can a poem absorb? Anthony Hecht's "Lizards and Snakes" comes close to the limit. The poem is essentially iambic, but here is a line in which three of the five feet are non-iambic substitutions. Can you scan it and spot the variations?

In the set of the jaw, a fierce pulse in the throat

The most logical way to scan this is to read the opening six words as two anapests. The other substitution is the trochee in "pulse in."

With so many variations, why do we call the poem iambic? Because *most* of the lines are largely iambic, with no more than one or occasionally two substitutions. When we come to a line like the one just quoted, we retain the memory of that iambic beat and assume that the poem will return to it, as indeed it does. If the poem contained very many lines with so few iambs, we would begin to conclude that it was unmetered.

The Appeal of Meter

Metered verse dominated British and American poetry for some 500 years. During our own century, varieties of free verse with its unique systems of rhythm became a firm part of our tradition. As I mentioned in the last chapter, the 1980s and 1990s have produced a renewal of interest in metrical systems under the general heading of **New Formalism**. Although it is not a dominant movement, it has many enthusiastic adherents.

When one is introduced to meter, it may seem mechanical and limiting. There are new terms to master, just as there are when one is learning the grammar of a foreign language. But poets who prefer to work metrically don't usually start out by selecting a meter as if it were a mold into which one could pour words. Instead, they are more likely to let a poem begin intuitively and see what kind of line develops. If you have been reading metered poetry, your initial lines may suggest a metrical pattern that seems natural and appropriate for your material.

Once we get beyond the introductory stage in metrics, it becomes clear that what we speak of as an iambic pentameter or a trochaic trimeter line is an abstract concept to work with rather than an accurate description of the completed poem. Poet and reader keep that metrical beat in mind, but the pleasure comes in the interplay between that pattern and the variations that the poem presents.

Those who listen to jazz know what it is to improvise around the melody, alternatively straying from it and returning to it. Stray too far and too consistently, and the memory of the melody is lost; stick too close, and you run the risk of monotony. In the same way, those who enjoy working with meter find pleasure in variety without losing contact with the traditional rhythm.

There are two other benefits to writing in meter that its proponents often mention. One is that using a metrical pattern frequently leads to finding words and phrasing that one didn't think of at first. That is, the meter (and the rhyme too, if it is used) often pushes the poet into exploring possibilities that might not have been tried with a less-structured system.

Second, many poets like the opportunity of emphasizing or highlighting a word or phrase through the natural stress of a metrical foot or, stronger still, through substitution. We have seen how using the heavy initial beat of a trochaic foot in a basically iambic poem can add emphasis, and how the lilting quality of an anapest can give a lift to a line that is otherwise consistently iambic or trochaic. This provides a delicate control of language not possible when writing prose.

The choice of whether to work with meter or not is a personal one, but like so many aspects of the arts, it is not a true choice until one has tried both possibilities. Many prefer the looser structure of free verse; but there will always be poets for whom meter is a valuable asset.

7
UNIQUE RHYTHMS

Assets and liabilities of working with unique rhythms. Visual patterns of typography. Rhythms of syntax and phrasing. Rhythms of speech. Developing your own rhythms.

The term **unique rhythms** describes rhythms that are devised to meet the needs of an individual poem. Since they do not rely on the formal patterns we have been calling traditional rhythms, they are unique to each work.

In our own century, unique rhythms are associated with **free verse**. Free verse abandons meter for other rhythmical devices, and it drops regular rhyme in favor of looser sound systems such as assonance and consonance. But poetry that makes use of unique rhythms was popular centuries before the term *free verse* was coined. The irregular patterns of unique rhythms are rooted in a variety of ancient sources, including the Bible.

Freedom: Assets and Liabilities

When working with unique rhythms, you are free to devise your own systems. There is no consistent pattern to serve as a guide. In early drafts, the writing may be highly intuitive.

There are advantages and disadvantages to this. On the one hand, it will seem as if anything is possible—a heady sensation. On the other hand, it is more difficult to determine what is really effective and what "doesn't work." Because the measures of success are less precise, one is never quite sure when the poem has reached its full potential.

If you find working with unique rhythms less demanding than metrics, it may mean that you are not placing enough demands on yourself. You may wish to try several different rhythmical approaches to the same poem, reading each version aloud.

Although unique rhythms are more difficult to categorize than formal rhythms, there are three basic approaches. You can't use them as a way to characterize an entire poem the way you can say of a metered work, "It is in iambic pentameter." But you will find yourself drawing on one or more of these three techniques as you devise the best set of rhythms for an individual poem.

The first approach is to create visual patterns on the page known as **typographical** rhythms. The second is to establish rhythms through repeated patterns in **syntax** (sentence structure) and phrasing. The third is to echo the rhythms of speech, sometimes described as **breath units**.

Each poem has a different combination of these techniques, but for purposes of analysis, it helps to look at them individually.

Visual Patterns of Typography

This method of creating rhythmical effects is not strictly a matter of sound. Since it depends heavily on how the poem looks on the printed page, it is often called **visual rhythm**. But actually there is no clear separation between visual and auditory rhythms. The way a poem is arranged on the page is going to affect the way it is read in some way. **Typography**, then, refers to the arrangement of words on the page, but it is linked closely with the sound of a poem.

Turn now to Denise Levertov's free-verse poem "Merritt Parkway," on page 119. Read it a couple of times just for the sense of motion. The typography of the lines is clearly designed to suggest both the motion and our mood as we drive.

Although the structure is not formal as in the stanzas of metered verse, there are cues that establish form. Notice, for example, the phrase "keep moving—" which appears in the third line and again a little more than halfway through. In each case the words are used to introduce a new block of images—the first indented to the right and the second brought out to the left.

The images tend to be linked visually more than by the sound of the words, but notice how at the end the poet employs not only alliteration but onomatopoeia in the echo of cars sliding by on the highway:

in six lanes, gliding

north & south, speeding with

a slurred sound—

When extra space is left at the beginning or the end of a line, or spaces are left between words within the line, the effect is called **horizontal rhythm**. The term is helpful because it is a reminder of how important white space is—the portion of the line not filled in with words. Painters call it "negative space"—the area between specific forms. Poets and painters share the ability to create significance from nothing.

In the same way, when extra spaces are left between lines, the result is **vertical rhythm**. Traditional stanza forms, of course, often make use of vertical rhythms by leaving an extra space between each stanza. But when working with unique rhythms as Levertov does in "Merritt Parkway," those spaces become irregular and in many cases closely tied to the meaning.

One note of caution, however: Simple, obvious use of typography can be just as damaging to a free-verse poem as simple, singsong use of meter and rhyme can be to traditional work. Because typographical arrangements are so blatant, so immediately apparent, they have to be used with considerable subtlety. Every writing class has been subjected to some version of this:

>And on that happy afternoon we
> all
>   fell
>   down
>   laughing.

What do you have to do to achieve real freshness and ingenuity in typography? E. E. Cummings' poem "Buffalo Bill's" (p. 117) is one example. Turn to it now and read it over several times for the pleasure of it. Then study it carefully, looking for the ways in which he controls the speed of your reading and provides elements of surprise through typographical arrangement.

Those run-together phrases are a sample of compressed horizontal spacing. Cummings actually speeds up your reading with that technique. This may not apply to your first reading, of course, since it takes time to figure out lines that are printed without spaces. But once you are used to the poem, these lines seem to ripple by as if they were moving:

>and break onetwothreefourfive pigeonsjustlikethat
>   Jesus
>   he was a handsome man

Here the word "Jesus" appears to be linked syntactically with Buffalo Bill's shooting ability; but then it leaps forward to become linked with how handsome he was. It is essentially a visual trick, tripping our expectations through an unexpected shift in rhythm. Of course, the same device of syntactical ambiguity can be used in metered verse, but the effect is heightened here by hanging the word between the two lines.

Notice, incidentally, that Cummings uses a form of syllabics in addition to typography. His run-together phrase "onetwothreefourfive" has exactly the same number of syllables as "pigeonsjustlikethat"—linking the number of his rapid-fire shots and the series of clay pigeons on a skeet range. This is a good example of the fact that when working with the unique rhythms of free verse, you can combine several techniques.

When we analyze poems like "Merritt Parkway" and "Buffalo Bill's" it should become apparent that much of what appeared on first reading to be arbitrary placement is in fact carefully planned to create an effect. Levertov's horizontal and vertical rhythms create our sense of cars moving on the highway, and Cummings controls the speed of our reading with precision and plays tricks with our expectations.

It is also true, however, that one cannot find a rational explanation for every typographical element. Like the brush strokes of a painter, many decisions that go into making a poem are intuitive. If it were not for this aspect, typographical rhythms would tend to seem contrived, even forced. This is why it is important to keep working on different versions of the same poem, writing out each and reading them aloud. Trust your ear as much as your mind.

One extreme form of typography is the "shaped poem," which molds the shape of the work into the object it is describing. This form was particularly popular in the seventeenth century and is well illustrated by Herbert's "The Altar" and "Easter Wings," as well as by Herrick's "The Pillar of Flame," each of which resembles the object suggested in its title. More recently, contemporaries like Allen Ginsberg have published poems in the shape of atomic clouds and, with the aid of punctuation, rockets.

Shaped poetry—also called **concrete poetry**—does have certain limitations. As a poem begins to rely more and more on its shape, it generally makes less and less use of the sound of language, rhythms, or metaphor. Even the theme becomes simplified. It is as if concern for the visual effect overpowers all other aspects. One can, for example, repeat the word *death* all over the page in such a way as to resemble a skull. It takes time and patience to do this, but the result is more like a cartoon than a poem. In general, the more extreme experiments in shaped poetry are remembered more for their curiosity value than for their literary worth.

Even nonpictorial use of typography has its drawbacks if used to an extreme. Sophisticated poetry depends at least in part on maintaining unity and flow. As you increase the rearrangement of words and lines on the page, the poem becomes more fragmented and, as a result, less of an organically unified work.

Rhythms of Syntax and Phrasing

Syntax is sentence structure. **Syntactical rhythms** are created by repeating a particular grammatical form such as a question or assertion.

Rhythms of syntax almost always contain a word or phrase that is repeated. If, for example, you start a sequence of lines with a question like "Who shall soothe…? Who justify…? Who speak…?" the pattern is recognized both by the repetition of syntax (the series of questions) and by that recurring word who.

Here is a sample of syntactical rhythm from Walt Whitman's "Passage to India." Notice how the repeated grammatical form and the repeated *who* serve in tandem to create the rhythmical effect.

> Ah who shall soothe these feverish children?
> Who justify these restless explorations?
> Who speak the secret of impassive earth?
> Who bind it to us? what is this separate Nature so unnatural?
> What is this earth to our affections?…

Why doesn't the repetition become boring? Mainly because the *content* is not repetitious, only the grammatical *form* and the key word *who*. There are limits, of course, to how long you can sustain a run like this, but much depends on the degree to which you can continue to offer fresh material while at the same time maintaining the rhythm with the grammatical form.

Allen Ginsberg wrote "Howl" in 1959, 104 years after Whitman first published "Leaves of Grass," and his indebtedness is clear. Here he describes "the best minds of my generation":

> who bared their brains to Heaven under the El and saw
>   Mohammedan angels staggering on tenement roofs
>   illuminated,
> who passed through universities with radiant cool eyes
>   hallucinating Arkansas and Blake-light tragedy among the
>   scholars of war,
> who were expelled from the academies for crazy & publishing
>   obscene odes on the windows of the skull,
> who cowered in unshaven rooms in underwear, burning their
>   money in wastebaskets and listening to the Terror through
>   the wall, …

Ginsberg is clearly influenced by Whitman, but both of them drew on a still earlier source, the Bible. Although the version Whitman knew was in English (the King James translation), and Ginsberg's version was in the original Hebrew, both men were strongly influenced by the rhythmical patterns found there. Compare, for example, the selections quoted from these two poets with this passage from Job 38:34:

> Canst thou lift up thy voice to the clouds,
>   that abundance of waters may cover thee?
> Canst thou send lightnings, that they may go
>   and say unto thee, Here we are?
> Who hath put wisdom in the inward parts?
>   or who hath given understanding to the heart?
> Who can number the clouds in wisdom?
>   or who can pour out the bottles of heaven?

Here too, it is the entire syntactical unit that is repeated to achieve the rhythm. The repeated words are merely cues which signal the repeated form. For further examples, read over the rest of the Book of Job and review the Psalms. Then go back and study the complex system of syntactical rhythms in Genesis. Doing this makes one far more open to the rhythms not only of Whitman and Ginsberg but of Ferlinghetti, Gregory Corso, John Ashbery, Amiri Baraka, and many others writing today.

Syntactical repetitions do not have to be thundering to succeed. The technique used by Anita Endrezze in the second stanza of "Song Maker" (p. 116) is essentially the same, though the tone is softer. Her syntactical repetition becomes almost a chant:

> Didn't he make songs people still sing
> in their sleep?
> Didn't coyotes beg him for new songs
> to give to the moon?
> Didn't he dance all night once and laugh
> when the women suddenly turned
> shy at dawn?
> Didn't he make a song just for me,
> one blessed by its being sung only once?

Those repeated questions, each starting with "Didn't he," become a part of the song. In this way, an aspect of style becomes an aspect of the theme.

A similar technique is used by Lisel Mueller in "Night Song" (p. 120) and is sustained throughout the poem. Here is the first stanza:

> Among rocks, I am the loose one,
> among arrows, I am the heart,
> among daughters, I am the recluse,
> among sons, the one who dies young.

The simplicity of the form is deceptive. If you read the poem over as a whole, you will see how the speaker finally becomes a symbol of poets everywhere. "Among the bones you find on the beach," she concludes, "the one that sings was mine."

Both Mueller's poem and the earlier examples, by the way, demonstrate the close relationship between syntactical rhythms and typography. If we wrote out "Night Song" or the selection from Job in lines of prose, the rhythm would still be unmistakable, just as it is in certain types of traditional oratory:

> Among rocks, I am the loose one; among arrows I am the heart;
> among daughters, I am the recluse; among sons, the one who
> dies young.

Because the poet controls the arrangement on the page, however, she can place each repeated phrase at the start of a new line. In this way, typography emphasizes the syntactical rhythms already there. This is one of the advantages poets have over writers of prose.

We think of syntactical rhythms as repeating whole syntactical units, as in the examples just given. But sometimes the effect can be achieved simply by repeating key words in a regular pattern. Lucille Clifton's poem "What the Mirror Said" (p. 126) appears to be a merry bit of self-affirmation almost without form. Here are the first 14 lines with the structure indicated:

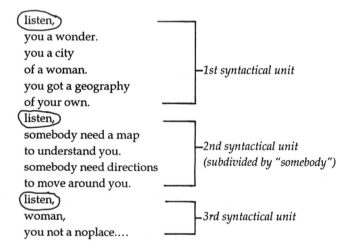

One of the pleasures of this poem is that it appears to be so spontaneous. But behind that apparent spontaneity there is a syntactical rhythm.

Rhythms of Speech

The rhythms of common speech can be found in all kinds of poetry from metered verse like T. R. Hummer's "The Rural Carrier" to the free verse of Lucille Clifton's "What the Mirror Said" which we have just examined for its syntactical patterns. Making use of speech patterns is essentially a nonintellectual act. It depends largely on the poet's ear.

One way to develop spoken rhythms is to imagine a persona speaking the lines. This can be done while you are composing as well as when you are revising. Short lines with abrupt phrasing, for example, generate a different set of rhythms than do long lines, especially if such lines are further divided by clauses or phrases. You can describe such contrasts in terms of horizontal rhythms (short lines have a lot of white space) or syntactical rhythms (if those phrases take on a pattern), but occasionally poets must set aside categories and trust their inclinations.

To contrast two dramatically different approaches, review the opening four lines of two poems that are now familiar to you: Lucille Clifton's "What the Mirror Said" and Walt Whitman's "The Dalliance of the Eagles":

> listen,
> you a wonder,
> you a city
> of a woman.

> Skirting the river road, (my forenoon walk, my rest,)
> Skyward in air a sudden muffled sound, the dalliance of the eagles,
> The rushing amorous contact high in space together,
> The clinching interlocking claws, a living, fierce, gyrating wheel,

Long before we start analyzing the rhythmical effect of these two passages, the ear responds to the illusion of two radically different tones of voice. The first is abrupt, enthusiastic, attention-getting; the second is leisurely, observant, concerned with detail.

Some poets like to describe such differences of line length in terms of **breath units**. On a literal level, the phrase suggests that a line is broken where the reader of the poem would naturally take a breath when reciting aloud. But this is complicated in poems that are presented through a persona, an implied speaker who may have cadences of his or her own. On a less literal level, breath means "spirit," and each poem has a spirit of its own that is reflected in every line. There is a breathless, eager spirit to Clifton's poem and a measured, deliberate quality to Whitman's.

Phrases like "breathless spirit" and "deliberate quality" are rather loose ways of describing rhythms, but they are appropriate. They demonstrate one of the differences between the approach of those primarily concerned with literary criticism and those who are involved in the creative act of writing poetry. It is the critic's job to analyze as fully, as deeply, and as precisely as possible. In some cases, the individual poem is less important than the literary principles it illustrates. This kind of study requires an extensive critical vocabulary and an analytical frame of mind. The poet, on the other hand, needs only as many critical terms and concepts as are needed to describe what he or she has done—a practical, working vocabulary—and an inventive frame of mind spinning with images and rhythms. A great deal of the creative process consists of making nonintellectual decisions. We call it "intuitive," but this does not mean that it simply bubbles up from our psyche. Part of it is "built in"—like having a good ear—and an equally important portion is acquired from reading a great deal of poetry.

Does all free verse contain some kind of rhythmical system? That depends on how broad your definition of verse is. **Prose poetry**, for example, is a hybrid form written in short lines that look essentially like a prose paragraph. Prose poems occasionally have less rhythm and fewer sound linkages and figurative language than the prose of, say, Dylan Thomas in "August Bank Holiday" quoted in Chapter 5. Some feel that prose poetry is a contradiction in terms, but its defenders point to examples that achieve a compression of statement and contain echoes of speech rhythms.

Although exceptions may be found, almost all poetry contains rhythmical patterns of some sort. For many poets, it is one of the strengths and pleasures of the genre, a fundamental asset that sets poetry apart from prose.

Developing Your Own Rhythms

When you begin composing a new poem, let the first few lines speak to you. Often they will suggest the kinds of rhythms that are appropriate for that particular poem. Your emotional involvement with the material, your personal preferences, and the nature of the subject matter will all influence what develops. And because so many factors are involved, the result will be unique.

As the poem takes shape, consider some of the general patterns we have examined in this chapter—the typography, vertical and horizontal rhythms, repetition of syntactical patterns and phrasing, and, if appropriate, echoes from common speech. Keep your rhythms subtle. Try not to overwork any one device so heavily that the technique becomes obtrusive. Experiment with a number of different approaches and trust your feelings.

If you are just beginning to write free verse, you may be tempted to establish a personal "style" by adopting a single rhythmical system and repeating it in poem after poem. This is limiting, however. Most accomplished poets vary their methods, particularly early in their careers. Variety helps one to grow.

With this in mind, here is an exercise that will help you keep your options open. First, read the three prose sentences quoted in the next paragraph. Forget that they have been taken from a poem you have studied. Imagine that this is simply a prose passage that happens to be highly charged with visual and auditory images:

"The wind's untiring saxophone keens at the glass. The lamp sheds a monochrome of stainless steel and linens, the nurse in her snowy dress firm in her regimens. The form in the bed is a soul diminished to a fledgling, fed on the tentative balm of spring, sketch for an angel, half-finished, shoulder blades the stubs of wings."

After you have become familiar with the passage (you may want to look up a couple of words), convert it to two quite different poems using the same wording but breaking the lines in different ways. Consider both horizontal and vertical rhythms, stressing different words by your choices. You may not be able to improve on the original version that is printed in Chapter 11, but you will come to understand how fluid this approach to rhythmical language is. You may also discover how deeply the rhythmical patterns affect the tone and even the statement of a poem.

Another helpful exercise is to take a descriptive prose passage from an article about nature or travel. This time, don't limit yourself to the wording of the original. Find your own language to add freshness and intensity to the passage and then, as before, devise two different rhythmical approaches. This is the kind of "sketching" that will make your poetry journal an effective part of your development.

In addition to exercises like these in your journal, spend some time each day examining the rhythms of published poetry. Since most poetry contains rhythmical patterns of some sort, every anthology and literary quarterly can serve as a source for study. By combining practice work in your journal and extensive, careful reading, you will soon acquire a facility in poetic rhythms.

8
TONE

Tone as an essential aspect of meaning. Tone defined as your attitude toward your subject. The role of a persona—close identity versus distance. Tensions in tone. Varieties of irony. The caustic tone of satire. Keeping the tone honest.

"I want that."

This looks like a clear, unambiguous statement. How could we mistake its meaning? Easily. In fact, we can't even respond until we identify the speaker and the tone of voice.

Suppose, for example, that the speaker is a stranger on a dark street and he is holding a gun. That's going to evoke one set of responses. But what happens when the same words are said with a laugh by a friend as you both gaze longingly at an elegant BMW? The whole meaning shifts.

Now imagine a situation in which there is no threat and no humor involved: The same words are said by a sobbing child in a supermarket, pointing to a sugar-coated breakfast cereal you detest. And what happens to the statement when it is the retort of someone who has just discovered her tax rate has been doubled—"I want that like a hole in the head" ?

In spoken language we respond not only to the literal meaning of a statement, the **denotation**, but almost always to the implied meanings, the **connotations**. We infer such meanings from the circumstances and the tone of voice. As you can see from those examples, tone in everyday speech is not just an adornment to language; it is a fundamental aspect of meaning.

The same is true of poetry. Tone is revealed by your attitude toward your subject and in some cases by the attitude of the persona or implied speaker of the poem as well. In every poem the tone is an essential part of the meaning.

Your Attitude Toward Your Subject

When we refer to the **tone** of a poem we use such words as cheerful, reflective, somber, wry, and angry. Keep in mind, however, that there are really as many different shadings of tone as there are different tones of voice and that there are no sharp divisions between them. Like the names of colors, they are convenient segments of a spectrum.

Oddly, you may not even know what your attitude toward your subject is when you start a new poem. You can be drawn toward an occurrence, an experience, a relationship, a setting without knowing why. It may take one or two drafts of a poem before you realize that what attracts you to the material is a sense of love or perhaps anger or a feeling of nostalgia. The very act of translating experience into lines of verse occasionally opens up veins of emotions you hadn't expected—some stratum of love for someone you thought you hated, a hidden fear of a situation you thought you enjoyed, anxiety in an area where you thought you were secure. In such cases, developing a poem with true honesty may take considerable courage.

A *cheerful* or *comic tone* is too often avoided on the grounds that the writer won't be taken seriously. There is an unfortunate confusion in the English language between *serious* as a furrow-browed emotion and *serious* meaning complex or insightful. It is quite possible for a poem to be cheerful, even comic and still offer genuine feelings and significant insights that are worth thoughtful consideration.

Lucille Clifton's "What the Mirror Said" (p. 126), for example, is comic in tone. The speaker looks in the mirror and compares herself with a whole country. She is so complex that someone would have to have a map to understand her. We smile. It's a comic use of **hyperbole**. But we also respond to the deeper implications. This is clearly a woman's statement, and the as-if-spoken cadences suggest that she is black. The poem is an assertion of self-worth on both counts. The true theme of the poem is rooted in the two major social issues of black and female self-esteem.

A *reflective tone* is a broad and inclusive category. In many cases, the poet has seen something that he or she wishes to share with readers. "Look, in these pools, how rocks are like worn change," Wilson says at the opening of "On a Maine Beach" (p. 118). He goes on to describe the scene and also to draw an analogy from it. In the same way, Maya Angelou draws the reader into her kitchen in "This Winter Day" (p. 124) and points out how the vegetables she is cutting up "leak their blood selves in the soup." At the end of the poem she tells us that making soup is a kind of bulwark against the rain outside.

The subject matter of Walt Whitman's "The Dalliance of the Eagles" is more dramatic, but essentially he, like Wilson and Angelou, is pointing out something and saying, "Look!" They are all reflective in that they are urging us to look more closely at the world about us.

Somber tones often dominate student poems. Remember, though, that listening to a whiner isn't much fun; reading complaints in verse can be just as bad. On the other hand, it is possible to be somber without being depressingly negative.

Michael Ryan's "Milk the Mouse" (p. 115) presents a somber, even harsh picture of the speaker's father, a man who would pinch his son and tell him to "Be strong Be tough!" What keeps this from being another one-sided account of child abuse is the recognition at the end of the poem that for all his apparent cruelty the father is actually speaking to himself. The man, a regular drinker, is pathetically urging himself to be strong and tough.

Chase Twichell's poem "Rhymes for Old Age" (p. 122) is another good example of a poem in which the tone is somber without being depressing. The subject is an old woman who is close to death. Twichell stays clear of sentimentality by using starkly clinical details; on the other hand she avoids cold detachment by showing a deep compassion for the subject of her poem. Establishing just the right tone in a poem requires careful adjustment.

A *wry tone* is an excellent way to avoid self-pity. Theodore Roethke in "The Waking" (p. 117) is talking about the brutal fact that we are mortal. If he had started with "We're hopeless, born only to die," many readers would quickly move on to another poem. After all, only teachers and parents are obliged to finish unpromising verse. The tone of that opening line seems to promise unrelenting, self-pitying despair. Instead, Roethke begins with "I wake to sleep, and take my waking slow." The tone of the metaphor is light, almost whimsical, and his determination to make the most of life while it lasts provides a wry acceptance of our mortality.

This does not mean that he is cheapening a serious subject by trying to make a joke out of it. Those lines toward the end indicate how serious he is:

> This shaking keeps me steady. I should know.
> What falls away is always. And is near.

But even recognizing the eternal quality of death ("What falls away is always") and his advancing age ("And is near"), he still ends with the notion that he will be learning, growing, until the very end.

Anger and *protest* have long been expressed in poetry. Some of the strongest examples come from the Hebrew prophets. They tended to stand outside the mainstream of their own cultures and were highly critical of the societies of their day. Their language was blunt and direct. Take this brief example from Isaiah 3:24:

And it shall come to pass, that instead of sweet smell
　　there shall be stink; and instead of a girdle, a rent;
And instead of well set hair, baldness; and instead of
　　a stomacher, a girding of sackcloth;
And burning instead of beauty.
Thy men shall fall by the sword,
　　and thy mighty in the war.

The following (Isaiah 33:1) is an attack on those in power. It is not far in spirit and to some degree in technique from the attacks made in the 1960s by poets like Allen Ginsberg, Gregory Corso, and others.

Woe to thee that spoilest, and thou wast not spoiled;
　　and dealest treacherously, and they dealt not treacherously with thee!
When thou shalt cease to spoil, thou shalt be spoiled;
And when thou shalt make an end to deal treacherously,
　　they shall deal treacherously with thee.

In this country, African Americans have struck the same note. For generations, slaves identified themselves with the oppressed Jews of the Old Testament; this link is reflected in the spirituals. The protest poetry of today, however, is released from the sense of resignation that characterized many of the spirituals. In many respects, it is closer to the bitter sense of outrage that is so much a part of the works of Isaiah, Jeremiah, and Ezekiel.

Clarence Major speaks for many black poets with this statement from the introduction to his anthology, *The New Black Poetry*:

Our poetry is shaped by our experience in the world, both deeply personal and social....We constantly mean our poems to reshape. the world; in this sense all excellent art is social....

You and Your Persona

When we discuss a poem, we never know for sure whether the speaker in the poem represents the poet or an imagined character. For this reason, it is best to refer to "the **persona**," "the speaker," or "the narrator."

As a poet, however, you have a choice as to whether you wish to place yourself in your poem, using *I* to introduce yourself and your feelings, or whether you wish to present your poem through a character who is someone else. This distinction is referred to as **distance**, a term that we will return to in the section on fiction.

Since contemporary poetry is often personal, it is frequently set in the first person. This trend is reflected in the poems included in Chapter 11—poems with which you are now familiar. Robley Wilson's rock pool in Maine, Maya

Angelou's kitchen on a rainy day, Ann Leventhal's terrible phone call when she learns that a relative has been killed in a plane crash: All these have the illusion of a recent experience. They may actually be fictionalized, so we refer to the speaker in each case as the persona, but the feeling we have is that the speaker and the poet are one.

Some poems increase the distance by having the persona or narrator recall an episode from the past. The narrator in Richard Wilbur's "The Pardon" describes the day he discovered the body of his dog. The insight and the language at the end of that poem is clearly that of an adult looking back. The same is true of the narrator's view of his childhood in "Fern Hill." Here too, the conclusion—"...I sang in my chains like the sea"—is one that seems unmistakably that of an adult who is well aware of his own mortality.

Then there are poems in which the first person, *I*, does not appear at all. Chase Twichell's view of the old and dying woman in "Rhymes for Old Age" does not identify the viewer, nor does Donald Hall's "Names of Horses." It seems natural, however, to refer to an *implied* persona when discussing the tone since in each case the sense of compassion comes through almost as if someone were talking.

Finally, there are those poems in which the narrator is clearly someone other than the poet. T. R. Hummer, for example, seems to be intentionally separating himself from his narrator right from the start in that lengthy, almost comic title, "The Rural Carrier Stops to Kill a Nine-Foot Cottonmouth." The poem would have taken on a different tone if he had called it, "The Day I Killed a Cottonmouth." Identifying the persona in the third person as a rural letter carrier allows the poet to distance himself from his narrator almost as if this were a short story.

In some cases, the poet is even further removed from the persona, criticizing the character through his or her own words. We have already seen how Gwendolyn Brooks uses "we" in "We Real Cool" to describe a character who is one of the pool players at the Golden Shovel. The narrator reveals himself (we assume "he" perhaps unfairly) and his future without quite realizing how much he is saying. The poet criticizes his way of life through his own words.

Creating Tension Through Tone

If you study a sophisticated poem carefully, you will almost always find some sort of contrast, mixed emotion, or apparent contradiction in tone. These are the crosscurrents that help to keep a poem from becoming static. They are ways of creating poetic **tension**.

Contrasts in attitude are common and fairly easy to identify. We have already touched on a few: Brooks' easygoing use of street language contrasted with the jolting prophecy at the end of "We Real Cool"; Hecht's merry anecdote played against the darkly dramatic image of the devil in "Lizards and Snakes"; Dylan Thomas' dreamlike description of an apparently ideal childhood played against a dark recognition of mortality in the last stanza.

Another poem that depends heavily on contrast throughout is "Pilot Error" by Ann Z. Leventhal (p. 127). Written in a stark, almost prosaic style without figurative language, the poem regularly repeats the contrast between the terrible news about the narrator's friend and the numbed response—folding laundry. The almost telegraphic style echoes that of a mind in a state of shock. In this poem the contrast is not held off until the last stanza, as it is in the examples given earlier. Read it again and notice how the contrast between the unfolding story of the accident and the folding of linen is repeated in each of the eight stanzas.

Poems presented through a persona who is distinctly different from the poet sometimes contain an even more subtle tonal tension—the tone of the speaker running against the apparent feelings of the poet. Returning to "We Real Cool," contrast the cynical indifference in the words of the speaker with the actual concern of the poet.

Ambivalence—conflicting emotions about a person, place, or thing—was introduced in Chapter 2. It is an important concept because poems without mixed feelings are apt to be simple—as in greeting-card verse. Ambivalence in tone is a reflection of the mixed feelings you may have about a character in your poem. We have already seen how Michael Ryan's persona had conflicting feelings about his father—hate and pity. More subtle, however, is the way the tone of the poem shifts from harsh protest in the opening stanzas to a more mature mix of resentment and pity in the last stanza.

Varieties of Irony

All forms of irony are based on a reversal of some sort. We expect a logical order in our world and are jolted when, say, the fire truck catches fire or the Olympic swimming champion drowns in his backyard pool. Since these involve our assumptions about the world around us, they are called examples of **cosmic irony**.

Irony can also appear in the form of a statement which unwittingly suggests future events either directly or indirectly. "I bring good news," the messenger in *Oedipus Rex* says, and the audience shudders, knowing that disaster is at hand. Since this is most closely associated with plays, it is called **dramatic irony**. More will be said about this in the chapters on drama.

The type of irony most frequently found in poetry is **verbal** or *conscious* irony. The terms are used interchangeably. It is verbal in that it is usually based on words rather than events, and it is conscious in that it is not a statement given by innocent speakers as in the case of dramatic irony.

Verbal irony often is achieved through the bringing together of elements we normally consider opposite in one way or another. There are several examples in these lines from Richard Wilbur's "The Pardon" (p. 122). The scene, you will remember, is the one in which the persona dreams he sees the ghost of his dog. In the following quotation, I have indicated with arrows how the overtones of certain words are pitted against those of other words in the same line.

I felt afraid again, but still he came

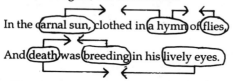

It is ironic to have a hymn associated with a "carnal sun" and a swarm of flies. It is equally ironic to think of death as "breeding." And there is a grim irony in those "lively eyes" of a dog that died some time ago.

There is another sample of irony in Chase Twichell's "Rhymes for Old Age" that you may have spotted in earlier readings of that poem. She describes the process of dying this way:

> One slips into it undressed,
> as into first love…

When an ironic contrast is phrased in a way that makes it sound like a complete contradiction, it is called a **paradox**. John Donne, for example, in his sonnet "Death Be Not Proud" ends with these lines:

> One short sleep past, we wake eternally,
> And death shall be no more; Death, thou shalt die.

On one level it is illogical to say that death shall die, but as a description of eternal life, it makes sense metaphorically.

All these examples are contained in specific phrases. There are also broader ironic contrasts that are in some cases at the very heart of a poem as a whole. As we have already seen, "Fern Hill" appears to describe unending youth; yet the real concern of the speaker at the end of that poem is focused on the word "dying." And in Ann Leventhal's "Pilot Error" there is an unstated irony in the way the persona's apparently emotionless responses to terrible news reveals her true emotions.

Poets do not usually add irony to a poem the way a cook adds seasoning to a bland recipe—though the results may be similar. Instead, ironies suggest themselves either in the original conception or in the revisions.

But you can't be passive either. You should be willing to probe your own ambivalences honestly, looking for elements of hate in love, hidden longings in hatred, or subtle desires buried in fears. In addition, explore the possibilities of ironic contrasts in the material at hand. Just as the process of dying is in some ways like lovemaking, so also the kindness of a parent may in some ways be cruel; aspects of combat may seem peaceful; a motorcycle's roar may be a lullaby.

The Caustic Tone of Satire

Satire criticizes or ridicules through some form of exaggeration. In mild satire the exaggeration may be only a matter of selecting some characteristics and neglecting others. The tone may be a gentle kidding. At the other extreme, it may be wildly exaggerated and the tone vitriolic.

Satire and irony can, of course, be used independently from each other. All the examples of irony above are nonsatiric, and the first example of satire below does not use irony. But ridicule is particularly effective when it is presented "with a straight face." That is, the cutting edge of satire is sharpest when the poet gives the illusion of presenting an unbiased view. It is the tension between the poet's apparent honesty and the actual intent that makes satire almost invariably ironic. In fact, when satire is presented without irony the result often appears rather crude. Such is the case with Kingsley Amis' "A Tribute to the Founder." In this first of four stanzas, the intent to ridicule is clear, but because the material is presented directly rather than ironically the attack lacks subtlety:

> By bluster, graft, and doing people down
> Sam Baines got rich, but mellowing at last,
> Felt that by giving something to the town
> He might undo the evils of his past.

There is, of course, irony in the title, since "tribute" is not intended literally. But the first line destroys all chance of sustaining subtlety. As soon as we see the words "bluster, graft, and doing people down" we know exactly where the poet stands, which is no sin in itself unless one asks more of poetry than one does of a good newspaper editorial.

William Jay Smith describes essentially the same sort of individual in his poem "American Primitive," and he also is satiric. But notice how different the effect is when irony is sustained:

> Look at him there in his stovepipe hat,
> His high-top shoes, and his handsome collar;
> Only my Daddy could look like that,
> And I love my Daddy like he loves his Dollar.

The lines flow like the ripple that runs silently down the length of a bull whip; and with his final word comes the "snap" which is sharp enough to make the most sophisticated reader jump. This is still fairly light verse, but the satire, sharpened with irony, draws blood. The tension here lies in the contrast between the *apparent* tone of sentimental tribute and the *actual* tone of cutting protest.

Moving further—much further—in the direction of subtlety and complexity, we have a third example of satire in Eliot's "The Love Song of J. Alfred Prufrock." The poem is an entire course in satire and deserves much more careful scrutiny than I can give it here. One brief excerpt from its total of 131 lines will have to serve as appetizer.

Like the other two poems, this one aims its attack at an individual who represents a general type. Unlike the other two, the attack comes not from the poet directly but indirectly through what the character says about himself. If you read this passage carefully, you will see that he repeatedly veers from self-deprecation to self-defense, employing both in a pattern of self-deceit which almost deceives us, the readers.

> Should I, after tea and cakes and ices,
> Have the strength to force the moment to its crisis?
> But though I have wept and fasted, wept and prayed,
> Though I have seen my head (grown slightly bald) brought in
>   upon a platter,
> I am no prophet—and here's no great matter;
> I have seen the moment of my greatness flicker,
> And I have seen the eternal Footman hold my coat, and snicker,
> And in short, I was afraid.

At first we may be tempted to see him as he sees himself: A man who recognizes the superficiality of his own society ("tea and cakes and ices"), has tried to rise above it ("wept and fasted"), is aware of his failure ("I have seen…my greatness flicker"), and is uneasy about death ("I was afraid").

But if we look more carefully, we see an aging man who has chosen to live in this particular society and has neither the strength nor the courage to leave it. He uses such absurd exaggeration ("wept and fasted") that we can't take him seriously. There is irony in the fact that he reveals his weaknesses through his defense of himself. He is being satirized through his own words.

Satire on television and in magazines like *Mad* and *National Lampoon* tends to be highly exaggerated and, like cartoons, obvious. It is one-shot entertainment. Satire in sophisticated poetry, however, is usually more subtle and frequently based on many aspects of character.

Keeping the Tone Honest

Tone is not your first concern when you begin a new poem. You don't select a tone in advance any more than you rationally decide the mood of the day when you first wake up. Tone develops as the poem develops. It takes shape through successive drafts.

At some point in the revision process, however, you should take a close look at the tone you have adopted. There are two levels on which your tone may need further adjustment. On the deepest level there is the matter of honesty. When examining the tone of a poem you are working on, be sure to ask this crucial question: Is this what I *really* feel? Does the poem, for example, merely echo conventional sentiments (mothers and nature are wonderful; war and poverty are terrible), or does it honestly explore the complexity of what you feel?

More subtly, have you been softening the implications of your poem through psychic modesty? That is, have you been reluctant to reveal your private feelings? If so, the poem will probably lack a sense of power and authenticity. You would do better to present your feelings through a persona so as to mask your own involvement while still being true to the subject matter.

Modesty isn't always the problem. Exaggerating a personal agony or a painful experience can sometimes result in **sentimentality**. Intentional sentimentality is a form of dishonesty because it cheapens genuine feelings. It is contaminated with details selected primarily for their capacity to stimulate the tear ducts. It's a trick rather than a sharing of true emotions. But what about *unintentional* sentimentality? That is far more common. Occasionally you may honestly feel that you are the most miserable, most misunderstood person on earth or, on a happier note, that the person you love really is perfect. Remember, though, that if the poem sounds sentimental to others, its effect will be spoiled. Perhaps a wry, slightly distanced tone would help to provide perspective and hold your readers.

In the same way, if you overdramatize a conflict or protest, going beyond your real feelings, your poem may lose some of its dramatic impact and may come across as **melodrama**. When readers have the feeling that emotions like rage or indignation have been pushed artificially for their own sake, they will not take the poem seriously. This is counterproductive. You might consider some form of irony. As a general rule, the most appropriate tone to adopt is an honest reflection of how you feel about your subject.

When you are sure that you have come to terms with your feelings on that deepest level, it is appropriate to examine your tone on a more craftsmanlike level: How successful have I been in communicating my tone to my readers?

Never mind saying, "But what I *really* felt was...." Remember that a poem must reach readers on its own without your explanations. And readers are entirely dependent on the signals embedded in the work itself. The overtones of every word and phrase contribute to the overall effect. A soft word or phrase can weaken the impact of a protest poem; a harsh detail can send an unwanted jolt through a gently contemplative poem. As we have seen, tonal tensions are often effective, but make sure they are intentional and appropriate.

Ask yourself, too, whether the poem's tonal signals all repeat the same note. Poems that do this can lose effectiveness, just like a musical piece that strikes the same chord too often. This problem is relatively easy to correct if you can make use of ambivalent feelings—like the way Michael Ryan in "Milk the Mouse" mixes his narrator's bitter resentment of his father with an element of pity.

If you remember that the tone of your poem is an essential part of the meaning, you will understand why the revision process is not complete until you have established just the right tone.

9
FROM UNITS TO UNITY

Structuring a poem through visual and nonvisual techniques. Visual patterns. Traditional stanzas. The shape of fixed forms. The irregular spacing of free verse. Internal structure through narrative sequences, themes, image clusters, and repetitions. Revising for structure and unity.

Until now we have been examining aspects of poetry as if they were separate elements. This approach is necessary for analysis. But a poem, like any art object, is a single, unified creation. This chapter deals with the ways in which a poem can be structured so as to become an artistic whole.

There are several different approaches to structuring a poem. First, there are the visual techniques like traditional **stanzas**, **fixed forms**, and the irregular stanzas and spacing of free verse. Then there are a variety of internal, nonvisual ways to achieve structure such as narrative sequences, thematic patterns, image clusters, and repetitions in phrasing.

These techniques of ordering and unifying a poem may be fairly subtle. When we read a successful poem for pleasure, we may not be fully aware of what went into its construction. But as writers we should be able to identify them and to keep them in mind as we work—both during the creative stage and in the course of revising.

Visual Patterns

Every poem has a shape when printed on the page. You see and respond at least unconsciously to that shape even before you read the first line. Some poems are long and skinny—a slender vine. Some sprawl across the page, the width varying, the spaces irregular. Others are in fairly regular rectangles of print, each unit separated uniformly from the preceding one.

Here, for example, is what your first impression of a particular poem in Chapter 11 might have been before you even read it:

```
XX XXXX XXXX XX
XXXX XXXXXX XX

XXXX XXXX XX
XXXXXX XXXXXXXX XX

XXXX XXX XX
XXXX XXX XX

XXXX XXXX XX
XXX XXXX
```

Do you recognize it? Even if you don't, you can tell a good deal from this quick glimpse at the shape. First, it is clearly made up of couplets. The vertical rhythm— a space after every two lines—is enough to tell you that before you read it. Tradition tells us that it will probably be rhymed and will almost certainly be metered. It seems likely that it will be organized in a series of relatively separate units. It's so short that it probably doesn't tell a story. That means that it may have to be pulled together by some thematic implication at the end.

When you actually read the poem, Gwendolyn Brooks' "We Real Cool," these expectations are generally fulfilled. Each couplet is an almost separate unit, and the theme of the poem is entirely dependent on the jolting last line, "We die soon."

Here is a visual pattern taken from a another poem, one that is structured in quite a different way.

```
XXXXXXX XXXXX
XXXXXXX
        XXX XXXX XX
        XXXX X XXXXXXXXXXXX XXXXXX
                              XXXXXXXX
XXX XXXXX XXXXXXXXXXXXXXXXXXXX XXXXXXXXXXXXXXXXXXXX
                                        XXXXX
XX XXX X XXXXXXXX XXX
              XXX XXXX X XXXX XX XXXX XX
XXX XX XXX XXXX XXXX XXXXXXXX XXX
XXXXXX XXXXX
```

This one certainly isn't couplets. Nor is it based on any other stanza form. It's not short enough to be a haiku or square enough to be a sonnet. All those irregular lines (extreme horizontal rhythms) assure us that this must be free verse. And rather erratic free verse at that. With no recurring units, it is probably going to be one of those poems that are unified by theme, not by a story sequence or by any regularly recurring phrase.

The poem, as you probably guessed, is E. E. Cummings' "Buffalo Bill's," and every prediction we made was correct. We were braced for an erratic structure, and we were quite right about having to read the entire work before we made sense of it.

There are an infinite number of visual patterns available for the poet, but they generally fall into three groups: the regular (recurrent) stanzas of metered poetry, the fixed forms such as the haiku and the sonnet, and the irregular or **nonrecurrent stanzas** or spacing of much free verse.

Traditional Stanza Patterns

Stanzas in metered verse are normally of uniform length and are separated by a space. When stanzas are used, the pattern is what the reader notices first. That was what made it so easy to spot the **couplets** in "We Real Cool" and to predict that it would probably be a metered poem. The same is true of Maxine Kumin's "Morning Swim." It is longer, but those pairs of lines, each separated by a space from the next pair, almost guarantee that the poem will be metered and probably rhymed as well.

Every traditional stanza has both advantages and disadvantages. Couplets, as I pointed out in Chapter 5, are less popular today than they were in the eighteenth century partly because they can easily become monotonous. How does one bind such short units together into a whole? Brooks in "We Real Cool" does it partly by echoing the rhythm of rap, a street chant. And the piece snaps into focus with that last line in which the true theme of the poem is revealed. The structure, then, is in the short units of couplets, but the unity is essentially thematic.

Maxine Kumin's couplets are visually similar, but they are used in an entirely different way. Almost every pair of lines is a separate image introduced as delicately as one moves into cool water, step by step. The unity of the poem comes partly from the narrative—a gentle sequence of events—and partly from the theme. The poem comes together at the end with a subtle echo of a childhood rhyme called "This is the House that Jack Built."

The **triplet** (three lines to a stanza) offers a larger unit. There is less danger of fragmentation. Still more popular, the **quatrain**, an easily identifiable four-line stanza, comes closer to the paragraph of prose in that it can be used to present more of a complete idea or impression. It is not surprising that the narrative sequence of Richard Wilbur's "The Pardon" is based on quatrains.

Although some are run-on stanzas (both the sense and the syntax continue unbroken into the next stanza), the four-line units remain the basic organizational structure.

The longer forms—**quintet** or **cinquain** (see "Those Winter Sundays" by Robert Hayden, p. 113), **sestet, septet,** and **octave**—all share the advantage of providing a solid block of lines in which entire sets of images or extended metaphors can be developed.

The subtleties of some of these organizational techniques are not always identifiable at first glance. You have to study Anthony Hecht's "Lizards and Snakes" (p. 111) fairly carefully, for example, before you can see that while the poem is printed as three octaves (eight lines each), the rhyme scheme divides each stanza in half as if it were made up of two quatrains. This is a basic part of the organizational structure of the poem, but the casual reader may well miss it.

Some of these stanza forms, by the way, serve not only as regularly recurring units but as components in more complex schemes. The triplet, for example, is the basic unit of the **villanelle**, just as the octave and sestet become subdivisions of the **sonnet**—forms that I will turn to later in this chapter.

Regular stanzas are just as important in syllabics as they are in metered poetry. With that form, you remember, the number of syllables in each line matches the number in the corresponding line of the other stanzas. As we saw in Dylan Thomas' "Fern Hill," the length of the lines can vary, but the pattern of line length established in the first stanza is precisely matched in the other stanzas syllable by syllable. That is, all first lines have the same number of syllables, as do all second lines, and so on. The poem is not metered, but the stanzas are very similar in shape. All this may seem cumbersome when described in the abstract, but if you read "Fern Hill" once again just for the pleasure of it (an excellent antidote to close analysis), you will see how the anatomy of form is hidden in an effective poem just as it is in a painting.

The Shape of Fixed Forms

In addition to types of stanzas, there are many traditional verse forms that provide the poet with structure while allowing a good deal of freedom within the pattern. Most are metered, but not all.

One of the simplest of these forms is the **haiku**, described in Chapter 4. It is, you remember, a syllabic system in which the first line has five syllables, the second has seven, and the third has five. There is no meter and generally no rhyme. As with many other fixed forms, the visual shape prepares us for a certain type of poem. Seeing those three lines, we expect either a single image or a very delicate contrast of some sort. We don't say, "Is there more?" because the form itself informs us in advance that it will be a miniature.

The **ballad** is a longer, looser form associated with narrative poetry and verse to be sung. The ballad stanza is a quatrain which alternates lines of iambic tetrameter with iambic trimeter. The rhyme scheme is *abcb*. Early ballads tended to be simple in plot, with lively action reported by someone outside the story. Ballads today often follow those conventions.

Coleridge adapted the ballad form to develop a highly sophisticated poem in "The Rime of the Ancient Mariner." Although he allowed himself occasional variations in traditional ballad meter, here is a dramatic stanza that contains only one rather inconspicuous substitution.

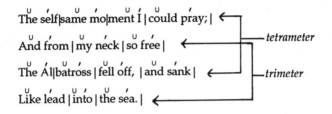

Although Coleridge used the ballad form to create a complex work, we still tend to think of ballads as entertaining stories set to verse, often with musical accompaniment. When selecting a verse form, it is generally a good idea to use one that harmonizes with the tone and subject matter you have in mind.

The **sonnet** is a metered and rhymed poem of 14 lines, almost always in iambic pentameter. Unlike the ballad, it is not really long enough to tell a rambling story, yet it has sufficient length to develop far more intricate statements than are possible in a haiku.

There are two basic types. The **Elizabethan sonnet** is the form made famous by Shakespeare. It can be thought of as three quatrains and a final rhyming couplet: *abab, cdcd, efef, gg*. The first eight lines are referred to as the **octave** and the last six as the **sestet**. Often there is some shift of mood at the beginning of the sestet, providing poetic tension. In these cases, the unity of the poem is established with the resolution in the final rhyming couplet.

If you have been reading sonnets, you can identify the form in advance just from the basic 14-line shape. Occasionally Elizabethan sonnets are printed as an unbroken block, but more often they are printed as an octave and a sestet. That concluding couplet is a distinguishing characteristic both in rhyme and, usually, in the subject matter as well.

The second basic type, the **Italian sonnet,** is also based on 14 lines of iambic pentameter, but it is usually arranged as two quatrains and two triplets: *abba, abba; cde, cde*. You can differentiate it from the Elizabethan sonnet immediately from the fact that it has no concluding couplet.

One tends to associate the sonnet with earlier literary periods and with elevated language, but the form has such versatility that many contemporary poets have used it. In fact, Vikram Seth (rhymes with "great") has written an entire novel of Elizabethan sonnets called *The Golden Gate*. The individual sonnets are relatively simple, highly accessible, and are based on tetrameter rather than pentameter. Although they lack density, they read like 14-line stanzas and serve as the poem's basic organizing unit.

The Elizabethan sonnet reprinted in Chapter 11 is T. R. Hummer's "The Rural Carrier" (p. 114). Although Hummer uses slant rhymes liberally, he follows the basic sonnet pattern. Remarkably, he does this while maintaining both the diction and the phrasing of informal speech. A rural letter carrier tells about the day in which he killed a nine-foot cottonmouth snake and discovered some startling similarities between men and snakes.

The internal structure of the poem is maintained with a muted but traditional rhyme scheme: *abba, cddc, efef, gg*. This pattern subtly divides the octave (first eight lines) into two quatrains, and the sestet (last six lines) into a quatrain and a final rhyming couplet. True to tradition, the rhyming couplet at the end draws the theme together.

There are other aspects to the structure of this poem that I will return to shortly. At this point we are only concerned with the ways in which an apparently informal as-if-spoken poem is given a shape through a traditional verse form.

The **villanelle** is the most complex verse form I will discuss in this text. It has some of the intricacy of a crossword puzzle, but its repetitions have a haunting quality that can be highly effective.

The villanelle has 19 lines divided into five triplets and a final quatrain. Like the sonnet, it is usually written in iambic pentameter. Simple enough so far. But unlike the sonnet, it has only two rhymes. The pattern is a somewhat demanding *aba, aba, aba, aba, aba, abaa*. As you can see, it is a good idea to select rhyme endings that are rich in choice. It is not considered dishonest to use a rhyming dictionary, but don't let the demands of the rhyme tempt you into poor word choices. That is called "forcing the rhyme."

There is one more requirement: the first line is used as a **refrain** that is repeated to form lines 6, 12, and 18; and the third line is repeated to form lines 9, 15, and 19. This means that those two refrains appear alternately as the last line of each stanza until the end of the poem (lines 18 and 19), where they are used together as a couplet. The refrains are used like the chorus of a song to enhance unity.

"The Waking" by Theodore Roethke (p. 117) is a villanelle. The opening phrase, "I wake to sleep," is central. It suggests that life is a gradual waking followed by death, an eternal sleep. He goes on to say that with this in mind he will prolong this waking process as long as he can: "...take my waking slow." This key concept is, because of the villanelle form, repeated in the even-numbered stanzas: second, fourth, and sixth.

The other key concept is that one gains experience simply by moving through life toward inevitable death: "I learn by going where I have to go."

This is repeated in the odd-numbered stanzas, three and five, as well as in the final stanza.

If you look at how these two key concepts are used, you will see how the seeming complexity of the form allows a poet to highlight certain themes. Form and content work together.

Here are the first two stanzas with annotations showing the meter and those two refrains that are repeated alternately in the other stanzas:

I wake | to sleep, | and take | my wak|ing slow. | *1st refrain (repeated at end of even-numbered stanzas)*

I feel | my fate | in what | I can|not fear. |

I learn | by go|ing where | I have | to go. | *2nd refrain (repeated at end of odd-numbered stanzas)*

We think | by feel|ing. What | is there | to know? |

I hear | my be|ing dance | from ear | to ear. |

I wake | to sleep, | and take | my wak|ing slow. |

If you look carefully at the whole poem printed on page 117, you will notice that Roethke takes certain minor liberties with the form. Some of the rhymes, for example, are slant rhymes, and one of the refrains is subtly altered (without giving up the pentameter). But he is essentially faithful to the form, and if you enjoy this kind of challenge you will want to match his fidelity.

Why bother? The parallel with music is helpful here. Form in varying degrees gives structure, and a basic structure gives pleasure. It's as simple as that. Each composer or poet has a different view of the ideal balance between form and free flight, but most syllabic and metered poetry, like most music, establishes a tension between an idealized form and variations on that form. We recognize the pattern in spite of the variations, and this contributes to a sense of overall unity.

The Irregular Spacing of Free Verse

The units in free verse tend to be unique in that they vary in length and are tailored to fit the needs of the individual poem. But some free verse poems use regularly recurring stanzas as an organizing structure just as if they were metered. Lisel Mueller's "Night Song" (p. 120), for example, is unmetered, unrhymed, and does not employ syllabics, but it is presented in regular quatrains. The rhythm, you will remember, is syntactical, based on the repetition of the phrase, "Among...., I am the...." But by dividing the poem into three end-stopped quatrains, Mueller has created four-line units that provide the structure she needs.

Ann Leventhal's "Pilot Error" (p. 127) is also unmetered, but it is presented in triplets as regular as any traditional poem. The organization is essentially narrative in that there are two telephone calls, the first reporting the accident and the second announcing the death of the narrator's friend. The first four stanzas conclude abruptly with an end-stopped line, "tight fists." The concluding four stanzas focus on the second call. The structure is partly narrative, but the use of visually identifiable stanzas helps to provide the structure.

In other free-verse poems, the stanzas are of unequal length, determined more by content. In such cases, the stanza is very much like a prose paragraph.

A poem like "Merritt Parkway" by Denise Levertov (p. 119), on the other hand, makes very little use of definable stanzas. There are double spaces that divide the material, but the structure relies far more on the horizontal spacing, sliding the lines left and right. If you look at any four or five lines, the visual impression of the spacing seems arbitrary. The unified effect doesn't achieve its goal until you see the entire poem—like looking down on highway traffic from an overpass.

Internal Structure

Internal structure is nonvisual. You can't see it in that first glance. The patterns are there but are buried in the poem itself and are revealed only when you read the poem carefully. The four basic techniques of internal structure are narrative sequence, thematic patterns, image clusters, and repetitions in phasing.

A **narrative** is a story, a sequence of events. It is as natural a structure for poetry as it is for prose. Storytelling was, after all, one of the original purposes of poetry. Epics like the *Iliad* and the *Odyssey* were long stories set in verse primarily to aid memorization. Unwritten epics have been recorded in Africa, India, Yugoslavia, and elsewhere. What we call the *literary ballads* of the nineteenth and twentieth centuries have their roots in poetry intended to be sung and often presented by individuals who could not read. Narrative sequence, like meter and rhyme, made the works easier to remember.

Anthony Hecht's "Lizards and Snakes" makes effective use of narrative sequence. It tells a story. It does other things also, but its primary organizational technique is to keep the reader wondering what will happen next.

In addition to plot, narrative poems often have a speaker who helps to unify the work. In the Hecht poem the identity of the narrator is not clearly defined. We know only that he and his friend, Joe, were a part of the action and he is now looking back after what appear to be a number of years.

"The Pardon" by Richard Wilbur (p. 122) is another good example. It begins with the summer day on which the persona, a boy of ten, finds the body of his dog. It continues through the burial and, considerably later, a nightmare. On waking he begs "death's pardon." This is a highly sophisticated poem with a complex theme, yet it is organized and unified with a relatively simple story line.

In these examples, the story is what you respond to first. The term *narrative*, however, also refers to poems that are organized by a much less dramatic sequence of events. In Maxine Kumin's "Morning Swim" there is not much of a story line, but what happens does order the poem. And in Walt Whitman's "The Dalliance of the Eagles" the observer does nothing but observe. Still, the eagles come together, lock, and then separate, each moving off on a "separate diverse flight." The events serve as the organizing principle of the poem.

One of the most fascinating uses of narrative sequencing in this volume is in Donald Hall's "Names of Horses" (p. 112). Turn to it now and see if you can on your own sort out the three different narrative sequences that are woven together in that poem.

The first of these sequences is based on seasons of the year. It starts out "All winter" and moves in the second stanza to "April," turns to summer with "noon's heat" and finally to the fall with "one October" in the fifth stanza. This use of seasons is clear and fairly common as a device. But there is a second and longer sequence that is based on the stages of a single horse's life. The first four stanzas focus on the mature years when the horse can do heavy work; the fifth stanza starts when he is "old and lame" and is taken out to be shot, and the seventh stanza deals with the horse after death, when the roots of trees "pushed through the pale curves of your ribs."

The third cycle is the longest and most subtle. Far lengthier than the seasons of a single year, longer even than the story of one horse's life and death, it is that succession of horses moving through the same cycle "generation on generation." This generational sequence is the underlying narrative thread and the primary concern of the poem. We know that from the last line, a moving tribute to the long series of horses over the years: "O Roger, Mackerel, Riley, Ned, Nellie, Chester, Lady Ghost."

Just as a complex sound like a sustained note on a cello can be analyzed precisely as having sound waves of high, medium, and low frequency working together to produce a single note with rich overtones, so a poem can combine narratives of differing length to produce a single, unified effect. This is what we mean when we say that a poem has **resonance**.

When there is little or no story line, a poem can be ordered just as successfully through the **theme** or **tone**. Unity of theme is just as important in a poem as it is in an essay. Think of it as a kind of gravitational force that keeps a poem from flying apart. Even when it is not stated explicitly, it is felt. Thematic unity usually occurs naturally in a short piece, but you may have to pay more attention to it in longer works. "Fern Hill" and "Names of Horses" are relatively long poems that contain a number of divergent elements, but each is unified in the concluding lines.

Think twice, however, before ending a poem with an abstract summary. This may be very tempting—particularly if the theme is still a bit fuzzy in your own mind. And you can find successful examples—particularly in work from previous centuries. But you run the risk of oversimplifying a successful poem and undercutting its subtlety. Notice how often the concluding lines of a contemporary work unify the poem not with a simple summary but indirectly through a fresh and powerful metaphor: "I sang in my chains..." in "Fern Hill," the hymn "Abide with Me" in "Morning Swim," and that list of actual horses in "Names of Horses."

In many cases the true binding force of a poem is not a single, unchallenged idea or feeling but thematic or tonal *contrast*. This technique, so common in the essay, plays one attitude or tone against another. You might think that divergent views or feelings would lead to *dis*unity, but instead they provide a clear structure, and through this a sense of order. We have already seen how the apparently "cool" attitude of the narrator in Gwendolyn Brooks' "We Real Cool" is played against that harsh ending, "We / Die soon." The contrast is a miniature version of the one in "Fern Hill," where the idyllic view of the speaker's youth is brought up short at the end with the awareness of death.

The tonal contrast in Ann Leventhal's "Pilot Error" has already been examined as an example of poetic tension in the previous chapter. The terrible drama of a fatal plane accident is contrasted with the numbed response of the persona. But instead of withholding this contrast until the end of the poem, the poet uses it in each of the seven stanzas. The unity of the poem is drawn from the fusing of these two elements in the last stanza.

The contrasting elements do not have to be of equal weight. As we have seen before, the protest against the father in Michael Ryan's "Milk the Mouse" (p. 115) seems to dominate that poem. The counter view that comes when we realize that the father was "speaking / to himself, of course, to the child inside him aching...." This is revealed only in the last two stanzas. Still, the contrast provides the structure of the poem. Without it the poem would be just another anti-parent protest.

A third and even more subtle method of providing structure in a poem is to establish **image clusters**. This often occurs quite unconsciously in early drafts. If we write about tidal pools, snails and barnacles naturally come to mind. And if our subject is life on a farm, then barns, cows, and fields will doubtless play a part just as they would if the topic came up in conversation.

But a *system* of related images requires a little more planning. Often it develops only after successive drafts. As I pointed out in the chapter on images, Robley Wilson's poem "On a Maine Beach" (p. 118) is organized around groups of closely related images. Remember that although the poem is written without stanza divisions, its rhyme scheme is based on a four-line unit as if it were written in quatrains. If you look closely you will see that each unit is dominated by certain key images: the rock pools, the "mainspring," the tides, and in the concluding four lines, "old coins."

The organizational structure, then, is based partly on a series of closely related images, and each series is subtly reinforced with "stanzas" that are formed by a loose rhyme scheme. Overall unity is achieved both by the setting and by the final two lines in which the roundness of pools and of mainsprings are fused in the phrase "round lifetimes," and the motion of the tide is repeated in "beach rhythms."

Another good example of image clusters is in Hall's "Names of Horses," which we have been examining for its narrative sequences. It is not surprising that the first stanza, dealing with winter, would have "sledges of cordwood," but the harshness of a rural winter is also reflected in the horse's "brute shoulders." In the third stanza, dealing with summer, we are introduced to the "chaffy barn," and the fourth stanza describes how on Sundays the horse "grazed in the sound of hymns." It is appropriate that on that day of rest we are given the image of the stall with its wood smoothed by rubbing as "the sea smooths glass." That process of rubbing the wood of the stall presumably went on in the winter too, but it is more appropriate and harmonious to introduce it in the quiet Sunday stanza.

Notice how when we discuss the pattern of images here and in Robley Wilson's poem it is natural to link them with stanzas. This is true whether the stanzas are made clear by spaces, as in the Hall poem, or are identified only through meter and the pattern of slant rhymes as in the Wilson poem. This is a reminder of how intermeshed content and form really are.

Finally, there are *repetitions* in phrasing. We have already seen how often repetitions have been used in poetry influenced by biblical verse in which key phrases return over and over. Such phrasing is not only a rhythmical device, it can be a part of the structure of the poem and in some cases a way of focusing the attention of the reader on an aspect of the theme. When such repetitions are regular, they are called *refrains*.

We have seen how the word "among" sets up a rhythm in Lisel Mueller's "Night Song" by being repeated at the start of all but two lines. But it is more than a matter of rhythm. The word itself has to do with the essential unity of the speaker with all of nature. And it is not just a matter of rhythm that led Gwendolyn Brooks to repeat the word "we" in every line but the last in "We Real Cool." The speaker is clearly thinking of very little but self, and his reiteration of "We...we...we" is a part of his tragedy.

Repetition of words and phrases is often associated with free verse, but the technique is built into fixed forms like the villanelle. The first step when working with a form that has regularly repeated lines is to determine what that key phrase or suggestion will be. In the case of the villanelle, each of two refrains is repeated four times, so it is essential that they not only conform to the meter but highlight aspects of the theme.

In Theodore Roethke's "The Waking," for example, we have the core of the theme in these two refrains:

> I wake to sleep, and take my waking slow.
> I learn by going where I have to go.

These two lines become the skeletal framework of the entire poem. While it is difficult to see the link between this structured use of repeated phrases and the explosive, apparently unstructured organization in Allen Ginsberg's "Howl" (see p. 74), the technique is essentially the same.

When we discuss all these visual and internal methods of organizing a poem and giving it unity, it is necessary to discuss them separately. Remember, though, that in many poems several different systems are used to achieve the same goals. To give one specific example, Hummer's "The Rural Carrier" makes use of the highly visual sonnet form, but it is also unified narratively (a dramatic story at that), and by a remarkable thematic linkage. The persona talks tough, but in the end he feels his spine "squirm" just as the snake's did—an honest confession about his sense of identity, the killer and the killed being similar in many ways. The poem, then, is woven together by form, by events, by tone, and by theme. The elements can be analyzed separately, but in the poem they are inseparable.

Revising for Structure and Unity

Let your mind run free in those early drafts. Explore your emotions. Discover your own true feelings. Try different versions until it "sounds right." Just when you finally feel satisfied and a bit pleased with yourself, look over your work with a cool, critical eye.

Start as your reader will start, with a quick look at the shape of the poem. Does it provide clues about how the poem is put together? If it is metered, have you left spaces to separate stanzas, or is there some good reason for blending them? If it is free verse, have you made use of line length and spaces to indicate the structural pattern? Just as many artists look at "negative space"—the areas between shapes—you can determine just how you have used your white space.

Turning now to the internal structure of the poem, those elements that depend on a careful reading, ask yourself whether the poem is essentially narrative. If it is based on a personal experience, guard against cluttering the poem with details that are meaningful only to you. Weed out the extraneous. In other cases, you may almost miss the fact that the poem is essentially narrative. As we have seen, a poem doesn't have to tell a story blatantly to be narrative. A sequence of events can be subtle and still serve as the thread that holds the poem together.

If the poem is not drawn together by narrative, are you depending on unity of theme? If so, remember the advantages of having two contrasting or even opposing thematic suggestions. The tension you achieve may provide energy as well as structure.

Take a close look at the images you have used. In the process of writing, you selected them line by line. Now look at them in the context of the whole poem. Is it possible to revise some so that they will be clustered, harmonizing with one another in groups and providing patterns? This is a subtle technique that is often ignored.

Finally, have you considered repetition of key words or phrases? If you were working with a fixed form like a villanelle, you had to. But if the structure you are using is looser, you might consider the technique as the unique solution to the needs of your poem. Our training in writing prose has made us determined to avoid redundancies, but in poetry they can be highly effective.

There is a subtle difference between the creative stage of writing a poem and the revision stage. When you begin with a new poem, you tend to write for yourself. You are trying to catch genuine feelings and translate them into imagery. But as you move into your revisions, your attention should turn toward your readers. Exactly what is going to come through to them?

For this reason, it's important to keep reading your early drafts as if you were a stranger to the material. Separate what is really there from what you hoped was there. Will it pull together for your readers? Try it out on friends or classmates. Yes, you want to be true to your feelings, but a poem is not entirely private property. It belongs in part to your readers.

As you move into those final drafts, make sure that the various elements have coalesced to create a unified work of art.

10
WRITING POETRY ON YOUR OWN

The three requirements for continued development: reading poetry critically, writing regularly, evaluating your own work honestly. The basic critical questions that lead to effective revision. Drawing from the fellowship of poets.

A textbook can introduce you to the wide range of possibilities in poetry, and courses in writing can speed your early development. But the goals of both are to help you work on your own. Poetry is partly a craft, and that can be taught; but it is also an art, and that must come from within you.

If you find the writing of poetry becoming important to you, take the time to examine why. Poetry won't support you financially, but it can enrich you in other ways. If you make the effort, it can become a valuable part of your life. Like playing the violin, painting, or any other artistic endeavor, a commitment to poetry is self-reinforcing: The more you do to expand your abilities, the more poetry does to expand your life.

Developing as a poet is a continuing process, and a complex one. Publication is certainly a legitimate lure; but if it becomes the sole motive, you may end up manufacturing a product to be sold. When you place that much emphasis on the marketplace, you may neglect the development of your own voice.

How do you keep expanding your abilities on your own? There are three aspects to the process, and they are equally important. In fact, if you ignore any one of them, you probably won't grow, and without a sense of growth you won't find enough satisfaction to continue. The first of these essentials is reading published poetry critically, the second is writing regularly, and the third is learning how to evaluate your own work objectively.

Reading Poetry Critically

Poets read the work of other poets. Serious poets read poetry seriously—that is, critically. This does not mean that they are necessarily critical in the negative sense—wonder, admiration, and sheer envy all have their place; but it does mean that they read analytically.

Is there a risk that you will become imitative? Not if you read widely. And consider the alternative: If you do not read other poets, you will end up imitating yourself, a sterile route. Besides, occasional imitation of poetry you admire is an effective form of study. Though imitations should remain in your journal, the process will bring you close to the model. When you return to your own original work, you will draw on what you have learned.

When students tell me that they are "very serious" about poetry, I don't ask how much they have written; I ask what was the last volume of poetry they read through to the end and what poetry journal they subscribe to. This isn't intended as a put-down. It is merely based on what I have observed: developing poets are readers even when they are not taking courses.

How do you find out what to read? If you are in school, take literature courses as well as writing seminars. Don't shun work written from earlier periods. It all has a bearing on your own work. If you are not taking classes, buy anthologies and read poetry journals. Find out what poets speak to you. Then order collections of their work. Expensive? No more so than records and tapes of music or a dinner for two.

Reading critically requires more concentration than passive reading. It means applying what you have drawn from this and other analytical texts to what you are reading. It means marking up your own copy or photocopies of work printed in library books. It means commenting on these poems in your journal—not just likes and dislikes, but analytical aspects.

In short, when you read poetry critically you adopt poets as your teachers. You will enjoy the works of some more than others, but you will learn from them all if you respond as a fellow poet.

And don't forget the auditory aspect. If you are near a library, try to attend poetry readings there as often as possible. Even if you live miles from the nearest library and commute to a mindless job in a cultural desert, there is a solution for you: Buy an inexpensive portable cassette player, record two new poems each evening, reading aloud from a collection, and then play them as you drive to work.

Writing Regularly

Poets write regularly. Even when they have full-time jobs, they write regularly. Even when they have children or financial problems or are splitting up with their partners, they write. I have met poets who get up at 5:00 A.M. to write before going to work, and others who reserve the late hours of the night for composition. But they write. Regularly.

True, a busy schedule does not allow for long blocks of time. But one of the blessings of poetry is that it doesn't necessarily require lengthy work sessions. Unlike a novelist, a poet can often recapture the mood of an unfinished poem in minutes and make good use of a spare half hour a day. Thirty minutes a day may be frustratingly brief, but for most it is more productive than having a whole day for work once a week. Poems are relatively short, intense works, and they can take root in the chinks that remain in a tight schedule.

For most poets, even writing fragments on a regular basis is ultimately more fruitful than waiting for a summer vacation. Fragments have a way of generating work that can be developed. Waiting for ideal working time generates nothing.

Evaluating Your Own Work

Neither reading carefully nor writing regularly will help you to develop as a poet if you don't learn to examine your own work objectively. Too many would-be poets maintain such faith in intuitive writing that they insulate themselves against change and growth.

Evaluating your own work starts with asking the right questions. It is often helpful to have the reactions of a fellow poet or a group, but make sure that you are turning to individuals who read poetry. Well-meaning friends may not know what questions to ask or how to advise. As a result, they tend to respond subjectively. "I like it. Sort of," one may say, playing it safe. Another reads the same poem and shrugs. "It doesn't do much for me," he says. A third complains, "Why don't you write about something cheerful?" Reactions like these will tell you more about the speaker than about your poem.

The kind of criticism that will be the most help to you as a practicing poet will be highly specific. It will focus on phrasing, on imagery, on rhythm. What you as writer need to find out is precisely what came through to the reader. In the process you may learn what didn't come through as well.

A helpful critic might say something like this: "Your three opening images are really dramatic and got me into the poem, but I lost track of them later. I don't see what you are doing with them. And I can't hear any sound devices in this poem." You may be tempted to use the well-worn defense, "That's the way I intended it." But resist that impulse! Ask yourself whether it might be possible to develop those opening images and whether you could do more with the sounds of the poem.

There is a distinct advantage to having your poem discussed by a group rather than evaluated by a single reader. No matter how specific and articulate your reader is, personal feelings may affect the critique. With a group you can weigh what is a chance misreading against what is a general impression. If several readers feel your poem is too static and needs some kind of tension in tone or attitude, that is worth more careful consideration than if only one had that feeling. This is not to say that you should blindly follow majority rule, but it is important to understand how your work is being perceived by a number of careful readers.

Valuable as group reaction is, the final decisions are your alone. You have to be able and willing to ask yourself the kinds of critical questions that will lead to improvement.

The Basic Critical Questions

Here are six questions often asked in writing classes by individual readers who know how to help a poet. They are also questions you will find helpful in analyzing your own work. I present them not as a simple checklist but as a description of the range of concerns that will be important to you as you revise. Eventually they will become internalized.

Each of these topics has been the subject of at least one chapter, though the order here has been changed slightly. The discussions will vary with the poem and with the inclination of the group, but it is often helpful to begin with those aspects that strike the reader first—key images, for example. The more complex concerns, such as tone, unity, and theme, are sometimes best postponed until later in the discussion.

• First, *are the images effective?* In a difficult poem, isolated images may be all that reach the reader the first time through. These may be vivid visual details used for their own sake, or they may be vehicles for metaphors; but the poet needs to know what has really made an impression. It is mainly by listening to the reactions of others that you will be able to judge for yourself what is a fresh image and what is bland, flat, or too familiar.

• Second, *is the diction fresh?* The concern here shifts to individual words and phrases. Make sure that all your readers have a copy of your work in front of them. They will be looking not only for clichés but for familiar phrasing, echoes from song lyrics, and conventional adjectives that are either unnecessary or poorly selected. If a reader says, "Some of your phrases seem sort of hackneyed," don't get sulky or defensive. Ask "Which ones?"

Occasionally critics will tell you that your poem or a part of it seems "prosaic" or "prosy." This may come from using too much abstract language (references to "love" and "trust" when what you had in mind was a particular person); or you may be describing a scene without focusing on key images. In either case, encourage your critic to identify specific lines so you can decide whether the problem lies in images, diction, or the degree of compression.

If you are working alone—as you probably will much of the time—you will have to serve as your own critic. These same questions become the basis of your own analysis.

• Third, *are there sound devices?* True, some poems depend heavily on sharpness of image and do not make use of such techniques as rhyme, assonance, alliteration, consonance, and onomatopoeia. But if you choose that route, make sure that it is by conscious decision, not forgetfulness.

Occasionally the problem may be just the reverse: sound devices that are obtrusive. As was pointed out in Chapter 5, rhyming couplets can do this, particularly when they are emphasized with regular, end-stopped lines. Contiguous alliteration can also become blatant. Just how much is too much obviously is a matter of individual opinion, but if several readers express the same complaint, the line certainly deserves reconsideration.

• Fourth, *does the poem make use of rhythm?* Here again it is important to urge your critics to be as specific as possible. If the poem is metered, where does the meter become monotonous and where, on the other hand, do the metrical substitutions become so numerous that the flow of reading is interrupted? Even if your critic is unable to scan metered poetry, he or she should be able to detect awkwardness in the rhythm. And if the poem is free verse, what rhythmical systems are being used? Don't instruct your critics: let them tell you what they have perceived in their reading.

Rhythm, of course, is closely connected with the sound linkages—rhyme, assonance, alliteration, and the like. You may find it valuable to read your work out loud to your group or, if you are working alone, to yourself. Some poets use cassette recorders for their own work. But it is still important to have copies to look at. As we saw in Chapter 7, some rhythms—particularly in free verse—depend on seeing as well as hearing the work.

• Fifth, *what is the tone?* The answers may surprise you. Those choice samples of wit may have eluded your readers. And what you took most seriously may not have had the impact you intended.

Equally important, you will want to determine whether the tone has developed some kind of tension—one attitude or reaction played against another. If it does not, have you considered all the aspects of your subject? Did you honestly have such a clearly defined attitude? Is there really only one way of looking at the subject? Sometimes what you thought was a finished poem ends up being a portion of a longer, more complex poem involving some kind of contrast or ambivalence.

Occasionally the tone or even the central theme of a poem may shift as you are working on it. There is no harm in this, but make sure that each line and every image in the new version really belongs there. This is particularly important when your attitude toward your subject has changed between, say, the third and fourth draft. Make sure that your original approach doesn't "show through" as an inconsistency in the later draft.

• Sixth, *how is the poem constructed and how do those various parts achieve unity?* Frequently this will turn into a discussion of the poem's theme or central concern. This is important, of course, but it shouldn't obscure the question of how the elements of the poem are put together.

A sense of structure and unity, you remember, can be aided by the visual pattern—the shape of traditional stanzas, fixed poetic forms, or the irregular spacing of free verse. There are endless alternatives here. Also there are the internal and nonvisual structural elements such as narrative, image clusters, and repetitions. Even after you are sure of the theme of a poem, there remain many alternatives as to how you can best present it. Keep in mind that the internal arrangement of the poem is actually a part of its statement. Ask yourself, is the structure doing enough?

The Fellowship of Poets

When you take a course in creative writing, you usually draw a good deal from those who share your interests. That sense of comradery keeps you going. After graduation, however, you may feel strangely isolated, wondering what happened to all those people who took poetry seriously. Rest assured on this score: there are tens of thousands of people who share your enthusiasms. Anyone who has judged a national poetry contest can tell you that the number of poets in this country is astounding. The problem is not numbers, it is distribution. They are scattered across a very large country.

You have to make a special effort to bridge the gap between you and other poets. If there is a reading in the area, take the time to attend. Better yet, order the latest volume by the poet who is giving the reading and study his or her work in advance. The reading will be far more meaningful if you do.

In addition, you may be able to find a poetry group whose members meet regularly to discuss their work. If it is a harmonious, supportive group, you can draw a good deal from it—both in critical insight and in your sense of worth. If are tempted to start your own group, much will depend on the tone you set at the first meeting. You may wish to use the list of basic critical questions described in this chapter as an initial guide. The most helpful approach is to steer a middle course between excessive politeness on the one hand and potentially damaging bluntness on the other. Remember that the goal of both writer and critic is to improve the work.

Finally, make use of poetry journals. They are edited and supported by people like you, and they depend on subscribers for survival. A brief list of quarterlies appears in Appendix B. Use this as a start, reading sample copies in your local library. As soon as you find which publications print work you enjoy, subscribe. You will read the poetry much more carefully if you own your own copy, and you can mark up poems as you wish. The cost for two subscriptions will be less than the cost of a ticket to a rock concert or a trip to the supermarket, and what you get will last a good deal longer.

There is a fellowship of poets in this country, and its members are connected across great distances through quarterlies, journals, and slim volumes of poetry. If they speak and you do not listen, you are not a part of that group. If you isolate yourself, you have walled yourself off from those who can help you grow. Developing as a poet does not mean grinding out more lines and chalking up publications; it means joining that fellowship of practicing poets—both the published and the unpublished—and sharing their values.

11
POEMS
FOR STUDY

Lizards and Snakes

ANTHONY HECHT

On the summer road that ran by our front porch
       Lizards and snakes came out to sun.
It was hot as a stove out there, enough to scorch
       A buzzard's foot. Still, it was fun
To lie in the dust and spy on them. Near but remote,   5
       They snoozed in the carriage ruts, a smile
In the set of the jaw, a fierce pulse in the throat
Working away like Jack Doyle's after he'd run the mile.

Aunt Martha had an unfair prejudice
       Against them (as well as being cold   10
Toward bats.) She was pretty inflexible in this,
Being a spinster and all, and old.
So we used to slip them into her knitting box.
       In the evening she'd bring in things to mend
And a nice surprise would slide out from under the socks.   15
It broadened her life, as Joe said. Joe was my friend.

But we never did it again after the day
    Of the big wind when you could hear the trees
Creak like rockingchairs. She was looking away
    Off, and kept saying, "Sweet Jesus, please   20
Don't let him hear me. He's as like as twins.
    He can crack us like lice with his fingernail.
I can see him plain as a pikestaff. Look how he grins
And swings the scaly horror of his folded tail."

Names of Horses

DONALD HALL

All winter your brute shoulders strained against collars, padding
and steerhide over the ash hames, to haul
sledges of cordwood for drying through spring and summer,
for the Glenwood stove next winter, and for the simmering range.

In April you pulled cartloads of manure to spread on the fields,   5
dark manure of Holsteins, and knobs of your own clustered with oats.
All summer you mowed the grass in meadow and hayfield, the mowing
    machine
clacketing beside you, while the sun walked high in the morning;

and after noon's heat, you pulled a clawed rake through the same acres,
gathering stacks, and dragged the wagon from stack to stack,   10
and the built hayrack back, uphill to the chaffy barn,
three loads of hay a day, hanging wide from the hayrack.

Sundays you trotted the two miles to church with the light load
of a leather quartertop buggy, and grazed in the sound of hymns.
Generation on generation, your neck rubbed the window sill   15
of the stall, smoothing the wood as the sea smooths glass.

When you were old and lame, when your shoulders hurt bending to graze,
one October the man who fed you and kept you, and harnessed you every
    morning,
led you through corn stubble to sandy ground above Eagle Pond,
and dug a hole beside you where you stood shuddering in your skin,   20

and lay the shotgun's muzzle in the boneless hollow behind your ear,
and fired the slug into your brain, and felled you into your grave,
shoveling sand to cover you, setting goldenrod upright above you,
where by next summer a dent in the ground made your monument.

For a hundred and fifty years, in the pasture of dead horses,   25
roots of pine trees pushed through the pale curves of your ribs,
yellow blossoms flourished above you in autumn, and in winter
frost heaved your bones in the ground—old toilers, soil makers:

O Roger, Mackerel, Riley, Ned, Nellie, Chester, Lady Ghost.

Those Winter Sundays

ROBERT HAYDEN

Sundays too my father got up early
and put his clothes on in the blueblack cold,
then with cracked hands that ached
from labor in the weekday weather made
banked fires blaze. No one ever thanked him.

I'd wake and hear the cold splintering, breaking.   5
When the rooms were warm, he'd call,
and slowly I would rise and dress,
fearing the chronic angers of that house,

Speaking indifferently to him,   10
who had driven out the cold
and polished my good shoes as well.
What did I know, what did I know
of love's austere and lonely offices?

Morning Swim

MAXINE KUMIN

Into my empty head there come
a cotton beach, a dock wherefrom

I set out, oily and nude
through mist, in chilly solitude.

There was no line, no roof or floor   5
to tell the water from the air.

Night fog thick as terry cloth
closed me in its fuzzy growth.

I hung my bathrobe on two pegs.
I took the lake between my legs.   10

Invaded and invader, I
went overhand on that flat sky.

Fish twitched beneath me, quick and tame.
In their green zone they sang my name

and in the rhythm of the swim   15
I hummed a two-four-time slow hymn.

I hummed *Abide with Me*. The beat
rose in the fine thrash of my feet,

rose in the bubbles I put out
slantwise, trailing through my mouth.   20

My bones drank water; water fell
through all my doors. I was the well

that fed the lake that met my sea
in which I sang *Abide with Me*.

The Rural Carrier Stops to Kill a Nine-Foot Cottonmouth

T. R. HUMMER

Lord God, I saw the son-of-a-bitch uncoil
In the road ahead of me, uncoil and squirm
For the ditch, squirm a hell of a long time.
Missed him with the car. When I got back to him, he was all
But gone, nothing left on the road but the tip-end   5
Of his tail, and that disappearing into Johnson grass.
I leaned over the ditch and saw him, balled up now, hiss.
I aimed for the mouth and shot him. And shot him again.

Then I got a good strong stick and dragged him out.
He was long and evil, thick as the top of my arm.   10
There are things in this world a man can't look at without
Wanting to kill. Don't ask me why. I was calm
Enough, I thought. But I felt my spine
Squirm, suddenly. I admit it. It was mine.

Milk the Mouse

MICHAEL RYAN

He'll pinch my pinky until the mouse starts squeaking.
The floorlamp casts a halo around his big, stuffed chair.
Be strong Be tough! It is my father speaking.

I'm four or five. Was he already drinking?
With its tip and knuckle between his thumb and finger,   5
he'll pinch my pinky until the mouse starts squeaking

Stop, Daddy, stop (it was more like screeching)
and kneels down before him on the hardwood floor.
Be strong Be tough! It is my father speaking.

What happened to him that he'd do such a thing?   10
It's only a game, he's doing me a favor
to pinch my pinky until the mouse starts squeaking

because the world will run over a weakling
and we must crush the mouse or be crushed later.
Be strong Be tough! It was my father speaking   15

to himself, of course, to the child inside him aching,
not to me. But how can I not go when he calls me over
to pinch my pinky until the mouse starts squeaking
Be strong Be tough? It is my father speaking.

The Dalliance of the Eagles

WALT WHITMAN

Skirting the river road, (my forenoon walk, my rest,)
Skyward in air a sudden muffled sound, the dalliance of the eagles,
The rushing amorous contact high in space together,
The clinching interlocking claws, a living, fierce, gyrating wheel,
Four beating wings, two beaks, a swirling mass tight grappling,   5
In tumbling turning clustering loops, straight downward falling,
Till o'er the river pois'd, the twain yet one, a moment's lull,
A motionless still balance in the air, then parting, talons loosing,
Upward again on slow-firm pinions slanting, their separate diverse flight,
She hers, he his, pursuing.   10

Song Maker

ANITA ENDREZZE

There is a drunk on Main Avenue, slumped
in front of the Union Gospel Mission.
He is dreaming of pintos the color of wine
and ice, and drums that speak the names
of wind. His hair hides his face,   5
but I think I know him.

Didn't he make songs people still sing
in their sleep?
Didn't coyotes beg him for new songs
to give to the moon?   10
Didn't he dance all night once and laugh
when the women suddenly turned
shy at dawn?
Didn't he make a song just for me,
one blessed by its being sung only once?   15

If he would lift his face
I could see his eyes, see
if he's singing now
a soul dissolving song.
But he's all hunched over   20
and everyone walks around him.
He must still have strong magic
to be so invisible.

I remember him saying:
Even grass has a song,   25
'though only wind hears it.

Bedtime

DENISE LEVERTOV

We are a meadow where the bees hum,
mind and body are almost one

as the fire snaps in the stove
and our eyes close,

and mouth to mouth, the covers   5
pulled over our shoulders,

we drowse as horses drowse afield,
in accord; though the fall cold

surrounds our warm bed, and though
by day we are singular and often lonely.   10

"Buffalo Bill's"

E. E. CUMMINGS

Buffalo Bill's
defunct
     who used to
     ride a watersmooth-silver
               stallion   5
and break onetwothreefourfive pigeonsjustlikethat
                    Jesus
he was a handsome man
          and what i want to know is
how do you like your blueeyed boy   10
Mister Death

The Waking

THEODORE ROETHKE

I wake to sleep, and take my waking slow.
I feel my fate in what I cannot fear.
I learn by going where I have to go.

We think by feeling. What is there to know?
I hear my being dance from ear to ear.   5
I wake to sleep, and take my waking slow.

Of those so close beside me, which are you?
God bless the Ground! I shall walk softly there,
And learn by going where I have to go.

Light takes the Tree; but who can tell us how?   10
The lowly worm climbs up a winding stair;
I wake to sleep, and take my waking slow.

Great Nature has another thing to do
To you and me; so take the lively air,
And, lovely, learn by going where to go.   15

This shaking keeps me steady. I should know.
What falls away is always. And is near.
I wake to sleep, and take my waking slow.
I learn by going where I have to go.

On a Maine Beach

ROBLEY WILSON

Look, in these pools, how rocks are like worn change
Keeping the ocean's mint-mark; barnacles
Miser on them; societies of snails
Hunch on their rims and think small thoughts whose strange
Salt logics rust like a mainspring, small dreams   5
Pinwheeling to a point and going dumb,
Small equations whose euphemistic sum
Stands for mortality. A thousand times
Tides swallow up such pools, shellfish and stone
Show green and yellow shade in groves of weed;   10
Rocks shrink, barnacles drink, snails think they bleed
In their trapped world. Here, when the sea is gone,
We find old coins glowing under the sky,
Barnacles counting them, snails spending slow
Round lifetimes half-awake. Beach rhythms flow   15
In circles. Perfections teach us to die.

In a Station of the Metro

EZRA POUND

The apparition of these faces in the crowd;
Petals on a wet, black bough.

Merritt Parkway

DENISE LEVERTOV

As if it were
forever that they move, that we
   keep moving—
      Under a wan sky where
     as the lights went on a star   5
         pierced the haze & now
    follows steadily
        a constant
    above our six lanes
    the dreamlike continuum...   10

And the people—ourselves!
   the humans from inside the
   cars, apparent
   only at gasoline stops   5
        unsure,
   eyeing each other

       drink coffee hastily at the
     slot machines & hurry
  back to the cars
    vanish   20
    into them forever, to
    keep moving—

Houses now & then beyond the
sealed road, the trees / trees, bushes
passing by, passing   25
   the cars that
     keep moving ahead of
    us, past us, pressing behind us
         and
      over left, those that come   30
    toward us shining too brightly
moving relentlessly

   in six lanes, gliding
   north & south, speeding with
   a slurred sound—   35

The Bay at West Falmouth

BARBARA HOWES

Serenity of mind poises
Like a gull swinging in air,
At ease, sculptured, held there
For a moment so long-drawn-out all time pauses.

The heart's serenity is like the gold   5
Geometry of sunlight: motion shafting
Down through green dimensions, rung below rung
Of incandescence, out of which grace unfolds.

Watching that wind schooling the bay, the helter-skelter
Of trees juggling air, waves signalling the sun   10
To signal light, brings peace; as our being open
To love does, near this serenity of water.

After Spring

CHORA

After spring sunset
Mist rises from the river
Spreading like a flood

Night Song

LISEL MUELLER

Among rocks, I am the loose one,
among arrows, I am the heart,
among daughters, I am the recluse,
among sons, the one who dies young.

Among answers, I am the question,   5
between lovers, I am the sword,
among scars, I am the fresh wound,
among confetti, the black flag.

Among shoes, I am the one with the pebble,
among days, the one that never comes,   10
among the bones you find on the beach,
the one that sings was mine.

The Guild

SHARON OLDS

Every night, as my grandfather sat
in the darkened room in front of the fire,
the liquor like fire in his hand, his eye
glittering meaninglessly in the light
from the flames, his glass eye baleful and stony,   5
a young man sat with him
in silence and darkness, a college boy with
white skin, unlined, a narrow
beautiful face, a broad domed
forehead, and eyes amber as the resin from   10
trees too young to be cut yet.
This was his son, who sat, an apprentice,
night after night, his glass of coals
next to the old man's glass of coals,
and he drank when the old man drank, and he learned   15
the craft of oblivion—that young man
not yet cruel, his hair dark as the
soil that feeds the tree's roots,
that son who would come to be in his turn
better at this than the teacher, the apprentice   20
who would pass his master in cruelty and oblivion,
drinking steadily by the flames in the blackness,
that young man my father.

Even with Insects

ISSA

Even with insects ...
Some are hatched out musical ...
Some, alas, tone-deaf

The Pardon

RICHARD WILBUR

My dog lay dead five days without a grave
In the thick of summer, hid in a clump of pine
And a jungle of grass and honeysuckle-vine.
I who had loved him while he kept alive

Went only close enough to where he was   5
To sniff the heavy honeysuckle-smell
Twined with another odour heavier still
And hear the flies' intolerable buzz.

Well, I was ten and very much afraid.
In my kind world the dead were out of range   10
And I could not forgive the sad or strange
In beast or man. My father took the spade

And buried him. Last night I saw the grass
Slowly divide (it was the same scene
But now it glowed a fierce and mortal green)   15
And saw the dog emerging. I confess

I felt afraid again, but still he came
In the carnal sun, clothed in a hymn of flies,
And death was breeding in his lively eyes.
I started in to cry and call his name,   20

Asking forgiveness of his tongueless head.
…I dreamt the past was never past redeeming:
But whether this was false or honest dreaming
I beg death's pardon now. And mourn the dead.

Rhymes for Old Age

CHASE TWICHELL

The wind's untiring saxophone
keens at the glass.
The lamp sheds a monochrome
of stainless steel and linens,
the nurse in her snowy dress   5
firm in her regimens.

The form in the bed
is a soul diminished
to a fledgling, fed
on the tentative balm of spring,   10
sketch for an angel, half-finished,
shoulder blades the stubs of wings.

Darkened with glaucoma,
the room floats on the retina.
The long vowel of *coma*   15
broods in the breath, part vapor.
What has become of the penetralia?
Eau de cologne sanctifies the diaper.

Flood and drag, the undertow.
One slips into it undressed,   20
as into first love, the vertigo
that shrinks to a keepsake of passion.
Sky's amethyst
lies with a sponge in the basin.

Balances

NIKKI GIOVANNI

in life
one is always
balancing

like we juggle our mothers
against our fathers   5

or one teacher
against another
(only to balance our grade average)

3 grains salt
to one ounce truth   10

our sweet black essence
or the funky honkies down the street

and lately i've begun wondering
if you're trying to tell me something

we used to talk all night   15
and do things alone together

and i've begun

(as a reaction to a feeling)
to balance
the pleasure of loneliness   20
against the pain
of loving you

We Real Cool

GWENDOLYN BROOKS

The Pool Players.
Seven at the Golden Shovel.

We real cool. We
Left school. We

Lurk late. We
Strike straight. We

Sing sin. We   5
Thin gin. We

Jazz June. We
Die soon.

This Winter Day

MAYA ANGELOU

The kitchen in its readiness
white green and orange things
leak their blood selves in the soup.

Ritual sacrifice that snaps
an odor at my nose and starts   5
my tongue to march
slipping in the liquid of its drip.

The day, silver striped
in rain, is balked against
my window and the soup.   10

Fern Hill

DYLAN THOMAS

Now as I was young and easy under the apple boughs
About the lilting house and happy as the grass was green,
      The night above the dingle starry,
        Time let me hail and climb
    Golden in the heydays of his eyes,   5
And honoured among wagons I was prince of the apple towns
And once below a time I lordly had the trees and leaves
        Trail with daisies and barley
      Down the rivers of the windfall light.
And as I was green and carefree, famous among the barns   10
About the happy yard and singing as the farm was home,
      In the sun that is young once only,
        Time let me play and be
    Golden in the mercy of his means,
And green and golden I was huntsman and herdsman, the calves 15
Sang to my horn, the foxes on the hills barked clear and cold,
        And the sabbath rang slowly
      In the pebbles of the holy streams.

All the sun long it was running, it was lovely, the hay
Fields high as the house, the tunes from the chimneys, it was air 20
        And playing, lovely and watery
          And fire green as grass.
        And nightly under the simple stars
As I rode to sleep the owls were bearing the farm away,
All the moon long I heard, blessed among stables, the nightjars 25
        Flying with the ricks, and the horses
        Flashing into the dark.

And then to awake, and the farm, like a wanderer white
With the dew, come back, the cock on his shoulder: it was all
        Shining, it was Adam and maiden,   30
        The sky gathered again
      And the sun grew round that very day.

So it must have been after the birth of the simple light
In the first, spinning place, the spellbound horses walking warm
        Out of the whinnying green stable   35
            On to the fields of praise.

And honoured among foxes and pheasants by the gay house
Under the new made clouds and happy as the heart was long
        In the sun born over and over,
           I ran my heedless ways,   40
        My wishes raced through the house-high hay
And nothing I cared, at my sky blue trades, that time allows
In all his tuneful turning so few and such morning songs
        Before the children green and golden
           Follow him out of grace,   45

Nothing I cared, in the lamb white days, that time would take me
Up to the swallow thronged loft by the shadow of my hand,
        In the moon that is always rising,
           Nor that riding to sleep
        I should hear him fly with the high fields   50
And wake to the farm forever fled from the childless land.
Oh as I was young and easy in the mercy of his means,
        Time held me green and dying
        Though I sang in my chains like the sea.

What the Mirror Said

LUCILLE CLIFTON

listen,
you a wonder,
you a city
of a woman.
you got a geography   5
of your own.
listen,
somebody need a map
to understand you.
somebody need directions   10
to move around you.
listen,
woman,
you not a noplace   15

anonymous
girl;
mister with his hands on you
he got his hands on
some   20
damn
body!

Pilot Error
(For Juliet Leventhal Balgley 1914–1965)

ANN Z. LEVENTHAL

The phone rings on a Sunday afternoon.
"There's been an accident," Juliet's
husband says. I go on folding laundry,

matching every corner, every seam
exactly, caressing terry velvet   5
on Sunday, after the phone rings,

I stack the towels, make
of them four piles, four
pillars. "The plane went down,

Juliet's not expected..." I shake   10
out socks, press them flat together,
roll them into neat, tight fists.

"I'll get back to you," he says.
I go back to laundry, the white
sheets I pull from the line—day-   15

filled blanks—stiff, cool, I
stretch them wide across my breasts.
Juliet is not like her name, not

fourteen but fifty, and thickly warm
as the furnace that holds off winter.   20
The phone rings. I carry inside

my basket of clean and the phone talks
funeral, me asking when as if there is
still a clock and there is still time.

Haiku

ETHERIDGE KNIGHT

1

Eastern guard tower
glints in sunset; convicts rest
like lizards on rocks.

4

To write a blues song
is to regiment riots
and pluck gems from graves.

5

A bare pecan tree
slips a pencil shadow down
a moonlit snow slope.

In the Attic

DONALD JUSTICE

There's a half hour towards dusk when flies,
Trapped by the summer screens, expire
Musically in the dust of sills;
And ceilings slope towards remembrance.

The same crimson afternoons expire   5
Over the same few rooftops repeatedly;
Only, being stored up for remembrance,
They somehow escape the ordinary.

Childhood is like that, repeatedly
Lost in the very longueurs it redeems.   10
One forgets how small and ordinary
The world looked once by dusklight from above ...

But not the moment which redeems
The drowsy arias of the flies—
And the chin settles onto palms above   15
Numbed elbows propped on rotting sills.

River Sound Remembered

W. S. MERWIN

That day the huge water drowned all voices until
It seemed a kind of silence unbroken
By anything: A time unto itself and still;

So that when I turned away from its roaring, down
The path over the gully, and there were   5
Dogs barking as always at the edge of town,

Car horns and the cries of children coming
As though for the first time through the fading light
Of the winter dusk, my ears still sang

Like shells with the swinging current, and   10
Its flood echoing in me held for long
About me the same silence, by whose sound

I could hear only the quiet under the day
With the land noises floating there far-off and still;
So that even in my mind now turning away   15

From having listened absently but for so long
It will be the seethe and drag of the river
That I will hear longer than any mortal song.

Comparatives

N. SCOTT MOMADAY

Sunlit sea,
the drift of fronds,
and banners
of bobbing boats—
the seaside   5
of any day—
except: this
cold, bright body
of the fish
upon the planks,   10
the coil and
crescent of flesh

extending
just into death.

Even so,   15
in the distant,
inland sea,
a shadow runs,
radiant,
rude in the rock: 20
fossil fish,
fissure of bone
forever.
It is perhaps
the same thing,   25
an agony
twice perceived.

It is most like
wind on waves—
mere commotion,   30
mute and mean,
perceptible—
that is all.

One Art

ELIZABETH BISHOP

The art of losing isn't hard to master;
so many things seem filled with the intent
to be lost that their loss is no disaster.

Lose something every day. Accept the fluster
of lost door keys, the hour badly spent.   5
The art of losing isn't hard to master.

Then practice losing farther, losing faster:
places, and names, and where it was you meant
to travel. None of these will bring disaster.

I lost my mother's watch. And look! my last, or   10
next-to-last, of three loved houses went.
The art of losing isn't hard to master.

I lost two cities, lovely ones. And, vaster,
some realms I owned, two rivers, a continent.
I miss them, but it wasn't a disaster.   15

—Even losing you (the joking voice, a gesture
I love) I shan't have lied. It's evident
the art of losing's not too hard to master
though it may look like (*Write* it!) like disaster.

Ice River

DAVID BAKER

Only after a couple of months of hard
cold, by mid-January usually,
no sooner, is the river ready, shards
of ice dropping to it from the white trees.
Before this, even in the early snow,   5
a frost-crust on mud and weed, it runs slowly

on, and on past wherever I might stand
to watch it, finally, freeze. Now it has.
I walk out toward that blue light at the bend
in its banks, the cold end of day, out past   10
the shore and skid of frozen mud to where
the snow lies flat as a road: the river

itself. I have waited this long to be
alone and small. Here the only sound is that
dull chewing, boots on snow. Even the trees   15
along the banks loom close, bent, the wet
rock-face bearded with long ice. I have come
back as to some trackless past, and I'm numb

with cold. Nothing moves, or appears to. Yet
under this sheet—snow on ice, thin inches   20
of support—the river runs black and fast.
As I walk I feel its deep pulse in the clenched
sagging of my weight. Even now, the ice
cracks a little, and small shoots pass

from my steps, to the river-edge, like roots.   25
In a few months I may return to fish

or walk long on the green land. Still, this mute
day is ending now, no sun, only this:
wind pulling in the heavy trees, the faint
light of snow, the blood stopped cold in my feet.   30

12
THE CREATIVE PROCESS

Factual versus creative writing. Blending experience and invention. Simple versus sophisticated fiction. The forms of fiction. Three motives for writing fiction.

We start telling stories almost as soon as we can put sentences together. Whenever we talk about characters doing something, we are narrating a story.

At first, we may make no sharp distinction between what is make-believe and what really happened. But as we get older, we learn that this can get us into trouble. That's when we discover that fiction is one way to make things up without being called a liar.

That's an important lesson to remember because it reminds us that there are two significantly different types of stories. The first is *factual*. Factual writing that deals with characters and a plot is a type of a story, but we usually describe it with more precise terms like biography, autobiography, journalism, social history, and the like. When we work with these forms, we are committed to reporting the events as they occurred. We may offer opinions or even present an argument, but first we have to get the facts right.

The other way of telling a story is called *imaginative* or **creative writing**. Fiction, narrative poetry, and drama are all *creative* in the sense that we are creating some or all of it from our own imaginations. Our first loyalty is not to events that have occurred but to the artistic object we are creating.

Blending Experience and Invention

Fiction, then, tells an untrue story in prose. It is "untrue" in the sense that it is at least partly made up. It is an artistic creation that stands on its own no matter how much it may make use of characters, events, and settings from life. As writers, we are free to take on a different personality and even to assume the existence of dragons or life on Mars without being called liars. A story or novel cannot be criticized for being "untrue"; it is judged on whether it *seems* true.

One of the best ways to achieve this sense of authenticity, however, is to draw heavily on the world you know best—your own life. Some beginning writers feel that their lives have been too ordinary, but everyone has had complex relationships with parents or foster parents, everyone has had to deal with people their own age, everyone has had defeats, successes, and learning experiences. And every experience is unique.

This does not mean, however, that *unrevised* experience makes good fiction. Our lives are a jumble of unconnected events and repetitious activities. There is nothing as dull as a step-by-step account of what has happened to you over the length of an average day. Even a specific event almost always needs extensive revision before it becomes a successful story. Usually there are many unrelated details that need cutting. Sometimes the event was too mild or, conversely, too melodramatic for fiction. So we begin cutting this and adding that. Our goal is not a factual record of events as they occurred but an artistic creation with its own sense of unity and significance. To some degree we do this without thinking when we tell a friend about something that happened to us. But with fiction, we are liberated from what actually happened. In some ways a work of fiction is to factual writing what a painting is to a photograph.

Simple versus Sophisticated Fiction

As soon as we talk about the *merit* or *worth* of an artistic work, we enter the slippery area of what is *good* and what is *bad*. It is so difficult to defend the worth of a story that some people duck the issue entirely by saying, "I only know what I like." Personal preference, of course, is everyone's privilege. Some like gentle stories, some want heavy drama; some prefer stories about women, others like to read about men. Arguing seriously about our preferences is as pointless as debating whether dogs are better than cats.

There is, however, one distinction about which we can reach a measure of agreement: Some stories, like some poems and plays, are relatively **simple** while others are significantly more **sophisticated**. This is a notion that is enormously helpful for writers and underlies all of the analysis in this book.

Essentially, sophisticated works "do" more in the sense that they suggest more, imply a greater range of possibilities, develop more subtle shadings of meaning than simple works do. This text is concerned with sophisticated writing, but that does not imply that such work is "better." It is simply "other" in the sense that the biologically simple crayfish is different from the far more sophisticated porpoise.

The span between the simplest fiction and relatively sophisticated fiction is enormous. Compare a comic strip about adolescents like *Archie, The Jackson Twins*, or *Gil Thorpe* with a novel about adolescents like Knowles' *A Separate Peace* or Salinger's *Catcher in the Rye*. They are similar in that they are both samples of fiction as I have been defining it—they both tell untrue stories in prose. Further, they both have plot, characters, setting, and themes. And they share certain basic techniques: dialogue, thoughts, action, description, and exposition. They even use the same subject matter: that highly charged period between childhood and adulthood. And before we brand one as "good" and the other as "bad," remember that many intelligent adults read the comics in the morning paper, and *Catcher in the Rye* is still barred from some secondary schools as immoral and unacceptable.

But obviously they are utterly different forms of fiction. Archie as a fictional character is *simple*; so are the stories in which he appears. There are only a limited number of suggestions or implications that can be made from the highly conventional, monotonously repetitive types of situations in which he is placed. On the other hand, Holden Caulfield is a sophisticated character, and the novel in which we come to know him is sophisticated as well. It is important here to distinguish this literary use of *sophisticated* from its popular use, which describes merely personal characteristics. Mark Twain's Huck Finn, for example, is certainly unsophisticated as an individual, but the complexity and intricacy with which the author presents him is sophisticated.

As in poetry, there are an infinite number of gradations between the simplest forms of fiction and the most sophisticated. Juveniles—stories and novels written for adolescents—are far more intricate in characterization and theme than comic strips. Gothic novels, for all their repetition of plots, have a certain sophistication of vocabulary; but they are not intended to be as subtle or insightful as literary novels. In fact, a standard, mass-market gothic novel manuscript might well be turned down by a publisher if it departed too far from the familiar and relatively simple pattern. In the case of murder mysteries, most of the sophistication takes the form of ingenious plots, but thematically they tend to be fairly simple. They are for most enthusiasts "a quick read."

Every magazine has a certain range in terms of fictional sophistication. Larger-circulation publications like *McCalls* and *Redbook*, for example, offer relatively simple fiction. For sophisticated short stories, one must turn to the literary journals and quarterlies like *Story* and *The North American Review*, or to the "qualities" like *The Atlantic* and *The New Yorker*. (A longer list appears in Appendix B.) These publications usually vary their offerings from relatively accessible pieces to works that, like sophisticated poetry, may require some effort on the part of the reader.

As a writer, how high should you aim? It would be a mistake to start out by attempting an extremely complex plot and an intricate theme. If you have one or two interesting characters and a single, insightful event, you can write a story that is fresh and rewarding.

As you gain experience you will want to examine what makes some works more sophisticated than others. Take a close look at the basic elements of the story: plot, characters, setting, and theme.

Starting with plot, it is obvious that all fiction, whether simple or sophisticated, is developed through a sequence of actions. Simple fiction, however, not only reduces the complexity of plot, but it usually avoids originality as well. Simple plots tend to be based on well-used conventions known in the magazine field as **formulas**. The pleasure some people derive from, say, husband-tempted-by-widow-next-door-but-finally-returns-to-wife is not the stimulation of fresh experience and insight but, rather, the tranquilizer of familiarity and repetition.

Sophistication of plot does not necessarily mean complexity. What one aims for is a situation and a sequence of actions that are fresh and provide new insights. The determining factor is not how many twists and turns the plot may take but how much is revealed about the characters and the theme of the story.

The same is true with the characters. In simple fiction, the characters may do a lot, but you never get to know much about them. It is possible to follow the adventures of a comic strip character for 20 years and still not know him or her the way you come to know the characters in a single sophisticated short story.

All fiction has setting, but simple fiction often relies on geographic clichés that are repeated over and over. Students in New York are described as living in Greenwich Village even though that area has not been a low-rent bargain for over 40 years; businessmen have their offices on Madison Avenue; San Francisco scenes are "in the shadow of the Golden Gate"; Paris stories have vistas looking out on the Eiffel Tower. "Originality" frequently takes the form of the exotic—a ski resort high in the Andes, a spy headquarters 400 feet below the Houses of Parliament, a royal palace constructed entirely in glowing Lucite on the planet Octo. Stories with exotic settings like these may *seem* original at first, but they are usually slightly disguised versions of other relatively simple stories.

Sophisticated fiction, on the other hand, tends to avoid both the hackneyed and the bizarre. The setting is used as a way of increasing credibility and placing the reader in the center of the story—regardless of whether it is based on an actual place or upon the dreamscape of the author.

Theme is another aspect of fiction that varies with the degree of sophistication. Simple themes suggest truisms that make no more impact on us than the background music in a restaurant. So-called detective magazines and their television counterparts reiterate endlessly, "Crime doesn't pay, but it's exciting to try." Many of television's situation comedies suggest repeatedly that "Nice girls eventually end up with nice boys, but only after being hurt." The fact that we know nice young women who have ended up with terrible husbands and fine young men who never married at all doesn't seem to weaken the popularity of this simple thematic concern.

Sophisticated fiction tends to have thematic concerns that suggest mixed feelings. Often this takes the form of ambivalence, a blending of love and hate for the same person at the same time. Further complexity is sometimes achieved with irony, a reversal of one's normal expectations.

Whenever you read fiction you evaluate the level of sophistication on the basis of elements like these, either consciously or unconsciously. And when you write, they are concerns that will hold your attention at every stage.

In addition to the content of a story, you will want to examine the way the material is presented. For purposes of analysis, it is helpful to see every sentence in a story as presented in one of five different ways or **narrative modes**: *dialogue, thought, action, description,* and *exposition.*

Dialogue and **thought** are two effective ways of suggesting character, and often they are used in tandem so that one sees a contrast between the inner and the outer person. In simple fiction, however, they are often stereotyped—predictable lines for predictable characters.

Action is the dominant mode for simple fiction—particularly for adventure stories. But as we will see in the examples included in this text, sophisticated fiction makes significant use of action too. The difference is that as the story begins to gain a greater range of suggestion, the action necessarily must take on a more subtle role of implication. Put another way, action shifts from being an end in itself to being a means of suggestion.

The same is true of **description**. In a sophisticated story, almost every phrase devoted to describing characters, places, possessions, and the like contributes to the theme or to some aspect of characterization.

The last of these five narrative modes, exposition, is perhaps the most dangerous. **Exposition** refers to those explanatory passages that give background information or commentary directly. "They lived in Chicago" or "He was more generous than they were" are expository statements if not presented through dialogue. In simple fiction exposition is used to point up the theme as one progresses through the story and, often, to sum it up directly at the end. "Down deep," we are told periodically, "Old Karl had a warm spot in his heart." And in case we missed it, we are given the clincher at the end: "Though his parting words were gruff, there was an undertone of kindness in the old prospector's voice. It was clear that he still knew the meaning of love."

Those who are used to sophisticated fiction grimace at this because it is a familiar convention. It is also close to the technique of the essay. A sophisticated story may use just as much exposition, but it will rarely label the theme that way. This is not because authors want to be evasive, but because the success of literarily sophisticated fiction depends on the degree to which readers have the feeling that they themselves have discovered the thematic suggestions in a story. It is similar to the way we make judgments about people and situations in actual life. We listen to what people say and watch what they do, and then we come to conclusions. In fiction, of course, the dialogue and action are carefully selected by the author, but when we read we like the illusion of discovering significances on our own.

The Forms of Fiction

We talk about fiction as if it falls into four precise categories: the short-short story, the story, the novella, and the novel. These terms are handy, but they are far from precise. There is no sharp line between one length and the next.

A **short-short story** is usually defined as a story of between 700 and 2,000 words. It can have real insights into character and feeling, but it is usually limited to just a few scenes and a short time span, and it generally focuses on a single character. A conventional-length **short story** usually runs from 2,000 to 6,000 words—from eight to 24 typed pages. It may deal with more characters and have a more intricate plot, but the theme is not necessarily more sophisticated. A **novella**, generally between 50 and 150 typed pages, is halfway between a story and a novel. Occasionally a magazine will include one or devote a special issue to several, but more often novellas are seen in published collections along with short stories by the same author.

The **novel** form is really more than just a story that has been expanded beyond 250 pages—or it should be. The length allows an author to do interesting things with the plot and to develop subplots. One can introduce many more characters than in a story or novella, and some of them can change and develop over the course of time. The theme of such a work can be broader and more intricate than in the shorter form.

When you start writing, the short-short story form is a good one to work with. In developing your creative abilities, it is important to try a number of different approaches—first-person, third-person, light tone, serious tone, close to experience, far removed from experience. You can achieve new skills and find your own voice better through a series of short-short stories than by locking yourself into a longer work too soon.

Three Motives for Writing Fiction

Whenever you become involved in creative work, it is worth asking yourself just what aspect of the activity is motivating you. This may help you to determine what direction you want to move in right from the start.

There are many reasons for writing fiction, but they tend to fall into three broad groups. Since each involves a different approach and different goals, it is important to examine them separately.

First, there is the *private motive*. This is expressed in writing that is mainly for personal pleasure. It is intended for an audience of one—yourself. Often it takes the form of journal entries. Spontaneous and usually unrevised, journal writing requires no special training. Entries may be valuable in recording or clarifying your own feelings or as a way of sketching out possible scenes in fiction, or they may be just good fun as a release, but they shouldn't be passed off as finished work.

The second is the *commercial motive*. In its pure form, **commercial fiction** writing is the opposite of private writing since it is motivated largely by outer rather than inner demands. It is writing for others. Commercial writers usually define their work as a craft rather than an art, and their primary goal is monetary reward. They produce entertainment. Many spend more of their time writing nonfiction than they do fiction since the demand is greater.

The fiction produced by commercial writers tends to follow certain familiar conventions—the love story, high adventure, war, crime—because there is a large market for that kind of writing. Like businesspeople, their goal is to supply what the market wants. Although there is a tendency for literarily minded individuals to look down on commercial writing, it is an honest profession that fills a need.

The third is the *literary motive*. Although it generates most of the fiction one reads in school and college, it is perhaps the most misunderstood. Writers in this area are like painters, sculptors, and composers who value the quality of the work they produce. Having an audience is obviously important, and being paid for one's efforts seems only fair; but making money is not the principal drive. Because of this, they do not generally tailor their work to meet the whims of the public, nor do they cater to commercial markets. They measure their efforts against what they consider to be the best fiction they have read.

Because literary writers require readers who have relatively sophisticated taste and experience, they must often (though not always) be content with a relatively small audience. Their novels may not be best-sellers, and their short stories frequently appear in "little magazines" that have small circulations and cannot pay their contributors lavishly. Many have to do something else for their major source of income. But they have a special satisfaction in knowing that they are reaching readers who will spend time with their work and will react to it with some sensitivity. In addition, they are working in one of the few areas where they do not have to compromise. For many, this is very important.

The literary motive is sometimes difficult for nonwriters to understand. It helps, though, to compare the literary writer with the opera singer who knows that rock singers earn ten times as much. Opera continues not because its performers like being paid less but because this is what they do best and enjoy most.

The emphasis in most creative writing courses is on sophisticated rather than simple work. The same is true of this text. This does not mean, of course, that personal entries in a journal are without value. Nor does it mean that commercial writing, which by definition is aimed at a wide audience, is to be scorned. What it does mean is that because sophisticated or literary writing requires careful study and a lot of practice, many people find writing courses and a text like this helpful. Selecting the kind of writing you want to do depends entirely on what motivates you.

Every writer—like every artist in the broadest sense—is driven by a combination of all three motives. Those who are primarily concerned with sophisticated writing, however, share a respect for literature as something of value in itself. With this as a base, there is no end of possibilities for fresh creativity.

13
THE SOURCES OF FICTION

Finding material; the danger of stale sources. The "seven deadly sins."
The authenticity of personal experience: family relationships,
male–female relationships, moments of growth and discovery,
memorable incidents. The necessity for invention. The metamorphosis
of experience.

Sophisticated fiction depends on fresh material. When we draw on our own lives honestly, we can be sure that we are being original. Each person's life experience is unique. But as I pointed out in the previous chapter, creative writing is almost always a blend of what we know well and what we have invented.

Where does the new material come from? Ideally, it springs from our imagination. Unfortunately, however, our memories are cluttered with old plots, characters, and settings half-recalled from what we have read in books and magazines and seen on television and in the movies. It is all too easy to draw on this material, often unintentionally. These subliterary **conventions** are like prefabricated units made up of **stock characters** and familiar plots. They are clichés on a big scale.

When commercial writers of fiction and film scripts adopt these conventions purposely, it is called **formula writing**. Like fast food, formula writing serves a wide market, but it usually sacrifices subtlety and insight. When conventional formulas work their way into an otherwise sophisticated story, they do real damage. As soon as readers recognize one of these familiar patterns, they are apt to slip into the glazed half-attention with which they often watch a routine television drama or listen to background music at a restaurant.

There are many such formulas, but here are seven that are particularly prevalent in the 1990s. I list them here not to discourage invention but to help you to distinguish true invention from mere imitation. Think of these as the seven deadly sins of fiction that, because of their associations, will defeat any effort to write insightful and convincing fiction.

- *The High-Tech Melodrama.* A **melodrama** is any piece of fiction or drama that is overloaded with dramatic suspense. Unlike true drama, it is overdone. Television's relentless drive for more viewers tempts many script writers to step over the line between drama and melodrama.

Everyone has a slightly different view of just where that line should be drawn, but regardless of labels, so-called suspense thrillers tend to have certain standard ingredients. Whether the protagonist is a solo detective, a cop, or a vice squad member, the props usually include both guns and late-model cars, and the plot turns out to be, at the mildest, some version of search-and-capture. More often, it's search-and-destroy. The high-speed chase is repeated as regularly as was the shootout in westerns of the 1950s. Replacing the magnum with a laser and moving the chase to another galaxy may be a challenge for the special-effects department, but the plot is remarkably similar, and the characters seem to speak the same lines.

It is not guns and uniforms by themselves that present the problem. If you have gone hunting, served on a police force, or been in the military, you should explore those experiences and find ways of sharing them with your readers. But serious problems arise when you start to borrow material from scriptwriters who themselves are borrowing from earlier scripts. Watch out for characters—male and female—who maintain their cool in times of stress and reveal nothing of themselves. Guard against that too-easy dichotomy between the good and the bad. Keep asking yourself: Where did I get this stuff? Is it used property?

- *The Adolescent Tragedy.* The adolescent period is an excellent one for sophisticated fiction as long as you keep your material genuine and fresh in detail. But there are three pitfalls: lack of perspective, unconscious borrowing from slick and conventional fiction, and sentimentality.

Lack of perspective occurs when the experience is too fresh. In such cases, you find yourself *in* the story rather than *above* it. You cannot control it. This may well be your problem if you find yourself calling your fictional characters by the names of their nonfictional counterparts. Another sign is when you find yourself reluctant to change the plot because "that's not the way it happened."

To avoid this lack of perspective, make sure that enough time has elapsed between the event and your attempt to convert it into fiction. The more emotional the experience, the more time will be required to gain some measure of detachment.

Unconscious borrowing from slick fiction is sometimes as difficult to spot as influences from television. But it does happen. Those who do not read stories in the women's magazines may find themselves reaching back to conventionalized plots half-remembered from comics like *Mary Worth*. Whenever one detects the slightest borrowing from such sources, it is important to ask, "Where did the rest of this come from?" Not only the plot but types of characters, lines of dialogue, and even descriptive details may be contaminated.

Sentimentality, the third danger in writing about adolescents, may come from secondary sources like magazines and television or may just as easily come from the simple desire to move the reader. The difference between the sentimental story and one that is genuinely moving is a matter of sophistication. When a story is simple and rigged to short-circuit the emotions of the reader, we say it is sentimental. These are the stories in which the lonely, misunderstood little boy, the plain little girl with glasses, the cripple, the blind girl, or the son of alcoholics is placed in some pitiable situation—any cold street corner will do, but a bombed-out village is better—simply to evoke tears.

But what if you really were the plain little girl with glasses or the son of alcoholics? The fact that the background is from life is never an excuse for fiction that *seems* like a sentimentalized treatment. Your job will be to find those unusual details or to explore ambivalences that will break the mold and convince the reader that this is a genuine experience.

- *The Twilight Zone Rerun.* Like the fiction of Edgar Allan Poe, the scripts of the television program "The Twilight Zone" are characterized by the strange and the bizarre. They usually depend on a gimmick. A **gimmick** is a tricky idea worked into fiction or a script, one that surprises and entertains. In one episode, for example, a nearsighted book-lover who is the sole survivor of World War III discovers an undamaged library for his uninterrupted use. As he runs toward the treasured books he trips and—you guessed it—breaks his glasses. Entertaining, yes, but it is *simple* entertainment. The trick becomes more important than the development of character or subtlety of theme. Like the anecdote or well-told joke, it depends on a punch line. Once read, there is little reason for going back to it.

- *Werewolves on Parade.* Werewolves and other assorted mutants seem to be coming back from their literary grave to haunt the silver screen and, in miniaturized form, creative writing classes.

When they are portrayed in their traditionally evil guise, the result is melodrama that runs the risk of evoking smiles rather than chills, and when for the sake of originality they are made into college-age men trapped in wolves' clothing, the story too often turns out to be a standard campus-life plot in costume. The film versions can, when well done, provide an evening of thrills, but the 2,000-word literary imitation hovers between a comic magazine and satire. The gimmick is so strong, so well known, that all attempts at characterization and thematic suggestion are buried.

- ***The Yuppie Gone Wrong.*** This is one of the most common patterns in college writing courses. The protagonist is a young, upwardly mobile individual who has put career and love of material objects ahead of personal relationships and spiritual values. He drives a Porsche, has a Jacuzzi, lives in Silicon Valley or some mythical place with the same climate. In the end, he pays for his sins and succumbs to drink, drugs, or a bullet. Sometimes all three.

These are morality tales with their roots in the Faust legend—medieval tales (and later operatic works) portraying a hero who sells his soul to the devil in exchange for knowledge and possessions.

It would be nice to think that such plots were inspired by the Faust tradition or by more recent works like Theodore Dreiser's *An American Tragedy* or stories like F. Scott Fitzgerald's "Winter Dreams," both of which build convincing characters with some of these same characteristics. But it seems more likely that the source is television.

In keeping with the times, the yuppie plot is occasionally refashioned with a young woman as unhappy protagonist. But if the original concept was hackneyed, the revised version will be no better. The problem with these stories is not that such characters don't exist but that the fictional version is based on an imitation which in turn is based on an imitation.

But suppose you knew a hard-driving individual who really did own a Porsche and tragically did commit suicide? It still will be a risky incident for fiction. Suicide is generally too big and complex a subject to handle convincingly in a short-short story. You may have to substitute some more subtle indication of a character's sense of defeat and despair. As for the other details, sometimes you have to revise life's events to keep them from echoing the conventions of simple fiction.

- ***The Temptations of Ernest Goodwriter.*** The protagonist walks up and down the beach, planning a great novel. He resists the invitations of fun-loving but superficial friends and spurns an offer to join a major advertising firm. In the end, he returns to his typewriter and his high literary principles.

Or perhaps he is in New York and will not change a word of a novel he has already written. Or he is in Los Angeles and is torn between writing a great novel and being paid a fortune to write hack scripts.

I don't know where this plot comes from—certainly not from television— and I admire the message, but unfortunately it makes very poor fiction. These stories are literarily simple because they pit the good against the bad in a sadly unrealistic fashion. In some cases the hero is so wooden you can't help hoping he or she will "go Hollywood," make a fortune, and live happily ever after.

- ***My Weird Dream.*** Recording your own dreams can be interesting, even significant. They are good material for a journal. But listening to someone else's interminable and incomprehensible dream is a punishment few of us deserve. In most cases, the dream story is far more fun to write than to read.

It does have a long history—though not one most contemporary readers are familiar with. In the 1920s it was called "**automatic writing.**" Writers simply typed whatever came into their heads for three hours and called the final fifteen pages a "story." Occasionally these "stories" were published, but no one has republished them—for good reason.

There was another flurry of interest in the late 1960s, when this kind of writing was defended as "literary tripping," a hallucinogenic voyage on paper. Again, the writing was more fun than the reading.

This technique of aimless composition is not to be confused with **stream-of-consciousness** writing. The latter, made famous by James Joyce, is designed to give the illusion of entering the mind of a fictional character. It is used as a part of a story—usually as the thoughts of a character we have already come to know through more conventional writing. As such, it is a literary device with a purpose. Recording a dream for its own sake may be of personal value to you, but the result belongs in your journal.

These, then, are seven of the most common causes for failure in short stories. You will be able to spot others. It is important to look closely at your plans for a new story, because time spent on shopworn material is time wasted.

These warnings, however, are rather negative. You may even feel intimidated by them. Don't be. Remember that creativity is essentially a positive process and that if you draw on the many fruitful sources for fiction, your work is bound to be fresh and original.

The Authenticity of Personal Experience

You know your own life better than anyone else does. When you write about your own experiences, your family, your friends, your neighborhood, your own feelings, you have inside information. If you select fresh details, you can draw your reader into the world you create.

Sometimes beginning writers avoid using their own experiences because they feel that their lives are too uneventful. But short fiction does not require high drama. Your life is filled with problem-solving, minor achievements, betrayals, reversals, and discoveries. You know more about the details than anyone else. And the people you grew up with—friends and relatives—have revealed themselves in interesting ways from time to time. If you learn how to draw on material like this and how to reshape it, you will have discovered how to use one of the basic ingredients of fiction.

A standard legal disclaimer states that "any similarity to persons or places is purely coincidental," but no one who writes fiction takes that seriously. A more honest statement would be that similarities to persons and places are frequent, intentional, and occasionally brazen, but generally fragmentary, inconsistent, and disguised with fanciful invention.

Using personal experience selectively and honestly is your best safeguard against work that is unconvincing. This is particularly true for those who are just beginning to write fiction. As you gain experience, you will learn how to keep one foot in the circle of familiarity while reaching out with the other. Memories of a summer job on a construction crew, for example, might allow you to explore what it would be like to be foreman or, pushed further, a civil engineer in conflict with the foreman. Some of the more demanding moments of baby-sitting might serve as the basis for a story dealing with the life of a single parent. At the outset, however, it is wise to stay relatively close to the original experience.

Finding a good incident with which to work may come easily, but often it will not. Even experienced writers have dry periods. Since "waiting for inspiration" is just a romantic way of describing procrastination, it is important to learn how to look for material in a constructive way. Here are some areas that are worth exploring.

Family relationships are natural subjects for fiction. Everyone has had either parents or foster parents; everyone has experienced in some proportion that mixture of love and resentment that is a natural part of that relationship. And that instable balance is normally in constant flux. In very general terms, it is apt to be a progression from idealization through disillusionment to a new acceptance, usually based on a fairly realistic evaluation. But this is a vast oversimplification, and stories based on a simple treatment of the theme "The day I discovered my father was no saint" are apt to turn out thin and unconvincing. The writer has to probe deeper in order to discover and dramatize those unique shifts in attitude. Often it is some *specific* characteristic of, say, the father, altered in some slight but significant way, that lends itself to good fiction.

In addition to child–parent relationships, there are a variety of other intrafamily attitudes that also shift significantly: brother and sister, two sisters and a maiden aunt, two brothers and their cousin, a daughter dealing with a stepfather, the reactions of three brothers to their uncle. Relationships like these keep shifting in real life, and the shifts are remembered because something was done (action) or said (dialogue) or thought in such a way as to dramatize the change. To some degree you can use such relationships directly, but often you will have to metamorphose experience into something related but different—a process I will explain shortly.

Relationships between girls and boys and between men and women are used repeatedly in fiction, and there are hackneyed situations that you should avoid. But in most cases you can find a safe path by asking these two essential questions: What *really* happened? And what was there about the action, the thoughts, the outcome that was truly unique? Of course there are those situations which at first glance seem too close to clichés to be credible or interesting. Occasionally lovers really do patch up quarrels while standing on the shore of Lake Placid under a full moon in June. But not often. You may have to douse the moon, change the name of the lake, and give the characters some uneasiness about that reconciliation if the story is to take on a sense of authenticity.

Some of the best relationships to examine are those with individuals who are much younger or older. The greater the gap in age, the more difficult it may be to enter the mind of the other individual. But you can always write the story from the point of view of the character who is about your own age.

A different way of stimulating your memory is to recall moments of intensity. Often these involve some kind of discovery about yourself or another person. As you examine the event (a good use for a journal), you may not really understand why the experience has remained so vivid in your memory. But you can be sure that if it is still clear there must have been some special meaning in it for you.

Such a memory may be fragmentary. Settings like a particular shopping plaza, a playing field or vacant lot where you used to play, a view from a car window, or a kitchen seen only once often stand out with extraordinary sharpness. They have remained for a reason.

Characters (not to be confused with "characters" who are held to be "unforgettable" by the *Reader's Digest*) may remain in your mind only from an overheard conversation or a quick glimpse: a subway attendant, a store clerk, a hitchhiker, an auto mechanic. And incidents do not even have to be directly connected with the observer. They may involve an argument overheard in a supermarket; the smashing of a window; an automobile accident; or the playful flirtation of a girl and three boys on a beach, a park, or a parking lot.

One of the first things to do with such a memory-fragment is to recall every possible detail: the visual minutiae, the sounds, and the intricacies of your own feelings. From these you may discover why that particular experience remained in your memory while so many others drifted beyond recall. The final story may or may not include you as a character, and it will probably be far removed from the facts of the original episode, but it will have the advantage of being rooted in a genuine and personally significant experience.

The Necessity for Invention

Valuable as personal experience is for the fiction writer, almost no work of fiction is a mirror image of actual events and characters. In fact, there are occasions when relying too heavily on actual events may restrict the development of the story or even undermine your ability to complete it.

Quite often, experience has to be altered simply because it is too personal. Failing to alter the events or some of the details may block our efforts to develop it at all. What is described as *writer's block* is frequently a reluctance to deal with what is still too close to us.

In addition, an episode from personal experience is almost always cluttered with details that have nothing to do with what you plan as the theme or central concern of the story. Or the sequence may be confusing to a reader. Occasionally the reverse is true: The life experience is too bland and needs intensifying.

As soon as you start inventing, you run the risk of adopting conventional plot patterns or familiar character types of the sort I have been warning you against. The best method of making sure that your material is fresh is to keep what you know as the base and make basic transformations in the setting, the plot, or the characters. This is known as **metamorphosing** your material.

Metamorphosis of Experience

When you metamorphose personal experience, you are reshaping the original material even before you write the first sentence. Don't confuse this with *revision*, a more subtle process that starts when you have finished the first draft. Metamorphosing occurs at the very outset and is a fundamental reshaping of experience, a transformation of events, characters, and places so that they form a coherent narrative known as fiction. Metamorphosing is at the heart of the creative process.

Some metamorphosing may occur unconsciously even before you start planning a story. Without being aware of it, we reshape memories, blocking certain events and inventing others. What we may think of as a character invented from nothing may actually be a disguised version of someone you know well or even a composite of two individuals.

This kind of metamorphosing can occasionally work against you. You may be censoring an experience by making a character better than she or he was in life or, conversely, blocking some act of kindness by a person you have generally disliked. That type of metamorphosing can sanitize experiences, making them too bland for fiction, or blunt the subtle contrasts in a character.

Our main concern here, however, is the conscious metamorphosing that serves as a constructive first step in the creative process. There are many different reasons for radically altering personal experience before converting it to fiction, but the most important is to *objectify the material*.

We all tend to be shy when we contemplate writing about our friends and relatives. We are apt to have feelings about them we don't want to advertise. Even if we feel very close to a parent, friend, or lover, we also see aspects in him or her that are less than perfect. Indeed, there may even be aspects of ourselves that are less than perfect. Most of us can recall a number of incidents we would never reveal to a friend, much less to total strangers. How can we put these on paper for everyone to read?

The answer is to disguise both characters and incidents through metamorphosis. That is, make them sufficiently different so that even before writing the first draft you are thinking about a *fictional* incident and a *fictional* character rather than the real-life model.

For starters, change the names. Let your fictional characters take on identities of their own. But it usually takes more than that; you have to break the mold set by the experience itself. Very personal experiences are often easier to handle in the third person ("he" or "she") than in the first. Consider telling the story through the eyes of a character not based on yourself. Painful childhood memories, for example, are sometimes made manageable by visualizing the story through the eyes of a parent.

Changing the setting often helps. Moving the story to another locale gives you a fresh vision. In the same way, radically altering the physical appearance or the age of your characters helps to give them a fictional identity. And it is easier to change the sex of a character than one might think. The transition often suggests new personality traits as well as freeing you from the real-life model.

How much should you metamorphose? Occasionally you will hardly have to make a change. Once in a while life provides a complete story, and all you have to do is cut superfluous details and ease the episode onto the page. But not often. There are two warning signs that are clear indications that more radical metamorphosing is required before going further. First, if you find yourself referring to your protagonist as "I" and to your other characters by the names of their actual models, it means you are still thinking of the piece as factual writing. Second, if you catch yourself saying, "I can't have them do that; it just didn't happen that way," you're in trouble. There is no clearer indication that your first loyalty is still to the events as they occurred. You have not yet begun to write fiction, an artistic creation in its own right.

Objectifying the characters and the events, then, is the first and most important reason for metamorphosing experience before you start writing. The second reason is to create *thematic clarity*.

Daily life consists of a great clutter of experience. Much of it is routine. If we reported everything that happened to us during a 24-hour period, we would end up with 100 pages of utterly boring material. It would have no thematic focus. Significant and interesting things do happen, but they are often embedded in unrelated events. Then too, just what is significant? Two friends recalling the same incident often focus on entirely different aspects. As writers, we have to identify the elements that seem to hang together, decide on which aspect interests us the most, and cut away everything else.

Suppose, for example, a couple with their two adolescent children plan to go on a picnic in the country on a hot August day, only to have the car break down in the city's most depressed neighborhood. And let us suppose that three weeks later each member of the family agrees to write a story based on this common experience. The father's story might be about a man who discovers that his wife, whom he always thought of as rather immature, has hidden strengths in time of crisis. Since this suggests a couple who really didn't know each other very well, his metamorphosing of the experience might include deleting the children and reducing the ages of the couple by ten years. (This might also allow him to create a fictional wife without risking a real-life divorce!)

The wife, on the other hand, might want to focus on her relationship with her 15-year-old daughter. Perhaps while the fictional husband and son in her story try to repair the car and later confer with a mechanic, mother and daughter get into a dispute, resolve it, and establish a far more honest relationship as a result. Conceivably, this story might end up dropping both the husband and the son just to highlight mother and daughter.

The 17-year-old son, on the other hand, being a rebellious sort, might write a satire lampooning a mechanically inept, emotionally immature family dealing with a minor mishap. He might well choose to exclude himself from this collection of incompetents. As for the daughter, perhaps she is genuinely concerned with social issues and decides to portray a rather sheltered, middle-class family being compelled to deal for the first time with an ethnic minority in a depressed neighborhood.

Each of these stories used the same incident as a starting point, but each has been metamorphosed before being committed to paper in order to highlight the aspect that interested that particular writer. All four writers began by identifying and clarifying a central concern, but the aspect each chose was entirely different from the other three.

The third function of literary metamorphosis is to *avoid the obvious*. Occasionally the patterns of experience are too neat, too contrived for fiction. Once in a while life not only imitates fiction, it even imitates hackneyed fiction. This is particularly true of heartbreaking experiences. Never mind protesting, "But it really happened that way!" You the author may have a genuine experience in mind, but your readers may see it as a scene borrowed from the soaps.

In such cases, metamorphosing will help you to gain control over material that may have been too close to you, too emotionally charged. With a little objectivity, you can delete the sentimental aspects and concentrate on that which is fresh, original, and insightful.

When you consider the extraordinary variety of experience stored in your mind and add to that the infinite number of variations you can devise for each, you can see how each new story is unique. This is the true meaning of *creative* writing.

14
A STORY BY
MELISSA PRITCHARD

Phoenix

Under the dressing room door, Phoenix sees the saleslady's feet pointed, suspiciously, straight at her. Stiletto pumps and cheap hose—aimed right at her, filthy hippy, sure-fire shoplifter, flower child/slut, rah, rah, rah, ...jeez. The minute she'd slunk through the revolving door in chewed-up bellbottoms, free-box overcoat, bare feet, and floppy leather hat slammed on her bramble of hair, a phalanx of salesladies had set tight lip and gimlet eye on her. No one stepped forth politely, May I be of assistance, May I hold your hat and coat as you browse through our racks? No, they'd stalked her, stepped when she stepped, kept strictest time. Now she's finally lugged an armload of fancy dresses into cubicle 4, kicking shut the door with her callused heel so the flimsy row of booths teeters on its brass hooves, and this one saleslady is stuck, feet aimed like weapons, three inches from Phoenix's.

She dumps the coat and hat in a corner, rolls off her smelly jeans, drops off her workshirt, same shit she's worn on the road for days. Her unwashed body looks fishy, hooked, sucked gray by fluorescence. Her eyes could double as deep sunk screws. Adios, Phoenix, California road queen; Hello, Mary Lou, long lost, impoverished grandchild. She see-saws a red mini-dress over her head, does the J.C. Penney spin, hands on poked-out hips. The red dress pushes her face into focus. Next we have Miss Mary Lou in a fashionable yellow paisley with black shoulder buttons like cootie heads. Oh, but the bummer is her *face*. She widens her eyes, squinches her eyes, stacks her hair, lets it drop. Tries a slew of angles, sticking out her tongue at the pasty skin, nasty bone, smarmy eye, queer mouth, stink-o nose. Hell with it. She forgets the other dresses, stuns the phalanx by putting down cash for the red dress along with two sets of white fishnet pantyhose. The dress gets folded into a shopping bag, the yellow paisley's stashed under her hat.

Down the block, in a Walgreen's ladies room, Phoenix shakes the paisley out of the greasy bin of her hat, climbs into the red dress, tugs her boots out of her pack, steps up to a sink loaded with wadded brown towels to wash her face with a squish of pink from the metal box, scrubs at her front strands of hair, rinsing them under the tap, turns a hot blower on her face. Galumphing in too-big boots down an aisle of the store, she palms a white lipstick, drops it in the shopping bag. Her road clothes, from the free box in Watsonville, get left on the pink, leaking floor of ladies.

Heading to a bus stop, Phoenix comes up to a crowd clamped around two drunks cuffing and mostly missing one another, one bubbling blood out of his smooshed nose like a trick he's learned. Passive crowd, wow, here's TV.

What's the deal? she asks around.

That guy in the black shirt says the other one took his money. Five dollars.

She pushes right up, lays two five dollar bills on the sidewalk between them. Smooshed-Nose squeezes up a bill between his fingers, churchlike. Black-Shirt, leering, pockets her money.

Gee thanks, sis. Whoa, you got bedroom eyes, anybody tell you? Real bedroom eyes.

You wouldn't be pulling my leg, would you?

I'd like an opportunity.

The crowd dirtylaughs a little.

Jeez. Buy yourself some food.

After the bus, Phoenix walks six or so blocks to her grandmother's. This near the bay, with its tobacco-black, rotting wharves, with the sun near setting, the air drenched in medieval gold, the sky shimming like milky grout between immense gray and rose sides of apartments, slipping in disciplined combings between precise forms, people move around the bases of these immaculate, climbing geometries, distracted, insignificant.

A ball-bellied black doorman, bursting out of green and gold livery, swings wide the glass door, so theatric and overly cheerful it embarrasses her. In the mirrored elevator, a circle glows around 14, a nightlight. She drubs the white thumb of lipstick around her lips, hefts her pack, steps out of the elevator into a lush carpeted hall with an odor of fried meat. Passes evenly spaced doors like a dream line of flat white cards, finally pressing an ivory button with the correct number. She hears muted shuffling before the brass spy cover slips open, and a gray eye takes up the roundness.

My gracious, dearie. It's our Mary Lou. Mary Lou's here. She's out in the hall, for heaven's sakes.

Phoenix hasn't heard that name, her old name, in weeks. The brass chain drops, her grandmother opens the door.

Oh, please—fastening on her grandmother like good, firm land, like the one place she's found safe in weeks—let it be what it was. Climbing past her parents and unremarkable childhood, going back in perfect time. Gramma's Mary Lou.

Her grandmother's furnishings are arranged exactly as they had been in the old house. Twin mahogany tables, green velveteen couch, Manet and Utrillo paintings in baroque frames, pigskin chests, carved ivory screens from China. She considers everything her grandmother's, but her grandfather lives here, taking sterner, darker steps to his wife's liltings and perchings, treading with the somber weight of park statuary.

Always, her grandmother has worn a beige or navy sheath with a Peter Pan collar and skinny belt, silk stockings with rubber and metal garters. Her black heels, from Italy, cost over one hundred dollars. This muted, diminutive form is balm and honey, from it proceeds a perpetual, subdued flow and bliss of wealth. Phoenix remembers never having enough of what could be purchased, the privacy of expensive things, the holy, counterfeit hush issuing from rare objects, exorbitant spaces. And Phoenix remembers this woman, this grandmother, in her navy or beige sheath with its hard, skinny belt and stiff sleeves, the pernicious blood sallowing her skin, the slushy blue hair and indulgent, dipped-in face, nourishing, no, bloating her!

Children never regret being spoilt. How could she resist being allowed to eat or not eat, do nothing or everything, breathe whenever or however she chose? Two weeks each August, as Mary Lou, she slept on starched, ironed sheets, woke at dawn to the hollow roar of zoo lions down the street. For breakfast, she was given coffee cut with milk in a doll-sized, pink and gold cup. She and her grandmother watched morning TV, *The Price Is Right*, comparing closest guesses. When her grandmother took a rest after lunch, Mary Lou watched *Queen for a Day*, hooked on the potent dreadfulness of grown-up lives. Domestic anguish separated and stacked like poker chips, every contestant's teary eye on the applause-o-meter…what happened to the women uncrowned by their tragedies, the ones going back to lives nasty enough to have earned them a spot on the show? These were upside-down fairy tales Mary Lou never missed.

Her grandfather, before his retirement, ate his eggs peppered and sunny-side up, read the *Sacramento Bee*, drove to work in a celery-colored Cadillac. After retirement, he ate the eggs and read the paper, but then, in Bermuda shorts and plain white T-shirt, weeded his kidney-shaped dichondra bed. When her grandparents turned in, as they called it, after lunch, Mary Lou got to watch more TV, drink ginger ale floats, shivering and indolent, in the green and white, air-conditioned house.

Her grandmother never learned to drive; a taxi took the two of them downtown to expensive stores, to the same dark restaurant with gold-corded menus, rigid tablecloths, pale curlings of butter and brittle rolls with airy centers. Mary Lou learned to heft silvery cool knives, cut into flushed slabs of prime rib, press down with etched fork, wrecking the French pastries.

Returning home, they counted on grandfather's whistlings and "whoo-whoo" ings as they modeled the fancy contents of their shopping bags. This train-sound, emanating from the blue cigarette haze that was killing him even as he sat in his leather chair, satisfied them by its ritual and variation; the more a thing cost, the more steam he blew. His immense white back was strewn thick as a lily pond with velvety splots of moles. His second-best feature was a library Mary Lou was free to muck through. He had been a surgeon so a number of shelves were taken up by fat, leather-bound medical texts. She tugged down the fattest first, its maroon edge whoofing into her belly, grew intimate with color plates of tropical afflictions, turning straight to distended and scabrous penises, uncircumcised, with melon-sized scrotums. Perplexed-looking men, each with a ballooned penis drooping past his knees. Elephantiasis, the small print diagnosis. From the first thudding of the book against her belly, Mary Lou took occult pleasure in imagining, within the colorful hyperbole of disease, what the dimension of normal, unafflicted men might be.

By the end of August, after this orgiastic submersion in television, perpetual sweets, and exotic male trauma, Mary Lou stepped from the plane, straining chubbily within one of too many new party dresses (a particular exasperation to her mother: why can't she just give you money so we can buy what you need, gym shoes, for one thing). Pale and secretive from her association with male anatomy, glutted on cookies and sleep, Mary Lou was at best, unresponsive. Her mother, handed back this doltish, monosyllabic daughter, this prepubescent lummox, realized how dearly she had purchased two weeks' freedom.

Did you at least swim, she asked.

Her grandparents' neighbors had a pool, but since her grandmother couldn't swim, she was, illogically, afraid Mary Lou might drown. Mary Lou agreed to swim once, with her grandmother sitting in a chair by the side, so she could answer her mother truthfully.

While Mary Lou was this mystery of malleable youth-stuff, keeping her family in hopes of some possible, still-dormant distinction, her grandmother regularly announced to dinner company that in all likelihood, her youngest granddaughter would marry Prince Charles. Their birthdates were the same, and could anyone overlook the uncanny resemblance to Princess Margaret? This logic stunned and enslaved Mary Lou, who looked forward to easy wealth, a royal and doting husband. These over-reachings for grandeur and class, irresistible since they involved her, set Mary Lou's mother on an opposite course of insane headaches, compelling her at times to peck at her spoilt daughter through the blankets with the heel of her cheap shoe. Having to live and breathe in a place of such disappointing proportions, her marriage—in suppressed fury over her own blown expectations—why should she remain calm, watching Mary Lou plumped and petted into a spoilt, naive princess, and by her husband's mother? Who else could she blame?

In those Augusts of Mary Lou's youth, blissful damage between the three women was wrought.

Now Phoenix wants to shake her grandmother like a toy bank, shake out of her things the way they were, plunder her childhood. Instead, she lies on starched, ironed sheets, listening to her grandfather cough-wheeze-cough for wrenching, blue minutes, her grandmother's voice in anxious, frail counterpoint.

Phoenix gets her own coffee, climbs a chair to search cabinets for her pink and gold cup. God, how do they manage? She winds up fixing eggs and toast while her grandmother dodders about, wondering what meal this is, which day this is, who's she, the maid? No, Phoenix repeats doggedly, I'm Mary Lou. Mary Lou. Your granddaughter.

Phoenix dials for a taxi while her grandfather chuffs and gasps over to his leather chair, the oxygen tank behind it, a khaki-green bullet.

Phoenix has chosen I. Magnin's; the shoe salesman is curt with her grandmother, dismissive of her. In Ladies Dresses, a saleswoman with a slipshod French accent is unctuous, bored. Phoenix's mother claims her grandmother buys clothes and never wears them; the sheaths, cashmere coats, shoe boxes, pile up and glut her closet, price tags still attached. Her grandmother insists Phoenix buy something, pick something, so they take the perfumed elevator up to Juniors with its strobe lights and Rolling Stones tape. Phoenix shoves around racks of leather, velvet and paisley while her grandmother, knees fastidiously crossed, perches on a blue neon wave. Phoenix chooses an embroidered suede coat with a fleece lining.

Her grandmother moves haltingly, as if her Italian shoes don't feel the sidewalk, as if they aren't connected to any ground. Phoenix steers her by the elbow to the sides of buildings, out of people's way, helps her up the shallow steps of the hotel and into the engulfing lobby with its diamondish sprays of chandeliers, oriental carpeting, arterial-blue leather couches. Phoenix tells the maitre'd her grandmother's name; they sit to wait on one of the leather benches. The grey mink stole (wrap, her grandmother calls it) keeps slipping off her hunched shoulders, her purse gapes, stuffed with loose bills, linting Kleenexes with scarlet cabbage kisses—a toy purse. Her silk stockings sag, her knees and thighs part, weak bannisters leading to an open darkness, similar to the purse.

When her name is called, they perk up. They remember how to do this, order the prime rib and Yorkshire pudding. But her grandmother doesn't touch hers; she rarely eats anymore, and Phoenix can't eat because she is newly conscious of her knife cooly plying into a bloody plank of flesh. The plates, untouched, are removed. They demand French pastries from the domed cart.

Her grandmother gouges at the iced Napoleon with oblivious greed, orders a second, eats that, while Phoenix aches over this hobbled outing, and worse, entertains Dostoyevskian ideas of stealing money from her grandmother's purse while she is busy talking about friends dead and dying. For a minute, Phoenix falls evilly silent over their coffees and third helpings, this time pastry swans and eclairs.

Grandmother? Thank you for the coat. I love it.

The coat, Mary Lou? I hope it's the right thing. Is it the right thing, this time of year?

Perfect, really. Thank you so much. Grandfather doesn't look very well.

We don't go out anymore, he has to be near his oxygen. Huffs and puffs so without it. Every morning, he takes the elevator to the garage to start the car, lets it run. Just sits down there in the car. He loves driving, poor man.

Women at surrounding tables clack mouths and dishes, shopping bags mulched around their feet, while Phoenix and her grandmother sit, ghosts, scarcely visible to one another. Phoenix doubts they are there except a waiter keeps bringing and removing things, and a water boy relentlessly splashes water. Her grandmother, forever a willing slave to fashion, has not said a word about her mini-dress, black boots, white lipstick. She doesn't see her, not as she is, maybe she sees nine-year-old Mary Lou with the Buster Brown haircut and freckles, in the lace-collared, velvet party dress. Prim and mute.

Phoenix navigates them to the marbled, heavily scented bathroom with its uniformed attendant, watches her grandmother scrabble out from her purse a twenty-dollar bill which the attendant impassively, dishonestly, accepts. She guides her back down the carpeted steps with slick brass railings. The doorman opens the taxi door. Oh, God, Phoenix is realizing. She did this for me. She has no vanity left for shopping, no appetite for hotel lunches. She did this for me.

After her grandparents turn in, Phoenix dials the number a friend in Big Sur had given her. A sullen female voice picks up.

Yeah?

Uh, my name's Phoenix, and a friend gave me your number, she said maybe I could crash at your place if I needed to.

Who's that?

Rain. We met up in Big Sur.

Oh sure, far out chick. Well, no biggy. Where are you now?

My grandparents' place, but I can't stay.

People drift in and out, it's definitely crazy, but if you like craziness, no problem.

Good. She has a place to go. She cleans the kitchen, makes two cheese sandwiches, wraps them and puts them on plates, sets a can of vegetable soup on the counter. Takes a hit off her grandfather's vodka, sponges off the dining room table. His ashes are all over the placemat and some egg yolk, so she washes and dries it. Her grandmother's place is spotless. Phoenix runs his glasses under water, polishes them. Otherwise the apartment's tidy. There's practically nothing to do. Finds a tube of glue and pieces together a broken cereal bowl. Opens the refrigerator, pulls out moldy fruit, turned milk, a flabby heel of lettuce. Patching and getting rid of chaos, infirmity, evidence of mental collapse. She stacks newspapers, lines up empty Coke bottles, goes into the library, folds her bed back into the couch.

She hears them in the bedroom, awake. They will be sitting on the worn edges of their beds, her grandfather in white undershorts and white T-shirt, her grandmother in one of her lacy, beige slips. Oh dearie this and dearie that, real conversation. She's never known what they say to one another every afternoon and so earnestly. They'll talk up to an hour. There will be her grandfather's mahogany dresser with the linen topcloth, the silver and copper handful of change by the photographs of her sister, Carol, and herself, when they were nine and fourteen, in black velvet dresses. There will be her grandmother's beige skirted dressing table with the silver-handled comb and brush set, bobby pins, buttons, foil-wrapped Sucrets in the green ivy dish. What they say is private, mysterious, but at least she knows how everything looks.

She stands in the hall, close to their sweet, familiar, failing voices, wanting to save and retrieve them, wanting as if it could be done. Grandmother and grandfather. Childhood.

She wipes the bathroom sink for them, rinses the cup.

Watching *M*A*S*H*, he mixes his five o'clock martini. During a commercial, Phoenix puts on her new coat, but halfway into his ritual "whoo-whoo's," her grandfather turns to suck oxygen from the green tank rising like an implacable landscape behind his leather chair. His face, purplish, stubbled, tries again. Whoo-whoo. She hates this obstinate courage, the need for it.

When her grandmother comes out of the bedroom in her silk navy sheath and real pearls, Phoenix mentions the soup and sandwiches for dinner, that she's going across the city to stay with friends, that she'll be taking a bus up to Mendocino to visit Carol. Specifically talks about a bus, about Mary Lou riding a bus, nothing about Phoenix hitchhiking her way up the coast.

They walk with her into the neat, narrow foyer, her grandmother pressing money into her hand, something she always does, something Phoenix, guiltily, counts on her to do. Kisses, embraces. Her grandmother tugs out the hanky she keeps stuffed in her sleeve, mops at her eyes.

You're the light of our lives, you know, dear, don't you?

The same doorman holds the door, his coat winging in the salt wind off the bay. She looks him halfway in the eye, says thanks.

On a city bus, wearing her coat, Phoenix irons the wrinkled hundred dollar bill with her palm. It smells of lilac. Dumb money, money she knew she would get, making her cry.

15
VIEWPOINT:
STRATEGIES
OF PRESENTATION

The means of perception defined. Variations in the means of perception (viewpoint). First versus third person. The focus of a story. Reviewing your options in viewpoint, person, and focus.

As soon as you settle on an incident that seems as if it would make good fiction, you have three areas of choice. First, through whose eyes is this story going to be presented? This is called the **means of perception**. Second, will you use the first or third **person**? Third, whose story is this? That is, what will the **focus** be?

Although these decisions are often made intuitively, it's important to test one's first inclination by examining the alternatives. In this way you will know what your options are and will be able to select the best strategy for presenting the material.

The Means of Perception

This term refers to the agent through whose eyes a piece of fiction appears to be presented. For example: "The boy looked at his grandfather, wondering if the old man had understood." Here the means of perception is the boy. We know what he is wondering and so we are "in his head." We don't know what the grandfather is thinking, and if the story continues in this vein we, like the boy, will not find out until the old man speaks or reveals his thoughts through his actions.

Means of perception is synonymous with **point of view** and **viewpoint**. I will use them interchangeably. Keep in mind, however, that these alternate terms are also used loosely to refer to attitude, as in the phrase "from the British point of view." It doesn't matter which term you use as long as you remember that when applied to fiction it is a precise literary concept—and an important one.

Stories written in the **first person** are almost always limited to a single means of perception. The "I" who begins the story will, in almost every case, be our only source of information. Shifting to another narrator is possible, but it breaks the mood so severely that it is rarely done. What many beginning writers don't realize, however, is that most **third-person** stories are limited to a single means of perception as well. Once the means of perception has been established—usually at the outset of a story—it is normally maintained right through to the end. In our example of the boy and his grandfather, for example, readers tend to assume that the story will be presented through the eyes of the boy, that we will know his thoughts and not enter the mind of other characters. It would be unusual to have the next line read, "Actually Grandfather did agree, but he knew that he could never tell the boy." This jumps from the boy's mind to that of the grandfather. It would be still more unusual by contemporary standards to have the author step in with an observation neither character could make such as "Little did either of them realize that later that day they would both take a trip to the hospital." That's called author's intrusion. Although it was popular in the nineteenth century and is found occasionally in novels today, it is rare in short stories, mainly because it breaks the reader's sense of identification with the character. In an anthology of 15 or 20 stories by different authors, it is unusual to find even one that does not limit the means of perception to a single character.

The primary advantage of limiting the means of perception to a single character, then, is that it effectively draws the reader into the story. It increases the natural tendency to identify with a fictional character—a feeling that should not be confused with sympathy, respect, or even approval. It creates the illusion of being someone else for a short period of time.

Another advantage, closely related, is that it allows the author to withhold information. Suspense is one of the pleasures of reading fiction, and suspense is achieved by not knowing what is about to happen. When our view of events is limited to that of a single character, we share his or her desire to find out what comes next.

There is a good example of this in the story "Phoenix." We are introduced to a young woman who visits her grandmother with the expectation of receiving a good meal and some money. Although she feels just a little guilty about it, this is in the back of her mind. It comes as a surprise to us—and perhaps to her too—that seeing her grandparents growing old and failing moves her, finally, to tears.

The author, of course, knew this would happen. Authors are omniscient about their own material. But she was careful not to start out explaining everything with a sentence like this: "Phoenix needed some money, and she knew her grandmother was good for it; but little did she realize that seeing her grandparents growing old and infirm would move her to tears." In such a statement the means of perception has shifted from the character to the author. Instead of having the story unfold in stages through action and dialogue, the very core of it has been given at the outset, as is often done in an essay. As readers, we have the sense that the story has been spoiled just as a good joke is spoiled when the punch line is given too soon.

Authors do occasionally give background or peripheral information in this direct, expositional way. And novelists often feel free to comment at greater length. But a short story is a far more concentrated form and depends on the reader entering the world of the protagonist from the outset. For this reason, it is a good tactic to plunge the reader into an ongoing situation and to present the material largely through the eyes of the central character.

It may seem at first that the single means of perception is too restrictive. How is the author to reveal the thoughts of other characters? The answer is fairly simple: the same way we determine what our friends are thinking. After all, we can't hear their thoughts either—much as we might like to. Instead, we listen to what they say and observe what they do.

How do we know that the grandmother in "Phoenix" loves her grand-daughter deeply even though we never enter her mind? First we hear the way she welcomes Phoenix (dialogue); then we see her take Phoenix shopping (action); then we hear her say "You're the light of our lives" (dialogue again). Fairly conclusive evidence!

Not only can we as writers indicate what characters think through what they say and do, we can reveal a lot by having a character say one thing and act in a contradictory way. Suppose, for example, the grandmother welcomes Phoenix warmly in the same way but after a half hour gets up and sends the girl on her way without a meal or as much as a dime. We as readers would come to the conclusion that the grandmother didn't love her granddaughter at all. No need to enter her mind; no need for an author's statement like "Actually she detested her granddaughter." We would not only know that, we would also conclude that the grandmother was a bit of a hypocrite.

Actually you can show just about anything about a character's thoughts and attitudes without ever entering his or her mind. Action and dialogue are all you need—just as in life.

Variations in the Means of Perception

Although most contemporary fiction limits the means of perception to a single character, some long stories and a good many novels do not. Since this approach is usually reserved for longer works, it is not represented in this text. One of the best examples of this technique is "The Short Happy Life of Francis Macomber" by Ernest Hemingway. This frequently anthologized story is unusual in that the point of view shifts not only from character to character but at one point even enters the mind of a wounded lion. Such an approach is sometimes described as a limited **omniscient point of view** because although there appears to be a narrator who knows all, our view of individual scenes is limited to that of a single character. In most stories of this type, lengthy sections of the story are given to first one and then another character. A fully omniscient viewpoint sounds like someone telling a story aloud and frequently commenting on the action and the characters. The process is not as popular as it was in the nineteenth century because the illusion of reality is broken for the reader every time the voice of the author is used. But varieties of the technique can be found in the works of a few novelists, such as John Fowles, Margaret Drabble, and Milan Kundera.

Another variation in point of view is what may be called the reportorial style. In such works the author, like a journalist, does not enter the mind of any character. Normally this tends to distance the material—making it read like a newspaper account. Or it may echo the tone of a fable or parable in which the thematic suggestion is more important than characterization or verisimilitude. In earlier periods, such works often presented a serious moral message such as the parables from the Bible; today they are more likely to be satiric in tone.

If this objective, reportorial style interests you, look up Shirley Jackson's frequently anthologized story "The Lottery." She does not enter the minds of her characters partly because she is dealing with a social issue, not with individual characters, and partly because the detached voice of a journalist helps to keep the story from becoming melodramatic. This reportorial style, however, does have limited application and perhaps for this reason is unusual in contemporary American fiction. There are good reasons why the single, clearly defined means of perception is generally preferred.

First versus Third Person

When children first start telling stories they often devise a mixture of autobiography and fantasy. Without thinking of technique they tend to select the first person.

"And I went down into Mr. Syke's field where the woods begin and I saw a little pond and right next to the pond lying down was a blue lion and I *ran!*"

This is a complete little story. It has a setting, a sequence of action, a climax with a protagonist pitted against a beast (the stories of five-year-olds are apt to be epic and archetypal), and a resolution. We can assume that the decision to use *I* rather than *she* or *he* has been made unconsciously. This is fine for a child of five, but when adults set out to write a literary short story they should take a second look at their first intuitive decision. It may be right for that particularly story, but then again it may not be. The best rule of thumb is this: Don't choose between first and third person on the basis of where the material came from. Instead, consider the advantages of each approach and select the one that seems the most natural for you in the writing and, in addition, has the greatest potential of developing into an effective story.

One type of story that lends itself to the first person is the reminiscence in which there is a significant gap between the events and the fictional narrator. The gap may be as little as an hour or as much as decades. Notice how these two openings suggest entirely different kinds of stories even though they are using the same situation:

> I'm never going back to that lake as long as I live—not after what happened to me this afternoon.

> I haven't gone back to that lake for 45 years—not after what happened to me as a kid.

In the first we expect to hear the story of a narrator who has just been through a dramatic experience. She (the character, that is, not the author) may be so close to the experience that she is not fully aware of its significance.

In the second, we can expect a character who is more acutely aware of the significance of the experience because so much time has passed. The character's view, of course, may be inaccurate, but probably not in the same way as the one in the first version.

A second and closely related advantage of first-person narration is that you can easily control the **voice**. At one end of the spectrum is what can be thought of as **neutral style**. (More about that in Chapter 24, "Style and Tone.") At the other end you can give the illusion of a storyteller speaking out loud. This as-if-spoken style is achieved by phrasing that echoes the spoken language.

> Swim in that lake?—No way! Not after the bummer of an afternoon I went through.

> No sir, swimming's not for me. I learned my lesson back when I was a youngster.

Very few authors indulge in phonetic spellings like "goin' " for "going" and " 'em" for "them" because they so easily become obtrusive. You can suggest a regional or foreign accent perfectly well through phrasing without altering the spelling of a single word. To achieve this, listen carefully to the way language is actually used and adopt some of the characteristic phrases you hear.

Even though Melissa Pritchard chose to write "Phoenix" in the third person, she often echoes the language of her protagonist just as is done in some first-person stories. But she is careful to use restraint. Phoenix is a character who embodies the spirit of the sixties, so as the author put it in her commentary published in *Story*, "I tried to reflect those feelings…by using the language of the time—excluding all of the 'far outs' and 'wows.' " Had she used too many of those characteristic words and phrases, the story might soon seem dated and, worse, strike some readers as satire. By using restraint, she catches the flavor without making the language obtrusive.

If you enjoy first-person stories that make full use of the as-if-told style, you should look up some of the widely anthologized stories such as Sherwood Anderson's "I'm a Fool," William Faulkner's "Spotted Horses" (two versions are in print, one of which is in the first person), and Eudora Welty's "Why I Live at the P.O." Keep in mind, however, that they represent a technique that is not widely used. Some authors feel that it is awkward maintaining the illusion of a nonstop talker. In addition, the technique depends as much on a good ear for dialogue as music depends on a good ear for tone.

A third valuable use of the first person is when the primary point of the story is to criticize or satirize the narrator. Readers tend to trust first-person narrators, and you as writer can achieve an effective irony by revealing the shortcomings of your protagonist through what he or she says and does. Sometimes this can be gentle. Those who have read *Gulliver's Travels* usually recall Swift's satire of the Lilliputians and other strange creatures who echo the foibles of our own society; but there is a more subtle satiric level in Gulliver himself. As the first-person narrator, he unwittingly reveals his conventional middle-class views through his descriptions and reactions.

Consider using this technique when dealing with a character who takes a situation too seriously. It is sometimes possible to allow the reader to smile at a character who is the all-too-serious narrator. A good example of this is seen in the Sherwood Anderson story I referred to above. The central character is a young man who is a far greater fool than he ever suspects, not because of what he has done but because of the melodramatic way in which he reports it.

Although the "I" of first-person stories is most often the protagonist, don't ignore the possibility of presenting a story through the eyes of a minor character. Children, for example, sometimes reveal more than they realize about their parents. Keep this in mind when you read Deborah Joy Corey's story "Three Hearts," which appears as Chapter 18. The first-person narrator there reveals more about her mother than she could ever understand at her age. In a sense, the mother is almost the protagonist.

For all the advantages of first-person writing, it is the third person that has a slight edge in contemporary fiction. This may be due to the fact that so many stories have originated with one or more personal experiences. Adopting the third person is an effective way of metamorphosing that material. It gives you as author a chance to look at both the characters and the action more objectively.

Melissa Pritchard made this choice when writing "Phoenix." When her story first appeared in *Story*, she wrote in an accompanying preface, "Some of the experiences I've written about are real. Some are imaginary....I made notes about my grandparents for years....But I had to wait for quite a while in order to get some distance from my feelings." Time gave her a chance to metamorphose some of the material, and using the third person rather than the first probably helped her to objectify Phoenix as a fictional character.

At first glance, there is not much difference between her third-person version—"Phoenix sees the saleslady's feet pointed, suspiciously, straight at her"—and a first-person version: "I see the saleslady's feet...." The gap is even less than in most third-person writing because, as I pointed out above, the writer often employs slang phrases that would have been used if the story were told in the first person in as-if-spoken style: "Oh, but the bummer is her *face*."

But unlike first-person stories, the third person does allow the author to insert occasional observations from an objective point of view. "Children," she writes, "never regret being spoilt." Notice how formal the language can get when Pritchard allows herself to speak as the observing author: "In those Augusts of Mary Lou's youth, blissful damage between the three women was wrought." That's not anything that would have gone through Phoenix's head at the time; that's the voice of the author commenting on her material.

Using the third person, then, allows the author to move back and forth between that which is clearly from the protagonist's point of view and that which is from the author's. As with most contemporary short fiction, however, authorial comments are kept to an absolute minimum. And they almost never present the central concern of the story. To do that is apt to spoil both the subtlety of the work and the reader's sense of discovery.

The primary advantage of the third person, then, is flexibility. The writer can use the protagonist as the primary means of perception while occasionally drawing on a more objective view for incidental or background information.

The popular notion that the first person provides a sense of immediacy or realism that cannot be achieved in the third person is not justified. As readers we enter a story using *he* or *she* just as easily as one that begins with *I*. But the decision of which to use should not be made carelessly. Your first inclination may be entirely justified, but do consider the alternative. If in doubt, convert a sample paragraph from first person to third or the reverse fairly early in the writing.

The Focus of a Story

The **focus** of a work of fiction is its center of attention. It answers these two closely related questions: "Whose story is it?" and "What is the central concern?" In determining the focus, we are deciding who the primary character is and what the theme of the story is. These questions are, of course, closely related; but for the sake of analysis we can treat them separately.

Shifting the focus from one character to another is a major undertaking, so consider it early—preferably while you are still in the planning stages and before you have even begun the first draft. Suppose, for example, Pritchard had decided to shift the focus of the story "Phoenix" from the girl to her grandmother. As usually happens, the means of perception would probably have to change as well. The opening scene would have to be shifted from the store (since the grandmother was not there) to the front hall when Phoenix arrives. The flashback picturing those summers when Phoenix, then Mary Lou, visited her grandmother would be seen through the grandmother's eyes.

It would be possible to maintain something close to the original theme. In this new version, perhaps the grandmother would see tears come to Phoenix's eyes and realize that the girl really did have a deep concern for her aging grandmother. More likely, however, the central concern or theme of the story would change as well. Perhaps it would concern a grandmother who is convinced that her hippie granddaughter was dropping in merely to get a meal and some money, but who realizes in the end that she had been guilty of placing the girl in a stereotype, that for all her strange appearance, her granddaughter is a complex and vulnerable young woman. Quite a change! But it demonstrates how altering the focus on character frequently shifts the theme as well. It also explains why reconsidering the focus should be done very early in the creative process—before one has invested hours of time on the first draft.

For other examples of shifts in the focus of a story, recall the example given in Chapter 13 about the four members of one family all writing about a hot August day when their car broke down. Each chose a different central character as the focus, and each chose a different thematic focus as well. If you are uncertain about the focus in a story you are planning to write, ask yourself these two questions: Which character interests me the most? What happens in this incident that makes it really worth sharing with readers?

You should be able to describe the theme or central concern in one complete sentence. Don't worry about the fact that different readers will have slightly different views of the theme as long as there is general agreement. A story that "means whatever you want it to mean" is probably a long journal entry waiting for someone to fashion it into fiction. The editors of *Story* describe "Phoenix" as "the story of a young girl's realization that her childhood is over when she must take care of the people who once took care of her." A somewhat narrower description might be, "It is a story of how even a dramatic change of life-style cannot obliterate the love we felt as children." These do not describe two different stories; they are merely two aspects of the same story. In testing the thematic focus of a story you have just begun, don't worry about being able to describe it in slightly different ways as long as it appears you will have general agreement from a group of readers.

Reviewing Your Options

When a story idea first comes to you, it will probably be a mix of personal experience and invention. Let it run through your head like a daydream. Don't concern yourself at this early stage about the means of perception, person, and focus. If you analyze too much too soon, you may lose the feel of the story.

There will come a point, however, when you feel you have enough to work with. This is when some writers like to make a few notes about plot and characters so they won't lose the original concept. This is also when you should consider some alternative strategies of presentation. Metamorphosing a story by altering the point of view, person, or focus at this stage may save you hours of rewriting later.

Begin by reviewing the means of perception. Make sure that the story is being presented through the right character. In most cases, that character will be the protagonist; but as we have seen, he or she could be an observer. It is well worth spending a few moments imagining your story through the eyes of other characters. It may even be worth your while to write alternative opening paragraphs from the point of view of two different characters. Even if you decide not to shift your original viewpoint, the exercise may well give you new insights into your story's potential.

When you have finished your first draft, take another look at how you have handled the means of perception in both the opening and closing. Stories with long, rambling introductions in the nineteenth-century manner seem dated today mainly because such passages are generally from the author's point of view. Contemporary fiction has muted the author's voice—especially in openings and closings. Readers expect to enter the mind of a character almost from the start.

In particular, guard against openings in which you as all-knowing author give away too much. In essays, the reader expects the theme to be clear and explicitly stated—often at both the beginning and the end. But fiction functions entirely differently. Readers discover significances by implication just as if they were going through the experience. That sense of discovery is spoiled when the theme is laid out in advance.

"It was a beautiful August day on Lake Docile, and there was little to suggest that before sunset Laura and Harry would learn much about the vicissitudes of weather and perhaps a bit about themselves as well." This is an exaggeration, but the principle is important: When you introduce a story in your own voice as author, you are apt to reveal too much. Remember too that for many contemporary readers, a story hasn't really begun until a particular character is doing something, thinking something, or saying something. With these points in mind, you may find that your first paragraph or even the first half page can be cut.

Conclusions can present the same kind of problem. Here again there is a temptation to step in as author and explain the story. If you do this too blatantly, you will be stating what the story should have shown through action and dialogue.

Often, endings consist of some small, apparently insignificant piece of action that may highlight the theme or possibly even reveal it. In other stories a line of dialogue may serve the same purpose. Sometimes there is a mix. Take a second look at the ending of "Phoenix":

> On a city bus, wearing her coat, Phoenix irons the wrinkled hundred dollar bill with her palm. It smells of lilac. Dumb money, money she knew she would get, making her cry.

This is an interesting mix of action (smoothing a hundred dollar bill), a smell (the lilac scent of the grandmother's perfume), a statement in the third person that closely resembles thoughts ("dumb money"), and a final action (crying). Although tears at the end of a story are the too-easy end of many rather simple stories, they are handled here with great restraint. Coming as they do from a streetwise and occasionally cynical young woman, they do not risk sentimentality. They contribute to the theme by revealing the vulnerability of the protagonist.

When reviewing the means of perception in your rough draft, try to resist the temptation to dazzle the reader with a tricky or bizarre point of view: the high-adventure sea story in which the use of the first person assures us that the hero will live turns out to be a note left in a bottle; the first-person account of an oversupervised little girl who turns out to be a happy little dog; the brother–sister story that turns out in the last sentence to have concerned two robots. All these have been done. But even if they had not, they all depend on a single trick. A trick, like the joke of a stand-up comic, may give momentary pleasure but is soon forgotten. Since sophisticated fiction is rooted in characterization and thematic insight, it has a lasting quality. Even if one is just beginning to write fiction, this is a goal.

Shifting a story from third person to first or the reverse is not as radical a transformation as changing the means of perception. But as we have seen, it involves more than changing *I* to *he* or *she*. Although it is technically a matter of style, its significance really has more to do with the relationship between the writer and her or his material. If you have any doubts about which approach is most appropriate for a particular story, try a half page each way and see which feels right. To a large degree, this is an intuitive choice.

Changing the focus, on the other hand, is major surgery. It is a terrible feeling to be working on what you hope is a final draft and to decide that the story really should be centered on a different character or a different insight. To avoid this, consider focus right at the start. Have you turned the spotlight on the right character? Do you really know what the story is suggesting? Sometimes it is worthwhile to write a full first draft without being sure, but don't forget to ask these questions when you finish. When you say that a story means whatever the reader wants it to mean, you are probably describing a story that is not ready to be read.

Viewpoint, person, and focus are fundamental. They determine *how* a story will be told just as plot determines *what* will be used. Trust your first inclination to get you started. But then review each factor to make sure that you have made the best possible choice.

16
A STORY BY
STEPHEN MINOT

Sausage and Beer

I kept quiet for most of the trip. It was too cold for talk. The car was getting old and the heater hadn't worked for as long as I could remember. My father said he couldn't afford to get it repaired, but he bought us a camping blanket which was supposed to be just as good. I knew from experience, though, that no matter how carefully I tucked it around me the cold would seep through the door cracks and, starting with a dull ache in my ankles, would work up my legs. There was nothing to do but sit still and wonder what Uncle Theodore would be like.

"Is it very far?" I asked at last. My words puffed vapor.

"We're about halfway now," he said.

That was all. Not enough, of course, but I hadn't expected much more. My father kept to his own world, and he didn't invite children to share it. Nor did he impose himself on us. My twin sister and I were allowed to live our own lives, and our parents led theirs, and there was a mutual respect for the border. In fact, when we were younger Tina and I had assumed that we would eventually marry each other, and while those plans were soon revised, the family continued to exist as two distinct couples.

But this particular January day was different because Tina hadn't been invited—nor had Mother. I was twelve that winter, and I believe it was the first time I had ever gone anywhere alone with my father.

The whole business of visiting Uncle Theodore had come up in the most unconvincingly offhand manner.

"Thought I'd visit your Uncle Theodore," he had said that day after Sunday dinner. "Wondered if you'd like to meet him."

He spoke with his eyes on a crack in the ceiling as if the idea had just popped into his head, but that didn't fool me. It was quite obvious that he had waited until both Tina and my mother were in the kitchen washing the dishes, that he had rehearsed it, and that I wasn't really being given a choice.

"Is Tina going?" I asked.

"No, she isn't feeling well."

I knew what that meant. But I also knew that my father was just using it as an excuse. So I got my coat.

The name Uncle Theodore had a familiar ring, but it was just a name. And I had learned early that you just do not ask about relatives who don't come up in adult conversation naturally. At least, you didn't in my family. You can never tell—like my Uncle Harry. He was another one of my father's brothers. My parents never said anything about Uncle Harry, but some of my best friends at school told me he'd taken a big nail, a spike really, and driven it into his heart with a ball peen hammer. I didn't believe it, so they took me to the library and we found the article on the front page of the *Herald* for the previous Saturday, so it must have been true.

But no one at school told me about Uncle Theodore because they didn't know he existed. Even I hadn't any real proof until that day. I knew that my father had a brother named Theodore in the same way I knew the earth was round without anyone ever taking me to the library to prove it. But then, there were many brothers I had never met—like Freddie, who had jointed a Theosophist colony somewhere in California and wore robes like a priest, and Uncle Herb, who was once in jail for leading a strike in New York.

We were well out in the New England countryside now, passing dark, snow-patched farm fields and scrubby woodlands where saplings choked and stunted each other. I tried to visualize this Uncle Theodore as a farmer: blue overalls, straw hat, chewing a long stem of alfalfa, and misquoting the Bible. But it was a highly unsatisfactory picture. Next I tried to conjure up a mystic living in—didn't St. Francis live in a cave? But it wasn't the sort of question I could ask my father. All I had to go on was what he had told me, which was nothing. And I knew without thinking that he didn't want me to ask him directly.

After a while I indulged in my old trick of fixing my eyes on the white lines down the middle of the road: dash-dash-dash, steady, dash-dash again. If you do that long enough, it will lull you nicely and pass the time. It had just begun to take effect when I felt the car slow down and turn abruptly. Two great gates flashed by, and we were inside a kind of walled city.

Prison, I thought. That's it. That's why they kept him quiet. A murderer, maybe. "My Uncle Theodore," I rehearsed silently, "he's the cop killer."

The place went on forever, row after row of identical buildings, four stories, brick, slate roofs, narrow windows with wire mesh. There wasn't a bright color anywhere. The brick had aged to gray, and so had the snow patches along the road. We passed a group of three old men lethargically shoveling ice and crusted snow into a truck.

"This is a kind of hospital," my father said flatly as we drove between the staring brick fronts. I had to take my father's word for it, but the place still had the feel of a prison.

"It's big," I said.

"It's enormous," he said, and then turned his whole attention to studying the numbers over each door. There was something in his tone that suggested that he didn't like the place either, and that did a lot to sustain me.

Uncle Theodore's building was 13-M, but aside from the number, it resembled the others. The door had been painted a dark green for many years, and the layers of paint over chipped and blistered paint gave it a mottled look. We had to wait quite a while before someone responded to the push bell.

A man let us in, not a nurse. And the man was clearly no doctor either. He wore a gray shirt which was clean but unpressed, and dark-green work pants with a huge ring of keys hanging from his belt.

"Hello there, Mr. Bates," he said in a round Irish voice to match his round face. "You brought the boy?"

"I brought the boy." My father's voice was reedy by comparison. "How's Ted?"

"Same as when you called. A little gloomy, maybe, but calm. Those boils have just about gone."

"Good," my father said.

"Funny about those boils. I don't remember a year but what he's had trouble. Funny."

My father agreed it was funny, and then we went into the visiting room to await Uncle Theodore.

The room was large, and it seemed even larger for the lack of furniture. There were benches around all four walls, and in the middle there was a long table flanked with two more benches. The rest was space. And through that space old men shuffled, younger men wheeled carts of linen, a woman visitor walked slowly up and down with her restless husband—or brother, or uncle. Or was *she* the patient? I couldn't decide which might be the face of madness, his troubled and shifting eyes or her deadened look. Beyond, a bleak couple counseled an ancient patient. I strained to hear, wanting to know the language of the place, but I could only make out mumbles.

The smell was oddly familiar. I cast about; this was no home smell. And then I remembered trips with my mother to a place called the Refuge, where the lucky brought old clothes, old furniture, old magazines, and old kitchen-ware to be bought by the unlucky. My training in Christian charity was to bring my chipped and dented toys and dump them into a great bin, where they were pored over by dead-faced mothers and children.

"Smells like the Refuge," I said very softly, not wanting to hurt anyone's feelings. My father nodded with an almost smile.

We went over to the corner where the benches met, though there was space to sit almost anywhere. And there we waited.

A couple of times I glanced cautiously at my father's face, hoping for some sort of guide. He could have been waiting for a train or listening to a sermon, and I felt a surge of respect. He had a long face with a nose so straight it looked as if it had been leveled with a rule. I guess he would have been handsome if he hadn't seemed so sad or tired much of the time. He worked for a paint wholesaler which had big, dusty offices in a commercial section of Dorchester. When I was younger I used to think the dirt of that place had rubbed off on him permanently.

I began to study the patients with the hope of preparing myself for Uncle Theodore. The old man beside us was stretched out on the bench full length, feet toward us, one arm over his eyes, as if he were lying on the beach, the other resting over his crotch. He had a kind of squeak to his snore. Another patient was persistently scratching his back on the dark-varnished door frame. Anywhere else this would have seemed perfectly normal.

Then my father stood up, and when I did too, I could see that what must be Uncle Theodore was being led in by a pock-marked attendant. They stopped some distance from us and the attendant pointed us out to Uncle Theodore. Then he set him free with a little nudge as if they were playing pin-the-tail-on-the-donkey.

Surprisingly, Uncle Theodore was heavy. I don't mean fat, because he wasn't solid. He was a great, sagging man. His jowls hung loose, his shoulders were massive but rounded like a dome, his hands were attached like brass weights on the ends of swinging pendulums. He wore a clean white shirt open at the neck and blue serge suit pants hung on suspenders which had been patched with a length of twine. It looked as if his pants had once been five sizes too large and that somehow, with the infinite patience of the infirm, he had managed to stretch the lower half of his stomach to fill them.

I would have assumed that he was far older than my father from his stance and his shuffling walk (he wore scuffs, which he slid across the floor without once lifting them), but his face was a baby pink, which made him look adolescent.

"Hello, Ted," my father said, "How have you been?"

Uncle Theodore just said "Hello," without a touch of enthusiasm, or even gratitude for our coming to see him. We stood there, the three of us, for an awkward moment.

Then: "I brought the boy."

"Who?"

"My boy, Will."

Uncle Theodore looked down at me with red-rimmed, blue eyes. Then he looked at my father, puzzled. "But *you're* Will."

"Right, but we've named our boy William too. Tried to call him Billy, but he insists on Will. Very confusing."

Uncle Theodore smiled for the first time. The smile made everything much easier; I relaxed. He was going to be like any other relative on a Sunday afternoon visit.

"Well, now," he said in an almost jovial manner, "there's one on me. I'd forgotten we even *had* a boy."

My face tingled the way it does when you open the furnace door. Somehow he had joined himself with my father as a married couple, and done it with a smile. No instruction could have prepared me for this quiet sound of madness.

But my father had, it seemed, learned how to handle it. He simply asked Uncle Theodore if he had enjoyed the magazines he had brought last time. We subscribed to *Life*, the news magazine, and apparently my father had been bringing him back copies from time to time. It worked, shifting the subject like that, because Uncle Theodore promptly forgot about who had produced what child and told us about how all his copies of *Life* had been stolen. He even pointed out the thief.

"The little one with the hook nose there," he said with irritation but no rage. "Stuffs them in his pants to make him look bigger. He's a problem, he is."

"I'll send you more," my father said. "Perhaps the attendant will keep them for you."

"Hennessy? He's a good one. Plays checkers like a pro."

"I'll bet he has a hard time beating you."

"Hasn't yet. Not once."

"I'm not surprised. You were always the winner." I winced, but neither of them seemed to think this was a strange thing to say. My father turned to me: "We used to play in the attic where it was quiet."

This jolted me. It hadn't occurred to me that the two of them had spent a childhood together. I even let some of their conversation slip by thinking of how they had grown up in the same old rambling house before my sister and I were born, had perhaps planned their future while sitting up there in that attic room the way my sister and I had, actually had gone to school together, and then at some point...But when? And how would it have happened? It was as impossible for me to look back and imagine that as it must have been for them as kids to look forward, to see what was in store for them.

"So they started banging on their plates," Uncle Theodore was saying, "and shouting for more heat. Those metal plates sure make a racket, I can tell you."

"That's no way to get heat," Father said, sounding paternal.

"Guess not. They put Schwartz and Cooper in the pit. That's what Hennessy said. And there's a bunch of them that's gone to different levels. They send them down when they act like that, you know. The doctors, they take a vote and send the troublemakers down." And then his voice lowered. Instinctively we both bent toward him for some confidence. "And I've found out—God's truth—that one of these nights they're going to shut down the heat *all the way. Freeze us!*"

There was a touch of panic in this which coursed through me. I could feel just how it would be, this great room black as midnight, the whine of wind outside, and then all those hissing radiators turning silent, and the aching cold seeping through the door cracks—

"Nonsense," my father said quietly, and I knew at once that it was nonsense. "They wouldn't do that. Hennessy's a friend of mine. I'll speak to him before I go."

"You do that," Uncle Theodore said with genuine gratitude, putting his hand on my father's knee. "You do that for us. I don't believe there would be a soul of us"—he swept his hand about expansively—"not a soul of us alive if it weren't for your influence."

My father nodded and then turned the conversation to milder topics. He talked about how the sills were rotting under the house, how a neighborhood gang had broken two windows one night, how Imperial Paint, where my father worked, had laid off a number of workers. My father wasn't usually so gloomy, but I got the feeling that he was somehow embarrassed at being on the outside, was trying to make his life appear less enviable. But Uncle Theodore didn't seem very concerned one way or the other. He was much more bothered about how a man named Altman was losing his eyesight because of the steam heat and how stern and unfair Hennessy was. At one point he moved back in time to describe a fishing trip by canoe through the Rangeley Lakes. It was like opening a great window, flooding the place with light and color and the smells of summer.

"Nothing finer," he said, his eyes half shut, "than frying those trout at the end of the day with the water so still you'd think you could walk on it."

He was interrupted by the sleeper on the bench beside us, who woke, stood, and stared down at us. Uncle Theodore told him to "Go blow," and when he had gone so were the Rangeley Lakes.

"Rangeley?" he asked, when my father tried to open that window again by suggestion. "He must be one of our cousins. Can't keep 'em straight."

And we were back to Mr. Altman's deafness and how seriously it hindered him and how the doctors paid no attention.

It was with relief that I smelled sauerkraut. That plus attendants gliding through with carts of food in dented steel containers seemed to suggest supper, and supper promised that the end was near.

"About suppertime," my father said after a particularly long silence.

Uncle Theodore took in a long, deep breath. He held it for a moment. Then he let it go with the slowest, saddest sigh I have ever heard.

"About suppertime," he said at the end of it.

There were mumbled farewells and nods of agreement. We were thanked for copies of *Life* which we hadn't brought; he was told he was looking fine, just fine.

We were only inches from escape when Uncle Theodore suddenly discovered me again.

"Tell me son," he said, bending down with a smile which on anyone else would have been friendly, "what d'you think of your Uncle Ted?"

I was overwhelmed. I stood there looking up at him, waiting for my father to save me. But he said nothing.

"It's been very nice meeting you," I said to the frozen pink smile, dredging the phrase up from my sparse catechism of social responses, assuming that what would do for maiden aunts would do for Uncle Theodore.

But it did not. He laughed. It was a loud and bitter laugh, derisive, and perfectly sane. He had seen my statement for the lie it was, had caught sight of himself, of all of us.

"Well," he said when the laugh withered, "say hi to Dad for me. Tell him to drop by."

Father said he would—though my grandfather had died before I was born. As we left, I felt oddly grateful that the moment of sanity had been so brief.

It was dark when we got back to the car, and it was just beginning to snow. I nestled into the seat and pulled the blanket around me.

We had been on the road about a half hour and were approaching our neighborhood by an odd route. My father finally broke the silence. "I could do with a drink."

This was a jolt because my parents never had liquor in the house. I knew about bars but had never been in one. I wondered if perhaps drinking was something men did—a kind of ritual.

"Sure," I said, trying to sound offhand. "It's fine with me."

"You like sausage?" he asked.

"I love sausage." Actually I'd never tasted it. My mother said you couldn't tell what they put in it.

"A little sausage and a cool beer is what we need." And after a pause, "It's a place I go from time to time. Been there since God knows when. Ted and I had some good times there back when. But..." He took a deep breath and then let it out slowly. "It might be best if you told your mother we went to a Howard Johnson for a hamburger, O.K.?"

"Sure, Dad."

We were on city streets I had never seen before. He finally parked in what looked like a dark, threatening neighborhood and headed for a place with neon signs in the window. I had to trot to keep up. As soon as we entered, we were plunged into a warm, humming, soothing, smoky world. The sound of music blended with voices and laughter. There was a bar to our right, marble tables ahead, booths beyond. My father nodded at a waiter he seemed to know and said hi to a group at a table; then he headed toward the booths with a sure step.

We hadn't got halfway before a fat man in a double-breasted suit came steaming up to us, furious.

"Whatcha doing," he said even before he reached us, "corruptin' the youth?"

I held my breath. But when the big man reached my father they broke out in easy laughter.

"So this is the boy?" he said. "Will, Junior—right?" We nodded. "Well, there's a good part of you in the boy, I can see that—it's in the eyes. Now, there's a girl too, isn't there? Younger?"

"She's my twin," I said. "Not identical."

The men laughed. Then the fat one said, "Jesus, twins sure run in your family, don't they!"

This surprised me. I knew of no other twins except some cousins from Maine. I looked up at my father, puzzled.

"Me and Ted," he said to me. "We're twins. Nonidentical."

We were ushered to a booth, and the fat man hovered over us, waiting for the order.

"Got sausage tonight?" my father asked.

"Sure. American or some nice hot Italian?"

"Italian."

"Drinks?"

"Well—" My father turned to me. "I guess you rate beer," he said. And then, to the fat man, "Two beers."

The man relayed the order to a passing waiter. Then he asked my father, "Been out to see Ted?"

"You guessed it."

"I figured." He paused, his smile gone. "You too?" he asked me.

"Yes," I said. "It was my first time."

"Oh," he said, with a series of silent nods which assured me that somehow he knew exactly what my afternoon had been like. "Ted was quite a boy. A great tackle. A pleasure to watch him. But no dope either. Used to win meals here playing chess. Never saw him lose. Why, he sat right over there."

He pointed to the corner booth, which had a round table. All three of us looked; a waiter with a tray full of dirty glasses stopped, turned, and also looked at the empty booth as if an apparition had just been sighted.

"And you know why he's locked up?"

"No," I whispered, appalled at the question.

"It's just the number he drew. Simple as that. Your Dad, me, you—any of us could draw the wrong number tomorrow. There's something to think about."

I nodded. All three of us nodded. Then the waiter brought a tray with the order, and the fat man left us with a quick, benedictory smile. We ate and drank quietly, lost in a kind of communion.

17
STRUCTURE:
FROM SCENES TO PLOT

Fictional scenes compared with episodes of daily living. Scene
construction in "Sausage and Beer." Varieties of plot patterns:
chronological, flashbacks, frame stories. Controlling the pace.
Coherence of plot. Building toward a concluding epiphany.

Clocks move at a steady rate. And in one sense, so do our lives. Awake or
asleep, we progress from birth to death at a steady pace.

But now take a moment to review what you did yesterday from the time
you got up to the end of the day.

Notice how naturally that chronology turned into a list of identifiable
events or episodes: getting dressed, eating breakfast, and, for students, attending classes, a coffee break with friends in the cafeteria, a conversation in the
hall, and lunch. For nonstudents, the events would be different, but the rhythm
from one unit of activity to the next is essentially the same. The point is that
while the *clock* moves perfectly regularly, our *life* as we look back is recalled as
a sequence of episodes.

These episodes have certain characteristics which every writer of fiction
should consider. First, we often identify them by where they occurred—the
setting. Second, we recall who was there—the characters. Third, such episodes
remain clear long after we have forgotten what came just before and just
afterward. Those unstructured periods of time that merely link one episode

with the next (walking, waiting, driving, watching television, sleeping) tend to blend together and blur quickly.

Finally, we don't always remember these events in the order in which they occurred. Students complaining about bad teachers they have had are not necessarily going to start with kindergarten; football fans recounting dramatic games they have watched are not going to begin with the first one they attended; and a man recalling his love for a woman is not necessarily going to begin with the day he met her.

Fiction tends to imitate these patterns. What we call *episodes* in life become **scenes** in fiction. These are the basic units. And their arrangement is what we call **plot**.

Scene Structure in "Sausage and Beer"

A scene in a short story is not as clearly defined as in drama, but generally speaking it consists of an episode that is identifiable either because of the setting or because of the characters involved. The reader senses a transition from one scene to the next whenever the author changes the setting or alters the "cast of characters" by having one leave or arrive.

If you examine the scenes in "Sausage and Beer," you will see that there are six of them:

1. The narrator is being driven by his father to see the boy's uncle on a cold January day. (Includes a flashback—a scene within a scene—in which the father invites his son to visit his Uncle Theodore.)

2. A short scene outside the hospital building. This is set off by a description of the hospital and grounds.

3. The waiting room. Father and son wait for Uncle Theodore to appear.

4. The visit with Uncle Theodore. This begins with Theodore's arrival and ends with the conclusion of visiting hours. Notice that the setting hasn't changed but there is a psychological break when Uncle Theodore appears.

5. A short scene in the car.

6. The important scene in the bar. Notice that this is not only a different setting, it is a different climate as well. The bar is warm and friendly.

Why six scenes? When the story was blocked out, this is what emerged. Initially, the number of scenes should probably be determined by the way in which the story comes to you. But once the first draft is down on paper, you should take a close look at the number and length of your scenes. Occasionally you will have to add a new scene. But more often you will find that you can cut. In this particular story, a two-page flashback was cut just before the story was published in *The Atlantic*, and another page was cut from the second edition of this textbook. A few more cuts were made for the fourth edition. Stories, like poems, are never really finished.

There comes a point where a story cannot be cut further without doing damage. In terms of plot alone, this story could be reduced to a single scene—the one at the hospital. But too much would be lost. The earlier scenes establish the relationship between father and son while also providing suspense, and the concluding scenes shift the story from a simple initiation (the boy introduced to the disturbing reality of mental illness) to a kind of first communion in which a young man is welcomed into the fellowship of adult life with all its distressing ironies.

The answer to the question of why the story is in six scenes is not a simple matter of rules. It is judgment. My sense is that more scenes would weigh the story down and less would begin to make it too sketchy, too simple. It is very helpful to have a rough idea of the scene pattern in advance—even a tentative outline. But it is equally important to be willing to make adjustments after the first draft, adding or cutting scenes where needed.

Varieties of Plot Patterns

The stories included in this volume all move chronologically from scene to scene. A majority of stories do—particularly those that are relatively short. But even in those cases, the writer is not bound to move relentlessly forward in time. The author—like the scriptwriter—is free to include glimpses of past action.

The **flashback** is a simple method of inserting an episode that occurred before the main flow (or **base time**) of the plot. The term "flashback," first used by film writers, describes more than a simple reference to the past seen through a character's thoughts or dialogue. A true flashback consists of a whole scene that took place before the main action of the story and is presented with setting and often with dialogue.

Take, for example, the flashback that occurs in the opening scene of "Sausage and Beer." The father and son, you remember, are driving in silence, and the earlier incident is dropped in almost as if in brackets:

> The whole business of visiting Uncle Theodore had come up in the most unconvincingly offhand manner.
> "Thought I'd visit your Uncle Theodore," he had said that day after Sunday dinner. "Wondered if you'd like to meet him."
> He spoke with his eyes on a crack in the ceiling as if the idea had just popped into his head, but that didn't fool me.

Notice that the reader is informed of the fact that the story is moving back to an earlier time by the brief use of the past perfect: "*had* come up" and "he *had* said that day." This is a standard method of entering a flashback in past-tense stories, even though many readers are not consciously aware that they are being signaled by a shift in tense. In fact, many *writers* have used the technique without knowing that the *had* form is called the past perfect. Never mind the terminology; *had* is the cue for your reader. After one or two sentences, shift back to the simple past: "It was quite obvious" and "asked."

How do you come out of a flashback? The most obvious way is to identify the transition directly: "But that was hours ago" or "But that was when he was much younger." More often, authors simply make sure that the new paragraph starts with a bit of action or a line of dialogue that clearly indicates to the reader that the story has returned to *base time*, the events and setting of the primary plot line. In this particular flashback the reader should be set straight by the paragraph that begins: "We were well out in the New England countryside now."

The same kind of cues are used when writing in the present tense. The shift in these cases is from the present to the simple past tense. There is a flashback in Melissa Pritchard's "Phoenix" that is handled in just this way. If you turn to page 153 you will see that it starts with:

> Two weeks each August, as Mary Lou, she slept on starched, ironed sheets, woke at dawn....

The shift is made clear by the reference to "each August" and to her childhood name of Mary Lou, but notice the use of the past tense in *slept* and *woke*. If you check the beginning of each paragraph, you will see that the author has continued with the past tense down to page 155. She signals the shift back to the primary time frame (the base time) with a double space, the use of "Now," and the return to the present tense ("Phoenix wants to shake her grandmother...").

In many cases, you can make the return to base time clear simply by starting a new paragraph and shifting the tense. But be sure that the setting is clearly different. If your flashback takes place in, say, a restaurant, be careful not to have your characters in another restaurant when you return to base time. There's no point in needlessly confusing your reader.

Multiple flashbacks are sometimes used when the author wants to suggest a complicated set of clues leading to a symbolic or a literal trial. Joseph Conrad's *Lord Jim* is in this form; so is William Faulkner's well-known "A Rose for Emily." Such an approach tends to fragment the story line, of course, and it may be for this reason that it is usually found in longer works and those that have a type of mystery or trial to maintain the story's unity and the reader's interest.

The **frame story** traditionally refers to a tale told by a character appearing in a larger work, such as the separate narrations within Chaucer's *The Canterbury Tales*. But by common usage it also refers to any story in which the bulk of the material is presented as a single, long flashback. It is possible to do this in the third person; but often a frame is achieved through the device of a narrator who recalls an incident that happened some time in the past.

"Sausage and Beer," for example, could have opened with the narrator looking back like this:

> As I stood with my wife waiting for the funeral to begin, I realized how little I had really seen of my father. It was as if he were a stranger until I was twelve. The turning point came one day when he took me to visit my Uncle Theodore.
> As I remember it, I had kept quiet for most of the trip. It was too cold for talk.

Notice the traditional use of the past perfect for a single sentence and then the simple past. And if the story were to have a complete frame, the ending might be rounded out with a return to the opening scene.

> Sitting there in the chapel, listening to the service intended to honor my father, I couldn't help feeling that he and I had experienced a more meaningful ritual there in that most secular bar years ago.

Such an ending seems wooden to me—a bit too obvious. But it does indicate how any story can be surrounded in a frame. Or, as an alternative, the frame can be left incomplete simply to avoid the danger of a needless summing up.

The use of the frame is well justified if there is a good reason for contrasting the attitude of the narrator at the time of the narration with that back when the event took place.

Controlling the Pace of Plot

Every reader is aware that some sections in a story move slowly or drag, while others move quickly. A writer, however, has to know *why* this has happened.

In part, the pace of fiction is controlled by the style—particularly the length and complexity of the sentence structure. This is discussed in Chapter 24. By far the greatest factor, however, is the **rate of revelation**. That is, a story seems to move rapidly when a great deal is being revealed to the reader; conversely, it slows down when the author turns to digression, speculation, description, or any type of exposition.

One can, of course, maintain a high rate of revelation simply by concentrating on what reviewers like to call an "action-packed plot." This is one of the recurring characteristics of many best-sellers, adventure stories, and stories of "true romance." Extreme examples are seen in television drama series and the comics. What these stories sacrifice is richness of suggestion and subtleties of characterization.

When you write sophisticated fiction you have to be on guard against two dangers: If you maintain a consistently high rate of revelation, entertaining your readers with a lively plot, you may bore them for lack of significance. They will find your work superficial. But if you become philosophically discursive or heavily symbolic, you may also bore your readers by lack of drama. Because of this, most successfully sophisticated stories shift the pace throughout the work.

Openings are frequently given a high rate of revelation. It helps to plunge into an ongoing situation that will arouse the reader's interest. "Sausage and Beer," for example, begins with the narrator driving with his father and wondering what his Uncle Theodore will be like. The question in the mind of the boy becomes the reader's concern too. In the case of "Phoenix," the opening wisely does *not* begin with Phoenix arriving in town or looking for a store; it begins with her in the changing room and with the saleslady standing just outside the door, keeping a sharp eye on this "filthy hippy, sure-fire shoplifter." There is no background, no introductory description. In fact, even though the story is written in the third person, the phrasing is close to what is going through Phoenix's head.

Both of these stories jump into a situation that arouses the curiosity of the reader. Once you have overcome the reader's reluctance to get started, you can afford to fill in the setting and provide background.

As a story develops, it is a good idea to continue alternating between the vitality of fresh plot development and the richness of description and exposition. In this way the pace of fiction often resembles that of a skater in that the forward thrust is followed by a glide. It's wise, of course, not to glide too long or the story, like the skater, will lose momentum.

As you read over your first draft, try to feel where the story slows its pace. If it is only a slight pause, you have no problem. The forward motion of the narration should carry the reader. But if not enough happens for too long, the story will "sag" and you need to revise.

On the other hand, too much emphasis on plot may make a story superficial or melodramatic—what we have been calling *simple* fiction. In those cases you may wish to moderate the dramatic action to the point where it can be handled in the relatively delicate form of the short-short story. A story ending with a fatal automobile accident, for example, may seem less like a routine television scene without the fatality; a story capped by a suicide (often a too-easy ending) may be more convincing if the protagonist shows his or her despair in a more subtle way.

When determining the pace of a story, consider the length. A short-short of six to eight manuscript pages, for example, may be based on a single scene and may move with essentially the same pace from beginning to end. The longer a story, the more natural it is to have multiple scenes; and as soon as you do, the pacing becomes important. "Phoenix," for example, seems like a relatively short story when printed, but it would come to about 14 double-spaced pages. A story of this length can afford a relatively slow-paced flash-back to fill in the protagonist's childhood contact with her grandmother. If the story were half the length, that section might have to be cut entirely or filled in with a few lines of exposition.

There are no easy rules to follow, but your sense of effective pacing will increase as you have more opportunities to read and to hear other readers respond to your work.

The Coherence of Plot

A diary may list the events of a day with great accuracy, but this is not a plot. A fictional plot is a weaving together of events that are interrelated and which work toward a conclusion. One event affects another, characters have an influence on one another, and elements that do not contribute to the whole—details left over from an actual experience, for example—are eliminated.

To what end? Short stories are rarely plotted with rising and falling action such as is common in traditional plays, but they do generally build toward what James Joyce called an *epiphany*. Although he used the term in a somewhat more limited sense, it has come to mean an important moment of recognition or discovery. It can take two different forms: either the reader and the central character learn something significant from the events of the story, or the reader alone makes such a discovery. Even stories that appear at first reading to be highly unstructured usually provide this important element.

In "Sausage and Beer" there are, I think, two such moments—one recognized by the boy and the other an insight perceived only by the reader. The first is given through the fat man at the bar who, in a serious moment almost at the end of the story, poses the question of why one of two brothers should live a normal life and the other should end up in a mental hospital. His answer is that it is just chance. We all run that risk. The boy and the reader come to realize this simultaneously.

The final sentence, however, offers an insight too complex for the boy to understand at this stage in his life. Father and son, having shared a difficult experience, are now sharing something like a communion—not a religious experience but a partaking of life itself.

The building of scenes and their arrangement as plot become more intu-itive after you have written several stories. But there are ways you can speed this process. First, examine the scene construction of short stories in print. Mark in the margin where the scenes begin and end. Study the transitions and the shifts in pace and in mood.

Second, study and question your own scene construction. Be on guard against two problem areas: the scattering of scenes that cover too broad a spectrum of time for the length of the story and, on the other hand, those long, talky, or highly descriptive scenes that sag for lack of development.

If the story seems too brief or thin or lacking in development, don't start padding the existing scenes with more explanation and longer sentences. Carefully consider whether the reader needs to know more about the characters or the situation through the addition of entire scenes. Conversely, if the story seems to ramble, don't think that the only solution is to remove a sentence here and a phrase there. Consider cutting or combining entire scenes.

Finally, ask yourself just what the reader learns from going through this experience. This shouldn't be a simple "moral" which the reader can shrug off as a truism, nor does it need to be a far-reaching philosophical or psychological truth. What most authors aim for in a short story is a subtle insight into character—some realization that the reader shares with the protagonist or discovers independently.

Most fiction, like drama and to a lesser extent narrative poetry, depends on plot to move it forward. Plot is the driving force. Readers may feel that this flow of action is uninterrupted, but writers know that it is made up of a sequence of related scenes. Fiction, like poetry and drama, is a construction of units in which the whole is greater than the sum of its parts.

18
A STORY BY
DEBORAH JOY COREY

Three Hearts

The morning after the big snowstorm Mama is real sick. Her hair has twisted itself into tight knots like spikes all over her head and she is so weak that her words are puffy and low. We are all up, listening to the radio that sits on top of the fridge to see if there will be any school. Bucky and I sit at the wooden table that wobbles on the crooked floor and wait with our elbows pressed like seams into the plastic tablecloth. Mama is lying on the kitchen couch, wrapped in a red robe, rolling her head from side to side, sighing.

Her eyes are like faded jeans and she sounds scared, so I go over and stand by her head. I take one of Daddy's newspapers from under the couch and fan her a bit. The newspaper leaves black on my finger and I rub it onto my soft corduroys. Mama has *nerves* and when my other brother, Eddie, drinks they get worse. She says that nothing could make her more weak than the fact that she has a fifteen-year-old child with a drinking problem.

Eddie has an angry streak like steel running through his heart. He quit school last year and now he sleeps all morning and stays out all night. He drinks with a man called Cake who lives on welfare and drives a big car. Mama and Daddy can't manage Eddie. They tried to make him go back to school, but whenever they brought it up his temper would roll, and he would slam himself at the walls. I remember Mama telling Daddy that maybe Eddie shouldn't go to school, that maybe his whole problem was that the teacher picked on him. But Daddy told her right up quick that Eddie had drinking in his blood just like Daddy's whole family did. Daddy used to drink on weekends. He'd go to the Legion every Friday night after supper and sometimes not come home until Sunday. The last time I saw my Daddy drunk, his lip was broken wide open and purple.

"Who did that to you?" Mama said.

"My old man." Daddy made the words sound like they were the last ones left in him. They echoed like a bobcat snarl.

Mama wrinkled her forehead. "Why?"

One of Daddy's eyes went wet. "Because he was drunk, too."

Mama blames herself for everything. When I smile at Mama, she always says, "Poor girl, she's got her Mother's crooked teeth," but I always say, "Mama, I grew these teeth, not you."

"I'm so warm," Mama says, and I think of calling Daddy at the County Garage to see what to do with her, but I figure he's sure to be out plowing the roads with all this snow. Mama is sicker than usual because Eddie didn't come home and she sat up all night waiting for him. In the night I could hear the rocking chair in Eddie's room moving back and forth like a song and I knew Mama had her face wrapped in her cool hands. I stroke Mama's hair and she says to the air: "You wonder if he's dead or alive."

The radio is playing "O happy day, when Jesus washed, my sins away," and I wonder how they get all those singers in the radio station so early in the morning. Bucky is still waiting at the table.

"I wish they'd say school's cancelled," he says.

"It is," I guess, and stand on the chair and press my face against the top part of the window so I can see out over the snow. In the shiny glass I can see my ghost looking back at me and I blow steam on the window and make three little hearts that Mama will complain about later. Big cutout flakes are still coming down and the veranda is a lake of snow, swirling up and around the railing and window in waves. I think of my feet sinking deep into the new snow—O happy day—and then I think of Eddie frozen in a snowbank.

"Upper Valley Elementary," Bucky yells. "We're closed. No school." He jumps up from the table and does a little circle. "Mama, where are my snow pants? Mama?"

He rubs Mama's face like he is polishing an apple and a smile sneaks out from under her half-moon lips.

When Eddie comes home, Bucky and I are in the hallway putting bread bags over our wool socks so our feet won't get wet. He comes through the door all dressed in black and loose and he looks like a puppet. A cigarette is burning at the side of his mouth and he steps over us as if we are stones.

"Eddie," Mama sits up. "Where have you been? I'm sick from waiting. What do you do all night?"

Eddie doesn't answer Mama. He gives her one of those stares that Daddy says could freeze hell and Mama stands up in front of him.

"Eddie," she begs and he uses his long blue hand to push Mama back down on the couch. Mama chokes back her air and cries like a baby that's got its feelings hurt. Eddie throws his cigarette in the sink and goes up the back stairs to his room and I know he is drunk by the way he smells. I twist a hole through the bread bag and listen for Mama to stop being sad. Bucky is all ready to go. Mama wipes at her face and pulls herself up. She ties her robe tight like a package and takes her pills from her pocket. She shakes them and reads the label.

"I need some sleep," she says to the bottle. Mama comes into the hallway and steps over the water spots that Eddie left. Her feet are pink and crusty. "Will you be warm enough?" She ties a green scarf around my neck and looks down at my face.

"Stop painting your lips with Mercurochrome," she says and she rubs my lips until they burn. "Double up on your mittens, Bucky."

Mama leans on the doorframe and watches us march out the door. "Have fun," she says, "your Mama's going to lie down."

The snow is white and heavy flour. Bucky pushes the wooden storm door closed behind us and we fall on our knees, piling the snow up at the door like we want to bury it.

"Now Mama can rest," Bucky says and he packs the cracks with lots of snow.

I love Bucky's face. It is pointed and always looks to smile like a dolphin's, and even though he is thirteen months younger than me, he seems older. We wade out to the yard and the snow is so deep and heavy that we just stop for a long time and look at things. The white cover is perfect except for Eddie's footprints in from the road. The tiny wind smells brand new and the telephone wires have so much snow on them that they are almost invisible. The snow-flakes try to get in our eyes and we squint at one another.

"Catch it on your tongue," Bucky says. We tilt our heads back and stretch our tongues on our chins. Bucky's tongue is watermelon color.

We pull our scarves up over our noses and my breath is warm and wet on the wool. I look back at the house and in the fuzzy snow it looks like a big blank face. The windows are as dark as molasses and nothing moves in them. I think of Eddie hidden in a stack of pillows with his mouth open, while the wind whispers around his window. I think how Daddy will pull him out of bed when he comes home. "I told you to look for work today," he'll say, and Eddie will squirm out of Daddy's hands like he always does.

"Let's make angels," Bucky says.

We look at the yard which is as smooth as a statue and we begin to drop down on our backs and slide our arms like we are trying to fly. We make so many angels that there is no untouched snow left and I tell Bucky if the birds were out, they'd think it was an angel graveyard. We wade around the house and look at all the high drifts. There is a huge drift in front of the shed that is connected to our house so we go around where there is a wooden ladder and climb up on the shed's roof. The roof is slippery, but we know if we fall we will just land in the soft snow and laugh. We slide down the roof into the drift and the snow comes up to our hips. Bucky almost can't get out of the snow and he pretends he is in white quicksand. He waves his arms and screams: "Help, I'm drownin', help me."

"Kick your knees," I say half-mad, and he pushes himself free, tee-heeing.

We're lined up on the roof like pigeons when we hear the snowplow coming. We push off together and land just in time to see Daddy going by. He honks and we rush out of the snow so we can run and see him. Swish, swish, swish, our legs are fat and noisy in our snow pants. When we get there, there is nothing but a swirl of white dust and the low growl of Daddy's machine going over the far side of the dirt road. After, everything is soft and still.

We scuff our boots through the snow and blank out five whole angels. There's a big bank of snow by the road and we make foot holes and climb up to the top. The snow is all packed hard and the top is as flat as a stage. As soon as I get up, Bucky pushes me off. That's what Eddie used to do when he played with us, that's exactly what he did. I slide down over the bank and land on my back.

"I'm the king of the castle and you're the dirty rascal," he sings and I don't move. I let the snow whip around my face and I stay perfectly still until the ends of my fingers go stiff.

"Sis," Bucky says, "Sissy, get up. C'mon, let's play. Come back up."

He climbs down beside me. "You're not dead," he says and kicks a pile of snow in my face.

Bucky starts to build a tunnel in the side of the bank. We dig and round it out like an igloo. It's real warm on the inside and when we are finished Bucky leans back against the hard wall and sucks the snow from his mitten.

"Bucky, don't eat snow, it's got worms in it."

"It does not." He wipes his nose with the back of his jacket sleeve.

"Mama says it does," I say.

"It's not snow, it's blubber," he says and just the thought of it makes me laugh.

"Get some icicles," he says.

"The icicles are always my job. Bucky says Eskimo women do all the stuff like that. "Anything they can do without their husband's help, they do. They're brave, " he told me once.

I climb up on the railing along the veranda and grab one big icicle to knock the rest down. The icicles tick off as I move across the railing and they fall like darts in the snow. I dig them out and carry them back as if they are kindling. We use the tips of the icicles to draw on the walls of the igloo. I always draw a trailer park because that is where I would like to live when I grow up, but Bucky does different things. Today, he draws Eddie with a huge set of drums. Eddie likes the Beatles. He combs his black hair down over his forehead and seals it with Dippity-Do so he looks like Ringo. Sometimes when Bucky and

I come home from school, Eddie is sitting in Daddy's brown recliner beating the arms of the chair with two wooden spoons. His timing is even and his blue eyes are storm clouds when he plays. "Get away from me," he always says.

We get tired and pile the icicles in the middle for firewood then lie on our backs and study the white walls. We never make any rules, but both Bucky and I know that whenever we build an igloo, he's the husband and I'm the wife. After a while, he leans over and kisses my cheek with his wet lips and then lies back down. We both close our eyes.

When our pretend night is over, Bucky sits up, rubbing himself all over because he is freezing. "Get up," he says. "We need more firewood."

My head is still empty from my rest when I poke it out of the tunnel. The air is thick and cold and the flakes have turned into small white dots. I run through the snow to the veranda and climb up to get the icicles. In the distance, I can hear Daddy's plow. I turn and brace my feet holding two big sticks of ice in my hands like swords. I wave them crossways when I see Daddy coming. I think of the people on *Gilligan's Island* waving to airplanes. Snow flies up from the road and Daddy gives a big toot when he goes by and it looks like the plow is empty, like it is driving itself.

I carry the firewood back to the tunnel and I start to feel dizzy when I can't find the igloo's hole. I carry the icicles along the bank thinking maybe I've lost my place and slowly the whiteness is all I can see. I dump the ice and start to crawl through the heavy snow on my knees, and I say, "Bucky, Bucky."

I look back along the bank for a piece of Bucky and I dig at a dark spot hoping it is his mitten, but it's just dirt or a shadow. I stop and listen for him and the weather squeezes in around me. When I get to the veranda, I don't remember running there. The door is piled high with snow and I pull at the handle but the door won't move. I brush the snow back from it with both hands. I get it open just a tiny crack, but I still can't get inside. I jerk the handle back and forth and bang the door hard. "Eddie, Eddie," I holler after each bang.

I get so tired from banging that the ghost in me takes over and I begin to dream. I am dreaming while my body bangs the door. I am all grown up with breasts like Mama and I am standing in front of the house screaming for Eddie to wake up. His window is black and empty. I'm screaming: "Eddie, help me. Bucky's suffocating. Eddie, help." I scream until my voice leaves me.

I dream that I climb up the side of the house toward the window. Splinters peel off the house and stick to my fingers until the tips turn purple and begin to bleed. The blood makes the wooden siding slippery and I start to slip back down to the ground. I leave long thin red strips like scratches on the house.

I am staring down, rubbing my frozen fingers together like I have just discovered them when Mama opens the door. Her face is foggy and I tell her fast what has happened.

"Go," she yells, pushing me out into the yard. "Show me."

I point at the flat side of the bank where I think the hole is and I'm scared that I am wrong and that Jesus won't wash my sins away. Mama's red robe works its way open in the front and her flowered nightie looks strange in the snow. I watch the soles of her feet right below me that are staring up with all their cracks and dryness and something about the way they twist and cuddle looks like two baby pigs. I wonder if they feel cold or if Mama has forgotten everything but Bucky. She is breathing with the wind.

"What happened?" She turns her eyes to me for the shortest second and I don't know what to say.

I remember how the plow shook the windowpanes in our house when it rumbled by. It reminded me of thunder.

"What happened?" she says again.

"The plow," I say, "the plow came by," and then I wished I'd blamed myself. That's what Mama would have done.

She has both arms in the snow and she is talking to herself like she is praying, like the bank is her altar. I look back at the house and wonder why Eddie hasn't heard us. Why he hasn't come to help? I am almost ready to let my tears out when Mama reaches way in with her head and all.

"Oh, my land," she says, her words just a whisper.

She pushes her shoulders in and she gets ahold of something and pulls two or three times. I can tell she is getting tired and I am afraid she will give up. She reaches one more time and hauls Bucky out by the arm. His body is limp and one double mitten falls to the white ground. He's flat on his back. Mama stares at his face which looks tired and sleepy and she shakes him.

"Bucky, Bucky, Bucky," she says quick, like his name is a rhyme. She puts her ear on his mouth and listens. She opens her thin lips and puts them on his in a circle. Specks of snow fall down and land on her hair. Bucky opens one eye and squints at the flakes.

"Bucky," Mama says soft and pushes her face against his cheeks, first one side, then the other. She holds his head on both sides. Bucky reaches his hand up and Mama pulls him to her chest and he snuggles into her flowered nightie. Mama's lips are shaking and her eyes are watery blue.

"It's all my fault," she says. She lifts Bucky up on his feet and keeps her hands under his arms. His face is red and full and I touch his bare fingers that hang in the wind like leaves.

"Come, baby," Mama says.

Bucky walks on his own, but Mama holds him tight. Mama's robe flies in the wind behind them and the way it swirls and prances makes me think she is dancing.

I fall back and let my bottom make a snug chair in the snow. I am jerky on the inside and my stomach feels small and hard. I thought Bucky would be dead and that his face would be caved in from the heavy snow. I pick up his mitten and try to forget the melted look that I thought he would have when Mama pulled him out. I take the mitten apart. The inside one is blue. The outside one is an old mitten of Eddie's and it is grey and full of holes. Each hole has a string of wool in it and I pull on the yarn to make the hole bigger, but the hole puckers together in a kiss. I fix every hole this way and the mitten rumples itself into a little ball.

I look at the house. Orange light comes from the kitchen and shadows move past the window in slow motion. I bet Mama is rubbing Bucky's chest with Vicks VapoRub. I think of his round chest that juts out in the middle and my throat goes all full and tight. I listen and everything is big and quiet and I wonder if Daddy will come home soon. I stuff Eddie's grey mitten inside of Bucky's and waddle myself free from the snow.

19
NARRATIVE TENSION

Tension defined. Techniques of creating tension: dramatic conflict between or within characters; curiosity aroused at the outset; the use of dramatic questions; creating suspense; the tensions of irony and satire.

Tension in fiction is what keeps the reader reading. Without it, a story will seem dull, even tedious. No matter how subtle or carefully written, a story is hardly a success if readers are not induced to finish it. Fiction needs some degree of internal energy, and that energy is created through tension.

There are many ways of creating tension, but they all consist of pitting one element against another. The most obvious kind of tension, the type we are most familiar with, is **conflict**. A more subtle form of tension is created by arousing *curiosity*. When curiosity is intensified and made dramatic, the result is **suspense**. And an entirely different but effective type of tension can be achieved through the use of **irony** and **satire**. Although there are no sharp lines between these five ways of generating tension, it helps to examine each separately.

Dramatic Conflict

Conflict is found in all types of narrative including plays, films, and some poetry. We call it "dramatic" partly because it is associated with plays like Shakespeare's *Henry V* and *Julius Caesar* but mainly in the general sense of being vivid or striking.

On its simplest level, dramatic conflict is the mainspring of simple fiction and drama. Adventure stories like Edgar Rice Burroughs' *Tarzan* series and, on a slightly higher level, Alexandre Dumas' *The Count of Monte Cristo,* and most television thrillers pit characters against each other with great regularity. Occasionally an individual faces a group such as a gang or posse. In other cases the opponent is some aspect of nature—the sea, a typhoon, a mountain. The conflict in such works tends to be simple, straightforward, and not complicated by inner debate. The plots have a certain similarity.

With associations like these, it is no wonder that some novice writers unconsciously avoid all forms of conflict and keep their characters passive or isolated. But there is no need to avoid conflict in even the most sensitive fiction. It will serve you well and will add essential vitality to your fiction as long as you make sure that it is reasonably subtle, insightful, and appropriate to your characters and to the length of your story.

The most striking example of conflict in the stories included here is in "Three Hearts." In the dramatic climax of this story a mother dressed only in her robe and nightgown digs frantically in the snow to save her son who has been buried by a snow plow. High drama indeed! In fact, it might even spill over into melodrama were it not for the fact that the characters are fully drawn. In melodrama, characters are mere vehicles for a tension-charged plot.

Actually, this story is made up of a series of conflicts that culminate in the final scene. The older son, Eddie, is in conflict with the whole family. And the father has earlier been in a drunken fistfight with *his* father. This is a family struggling with conflicts. Notice, however, that while the father and Eddie battle other members of the family, almost breaking it apart, the mother's conflict is with nature, in the form of snow, and her actions have the power to bring the family together in spite of her afflictions. More about that later. It is sufficient here to point out that a story can have a number of different types of conflicts, some more serious than others.

Inner Conflict

One of the characteristics of simple fiction is that conflict is rarely muddied by inner conflict. Superman does not question his almost neurotic fascination with crime; Dick Tracy is never seriously tempted to take a bribe. But look at the inner uncertainties of the mother in "Three Hearts": She would clearly like to retreat from responsibilities and stay in bed, wrapped in that red robe, "rolling her head from side to side, sighing." Yet she is the one who plunges into the snow to save her son. She is clearly being pulled in two directions, but ultimately it is her mature and loving side that wins.

In "Phoenix," the entire story revolves around the young woman's conflict between the streetwise survivor within herself who knows her grandmother is good for a hundred dollars and her less-cynical self who recalls her grandmother warmly and is deeply disturbed by how the older woman is failing. The inner conflict is further dramatized by her two names: Mary Lou and Phoenix.

In "Sausage and Beer," the father is torn between his sense of obligation to visit his brother in the mental hospital and an understandable wish to get out of there just as soon as he can. Like the characters in the other stories, he is "of two minds"—struggling with an inner debate.

An analysis like this is necessary to show how different types of conflict can be used within the same story. But I should make it clear that this is not how stories generally get written. One doesn't sit down with a determination to combine an inner conflict with an outer one. The usual beginning involves a character in a particular situation. A plot unfolds—part experience, perhaps, and part invention. Let it flow. The best time for a careful literary analysis is after you have completed the first draft.

Suppose, for example, that Melissa Pritchard had begun by writing a rather autobiographical account of how she as a free-spirited young woman visited her rather conservative grandmother. They meet, talk about the past, and then the girl goes on her way. The original concept might have come to mind because of the contrast between them, but the first draft as we are envisioning it would be bland, even dull. This is the point at which an author should turn analytical about his or her work and identify the problems as objectively as possible. In this case, she would undoubtedly see that the draft lacked tension, and she might decide to add an inner conflict in the girl's attitude toward her grandmother—a pull between her original motive of picking up some money and a growing concern for her grandmother as a person. Often, inner conflicts like these are intensifications of feelings the author actually had, but in some cases they are invented on the basis of "what if?" We don't know, of course, if this is how this story actually developed, but it is the way tension is often employed to revitalize an early draft that seems static or lifeless.

One word of warning: When working with internal conflict, be careful not to rely too heavily on your protagonist's thoughts. Long passages in which characters "debate" with themselves begin to sound like explanatory essays. Notice how in "Phoenix" our perception of that inner conflict depends largely on the very end of the story: "Phoenix irons the wrinkled hundred dollar bill with her palm. It smells of lilac. Dumb money, money she knew she would get, making her cry." Since this is money "she knew she would get," there is a streetwise portion of her who was calculating on securing money to survive; yet the lilac smell from her grandmother evokes the love she felt as a child and she is moved to tears. In addition, there is a conflict between the portion that disdains money and material possessions as "dumb" and the portion that didn't hesitate for a moment to accept the new coat and the hundred dollars.

Arousing Curiosity

Curiosity is what keeps a reader reading. It is essential. While it often takes time to develop conflict in a story, you can arouse the reader's curiosity in the very first paragraph.

It is well worth taking a close look at the first paragraph of a story to determine just how it draws the reader in. Here is a quick review:

"Sausage and Beer"

I kept quiet for most of the trip. It was too cold for talk. The car was getting old and the heater hadn't worked for as long as I could remember....There was nothing to do but sit still and wonder what Uncle Theodore would be like.

This story does *not* start with the boy waking up, having breakfast, brushing his teeth, and wondering what to do. It begins with a trip already in progress. And at the end of that first paragraph he (and the reader) wonders what Uncle Theodore will be like.

"Phoenix"

Under the dressing room door, Phoenix sees the saleslady's feet pointed, suspiciously, straight at her. Stiletto pumps and cheap hose—aimed right at her, filthy hippy, sure-fire shoplifter, flower child/slut, rah, rah, rah, ...jeez.

This story does *not* start with Phoenix walking down the street looking for a dress shop. It begins with her already in the dress shop, in the changing room, seeing the feet of the saleslady and imagining what is going on in the woman's mind. We are plunged into the girl's mind and are presented with some intensely mixed feelings about how she is perceived.

"Three Hearts"

The morning after the big snowstorm Mama is real sick.... Mama is lying on the kitchen couch, wrapped in a red robe, rolling her head from side to side, sighing.

Right from the start we know that a mother is "real sick" and that the story is being told from her child's point of view. If it had started with "My wife is real sick," there would be some concern, but the situation would seem less serious having an adult on the scene.

Notice too that it is a specific occasion. Compare that opening with this: "Mama was often sick in the mornings, lying on the couch...." There is less tension in habitual or repeated action than there is in a specific event. In this case, "The morning after the big snowstorm" fixes the event in time and assures us that the story has been launched.

None of these stories, however, relies on that single opening situation to sustain curiosity for the length of a story. Depending on a single dramatic event has its risks. If the reader has the feeling that there are only two possible outcomes, the result will seem too predictable. We see this too often in the sports story that poses the too-simple question, Will they win or lose? Or the mountain-climbing story that asks, once again, Will they make it to the top or not? One solution is to find a conclusion that is not quite one or the other. They lose the game but preserve their sense of honor. The climbers make it to the top but for complex reasons the victory brings no sense of satisfaction.

A more sophisticated approach, however, is to sustain the reader's curiosity through a series of interrelated *dramatic questions*.

Dramatic Questions

Important as it is to arouse the reader's interest in that first paragraph, it is equally important to hold the reader through to the end. The longer the story, the more challenging this becomes. The best solution is to pose a series of **dramatic questions**, each one taking over from the one before.

In "Sausage and Beer," for example, the initial questions have to do with where they are going and what Uncle Theodore will be like. The reader learns that they are going to a hospital, but the uncertainty about the uncle remains. After we meet Uncle Theodore, there is the uneasy question of just how irrational he will be. Back in the car there is still another trip to another new place, the bar. What will it be like? The plot, then, unfolds in stages, each revelation quickly followed by another question until the conclusion.

Melissa Pritchard's "Phoenix" begins with a possible confrontation with the salesgirl, moves directly to a possible confrontation with two drunks fighting on the street, and then presents us with the longer interrelationship with the grandmother. Each of these scenes poses a new set of questions.

Corey's "Three Hearts" is even more dramatic. We move almost at once from the daughter confronting a sick mother to the conflict between the rebellious Eddie and his family. Just as we begin to think that Eddie will be the main concern of the story, we are given a glimpse of the father's conflict with *his* father. Then the story can afford to glide a bit. There is a long scene in which the narrator and her brother Bucky play in the snow and build a kind of igloo. If the story had started with a long, quiet scene like this, we might begin to lose interest, but we remain curious because of the set of unresolved conflicts already described.

Suspense is simply a heightened form of curiosity. It too uses a dramatic question, but the volume has been turned up. That final scene in "Three

Hearts" is a good example of suspense. As the mother—all her maladies forgotten—digs in the snow for her son, we really don't know whether she will succeed or not.

Notice, however, that the suspense is limited to a specific scene. Even in novels, suspense is frequently limited to specific scenes rather than becoming the primary energizing force. So-called suspense thrillers will, of course, continue to be popular just as will television dramas of the same sort. The difficulty with suspense in sophisticated fiction is that it can easily overpower all other literary elements. Characterization, thematic suggestion, and tonal subtlety are apt to be sacrificed. The result is melodrama. But you can avoid that form of simple writing if you create credible characters first and then make sure that the suspenseful scene contributes to the theme of the story rather than dominating it.

Irony and Satire

Irony provides tension in quite a different way. While conflict is developed by generating tension between and within characters, and curiosity is generated by heightening the reader's desire to find out, irony plays the author's apparent intent against the actual meaning. As we will see, this seemingly unrelated technique is also a form of tension that in its own way provides energy and vitality in fiction.

Before one can use irony effectively, it helps to be able to identify examples and understand how it works. Actually there are three different but closely related kinds of irony that appear in fiction and drama.

Verbal irony occurs when characters make statements that are knowingly different or even the opposite of what they really mean. In casual conversation we sometimes call this *sarcasm*, though sarcasm is generally hostile and critical. Irony can take the form of simple understatement, as when someone describes a hurricane as "quite a blow." Stronger irony can be a full reversal of meaning, as if the same character, while watching his house being washed away in the storm, says "Great day for a sail."

Verbal irony in fiction occurs most often in dialogue. It suggests a character who is wry and given to understatement. As such, it is one more way dialogue can help define character. It is also possible to use verbal irony in passages of exposition. As I have already pointed out, author's intrusion is not widely used in contemporary writing, but it is always possible to adopt a wry tone when one does step into a story.

Dramatic irony is similar except that the character making the statement does not understand that it is ironic. The classic example is in Sophocles' play *Oedipus Rex*. When the messenger comes on stage saying "Good news!" those in the audience who know the story wince with the realization that the news will actually be catastrophic. For the others, the impact of the irony will be delayed until later in the play.

Dramatic irony could also be called unconscious irony in that the characters are not aware of it. We see it most often in comedy when characters say things that have a significance they don't yet understand. Another effective use is in first-person stories in which the narrators are not fully aware of how much they are revealing about themselves.

There is a good example of dramatic irony in "Three Hearts." While the two children are playing in the igloo, Bucky tells his sister to get some icicles. The narrator comments,

> The icicles are always my job. Bucky says Eskimo women do all the stuff like that. "Anything they can do without their husband's help, they do. They're brave," he told me once.

Neither of them, of course, is aware that this description of Eskimo women will apply to their mother. At the end of the story she will suddenly forget her ailments and without the help of her husband or her older son plunge into the snow to save Bucky. She will certainly prove herself to be brave. Bucky's comments turn out to be ironic—prophetic without his awareness.

The third type of irony is sometimes called **cosmic irony** or the irony of fate, though it may take the form of a very minor event. It refers to any outcome that is the opposite of normal expectations. One often hears it used in a careless way to describe anything that is unexpected. "Ironically," announcers sometimes say, "the weaker team won." True irony, however, is stronger than that. It is ironic for a composer like Beethoven to lose his hearing or for an Olympic swimmer to drown in his own bathtub. Life occasionally provides ironic twists that are too blatant for fiction. Bad enough that America's first major toxic-waste disaster should actually occur in something known as the Love Canal, but what story writer would have dared call the culprit the Hooker Chemical Corporation?

Ironic reversals in fiction tend to be muted so that they don't become obtrusive. One occurs in "Sausage and Beer" in the scene from which I quoted earlier—the visit with Uncle Theodore. Although one might expect that bizarre behavior would be the most disturbing aspect of such an experience, it is actually Theodore's one moment of lucidity that jolts the boy.

In "Three Hearts" it is ironic that while the mother appears at first to be the weakest and least functional of all the characters, she in fact is the one who through an act of heroism is able to bind the family together.

Irony provides tension in fiction because there is a strain between what is said and what is meant or between what occurs and normal expectations. The reader is caught off balance, jolted.

Satire is almost always rooted in irony. Essentially it is exaggeration for the purpose of ridicule. The writer usually adopts a solemn or serious tone when in fact he or she is making fun of the topic at hand. Occasionally the technique is reversed and a serious subject is treated as if it were high comedy. Either way, there is always a tension established between the apparent tone and the true intent.

Many readers have been introduced to simple satire through magazines such as *Mad* and, later, *National Lampoon*. Neither these nor the satiric sketches one often sees on television are very subtle. In fiction there is a greater range and greater subtlety. Quite often satire is used in a single scene or even with a single detail in a story that is not otherwise satiric. Phoenix, for example, satirizes the attitude of many people toward those in the counterculture by imagining what is going on in the head of the saleslady:

> Stiletto pumps and cheap hose—aimed right at her, filthy hippy, sure-fire shoplifter, flower child/slut....

It is a mild exaggeration, it is critical, and it has a comic touch. These are all the characteristics of satire in a single thought sequence. The same elements can be applied to an entire work.

Satire has a long and important history not only in fiction but in drama and poetry as well. It is often the voice of protest. As such, it sacrifices subtlety of character in order to stress the theme or message. In a sense, it is to mainstream literature what a political poster is to a painting.

If this approach interests you, keep in mind that there are two dangers in the writing of satire. The first is lack of focus. Decide in advance just what kind of person, institution, or tradition you wish to ridicule. Keep your satiric attack precise and detailed.

The other danger is a matter of excess. If your exaggeration becomes extreme, you will find the piece turning into slapstick. Such work may, like cartoons, be very funny, but also like cartoons quickly forgotten. If you want to study (and enjoy) some examples of light but durable satire, read some of the novels of J. P. Marquand or Peter DeVries. For heavier, more biting satire, try George Orwell's *Animal Farm*, a comic but ultimately savage attack on Soviet communism of the 1930s, or Joseph Heller's *Catch-22*, a funny yet bitter view of war.

Casual readers often sense the lack of tension without being able to identify it or suggest a remedy. "It doesn't grab me," they say; or, "It seems kind of flat." These are not literarily precise statements, but they are worth taking seriously. Better yet, try to evaluate your own first draft before anyone else reads it. Does it have the energy, the vitality needed to hold a reader who might have other things to do?

If not, see if there is the potential for at least implied conflict between two individuals or between one person and a group. Or is the story better suited for an internal conflict within a single character? Check to make sure that you have aroused the reader's curiosity early in the story and have provided a few dramatic questions to maintain interest. And if you have made use of suspense or shock, make sure you haven't overdone it.

If the story is critical of particular types of people or institutions or traditions, should it be presented with irony or even pushed into satire? Remember that in doing this, the story will become less penetrating in character development since satiric characterization stresses surface appearance; but it may create the result you want.

When you are starting a new story, tension will not be your first concern. Plot, character, and theme are quite enough to deal with at that stage. But once you have the basic framework clearly in mind, make sure you have provided enough tension to give your story a sense of vitality and life.

20
A Story by John Updike

Man and Daughter in the Cold

"Look at that girl ski!" The exclamation arose at Ethan's side as if, in the disconnecting cold, a rib of his had cried out; but it was his friend, friend and fellow-teacher, an inferior teacher but superior skier, Matt Langley, admiring Becky, Ethan's own daughter. It took an effort, in this air like slices of transparent metal interposed everywhere, to make these connections and to relate the young girl, her round face red with windburn as she skimmed down the run-out slope, to himself. She was his daughter, age thirteen. Ethan had twin sons, two years younger, and his attention had always been focussed on their skiing, on the irksome comedy of their double needs—the four boots to lace, the four mittens to find—and then their cute yet grim competition as now one and now the other gained the edge in the expertise of geländesprungs and slalom form. On their trips north into the mountains, Becky had come along for the ride. "Look how solid she is," Matt went on. "She doesn't cheat on it like your boys—those feet are absolutely together." The girl, grinning as if she could hear herself praised, wiggle-waggled to a flashy stop that sprayed snow over the men's ski tips.

"Where's Mommy?" she asked.

Ethan answered, "She went with the boys into the lodge. They couldn't take it." Their sinewy little male bodies had no insulation; weeping and shivering, they had begged to go in after a single T-bar run.

"What sissies," Becky said.

Matt said, "This wind is wicked. And it's picking up. You should have been here at nine; Lord, it was lovely. All that fresh powder, and not a stir of wind."

Becky told him, "Dumb Tommy couldn't find his mittens, we spent an *hour* looking, and then Daddy got the Jeep stuck." Ethan, alerted now for signs of the wonderful in his daughter, was struck by the strange fact that she was making conversation. Unafraid, she was talking to Matt without her father's intercession.

"Mr. Langley was saying how nicely you were skiing."

"You're Olympic material, Becky."

The girl perhaps blushed; but her cheeks could get no redder. Her eyes, which, were she a child, she would have instantly averted, remained a second on Matt's face, as if to estimate how much he meant it. "It's easy down here," Becky said. "It's babyish."

Ethan asked, "Do you want to go up to the top?" He was freezing standing still, and the gondola would be sheltered from the wind.

Her eyes shifted to his, with another unconsciously thoughtful hesitation. "Sure. If you want to."

"Come along, Matt?"

"Thanks, no. It's too rough for me; I've had enough runs. This is the trouble with January—once it stops snowing, the wind comes up. I'll keep Elaine company in the lodge." Matt himself had no wife, no children. At thirty-eight, he was as free as his students, as light on his skis and as full of brave know-how. "In case of frostbite," he shouted after them, "rub snow on it."

Becky effortlessly skated ahead to the lift shed. The encumbered motion of walking on skis, not natural to him, made Ethan feel asthmatic: a fish out of water. He touched his parka pocket, to check that the inhalator was there. As a child he had imagined death as something attacking from outside, but now he saw that it was carried within; we nurse it for years, and it grows. The clock on the lodge wall said a quarter to noon. The giant thermometer read two degrees above zero. The racks outside were dense as hedges with idle skis. Crowds, any sensation of crowding or delay, quickened his asthma; as therapy he imagined the emptiness, the blue freedom, at the top of the mountain. The clatter of machinery inside the shed was comforting, and enough teen-age boys were boarding gondolas to make the ascent seem normal and safe. Ethan's breathing eased. Becky proficiently handed her poles to the loader points up; her father was always caught by surprise, and often as not fumbled the little maneuver of letting his skis be taken from him. Until, five years ago, he had become an assistant professor at a New Hampshire college an hour to the south, he had never skied; he had lived in those Middle Atlantic cities where snow, its moment of virgin beauty by, is only an encumbering nuisance, a threat of suffocation. Whereas his children had grown up on skis.

Alone with his daughter in the rumbling isolation of the gondola, he wanted to explore her, and found her strange—strange in her uninquisitive child's silence, her accustomed poise in this ascending egg of metal. A dark figure with spreading legs veered out of control beneath them, fell forward, and vanished. Ethan cried out, astonished, scandalized; he imagined the man had buried himself alive. Becky was barely amused, and looked away before the dark spots struggling in the drift were lost from sight. As if she might know, Ethan asked, "Who was that?"

"Some kid." Kids, her tone suggested, were in plentiful supply; one could be spared.

He offered to dramatize the adventure ahead of them: "Do you think we'll freeze at the top?"

"Not exactly."

"What do you think it'll be like?"

"Miserable."

"Why are we doing this, do you think?"

"Because we paid the money for the all-day lift ticket."

"Becky, you think you're pretty smart, don't you?"

"Not really."

The gondola rumbled and lurched into the shed at the top; an attendant opened the door, and there was a howling mixed of wind and of boys whooping to keep warm. He was roughly handed two pairs of skis, and the handler, muffled to the eyes with a scarf, stared as if amazed that Ethan was so old. All the others struggling into skis in the lee of the shed were adolescent boys. Students: After fifteen years of teaching, Ethan tended to flinch from youth—its harsh noises, its cheerful rapacity, its cruel onward flow as one class replaced another, ate a year of his life, and was replaced by another.

Away from the shelter of the shed, the wind was a high monotonous pitch of pain. His cheeks instantly ached, and the hinges linking the elements of his face seemed exposed. His septum tingled like glass—the rim of a glass being rubbed by a moist finger to produce a note. Drifts ribbed the trail, obscuring Becky's ski tracks seconds after she made them, and at each push through the heaped snow his scope of breathing narrowed. By the time he reached the first steep section, the left half of his back hurt as it did only in the panic of a full asthmatic attack, and his skis, ignored, too heavy to manage, spread and swept him toward a snowbank at the side of the trail. He was bent far forward but kept his balance; the snow kissed his face lightly, instantly, all over; he straightened up, refreshed by the shock, thankful not to have lost a ski. Down the slope Becky had halted and was staring upward at him, worried. A huge blowing feather, a partition of snow, came between them. The cold, unprecedented in his experience, shone through his clothes like furious light, and as he rummaged through his parka for the inhalator he seemed to be searching glass shelves backed by a black wall. He found it, its icy plastic the touch of life, a clumsy key to his insides. Gasping, he exhaled, put it into his mouth, and inhaled; the isoproterenol spray, chilled into drops, opened his lungs enough for him to call to his daughter, "Keep moving! I'll catch up!"

Solid on her skis, she swung down among the moguls and wind-bared ice, and became small, and again waited. The moderate slope seemed a cliff; if he fell and sprained anything, he would freeze. His entire body would become locked tight against air and light and thought. His legs trembled; his breath moved in and out of a narrow slot beneath the pain in his back. The cold and blowing snow all around him constituted an immense crowding, but there was no way out of this white cave but to slide downward toward the dark spot that was his daughter. He had forgotten all his lessons. Leaning backward in an infant's tense snowplow, he floundered through alternating powder and ice.

"You O.K., Daddy?" Her stare was wide, its fright underlined by a pale patch on her cheek.

He used the inhalator again and gave himself breath to tell her, "I'm fine. Let's get down."

In this way, in steps of her leading and waiting, they worked down the mountain, out of the worst wind, into the lower trail that ran between birches and hemlocks. The cold had the quality not of absence but of force: an inverted burning. The last time Becky stopped and waited, the colorless crescent on her scarlet cheek disturbed him, reminded him of some injunction, but he could find in his brain, whittled to a dim determination to persist, only the advice to keep going, toward shelter and warmth. She told him, at a division of trails, "This is the easier way."

"Let's go the quicker way," he said, and in this last descent recovered the rhythm—knees together, shoulders facing the valley, weight forward as if in the moment of release from a diving board—not a resistance but a joyous acceptance of falling. They reached the base lodge, and with unfeeling hands removed their skis. Pushing into the cafeteria, Ethan saw in the momentary mirror of the door window that his face was a spectre's; chin, nose, and eyebrows had retained the snow from that near-fall near the top. "Becky, look," he said, turning in the crowded warmth and clatter inside the door. "I'm a monster."

"I know, your face was absolutely white, I didn't know whether to tell you or not. I thought it might scare you."

He touched the pale patch on her cheek. "Feel anything?"

"No."

"Damn. I should have rubbed snow on it."

Matt and Elaine and the twins, flushed and stripped of their parkas, had eaten lunch; shouting and laughing with a strange guilty shrillness, they said that there had been repeated loudspeaker announcements not to go up to the top without face masks, because of frostbite. They had expected Ethan and Becky to come back down on the gondola, as others had, after tasting the top.

"It never occurred to us," Ethan said. He took the blame upon himself by adding, "I wanted to see the girl ski."

Their common adventure, and the guilt of his having given her frostbite, bound Becky and Ethan together in complicity for the rest of the day. They arrived home as sun was leaving even the tips of the hills; Elaine had invited Matt to supper, and while the windows of the house burned golden Ethan shovelled out the Jeep. The house was a typical New Hampshire farmhouse, less than two miles from the college, on the side of a hill, overlooking what had been a pasture, with the usual capacious porch running around three sides, cluttered with cordwood and last summer's lawn furniture. The woodsy sheltered scent of these porches, the sense of rural waste space, never failed to please Ethan, who had been raised in a Newark half-house, then a West Side apartment, and just before college a row house in Baltimore, with his grandparents. The wind had been left behind in the mountains. The air was as still as the stars. Shovelling the light dry snow became a lazy dance. But when he bent suddenly, his knees creaked, and his breathing shortened so that he paused. A sudden rectangle of light was flung from the shadows of the porch. Becky came out into the cold with him. She was carrying a lawn rake.

He asked her, "Should you be out again? How's your frostbite?" Though she was a distance away, there was no need, in the immaculate air, to raise his voice.

"It's O.K. It kind of tingles. And under my chin. Mommy made me put on a scarf."

"What's the lawn rake for?"

"It's a way you can make a path. It really works."

"O.K., you make a path to the garage and after I get my breath I'll see if I can get the Jeep back in."

"Are you having asthma?"

"A little."

"We were reading about it in biology. Dad, see, it's kind of a tree inside you, and every branch has a little ring of muscle around it, and they tighten." From her gestures in the dark she was demonstrating, with mittens on.

What she described, of course, was classic unalloyed asthma, whereas his was shading into emphysema, which could only worsen. But he liked being lectured to—preferred it, indeed, to lecturing—and as the minutes of companionable silence with his daughter passed he took inward notes on the bright quick impressions flowing over him like a continuous voice. The silent cold. The stars. Orion behind an elm. Minute scintillae in the snow at his feet. His daughter's strange black bulk against the white; the solid grace that had stolen upon her. The conspiracy of love. His father and he shovelling the car free from a sudden unwelcome storm in Newark, instantly gray with soot, the undercurrent of desperation, his father a salesman and must get to Camden. Got to get to Camden, boy, get to Camden or bust. Dead of a heart attack at forty-seven. Ethan tossed a shovelful into the air so the scintillae flashed in the steady golden chord from the house windows. Elaine and Matt sitting flushed at the lodge table, parkas off, in deshabille, as if sitting up in bed. Matt's way of turning a half circle on the top of a mogul, light as a diver. The cancerous unwieldiness of Ethan's own skis. His jealousy of his students, the many-headed immortality of their annual renewal. The flawless tall cruelty of the stars. Orion intertwined with the silhouetted elm. A black tree inside him. His daughter, busily sweeping with the rake, childish yet lithe, so curiously demonstrating this preference for his company. Feminine of her to forgive him her frostbite. Perhaps, flattered on skis, felt the cold her element. Her woman-hood soon enough to be smothered in warmth. A plow a mile away painstak-ingly scraped. He was missing the point of the lecture. The point was unstated: an absence. He was looking upon his daughter as a woman but without lust. The music around him was being produced, in the zero air, like a finger on crystal, by this hollowness, this generosity of negation. Without lust, without jealousy. Space seemed love, bestowed to be free in, and coldness the price. He felt joined to the great dead whose words it was his duty to teach.

The Jeep came up unprotestingly from the fluffy snow. It looked happy to be penned in the garage with Elaine's station wagon, and the skis, and the oiled chain saw, and the power mower dreamlessly waiting for spring. Ethan was happy, precariously so, so that rather than break he uttered a sound: "Becky?"

"Yeah?"

"You want to know what else Mr. Langley said?"

"What?" They trudged toward the porch, up the path the gentle rake had cleared.

"He said you ski better than the boys."

"I bet," she said, and raced to the porch, and in the precipitate way, evasive and female and pleased, that she flung herself to the top step he glimpsed something generic and joyous, a pageant that would leave him behind.

21
CHARACTERIZATION

Characterization as an illusion based on three elements: Consistency of behavior and attitudes, complexity, and individuality. Techniques of developing these qualities including direct analysis, significant action, dialogue, thoughts, and physical description. Blending these various techniques.

Characterization, like all aspects of fiction, is illusion. When we as readers feel that a fictional character is "convincing," "vivid," or "realistic," it is not because that character resembles someone familiar; the illusion we have is of meeting and coming to know someone new.

It is not necessary, for example, to be a skier or a father to appreciate and understand Ethan in "Man and Daughter in the Cold." We don't have to be a young woman living an alternative life-style to respond to Phoenix in the story of the same name. Nor is it necessary to have known mental patients to have the illusion of having just met one in "Sausage and Beer." In each case, our sense of having come to know someone new is based not on familiarity but on the way that character is revealed in the course of the story.

Consider for a moment the full range of characters you feel that you have "met" through fiction. Stories and novels have allowed you to cross the barriers of time, age, nationality, social class, sex, and race. The illusion of reality is in no way dependent upon having been an old Caribbean fisherman, a nineteenth-century Russian countess, or a British country squire.

This illusion, or "willing suspension of disbelief," as it is sometimes called, has enormous power. How is it achieved? There are three elements involved: consistency, complexity, and individuality.

In practice, of course, making a character "come alive" on the page is not at all this mechanical. Most writers borrow heavily from people they have known and then metamorphose the details in a variety of ways, both consciously and unconsciously. This is the way they find those hundreds of minute details that go into a finely drawn character. But the reason for this dependence on experience is that it is the most natural way to develop consistency, complexity, and individuality.

Consistency

In real life we come to expect a certain consistency in our friends—patterns of behavior, outlook, dress, and the like. In spite of variations, some people tend to be naturally generous or constitutionally sloppy or ambitious.

In addition, these characteristics tend to be interlocked. If a man is an insurance executive, we don't expect him to be politically radical or to have a long black beard or to speak in incomplete sentences prefaced with "like" or to race his Harley Davidson on Sunday afternoons. It might be nice if he did, of course; and making such a contradiction plausible could be the start of a story. But that comes under the heading of *complexity*, which I shall turn to shortly. The point here is that consistency of character is one of the basic assumptions we make about people in real life, and it is also the fundamental assumption upon which fictional characterization is built.

In simple fiction, consistency is pushed to the point of predictability—and monotony. We know, for example, that Dick Tracy will never under any circumstances take a bribe or punch a sweet little old lady in the nose. It is most unlikely that Blondie will turn junkie. And Tarzan is not going to start wearing a suit. For many readers, these rigid conventions destroy the illusion of credibility; yet for others the illusion is so strong that they send letters and presents to these fictional characters in care of their local paper, utterly confusing art and life.

In sophisticated fiction, it is the minor characters who are usually the most consistent. The heavyset owner of the bar in "Sausage and Beer" has some important lines, but he is what E. M. Forster calls a "flat" character, one who is there merely to serve a function and so is not developed. He is completely consistent. In "Phoenix" the grandfather is present in a number of scenes and is important as visible evidence of how both he and his wife have aged, but he is unchanging and we see only one aspect of him. He is as "flat" as some detail from the setting.

A certain degree of consistency is necessary in major characters as well. As we have seen, Phoenix has mixed feelings about her grandmother—a genuine fondness combined with a slightly cynical recognition that a quick visit will probably net her some needed cash. In the interest of consistency, she still has mixed feelings at the end of the story. She doesn't fling her arms around her grandmother and refuse the gift, nor does she trash the place and take the silver. Either of those alternatives would violate consistency of character. In the same way, Ethan, the father in "Man and Daughter in the Cold," isn't suddenly converted into a daring skier by his daughter's example.

Complexity

To achieve complex characterization, you have to develop more than one aspect of a character. You can do this by establishing a pattern, countering it in some way, and showing how both elements are a part of the whole character. Or you may choose to reveal some previously hidden aspect of character.

You will have to go beyond the stereotypes of film and television, of course. We are all familiar with the hard-driving businessman who has a suppressed longing for simple pleasures and the man-hating woman who turns out to be secretly in love. To achieve real complexity, don't settle for patterns you have seen before.

In "Sausage and Beer," the complexity of Uncle Theodore takes the form of alternation: He appears at first to be quite sane and then reveals himself to be hopelessly out of contact with the real world. When, at the end of the visit, the boy assumes that a polite lie will do as well for a mad uncle as it does for any other relative, Theodore has an unnerving moment of lucidity.

More basic to the development of the story, however, is the complexity that I hope is apparent in the father. Before the visit, he is austere and distant. He is not the kind of man who confides anything. But visiting the hospital is an ordeal he shares with his son. After that he invites the boy to share a private corner of his life. The bar is where he once played chess with his brother, and it has apparently been a place of solace for him in recent years. There he reveals the warmer, more compassionate side of his nature.

Melissa Pritchard's story "Phoenix" is relatively short and in some ways straightforward. Yet there is a deceptive complexity in her central character. Although the complexity runs through the entire story, dramatized in the split between her childhood name of Mary Lou and her chosen name of Phoenix, it is highlighted at the end. As she spreads that hundred dollar bill and smells the lilac perfume her grandmother uses, the full measure of her mixed feelings is dramatized. That ending is a sudden revelation of her **ambivalence**, a mix of two opposing emotions. This is one of those revelations that are shared by the character and the reader at the same instant.

As I have already pointed out, the character of Ethan in "Man and Daughter in the Cold" does not go through some unrealistically radical change. What we see at the end of the story is not the creation of an Olympic skier or, conversely, a total coward who has to be carried down the slope by his daughter. Our insight into his character is both more subtle and more penetrating than that. We see at first that for all his admiration of his daughter, he is also jealous of her skill as a skier and, by extension, the energy and vitality of all young people. Finally, however, he recognizes himself as a part of a grand "pageant," the new generation surpassing the old in an endless sequence. The story is one more example of the fact that what we sometimes describe as character change is often a matter of a significant shift in attitude or insight.

To achieve complexity in characterization, then, you have to probe below the surface. Most stories provide some type of fresh insight—either one that the reader shares with the character, as in the stories already discussed, or an aspect that only the reader fully appreciates. If the change is too subtle or obscure, readers may have the feeling that the story lacks *closure*, that sense of being fully completed. "I'm not sure what the point is," they are apt to say. But on the other hand, if the change is too great or unconvincing, readers will feel that the character lacks consistency. "I just don't believe she would behave like that," they say, and the story has failed. The writer has to establish a delicate balance.

Individuality

Some characters are memorable and some are not. Occasionally we recall a particular character long after the plot has been forgotten. In other cases we have to ask questions like, "Wasn't there a father in the story somewhere?" or "I remember a brother, but how did he fit in?" The characters who stick in our memory are those that have a high degree of individuality.

If you write about two typical college students who share a typical college room, it is quite likely that the reader will soon lose interest even if these characters are based on individuals you know. And if you present a family that on the surface resembles those that appear so often in television sitcoms and in commercials, it is unlikely that any of those characters will linger in your reader's memory.

Often it is the unlikely occupation, the unusual commitment, the striking disability that serves to make a character vivid and memorable. A young woman who is the epitome of what we think of as a hippie is more striking than one who has simply dropped out of school. An uncle in a mental hospital is more distinctive than a mere eccentric relative who joins the family for dinner. Imagine how much would be lost in the story "Three Hearts" if the family were conventional and well adjusted.

Be careful, however, not to overdo the attempt to be different. There comes a point when it turns artificial and unconvincing. An inconsequential tale about two college roommates is not going to be improved by being metamorphosed into an inconsequential tale about two hunchbacks living in an abandoned fun house on the eve of World War III. Individuality for its own sake becomes a **gimmick**, a contrived and superficial attention-getter.

The most effective examples of individuality are credible and add to our understanding of character. In "Phoenix" the author is careful not to present the stereotype of a young hippie. The girl certainly looks like a cartoon of the type, but the author quickly gives us a glimpse into Phoenix's background and, at the same time, her mixed feelings about her free but perilous lifestyle. When she first sees her grandmother she sees the woman as the "good, firm land, like the one place she's found safe in weeks...." She is also described as "Climbing past her parents and unremarkable childhood, going back in perfect time." Her memorable appearance, then, is no longer just an attention-getter. It is a part of what makes Phoenix an interesting and complex character.

Individualization can be achieved with a relatively minor detail. Ethan, the father in "Man and Daughter in the Cold," is an enthusiastic skier, but he also has a serious asthmatic condition. He relies on his inhalator. Early in the story he "touches his parka pocket" to make sure that it is there; he is soon forced to use it before he can call his daughter; and then he must use it again. At first reading, this seems like simply an odd little dependency, a way of individualizing him as a character; but toward the end of the story we learn that his condition "was shading into emphysema, which could only worsen." What began as a minor detail takes on new significance with repetition and eventually highlights his dread of aging and his fear of death.

Direct Analysis of Character

Consistency, complexity, and individuality are the goals one works for in creating fictional characters. The techniques one uses to achieve these goals are more numerous. In addition to **exposition** (direct analysis), one can use a character's actions, dialogue, thoughts, and physical details. Each of these deserves a close look.

The direct approach is tempting because through exposition you can cover a great deal of material very quickly. Suppose, for example, "Man and Daughter in the Cold" had started this way:

> Ethan admired his daughter's skiing ability, but in some ways he was jealous of her youth and vitality. Later that day he would see her as a part of a pageant that would soon leave him behind.

This little paragraph presents a great deal of information about the character that the reader of the original version has to gather over the course of several pages. But what appears to be an advantage has serious liabilities.

First, an opening like this deprives the reader of the sense of discovery. The language of exposition, remember, is closer to that of case histories and newspaper articles than it is to fiction. In the actual opening, Updike begins not with analysis but with the exclamation of a minor character: "Look at that girl ski!" This assures us that she really is a good skier. Only later do we realize that it reflects the father's admiration too. The author has chosen to let us discover the significance of the father's admiration without laying it out for us in the opening page.

Another disadvantage of the analytical first paragraph is that it slows the pace. A line of dialogue like this one or a sudden bit of action gets the story moving right at the start.

The greatest danger of using too much exposition in presenting a character, however, is that you risk laying out too much of the theme. This is particularly true with statements about the protagonist. The analytical passage I invented, for example, not only reveals character in the manner of a case history, it reveals a good portion of the theme itself. The reader would lose the sense of discovery so necessary in good fiction.

This is not to say that direct analysis of character is to be avoided at all costs. It can be a useful way to reveal some minor aspect that simply isn't worth the space it would take to imply through action or dialogue. Such passages are rarely found in introductions. Instead they usually appear as unobtrusive comments in the body of the story. In Corey's "Three Hearts," for example, the author informs us through the narrator, "Mama and Daddy can't manage Eddie."

She probably wouldn't have been so direct if that had been the theme of the story, but Eddie is a minor character in a story essentially about the mother. The direct statement simply saves time. John Updike, more inclined to analyze than many authors, tells us directly that Ethan feels "jealousy of his students, the many-headed immortality of their annual renewal." This comes close to his theme—Ethan's concern about his own mortality. But we do not depend solely on such statements. The bulk of what we learn about Ethan is unfolded through Ethan's actions, his dialogue, and his thoughts.

Longer samples of exposition analyzing character are occasionally found in the novels of certain contemporary authors like Margaret Drabble, but it is an approach that is more closely associated with the nineteenth century than with contemporary work.

The Use of Significant Action

In simple fiction, we rely heavily on action to judge character. This is partly because most simple fiction is dominated by plot—a character does or does not kill the shark, find the murderer, deceive his partner. In sophisticated fiction, however, character development stems not only from major events but from subtle actions as well.

In "Sausage and Beer," for example, we are informed that the father is a withdrawn character by the fact that he gives his son so little information on the ride to the hospital. But the story doesn't stop with the visit. We learn more about the father's character when he invites his son to go to the bar. In fact, that bit of action is essential to the reader's understanding of the father as essentially a kind and loving man.

The development of the mother's character in Deborah Corey's "Three Hearts" relies even more on action. In our first view of her she is "lying on the kitchen couch, wrapped in a red robe, rolling her head from side to side, sighing." This is obviously not just a case of lethargy. She is ill. From that point, we think of her as incapable of managing this largely dysfunctional family. But at the end of the story we see her digging in the snow in a frenzy. She, not her husband or her dissolute son, is the one who saves Bucky. Without crossing over into melodrama, the story reveals her hidden strength through action.

The Use of Dialogue and Thoughts

Dialogue often is used in such close conjunction with action that it is hard to consider them separately. That long drive to the hospital in "Sausage and Beer" is a bit of action that presents us with our first view of the father, but the true import of that drive is in the frustratingly terse comments of the father. Either he is simply insensitive to his son's bewilderment or he is tense. His capacity for warmth and kindness is finally revealed toward the end of the story by the way he invites his son to the bar—both a significant action and a revealing bit of dialogue.

John Updike in "Man and Daughter in the Cold" relies heavily on dialogue to reveal the character of Becky, the 13-year-old daughter. As I pointed out earlier, our first view of her is not through description but indirectly through an exclamation of admiration: " 'Look at that girl ski!' " The speaker is a minor character, himself an expert skier. Later he elaborates: " 'She doesn't cheat on it like your boys—those feet are absolutely together.' " On a literal level, of course, he is only describing her skill at the sport; but right from the start we sense that she is competent and sure of herself.

She also has a sense of pride in her skills, even a cockiness. Referring to the lower slope, she says " 'It's babyish.' " And when they look down from the gondola and see someone take a terrible spill, she shrugs it off with the comment, " 'Some kid.' " The author adds that "her tone suggested that [kids] were in plentiful supply; one could be spared."

But Becky is not a self-centered egotist. She is deeply concerned with her father as they work down the slope in the dangerously bitter wind. " 'You O.K., Daddy?' " she asks. And later she suggests the easiest route down. Once back home she gives him a little lecture about how asthma tightens the bronchial passageways. Although he knows more about his condition than she does, her genuine concern is appreciated. As readers, we see another dimension of her character—her capacity to feel sympathy and warmth for others.

There are, incidentally, certain **conventions** connected with dialogue that readers generally expect. Conventions in writing are not rules, but they are patterns that are widely followed. If you decide to ignore them, make sure you have a good reason.

First, most stories use quotation marks around words spoken out loud and none around thoughts. The story "Phoenix" is a rare exception—perhaps in part because it uses so little dialogue. Readers are used to seeing full quotation marks to indicate spoken lines and apostrophes to set off quotations within quotations, as in the following:

> "He really liked the design," she said. " 'It's the best we've seen
> so far, ' he told me. Those were his exact words."

Second, most writers indent the first line of speech of each new speaker. This may appear to waste paper, but readers are used to it both in fiction and in drama. One advantage of regular indentation is that in lengthy exchanges between two characters, the reader does not have to be told each time which one spoke.

Third, "she said," "he said," and "I said" are used more like punctuation marks than like phrases, and for this reason they are repeated frequently. The prohibition against redundancy just doesn't apply to them. In fact, it sounds amateurish to keep using substitutions like "she retorted," "he sneered," "she questioned," "he hissed." They become obtrusive.

In this connection, guard against adding modifiers to "said." There is usually no reason to write "said angrily" or "said shyly" since almost always the tone is clear from the dialogue itself. If you really have to reverse the reader's first assumption, it may be more effective to use a separate phrase, as in,

> "Boy, are you dumb!" she said, rolling her eyes, but her tone was
> still loving.

Fourth, as I have suggested earlier, dialogue is rarely aided by phonetic spelling. There are some really successful exceptions, but in most cases it is possible to catch the flavor of an accent or dialect with appropriate phrasing rather than tinkering with conventional spelling. If you want to give the impression of a foreign language being spoken, consider the value of translating a few foreign idioms directly into English, as Hemingway occasionally did with his Spanish-speaking characters.

Finally, one way to compress dialogue and yet still provide a general sense of what is being said is to use **indirect discourse**. For example: "She said that she had missed the flight, that she would be there as soon as she could make another reservation." This may eliminate a paragraph of unnecessary dialogue. Indirect discourse can also be more extended and can use actual phrasing from the conversation without quoting directly and without using quotation marks:

> He greeted his sister warmly, remarking on how tall she had grown, how sophisticated she had become. How long, he asked, had it been since they had seen each other?

Thoughts are equally valuable as a method of revealing character and attitude. Thoughts can be presented in a way that sounds almost like dialogue without quotation marks; or, at the other end of the spectrum, they can seem closer to indirect discourse or even to exposition.

Here, for example, is a passage in which the thoughts are really an unspoken dialogue or, since there is only one speaker, a silent monologue:

> How strange, he thought, to have my own daughter lecturing me. But better, really, than when I have to lecture. Such warmth in her voice—warmth in this chilled air. How bright the stars are! There's Orion behind the elm. The snowflakes like sparks at her feet.

Here is a similar passage in which thoughts are not directly quoted. Notice that the first person has been replaced with the third person. The effect is more like indirect discourse.

> He found it strange to have his own daughter lecturing to him. Still, it was better than when he had to do the lecturing. He was moved by the warmth in her voice—a sharp contrast with the chilled air. He was struck by how bright the stars were. It was a pleasure to recognize Orion behind the elm. And there at her feet, he was dazzled by the snowflakes like tiny sparks.

These are both paraphrases of a passage from John Updike's "Man and Daughter." His own version is a combination of the two—starting with a statement of fact (exposition) and then presenting the thoughts indirectly in the third person as "inward notes":

> But he liked being lectured to—preferred it, indeed, to lecturing— and as the minutes of companionable silence with his daughter passed he took inward notes on the bright quick impressions flowing over him like a continuous voice. The silent cold. The stars. Orion behind an elm. Minute scintillae in the snow at his feet.

One word of warning: Be careful not to use dialogue or thoughts unrealistically to present facts to the reader. It is not at all convincing to have a character think, "I am 23 years old, tall, handsome, and was born in Omaha." And unless you're working with comedy, it doesn't help to borrow what has become a detective-story convention: "What's a tall, handsome, 23-year-old kid from Omaha doing in a situation like this?" Both dialogue and thoughts have to be motivated by the situation, not merely by the author's need to get the facts across.

Generally speaking, if dialogue is merely filling space and not contributing to the reader's understanding of character, replace it with a sentence or two of exposition. Whole blocks of trivial conversation can be condensed with a brief statement of fact like: "They greeted her warmly," "They talked of other matters for over an hour," or "They lingered at the door, saying their goodbyes." Far better to use summaries like these than to weigh your story down with conversation that is only padding.

When you do use dialogue, make every line reflect the character of the speaker and, whenever possible, provide new insights.

Using Physical Details

In the nineteenth century, stories and novels often provided lengthy descriptions of the main characters. This is rarely done today. Solid blocks of physical description tend to slow the story and break the illusion of the fiction. They are particularly cumbersome at the beginning of the work. Instead, contemporary authors tend to provide physical details in more fragmentary form and well after the story has been launched.

In "Sausage and Beer," for example, the father's appearance is left largely to the reader's imagination. There would be no need for the son to remark on his father's appearance, and the story is told almost entirely from the boy's point of view. Uncle Theodore, on the other hand, makes a dramatic visual impression on the boy, so it is natural to provide a detailed description:

> He was a great, sagging man. His jowls hung loose, his shoulders were massive but rounded like a dome, his hands were attached like brass weights on the ends of swinging pendulums.

The details here are not arbitrary; they provide some sense of what life is like for those who have spent years in an institution.

In "Phoenix," the story depends heavily on the contrast between the girl's present life–style and what she was like as the conventional Mary Lou. Rather than open the story with a heavy-handed and possibly patronizing description, however, the author has ingeniously provided a description by having the girl imagine what is going through the mind of the saleslady: "...filthy hippy, sure-fire shoplifter, flower child/slut...." For contrast, we are later given a glimpse of her childhood, again through her own thoughts, recalling her breakfasts with her grandmother, sipping "coffee cut with milk in a doll-sized, pink and gold cup."

When a fictional character is based on a person you know, should you describe the model directly? Generally speaking, it is a good idea to metamorphose the appearance for the same reason that you should give the character a fictional name from the start. But once you have visualized the character, don't hesitate to slip in physical details if they can aid in characterization.

In the case of Uncle Theodore, the actual uncle was tall, lean, and rather distinguished looking. Since I wanted to contrast the two brothers and also to stress the debilitating effect of living in an institution year after year, I borrowed the sagging physique of a stranger I once glimpsed in a hotel lobby years before.

Physical descriptions that help a reader to understand a character are not limited to physique and clothes. They may also include the house she or he lives in, the furnishings, the make and age of the car, the pet, the prints or paintings on the wall. Just remember, though, that physical details which do not add to characterization and are not essential to the plot are mere fillers. Providing details that do not contribute simply clutter the story and slow it down. Make every detail count, even if the suggestion is too subtle to be perceived on first reading.

Blending the Techniques

When we analyze how characters are revealed in fiction, the process seems enormously complex. The same is true when we explain any artistic technique in abstract terms, whether it be dance, music, or some aspect of painting. Actual practice requires a blend of unconscious decision-making along with conscious knowledge of craftsmanship.

The best way to develop what we think of as an "intuitive" ability to create believable characters in fiction is to read as much as possible. After an initial reading of a story for pleasure, go back over it and examine as a fellow writer just what the balance is between consistency and complexity. How is the character individualized? And how is the character revealed? Can you find samples of direct analysis on the part of the author? Could they have been avoided? How much has action contributed to your understanding? Or were dialogue and thoughts employed to a great extent? Exactly how much of a description were you given and how much is your impression based on the objects associated with that character? This is *active reading*—not for course credit but for your own development.

When you turn to the actual process of starting to write a new story, consider your characters carefully before you even outline the plot. Do you really know them? If you keep a journal, you may want to use it to record significant facts about the major characters in a new story: What kind of childhoods did they have? What kinds of parents? Where do they live and how do they spend their days—school? job? waiting for something to happen? What kind of music do they like and what kinds of people do they enjoy? You should be able to write a page or so about the protagonist of any new story. You may not use more than half of the details you devise, but it helps if you have far more information about a character than is needed. Conversely, there is no kind of action, dialogue, or thoughts that can successfully reveal a character who is not yet fully formed in your own mind.

Finally, after having completed your first draft, you may wish to review your work from the point of view of craft to make sure your characters are consistent yet complex, and that they have individuality. It is at this point that you can adjust the ways in which you have revealed your characters. Try to be as objective with your own work as you were when examining published stories.

In many cases the literary sophistication of a story is developed more from characterization than from complexity of plot. For this reason, those goals of consistency, complexity, and individuality will continue to be major concerns for you as long as you write fiction.

22
SETTING

The impact of immediate surroundings as seen through specific visual details. The geographic setting: "real" versus imagined places. Time—historical period, season, and hour of day. Revising the setting—heightening and muting of details.

A story seems strangely abstract and unconvincing until we can visualize where it is taking place. **Setting** or **orientation** is what fixes a work of fiction in place and time. Readers tend to be impatient about this, wanting to know about the immediate surroundings fairly soon. If you delay, it should be for a good reason.

Don't forget that setting involves not only a visual impression of where one is; it may also involve time—the hour of the day, the season, or occasionally the historical period.

Some stories, of course, make scant use of setting, but even the most dreamlike fantasies usually provide, as do dreams themselves, details that help readers to imagine themselves in a specific place. Without such details the characters may be unconvincing, and the story will fail to establish the illusion of reality. As writers, we have to judge which aspect of the setting is important for a particular story and how to present it convincingly.

The Impact of Immediate Surroundings

"Where am I?" is the stereotyped cry of those who are regaining consciousness. It is also the instinctive question of readers who have just begun a new story or novel. This is why most stories establish the immediate setting early. Like a stage set, the surroundings help to place readers in the story. A particular house, a room in that house, a field, a beach, a factory assembly line—these and countless other settings not only help to start a story and make the opening scene come alive, but they may contribute to characterization and theme as well.

Watch out, however, for the opening paragraph that is a solid block of descriptive exposition. Get your situation launched, have your characters do something or say something that engages the reader. *Then* work in where this is taking place. Often the setting can be presented in a series of separate details rather than as a single paragraph. "Sausage and Beer," for example, presents father and son first. It is not until the second page that the reader is told, "We were well out in the New England countryside now." In a similar way, "Three Hearts" begins with the fact that "Mama is real sick" and gives a fair amount of information about the family before the narrator presses her face against the window to look out at the snow that is to become a major element in the story.

The key to making the immediate surroundings vivid and convincing is *specifics*. Just as poems depend on the freshness of images, fictional scenes depend on precise, carefully selected visual details.

Read the following two descriptive passages.

> (A) It was a large, sparsely furnished room. A number of people wandered about, but it was hard to tell whether they were patients or visitors.

> (B) The room was large, and it seemed even larger for the lack of furniture. There were benches around all four walls, and in the middle there was a long table flanked with two more benches. The rest was space. And through that space old men shuffled, younger men wheeled carts of linen, a woman visitor walked slowly up and down with her restless husband.... Or was *she* the patient?

Passage A is brief and provides few details. There would be nothing wrong with such a description if the setting—a room—were not going to be used extensively. But the story, "Sausage and Beer," does make prolonged use of that room, so the version actually used (passage B) includes specific details that amplify each aspect.

In passage B, "large" is amplified with a phrase designed to help the reader feel it. The word "space" is repeated for effect. "Sparsely furnished" is made visual with specific examples. And the simple assertion that it was hard to tell which were the patients is dramatized by picturing a particular couple. This is not merely a matter of adding words; it is a careful selection of those visual details that will most successfully draw the reader into that room.

How much description should you provide? Much depends on whether the setting is going to be used in a significant way. Rambling descriptions of surroundings that are incidental merely slow the story. If, on the other hand, the setting you are dealing with is intended to reflect a character's personality, create a mood, or provide a contrast with some other scene, you have good reason to provide details. In "Sausage and Beer" there is not much description of the countryside on the way to the hospital because it would merely slow the story. Except for the cold, it has no real function. That waiting room, on the other hand, is worth describing not only because it introduces the boy to the unfamiliar world of the mentally ill, but also because it is later contrasted with the warm and happy world of those who, by chance, are not afflicted.

The pattern in "Phoenix" is somewhat similar in that the opening scene in the store is not described in any detail. It is enough to know that Phoenix is in a changing room where she can see the feet of the saleslady under the door. But her grandparents' apartment is central to the story since it represents the world Phoenix left and one that still attracts a part of her. For this reason, the author takes the time to give some highly specific details:

> Twin mahogany tables, green velveteen couch, Manet and Utrillo paintings in baroque frames, pigskin chests, carved ivory screens from China.

The primary question about setting every writer should ask early in the writing is, Just what aspect will contribute significantly to the story? For John Updike in "Man and Daughter," the scene is the descent down the slope in bitterly cold weather. This has to be vivid enough, dramatic enough to make the reader share the father's sense of alarm. It is this experience, after all, that will generate in him a deep awareness of his mortality, an awareness that is central to the story. Notice the use of metaphors in this passage:

> The moderate slope seemed a cliff.... The cold and blowing snow all around him constituted an immense crowding, but there was no way out of this white cave but to slide downward toward the dark spot that was his daughter.

The hillside is compared with "a cliff"; the cold presses in on him as if "crowding" him; the white of the snow seems like a "cave"; and as he looks down to his daughter she looks like a "dark spot" against the glare of the snow. This is a highly compressed descriptive passage. It is essential to the story because it helps us to share his fear and, beneath that, his awareness of growing older. It prepares us for that mix of feelings at the end of the story where he admires his daughter's energy and vitality while at the same time realizing that she and her generation "would leave him behind."

Where in the World?

Some stories are set in a particular geographic region or a specific city. This type of orientation is not at all necessary, but it can add a valuable new dimension to fiction. If you do decide to take advantage of this approach, your first question will be one of tactics—whether to identify an actual state or city or to create your own from imagination.

In some respects, there is a fallacy in the question. Since all fiction is only an illusion, you don't have a choice between a "real" location and one of your own creation. All fictional settings are imaginary, and everyone's use of, say, New York or Los Angeles is going to be a product of imagination.

Your true choice, then, is not, "Shall I set this story in a real city?" but "Shall I use the name and certain characteristics of a real city in the exercise of my imagination? Will it help my readers to see what I want them to see?"

There are two good reasons for drawing on a known city and naming it. First, it can serve as a geographic shorthand for the reader. There are features of our larger cities like New York, San Francisco, and Chicago that are known even by those who do not live there. In addition, using a real city can be a convenience for you as a writer *if* you know the area well. It will save you the trouble of making up your own map.

But there are a couple of dangers as well. Unless you are really familiar with the city you are using, you may begin to depend on scenes and details you have unconsciously absorbed from other stories and from television. Students who have never been to New York, for example, are apt to fall back on such standard conventions as a rainy night on Forty-Second Street, poodles on Park Avenue, hysteria on Madison Avenue, rumbles on either the Lower East Side or the South Bronx, and general perversion in the Village.

The same is true for Paris. If in blind ignorance the author spices a story with shots of the Eiffel Tower, cancan dancers, and prostitutes with hearts of gold, the fiction is bound to reflect the television programs and musical comedies from which this material was taken.

To avoid this, make sure you know the city well if you are going to name it, and try to focus your attention not on the most obvious aspects of the city but on districts and details that will seem authentic to your readers without being reminders of hackneyed stories and films.

Another problem with using a specific place is that you may find it difficult to metamorphose your material. That is, your fiction may become locked into the town or city. This is particularly common when the events have been taken from recent experience.

Perhaps for this reason, a majority of published stories are set in towns or cities that are linked to but not identified directly as real-life locations. John Updike describes this in his foreword to *Olinger Stories*:

> The name Olinger is audibly a shadow of "Shillington," the real name of my home town, yet the two towns, however similar, are not at all the same. Shillington is a place on the map and belongs to the world; Olinger is a state of mind, of my mind, and belongs entirely to me.

In this spirit, John Updike has used Olinger, Pennsylvania, in 11 short stories. The names and ages of the protagonists vary, but essentially they are the same boy. The approach is similar to that of Sherwood Anderson in *Winesburg, Ohio*. On a broader scale, William Faulkner blended historical and fictional elements this way in his stories and novels set in his imaginary Yoknapatawpha County, Mississippi.

None of the stories included in this volume are linked with a major city, but they all identify a specific geographic region. In "Sausage and Beer" the father and son are described as driving "well out in the New England countryside." Why New England? Partly because the author is familiar with it, but also because the bleak, snowy landscape helps to dramatize the chilly relationship between father and son. Later it provides a contrast with the warmth of the bar scene at the end of the story. The precise location is not important, but the New England climate does play a significant role in the story.

Both "Man and Daughter" and "Three Hearts" are clearly set in northern areas since both make significant use of snow. Notice that the geographic setting is not simply background. In each case it is an essential part of both the plot and the theme.

The most precisely set story is "Phoenix." In the second paragraph the protagonist is identified as a "California road queen." And careful readers will recall that her grandfather reads the *Sacramento Bee*—Sacramento being a relatively conservative, inland city and the capital of California—and that she is heading for Big Sur, a California coastal area often associated with alternate life-styles. These areas are not used in any detail, but the few geographic details help to ground the story, give it a sense of taking place in a specific part of the country.

Some fiction makes much more direct use of specific regions. There was a particular interest in this approach toward the end of the last century, and it became known as local color writing. Mark Twain, Bret Harte, and Sarah Orne Jewett are the best-known practitioners. A number of lesser-known writers, however, gave the term a bad reputation by concentrating on regional dialects and customs in a patronizing manner.

Regionalism in the best sense is flourishing today. Every area of the country is producing short fiction which draws heavily on local attitudes, values, and culture. There are several anthologies of short fiction that reflect these concerns. Writers with distinctly regional or ethnic backgrounds should consider drawing on those traditions.

Good regional writing depends on two elements: personal familiarity and respect. You really have to know what you are writing about if you are going to do justice to the people of a specific region or culture. It is important to write from the inside, not as an outside observer. And even though you may see their weaknesses and vulnerabilities, you have to have a basic respect for them if you are going to avoid a patronizing tone. This is the true distinction between local color writing in its worst sense and genuine regionalism. If you spend some time in New Mexico as a tourist, for example, you may gather some excellent material for a story about tourists in New Mexico, and you certainly will be able to draw on the physical characteristics of the area, but that doesn't mean that you are equipped to depict the life of a Navaho living on the reservation.

The Uses of Time

A story or novel exists in time as well as in space. Time includes the historical period, the season, and the hour of the day. As writer, you can ignore any one of these without disorienting a reader, but don't forget that any one of them can be used to make a real contribution.

Most short stories are set in the same historical period as the one in which they are written. This is partly because it takes time to establish the atmosphere of an earlier period, time that one can't easily spare in so short a form. In addition, if you move back to the nineteenth century it is difficult to avoid having your stories resemble historical romances and so-called costume gothics with their recurring plots and stereotyped characters.

There are, however, two ways of using an earlier historical period effectively without running the risk of echoing formulaic fiction. Both are approaches in which the writer maintains some personal link with the earlier time. First, it is sometimes possible to develop good fiction from extensive conversations with elderly people such as grandparents or others in an older generation. Thanks in part to portable tape recorders, there has been a growing interest in oral history of the immediate past. If your subject is willing, material gathered in this manner can provide the basis of fiction that has the true ring of authenticity.

You do have to pick your subject carefully, of course. Some people are more articulate than others. Some enjoy recalling their past, but others do not—occasionally for good reason. If your informant is agreeable, however, let him or her do plenty of talking. Occasionally you will have to ask questions in order to clarify certain facts, but try not to be too directive. Let your informant determine the direction of the conversation.

The most effective interviews are with those whose childhoods were significantly different from our lives today—those who came from Europe or Asia, those who endured the hardships of farming or factory work. Be very careful, however, not to sound patronizing or, even with the best intentions, sentimentally admiring. Since you are using borrowed material, your safest route is to maintain a fairly neutral tone. Let the story and its characters speak for themselves.

Be careful, too, not to turn your story into a simple **anecdote**. Anecdotes depend primarily on a turn of events, a clever little plot. This may be entertaining in conversation, but if you use it as the basis of a story you run the risk of trivializing your subject. To guard against this, concentrate on characterization. If you focus on the ambivalences of your protagonist, you will add depth that anecdotes normally lack.

The other use of the past applies only to those writers who are themselves old enough to remember when life was different. The accumulation of memory is one of the compensating benefits of age, and that layering of experience is an excellent source for fiction. One word of caution, however: Be careful not to lay undue emphasis on the differences between the period being described and the present day. If you draw too much attention to how inexpensive things were, for example, the reader may begin to view the material as quaint. Try instead to draw readers into that period; help them to share it.

The *time of year* is another aspect of time that is well worth considering. If the season has no real significance in a story, you can ignore it without the reader even noticing. But occasionally it helps to fix a story in a specific season and make use of it. "Sausage and Beer," for example, makes use of winter. The opening paragraph starts the story with the fact that "It was too cold for talk." The heater does not work. And at the hospital Uncle Theodore tells about his nightmarish theory that some night the hospital will shut off the heat and freeze the patients to death. It is not until the end of the story that this pattern of cold is broken. When father and son enter the bar together the boy discovers a "warm, bubbling, sparkling, humming…bit of cheerful chaos." The cold of a New England winter serves as a contrast with the warmth of friendship and, particularly, the newfound relationship between father and son.

Season can also be used as a method of metamorphosing a personal experience into something manageable. An episode that occurred in the heat of midsummer can sometimes be shifted to January merely to remove it from the confines of experience. Or an event that happened to take place in autumn might lend itself to spring and at the same time give you some sense of freshness and objectivity over your material. You must, of course, be on guard against the clichés of season. A first love that ends with a paragraph about the spring buds on the apple tree is as hackneyed as the story about an old couple that ends with the fallen leaves of November. Seasons can be enormously valuable—but only when they are used with subtlety and originality.

The *time of day* also has its share of clichés. A surprising number of stories begin with protagonists waking and wondering where they are. Fewer—but still too many—use the old film ending: watching the sun go down and "looking forward to another day."

In spite of these dangers, identifying the time of day can serve to orient the reader and to get the story moving. "Three Hearts," for example, begins with this sentence: "The morning after the big snowstorm Mama is real sick." This informs us about the snow that will become such a crucial part of the story and explains why the children are listening to the radio to see if school will be canceled. Equally important, it distinguishes this particular morning from other mornings. It launches the story right at the outset.

Even if you are not making specific use of the time of day, keep track of it in your own mind. This will help you to avoid careless errors in which a character refers to the morning coffee break one moment and quitting time five minutes later.

Carelessness in time sense can lead to another type of error which often takes this form: Two characters meet, sit down and talk for what in fact is only two minutes of dialogue, and then they part saying "It's been great to be able to talk this over with you." Since serious conversations are rarely that brief, be sure to provide some reference to the rest of their talk with a phrase like, "She kept on arguing, but her heart was not in it," or "The conversation turned to milder topics."

Whether you make direct use of the time of day depends on whether it is useful to the story. But remember that whatever scene you develop exists in the fictional time of the story, and the reader will expect it to be consistent.

Revising the Orientation

Revising aspects of place and time usually comes early in the writing of a story. It may, as I have pointed out, take the form of fundamental metamorphosing of the original experience. As the story develops, however, such sweeping changes become more and more difficult. A basic sense of geographic and seasonal setting tends to permeate a story so that revising it becomes a much more difficult matter than, say, changing a Nebraska farmhouse into a Chicago apartment or replacing the references to a winter scene with details about summer. If one has used place and season prominently, they become a part of the "feel" of the story. For this reason, it is best to make sure that the place and the season of a story are right before one has invested many hours of work.

Still, minor revisions of these details often go on through successive drafts. Heightening often is the result of chance. One selects a season, perhaps, because that is when the experience took place; and then various implications and suggestions come from the material and demand development. The use of cold as a vehicle to suggest separation and isolation in "Sausage and Beer" evolved in just this way.

In other cases, sharpening the visual details of a story is demanded because the action has gone on in a non-place. A surprising number of unsuccessful stories are placed in some ill-defined urban area which conveniently allows the protagonist to dodge city traffic one minute and, when the plot demands it, to be wandering "in the outskirts of town" the next. If you find yourself doing this, shift the story to a specific town or city that you know even if you do not use the name.

Muting aspects of setting may be necessary if you feel your use of place or season has become hackneyed. The kinds of clichés that damage fiction have already been described, but I should stress here that it is easy even for experienced writers to borrow from overworked conventions. Sometimes this happens because the experience has, infuriatingly, echoed a fictional cliché. There is no cosmic law that forbids life from imitating the worst in fiction. Occasionally a beautiful woman and a handsome man really do fall in love while strolling by the Eiffel Tower in Paris on a lovely June day. They may even live happily ever after. But who is going to believe it? Leave that plot to the musical comedy writers. If you really have had such a marvelous experience, find aspects of it that are further from the conventional pattern. This may involve moving the story to another setting or another season or both.

Occasionally the setting has to be revised because it has begun to resemble a literary convention. Stories about migrant workers tend to sound like John Steinbeck; hitchhiking stories often pick up the smells and sounds of Jack Kerouac's *On the Road* or motorcycle films; scenes involving city gangs frequently use standard details, including switchblades and leather jackets. One often has to mute these details and stress ones that the reader will see as if for the first time. Once again, be careful not to assume that details from your own life will necessarily be convincing as fiction. If you present a setting that your reader will associate with another author or with a film, song lyric, television commercial, or musical comedy, your story will be damaged by the association. Muting those details and highlighting other elements will be necessary, and usually you can do this without losing your original conception.

It is important to understand that a sense of place, historical period, season, and time of day are not adornments to a story. They are part of what you see and feel as you write; they are also the primary means by which your readers are going to enter your story and experience it as if they were physically present. It is this sense of being there that makes fiction an "as-if-real" experience.

23
IMPLICATION: METAPHOR, SYMBOL, AND THEME

The function of similes, metaphors, and symbols. Similes and metaphors defined. Vehicle and tenor distinguished. Symbols defined. Theme as commentary on the human condition. Revising thematic elements.

Similes, metaphors, and symbols can enrich your fiction. They add another range of meaning through implication, and they can do it economically. They are also one of the most effective means of communicating abstractions without making the passage sound like an essay. You can translate feelings like love and hate as well as concepts like liberty and courage into concrete entities that we can see, feel, smell, or hear.

It is a mistake to use these devices simply as adornment. When added artificially, they make a work of fiction seem "literary" in the worst sense. Their true function is to enrich your writing, not to weigh it down.

Similes and Metaphors Defined

First, some clear definitions. It is hard to discuss any work of fiction—our own or someone else's—if we start using words like simile, metaphor, and symbol interchangeably. Similes are easiest to understand because they are the most literal. A **simile** is a comparison in which we state that one item (often an abstraction) is *like* something concrete. Thus, "She fought like a lion" implies courage. Notice, however, that this is not a simple comparison as in "Lemons are like oranges." We are not suggesting that this woman used claws or bit her opponent. We are saying only that the way she fought brings to mind the ferocity of a lion. It's impossible to see an abstraction like courage, but we can easily visualize a lion in action.

A **metaphor** serves the same function, but it makes the comparison without *like* or *as*. The distinction is more significant than one might think since a metaphorical statement is literally untrue. It is only *figuratively* true. In this case we might have said, "She was a lion when fighting for civil rights." *Was* a lion? Well, was *like* a lion. When we explain metaphors it is natural to convert them back into similes.

Similes and metaphors are both called **figurative language** or **figures of speech** because they use words in a nonliteral way. Some authors use figurative language more than others. Updike, for example, frequently uses both similes and metaphors so that he can imply more in an economical manner. In "Man and Daughter" he presents an extraordinary simile right at the opening—the second sentence, in fact:

> "Look at that girl ski!" The exclamation arose at Ethan's side as if, in the disconnecting cold, a rib of his had cried out; but it was his friend....

The exclamation arose *as if his rib was speaking to him*? A careless reader could skip over that without noticing, but an active reader should pause long enough to make this quick interpretation: The admiration expressed by his friend seemed as if it had come from himself. A lesser writer might have said, "...as if it came from his own heart," but using the heart as the source or our emotions is a cliché. And besides, Updike can draw on an **overtone** or extended meaning for those who read the story twice: this father at the end of the story is seen as passing something on to this young woman; is it too much to recall that Eve is described as being made from Adam's rib? No harm if you missed this, but Updike is the kind of writer who likes to give his readers fresh pleasures in the second and third reading.

That was a simile because Updike used *as if*. Later, he uses a metaphor to describe how his protagonist, a teacher, reacted to growing older. Each succeeding class of student "ate a year of his life...." The students were not described as *like* some creature that consumed another year, they simply *were*. Literally untrue, of course, but figuratively it suggests in a single image what it might take a paragraph to explain without using a metaphor.

There is a tendency to think of figurative language as "literary" or elegant, but it is found just as frequently in stories that are written in a deceptively informal manner. Deborah Corey's "Three Hearts," for example, is written in the first person from the point of view of a young girl, yet it contains many similes and metaphors. She describes her mother's eyes, for example, as being "like faded jeans." This doesn't mean just the color; there is the implication of being worn out as well. Eddie has "an angry streak like steel running through his heart." The phrase *angry streak* alone is technically a metaphor, but it is so familiar that we don't picture the streak. Having a "streak like steel running through his heart" is both visually arresting and at the same time natural to a young girl's language. In another simile, Corey describes not only an action but an attitude behind the action. Eddie, returning after a night on the town, "steps over us as if we are stones." The frequency and vividness of these metaphors don't make the narrator sound precocious because they are the sort we often hear from children.

Vehicle versus Tenor

The terms *vehicle* and *tenor* are extremely helpful when we examine just how effective a simile or a metaphor is. And as we will see shortly, they are essential in understanding how a figure of speech differs from a symbol. The **vehicle** of a simile or metaphor is the image itself—usually a concrete object, something we can see or at least hear or feel. The **tenor** is the implied subject.

In the example from the Updike story, "as if...a rib...cried out," the vehicle *rib* is solid, something we can picture. The tenor or subject being described in his inner self, an abstract notion. In the second example from that story, *eating* is used as a vehicle to describe how the years pass. Even in describing it, we are tempted to say that time seems to *consume* the years, resorting to another metaphor.

In the final example from "Three Hearts," the one in which the brother "steps over us as if we are stones," the vehicle is the picture of someone stepping over stones in a field. The tenor is the total indifference with which Eddie treats his younger brother and sister.

The Distinctive Force of a Symbol

We are all familiar with **symbols** when they appear in fiction, but most readers and even some writers have difficulty explaining just how a symbol differs from a metaphor. It's important to know because only by understanding how symbols work can we evaluate symbolic elements in our own work.

Let's go back to our original example of the metaphor, "She was a lion in battle." The image of the lion is introduced simply for the purpose of comparison. There is no lion in the story. Contrast this, however, with a story set in Africa that deals with a real lion. By contrasting the animal with a man who is cowardly, it would be possible for the author to imply that the lion symbolized virtues of courage and perhaps dignity. In that case, the author's job is made easier by the fact that the lion is what is called a **public symbol**, one that is widely accepted. A **private symbol** is a rather misleading term for a symbol devised by the author. *Original* would be a far better term.

The difference between this symbolic use of the lion and the figurative use is clearer once you see that in the case of a metaphor, the vehicle is not a literal part of the fiction. With a symbol, on the other hand, the vehicle is an item in the story and its symbolic meaning, the tenor, is suggested through implication.

The difference between metaphors and symbols is best seen when they are used together in the same scene. At the end of "Sausage and Beer," for example, the waiter brings the order and then leaves "with a quick, benedictory smile." Translating that back to a simile: "with a smile *as if* it were the expression of a clergyman at the conclusion of a service." Father and son are then "lost in a kind of communion"—not a literal one. They are not, after all, in a church. In contrast, the sausage and beer that the waiter brings are real, not a figure of speech, and a careful reader will see that they serve as a symbol for the bread and wine of certain religious services. How can we be sure? Not because the author says so, but because there is evidence in the story in the form of the two metaphors. In addition, the image is highlighted in the title.

Sometimes complex symbols are found in stories that appear to be relatively straightforward. "Three Hearts," for example, ends with a complex symbolic detail that the narrator herself does not perceive. Bucky, the narrator's brother, has almost died because Eddie would not get out of bed to help. Bucky has survived only because the sickly mother has dug into the snow, found him, and performed mouth-to-mouth resuscitation. After their mother takes Bucky inside, the narrator picks up Bucky's mitten and the one that belongs to Eddie. (This was prepared for early in the story when Mama tells Bucky, "Double up on your mittens....")

Eddie's mitten is "grey and full of holes." She pulls on the yarn "but the hole puckers together in a kiss." She then does this with every hole and the mitten finally "rumples itself into a little ball."

The story, you remember, informs us in the third paragraph that Eddie has been a continual problem—a dropout who stays out drinking all night and sleeps during the day. The family members, especially the mother, treat him gently, even with love. In exactly the same way, Sissy ineffectively tries to mend Eddie's mitten, the hole puckers "in a kiss" and eventually "rumples itself into a little ball" just as Eddie himself sleeps inside, as useless as the little ball of yarn.

That "kiss," by the way, is not literal. It is a vehicle that describes the puckering of the yarn. The mitten, however, is real—not a figure of speech—and becomes a symbol for Eddie's damaged and hopeless state. The question to ask when distinguishing a metaphor from a symbol is simply this: Is the vehicle a figure of speech (like that metaphorical kiss) or does it, like the mitten, exist in the story?

For some readers, picking out figurative language and symbols may seem like a literary exercise that detracts from the pleasure of a story. Echoes, perhaps, from unhappy English classes! As a result, some student writers avoid any symbolic suggestion for fear of sounding artificial or self-consciously literary. Caution is wise, but avoidance is limiting.

A few reassurances may help. First, symbols are not a necessary ingredient in fiction. Excellent stories and novels—sophisticated in the best sense—are written without even the hint of a symbolic detail. Second, neither figures of speech nor symbols are the invention of teachers. They are a part of common speech. True, many are too well used to have an impact. When we hear that someone is proud as a peacock or smart as a whip we don't even see the image. But we also use fresh figurative language without much conscious thought, just as the narrator does in "Three Hearts." We dream in symbols. Fantasies tend to be symbolic. They have been a special concern of writers in every age because they allow us to imply so much more than we can when using straightforward, literal language.

Finally, very few stories are ruined if one does not at first see symbolic elements. Few works depend on them utterly. It's just that the stories become more meaningful if one can respond to the added dimension. It is possible to identify and enjoy a melodic line from a symphony played on the piano alone, but listening to the way it sounds with a full orchestra is a far richer experience.

Turning now to your own work, here is a cardinal rule to remember: keep it subtle. When readers recognize an unmistakable symbol, the illusion of reality breaks and the story seems contrived. Watch out for **public symbols**—those that are so widely known that they appear in song lyrics and political cartoons. The crucifix, Christlike characters named Chris, Adam and Eve on a Pacific isle, and the setting sun—all these are shopworn public symbols. They become obtrusive and dominate the story. The reader sees your intellectual intent looming like a cartoon and loses the sense of being in the story itself.

In the interest of subtlety, think twice before you let a story depend utterly on a symbol. Such works often end up sacrificing credible characterization for the sake of that central abstract idea. The best approach is to move cautiously and let the story suggest to you what might be made symbolic. Whenever possible, develop your symbolic material from the events, the setting, and the characters of the story itself. The goal is to have symbolic details serve the story, not dominate it.

The Importance of Theme

Journal entries don't usually have a theme. They record events or describe personal feelings, often without any unifying concern. Sophisticated fiction, on the other hand, almost always does. Readers expect it. If you don't provide some kind of theme, readers are apt to respond with questions like, "What's the point?" or "What are you getting at?" When writers claim that a story means "whatever you want it to mean," they are usually describing meaningless work.

There are many ways to define theme, but I have found that this is the most useful for writers: **Theme** is that portion of a work of fiction which comments on the human condition. If we think of it in this way, we will never confuse theme with plot. Plot is what happens. When we talk about plot, we name characters and describe events. When we talk about theme, we are making a statement about something that applies to us all.

The theme is usually implied rather than stated. But even when subtly presented, it is still a statement. For this reason, the theme of a story and sometimes even a novel can usually be described in one complete sentence. It's not always easy, and there is always room for debate, but the effort helps us to identify an aspect of the story that passive readers often miss. Equally important, it can clarify our thinking about own work.

Put in simplest terms, the *plot* of "Phoenix" is about a free-spirited girl who visits her loving grandmother and has mixed feelings about accepting money from her. The *theme*, on the other hand might be described as: "Although we can change our life-style in radical ways, we never quite let go of what we were before." There is nothing absolute about the wording, of course. With just a slightly different emphasis we might suggest the theme this way: "No matter how free and independent we think we are, there is a portion of us that still loves to be indulged like a child." These two thematic statements aren't contradictory; they simply focus on two closely related aspects of the same story.

In the case of "Three Hearts," a deceptively complex story, we might suggest a thematic statement such as, "The weakest member of a family occasionally turns out to be the strongest in a real emergency." Or, in a slightly different reading, we might describe it this way: "No matter how sympathetic a family is toward a dysfunctional member, he or she may end up beyond repair." The first is like describing a glass as being half full while the second describes it as half empty, but each applies to the same story. Each describes an aspect of the human condition.

Although authors are not always the best judges of their own writing, I can at least describe what I hoped would emerge as the theme in "Sausage and Beer." The theme that appears to me to be dominant in the final draft might be worded this way: "No matter how much we plan, chance plays a major role in how we turn out." But that doesn't include the sense of being initiated into the adult world. So perhaps this is closer: "When we discover just how much of our lives are controlled by chance, we become initiated into adulthood."

All thematic statements are necessarily simplifications—distillations of meaning. Sophisticated fiction usually has multiple themes. Often there is a dominant concern that provides thematic focus and then a cluster of related themes. For this reason, some critics prefer the phrase **central concern** rather than *theme*. The two terms are used in the same way.

In "Sausage and Beer," for example, I would like to think that there are two other important concerns which, though closely related, were not included in either of my attempts to describe the theme in a single sentence. First, there is the suggestion that two members of a family can remain distant from one another until they share some intense experience which is difficult for them both. In addition, I was concerned with how we tend to mark the really important moments in our lives with some kind of ritual. We may drink a toast, share a meal, or borrow, consciously or unconsciously, from established religions in order to elevate the occasion above the routine of daily life.

Analyzing the themes in published stories can be discouraging. It may seem as if authors somehow hold all those threads in their heads from the start. Not so. What you read in print is a final draft, and it is very unlikely that the author had all those intellectual concerns in mind when beginning the story. In the case of "Sausage and Beer," I started with an experience that was vivid in my memory. Only after metamorphosing it so it became independent from actual events did I begin to think about theme. My first concern was the notion that only by sharing an intense experience can one get to know a reserved parent. The element of chance that sends one brother to a life of hospitalization and allows another to live fully did not occur to me until well into the second draft. And the ritual element wasn't added until the third or fourth draft.

Here, then, is an important aspect of the creative process that can't be taught: A complex story speaks to its author through successive drafts. It, the story itself, develops certain characters, highlights certain scenes. But most important, it often informs the writer about new thematic possibilities. Each suggestion, of course, requires more rewriting. The author who quits after the first draft can never hear the story suggesting new implications to be developed. Although the notion of a dialogue between the story and the author is a metaphor, such a dialogue is often a fundamental part of the creative process.

When Themes Need Revision

A recurring problem in student fiction is settling for a theme that is simple and one-noted. Many of those plots I described earlier under the heading of the Seven Deadly Sins are one-noted. That is, they reiterate the same notion so relentlessly that the reader is quickly bored. Good characters remain good, corrupt characters are unrelentingly corrupt, and the theme is laid out as if in a sermon. In such cases, work to add related concerns. Reviewing the variety of related themes in the stories I analyzed above should help you to see how it is possible to broaden the implications of a story.

Closely related to one-note stories are those in which the theme is a **truism**. There is nothing fresh in a story that informs us as if for the first time that Materialism is not ultimately satisfying, Violence leads to violence, and It's tough trying to maintain spiritual values in a corrupt society. These are fine sentiments, but when every scene and every character of a story is clearly designed to make such an assertion, the story is apt to seem not only like a sermon but like a boring sermon. To avoid this, explore some aspect of the theme that readers haven't thought about before. Look for ironic contrasts, mixed feelings. After all, materialists aren't *always* miserable; and the kind, the generous, and the spiritual are not always the ones we really admire. Don't be afraid to develop the odd twists in human relationships.

Look at the fresh and interesting thematic suggestions that are made in the stories in this anthology. See if you can make your story probe something more complex than a generally held belief or truism.

In other cases, the theme remains inaccessible. It may be clear to you as author, but you may find that to your chagrin others simply don't get it. This is the advantage of working in a writing class or with a group of fellow writers. One is never quite sure of what comes across until one listens to readers—preferably readers who have read a good deal of sophisticated fiction.

If the theme needs clarification, resist the temptation to add a line of exposition explaining the story. See if you can find ways of dramatizing the theme through action, dialogue, or thoughts earlier in the story. You might also consider a concluding action that will bring the story into focus. If you review the endings of a number of stories you have previously read, you will see how many ways there are to highlight a theme in the final paragraph without explaining everything to the reader in the form of an analytical statement.

Theme is only one aspect of a story. The freshest and most insightful theme won't make a story succeed if the characters are not convincing and the action is not plausible. But without originality and complexity of theme, a story becomes nothing more than a simple piece of passing entertainment. A truly sophisticated work of fiction appeals to the mind as well as to the emotions.

24
STYLE AND TONE

A neutral versus pronounced style. The five factors that determine style: diction, syntax, density, balance of narrative modes, and tense. Varieties of tone. Consistency versus calculated shifts in style and tone.

Style is the manner in which a work is written. All fiction has style. You can't compose without it any more than you can write your name without revealing—for better or for worse—your handwriting. But it is important to examine just what your style is and then to judge whether it is the best possible approach for a particular story.

More than half the stories and novels you read maintain what can be described as a **neutral style**. That is, while the writing may have particular characteristics, the average reader is not aware of them. Some fiction, however, is presented in a highly distinctive manner. And some authors maintain such an individualized style in all their work that you can identify an isolated passage just as easily as you can recognize the voice of a friend on the telephone.

Should you adopt a distinctive style when you are just beginning to write fiction? The advantage is that your work gains a certain visibility, standing out from the rest; the disadvantage is that you limit your options when turning to new work and eventually may appear to be repetitious.

Style is placed last in this section on fiction because it doesn't usually become a conscious concern until one has had a good deal of experience. At first, we make stylistic choices intuitively. We write in the manner that feels appropriate. A complex, highly sophisticated story may encourage us to use lengthier sentences and longer words; a story with a tough, inarticulate protagonist may call for a sparse syntax and limited vocabulary even in the exposition.

But you can't always rely on your literary intuition. As you write more you will want to be able to adopt different styles knowingly. You will also want to be able to revise the style in first drafts. Such adjustments can make a radical difference. Eventually you may find yourself adopting a characteristic stylistic pattern in all your work, but try not to restrict yourself until you have explored a variety of approaches.

"Sausage and Beer" is written in essentially a neutral style. Here, to remind you, is the opening:

> I kept quiet for most of the trip. It was too cold for talk. The car was getting old and the heater hadn't worked for as long as I could remember. My father said he couldn't afford to get it repaired, but he bought us a camping blanket which was supposed to be just as good.

The same passage, however, could be written in a formal, even elegant style as if it were recalled years later by an elderly man. The result is not too far from how Henry James might have presented it:

> Being a reticent child raised in a family that did not encourage discourse with the young, I made no effort to initiate a conversation with my father for the entire duration of the trip. Ours was an aging automobile that, like some former beauty now facing the ravages of time, was incapable of warming either body or soul. Whether repairs to the heater were possible or not was a moot point since my father habitually exercised thrift by claiming abject poverty; but since he was not without some modicum of charity, he provided his passengers with a blanket that, having been designed for camping in the wilds, served in some minimal way to safeguard us against the ravages of frostbite.

At another extreme, we might try the same passage as if spoken by a rather resentful young man.

> I didn't open my mouth. Not for an hour. Why should I? It was incredibly cold as always, and all his fault. He'd do anything to save a buck—like not getting the heater fixed. Gave us a lousy camping blanket instead.

These two alternative versions describe the same situation, the same events, and basically the same characters. But from the outset the style suggests a different type of narrator, and as a result the stories, if developed, would end up being radically different. This demonstrates the fact that style isn't just a matter of external appearance like a coat of paint; style is an integral part of fiction in the same sense as are characters or plot.

The varieties of stylistic effect are infinite. Surprisingly, however, style is determined primarily by only five factors. These are **diction** (choice of words), **syntax** (sentence structure), **density** (presence or absence of figurative and symbolic language), the balance of **narrative modes** (dialogue, thoughts, action, and the like), and **tense** (past or present). Each of these deserves a close look.

Diction

Your choice of words is a more significant factor in English than in most other languages because there is such a radical difference in sound and tone between those words that came to us from the Norse and Anglo-Saxon and those that came from the Greek or Latin through French. To cite an extreme example, contrast your reaction to these two samples:

> Edgar got in the boat and gripped the seat, sweating like an ox. He hated the sea.

> Julius entered the vessel and embraced the cushions, perspiring profusely. He detested the ocean.

In the first, the nouns and verbs are without exception of Anglo-Saxon or Old Norse origin. In the second, every noun and verb is of Latin origin. Except for the articles and the conjunctions, these could be two different languages, each with its distinctive sound, and each with its own tone. Past generations were taught that words of Latin and Greek derivation were "elegant" and "refined," and some of that prejudice remains. You should feel free to use whatever the language has to offer, but remember that your choices will affect your style.

None of us has the time to look up the derivation of every word we use, but we all have a built-in awareness of the distinction between these two verbal heritages. One is dominated by short, abrupt sounds that imply simplicity, roughness, and in some cases obscenity; the other is characterized by longer words, smoother sounds, and a sense of elegance or even pomposity.

Aside from the derivations, there are the subtle distinctions between short words and long ones, harsh ones and smooth ones, crude ones and those that sound elegant. As with nonfiction writing, you will want to choose an appropriate *level of usage*. If the story is being narrated by a city dweller who is streetwise, your choice of words is going to be dramatically different than it would be if you were writing a third-person story in a neutral style. And of course the diction of each line of dialogue should be appropriate to the character who is speaking.

Fiction is not written word by word, however. When it is going well, let it flow. The time to take a close look at your diction is when you read over the completed first draft. Decide what effect you want to achieve, and revise accordingly.

Syntax

Syntax means sentence structure, and it has as much to do with the stylistic effect as does diction. If you turn back to the two alternative openings to "Sausage and Beer," you will discover, if you do some counting, that the long-winded version uses 120 words but combines them so that there are only three sentences. At the opposite extreme, the terse, as-if-spoken passage covers essentially the same ground with less than half the number of words, yet there are exactly twice as many sentences.

In general, long, complex sentences tend to slow the reader down, but this has advantages as well as disadvantages. It can add a certain elegance and sophistication that may be entirely appropriate to a particular story. Even when you are using the third person, those long sentences may serve as an echo of your protagonist's character.

Be careful, however, not to overdo it. If you extend this style beyond what you might hear from someone you know, you may inadvertently end up making the character seem like a satire of a pompous fool. My example, exaggerated for illustration, comes close to that. If you *intend* to satirize a wordy, slow-speaking character, fine. But it is not a happy experience to find that a story you wrote in a serious style is being read as a satire.

At the other extreme, those short, simple sentences can add energy and vitality to your writing. They help when you want to provide dramatic impact. But this style too can prove to be a disadvantage if pushed too far or if used too unrelentingly. Pages of short, extremely simple sentences can become as monotonous as the relentless beat of windshield wipers on a long drive.

Because of these risks, most writers prefer to revise the syntax either to echo particular characters (especially in dialogue) or to control the pace of the fiction. There are, however, some authors whose distinctive use of syntax has become a basic characteristic that runs through almost all their work. It helps to read these authors to see how they manage to maintain a distinctive style without becoming monotonous.

Henry James is a good example of a writer who fairly consistently used long, complex sentences and did it with great success. William Faulkner varied his syntax, but he occasionally indulged in prodigiously long sentences. And so did Thomas Wolfe. At the other end of the scale, Ernest Heming-way is known for his sparse, unadorned syntax, a style that has been widely imitated.

Sentence length is only one of several variables in syntax. Internal structure can be quite different. Faulkner's lengthy sentences tend to be loose, occasionally rambling, even grammatically confused, while those of Thomas Wolfe are often rhythmic. Punctuation is another factor. Although most authors are fairly conventional, there are those who echo the spoken language with more incomplete sentences and sometimes a greater use of dashes.

There is absolutely no need to adopt a distinctive pattern of syntax, but it is important to remember this: The best way to avoid stylistic monotony in fiction or nonfiction as well is to vary your sentence length.

Density

Density means compression. High density means that a great deal is implied about characterization and theme in a relatively compressed manner. Fiction can be fairly sophisticated and still lack density. We describe it as "a quick read" because we do in fact read it rapidly.

As I pointed out in the previous chapter, one way to achieve density is to use figurative language (similes and metaphors primarily) and symbolic details. Another way is to develop ambivalences and apparent contradictions. A third approach is dealing with a cluster of related themes rather than a single concern.

The degree of density is essentially a matter of choice. Some story ideas will come to you easily and don't merit being charged with real density. Others may develop complexities in characterization and thematic suggestion as you move through successive drafts.

Occasionally, you may find that you have taken on too much. The story begins to seem cluttered and confused. In such cases, you may want to back off and focus on a single aspect. The level of density may need to be reduced for the sake of clarity. In short, lack of density makes fiction seem slight; excessive density can make it turgid or, worse yet, confusing. Determine the level of density that is appropriate to your material.

The Balance of Narrative Modes

The third method of influencing your style in fiction is the balance of **narrative modes**. I am using *mode* in the special sense introduced at the beginning of the fiction section: dialogue, thoughts, action, description, and exposition.

A particular sentence may contain two or more modes, but usually one will dominate. The concept becomes helpful when a scene or a whole story stresses one mode more than the others. This is not necessarily bad; it may produce just the style you want. But be aware of how you are affecting your style.

Depending heavily on dialogue, for example, may be entirely appropriate if that mode is used effectively to develop theme and characterization. If you try such an approach, however, be careful that your work doesn't become "talky." That usually means that the dialogue isn't revealing enough. It has become mere padding.

When fiction is dominated by thoughts, the style may become heavy and slow. This is because of the significant difference between thoughts and dialogue: When characters talk, they interact with others, but when they think, they are in isolation. An extended passage of thinking is a monologue within the mind. All too easily it begins to sound like exposition—an author's analysis. When a character thinks to himself, "I've been too selfish about this whole thing," the reader may have the feeling that what is being presented as thought is really just a poorly disguised form of exposition. An extended passage in this vein will make the style heavy, slow, and possibly boring. Often you can correct this by presenting those thoughts through a more active mode like dialogue or action. It's far more effective to have a mother, say, digging desperately in a snowbank with her bare hands than to have her think, "Yes, when it comes to an emergency I guess I really do have more strength than the men in this pathetic family."

Action tends to enliven your style, but too much may give the piece a breathless effect. The story may seem superficial. Description and exposition are stylistically opposite to action. They can provide valuable information, but they add weight to your style. If overused, they can make a story seem sluggish.

The balance of modes is, like other aspects of style, something that comes naturally in first-draft writing. The time to examine it is when you have your first draft on paper. There is no reason whatever not to favor one mode over the others in a particular story, but try to judge as objectively as you can how this has affected your style. A few revisions at that stage may make a major difference in the overall effect.

Tense

The matter of **tense** has become a major controversy in the past decade. Traditionally, most short stories and novels were written in the past tense. Starting in the early 1980s, however, an increasing number of authors began using the present tense. Some people take this very seriously. An article in *The New York Times Book Review* attacked the practice on principle, and at least one editor refuses to print present-tense stories regardless of their worth. On the other hand, the number of present-tense stories in print continues to increase.

The effect of the present tense on style is highly subjective and difficult to judge. For some, it seems illogical and therefore disruptive to imply that events are occurring at the time of the telling. This is particularly bothersome in scenes of dramatic action. Out of context, it seems a bit odd to have a first-person narrator write, "She slaps me across the face and I am left speechless." This surely is an odd time to be writing a diary entry.

The counterargument is that you really don't respond to stories like these as if they are diary entries. Readers lose themselves in the action, and after the first paragraph the matter of tense is largely forgotten. Can you, for example, recall which two of the four stories in this volume are written in the present tense?

Present-tense enthusiasts often claim that fiction is livelier and more immediate in that tense. But if this were so, past-tense fiction would not have dominated fiction for over a century.

There is one good technical reason for adopting the present tense. If a story in the past tense contains a number of flashbacks, the author must cue the reader with the past perfect each time: "She had been an excellent lawyer in her thirties," for example. The flashback itself, you remember, reverts to simple past tense. But if the main part of the story is written in the present tense, the author can signal the start of those flashbacks simply by shifting to the past tense and staying there. Melissa Pritchard, for example, is one of the two writing in the present tense, and she is able to slide into a flashback simply by saying "Two weeks each August...she slept on starched, ironed sheets, ..." Had the body of the story been written in the past tense, she would have indicated the flashback with "Two weeks each August...she *had* slept on starched, ironed sheets." True, she could soon revert to the simple past, but the distinction between time present and events previous to that is somewhat more natural when the main body of the story is written in the present tense.

Another, more specialized stylistic use of the present tense is to add dramatic emphasis to a particularly vivid or significant scene in a story that is written primarily in the past tense. Here is a very brief example.

> She was utterly exhausted after seven hours of freeway driving that night and wondered if it would ever end. Suddenly lights flash in her eyes, she has the sensation of floating, of cold fresh air, and to her amazement she finds herself looking up at the stars. Not for more than a minute did she realize that her car was in flames some fifty yards from where she landed and that she could not move.

In this fragment (which you are welcome to use to launch a story of your own) the passage begins and ends with the past tense ("*was* exhausted....did she realize"), but the dreamlike nature of her experience at the moment of the accident is highlighted by shifting to the present tense.

It is odd that while the overall choice of tense is one of the most debated aspects of style today, its effect on fiction is almost entirely subjective. If you are uncertain which to use in a particular story, try an opening half-page first in past tense and then in present tense. One will seem better than the other, and you can invent a good explanation later.

Varieties of Tone

While style has to do with the manner in which a work is written—a distinctly literary element—**tone** deals with the emotional element. In general usage, it can refer either to the emotion within the work itself or to the author's implicit attitude toward that work.

These are not always the same. The tone of a work itself can usually be described with adjectives like "exciting," "sad," "merry," "eerie," or "depressing." The tone adopted by the author might be "serious," "flippant," "ironic," "satiric," "sardonic." To see the difference, imagine an apparently sad story about a young boy who loses his dog (a sad plot) written by one author in a serious manner and by another in a flippant or satiric manner. Same sad story; different tonal approach on the part of each author. When describing certain stories, then, it is important to distinguish the tone of the work itself from the author's tone. This is particularly important when irony or satire is used.

What tone should you adopt? Your first inclination may be the best, but not always. If you are writing a story that is at least partially based on personal experience, it will seem natural to present it with the emotional response you still feel.

This is reasonable, but remember that what you are writing is fiction, and you should be able to shift the tone if you feel that such a change would improve the story. Most of the time such changes take the form of light touches to stories that have become too heavy, too close to melodrama.

Be on the alert when working with a personal experience you recall with strong emotions—deep sorrow, strong anger, and the like. It may be that what are sincere emotions will appear sentimental or superficial in a short story if presented without relief. The same applies to experiences that were charged with excitement and fear. If you are not careful, they can become conventional thrillers. Remember that a story—particularly a relatively short one—is a rather delicate art form. Think of it as an electrical wire that cannot take too heavy a surge of voltage without burning out. By "burning out" I simply mean appearing ridiculous. It is not a pleasant experience to have readers respond to a scene you thought was moving or dramatic with chuckles and comments like, "Oh, come on now!"

The solution may be to back off from the material a bit. Look at your protagonist with a slightly detached attitude. See if there aren't some aspects of the situation that could be treated either lightly or at least with a hint of a smile. When you do this, you are establishing **distance** between yourself and your material.

In my own story, for example, I made a conscious effort to keep the asylum scene from turning excessively dark by working in some of the simple, humdrum complaints that the mad share with anyone living in an institution. Uncle Theodore's little worries about fellow patients were invented for this purpose. This is one of those cases in which the actual experience had to be softened to keep the scene from becoming melodramatic.

It is always possible and often advisable to add light elements to serious fiction. "Phoenix," for example, could have been written as a defense of alternative life–style living and a heavy–handed criticism of older people whose lives have become meaningless in spite of their wealth. Instead, the author opens with what is essentially a lightly satiric view of Phoenix with her "bramble of hair" and her "smelly jeans" and an "unwashed body" that looks "fishy." Later, the grandparents are treated with light, near-satiric touches to keep them from appearing too pathetic.

Keep in mind that you as author determine what the tone will be. Even when a story is based fairly directly on a personal experience, treat it as fiction and consider carefully just what kind of tone would be the most effective. The darkest experiences often have lighter elements that can be developed. If not, feel free to invent them. Touches of humor and irony can add yeast to work that would otherwise be heavy.

Occasionally, the tone should be shifted in the other direction. Genuinely comic stories (a rare species!) should never be made serious, but some first drafts are simply too light, too lacking in tension, too kind to the characters. You may have to take a closer look at your characters and see if you can dig deeper, present more honest insights. You may have to provide dialogue or perhaps a whole new scene to develop such a character more fully.

Finally, consider tonal consistency. As I have explained, some variation is often helpful, but having an apparently cheerful story end in disaster is risky. The story may seem to fall apart and become unconvincing. To a certain degree, the tone you set at the beginning establishes expectations in the reader. If you plan to have a strongly dramatic ending, it is often wise to provide a touch of harshness at the opening to prepare the reader. Even a small detail will suffice. Traditionally this is called **forewarning**. It serves as a kind of pre-echo, preparing the reader—at least unconsciously—for the darker tone to come.

Style and tone are enormously important, but don't let them distract you when you are starting a new work. You can suffer a serious case of writer's block if you stare at a blank piece of paper or a computer screen worrying about your options. As I have urged before, let the story develop. Have faith in your initial vision. Once you have a rough draft safely down on paper, then turn critic and examine these literary aspects.

Remember, too, that this chapter is largely a distillation of abstract concepts. For a real appreciation of what you can do with style and tone you have to read a lot of fiction. This chapter will help you identify and evaluate those literary elements, but your growth and development over the years will come from fiction itself.

25
WRITING FICTION
ON YOUR OWN

Learning from published fiction. A regimen for writing. Rewriting and more rewriting. Writing groups as support systems. Six critical questions for writers and readers.

Studying a textbook helps you to start asking the right questions about fiction. And taking a course develops your critical skills as well as the all-important ability to accept criticism with an open mind. But that's only the beginning. If you plan to develop and expand your writing abilities, you will have to work a good deal on your own.

Learning from Published Fiction

The key to developing as a writer is as simple as it is important: Spend at least as much time reading as you do writing. Surprising as it may seem, there are many who do not. As a result, they fail to expand their abilities because they have cut themselves off from the greatest resource a writer has: published fiction.

Reading, however, refers to two quite different activities. Passive or recreational reading is the sort we do when we want to turn off and be entertained. It is a relatively inexpensive, legal pastime and has no dangerous side effects.

We all need it from time to time—but we learn nothing from it. Active reading, on the other hand, is what writers do. It is analytical reading. When we read actively we are not only making value judgments ("terrible character development," "slow pacing," "skillful irony," and the like), we are examining portions of the work objectively ("a flashback within a flashback—interesting," "that house is becoming almost like a character!").

Active reading may require studying works you do not enjoy. In such cases, the pleasure you derive stems from a writer's curiosity and a sense of personal growth rather than from the immediate experience.

For some, active reading means keeping a pencil and paper handy for notes—not just plot development and names of characters but interesting techniques. Many find it helpful to keep a literary journal. Written comments about what you have read will bring the work back into focus just the way a photo album helps you to recall past experiences. Be sure to include notations about where the stories were published so that you can refer to them later.

At first you may have a problem knowing where to find good fiction. Anthologies provide a good initial step. They will introduce you to new authors. Some anthologies cover the past few decades. More recent short stories can be found in two annual collections, the *O. Henry Prize Stories* and *The Best American Short Stories*. These are in almost every library and can be ordered through your bookstore. In addition, the University of Illinois Press has been publishing four volumes of paperback collections (one author to each collection) annually since 1975. A list of these can be obtained by writing to the publisher, and individual volumes can be ordered directly or through your bookstore.

As for magazines, there are two large-circulation publications that include fiction in every issue: *The New Yorker* (at least one story every week) and *The Atlantic*, a monthly. There are also about 100 little magazines, many of them quarterlies, which publish stories along with poems, articles, and reviews. Some, like *The North American Review* and *Story*, specialize in fiction. More titles are listed in Appendix B.

How do you find these publications? Start by reading whichever magazines are available in your library. Then select one or two and subscribe. As I have mentioned before, a subscription costs less than many compact discs. When you have your own copy of the magazine you will be sure to read it, will feel free to mark it up, and will have it for future reference.

Writers of fiction are even more isolated than poets. They do not give readings as often, and they have difficulty finding individuals who are willing to read and criticize their work. Quarterlies and little magazines provide the best way for writers to stay in touch with others in their field.

If you decide to invest time and energy in writing fiction, make sure you invest at least as much time in reading what others have written. If you value fiction, you will not find the cost of books and subscriptions excessive. Your development as a writer will depend in large measure on how active and perceptive you are as a reader.

A Regimen for Writing

Everyone knows that when it comes to a weight-losing diet or a body-building exercise, a regular program is necessary. But for some reason, some writers still believe that they can rely on "inspiration." Those who wait for the perfect fictional idea to hit them forget that much of our progress as writers of fiction is a matter of trial and error. One great advantage of taking a creative writing course is that it provides deadlines. The writing gets done—sometimes good, and sometimes not-so-good. We learn either way. To put it bluntly, we learn nothing when we write nothing.

When you are not taking a course, it is important to set deadlines for yourself. If you are part of a small group of serious writers who are willing to meet every two weeks, those meetings will provide deadlines. Otherwise you may have to impose a schedule on yourself such as a completed story every two weeks. Those who submit work often use contest dates to prod themselves into intense activity. Due dates are listed in *Poets and Writers Magazine*, a highly useful publication (address listed in Appendix B).

Rewriting and More Rewriting

Those who have just started to write fiction usually spend very little time with revisions. It is not that they are so sure of themselves, it is simply a matter of not knowing how to evaluate what they have done. What is there on the page seems fine.

One of the functions of this textbook is to make the beginning writer less satisfied with his or her first draft. As one develops, the time one spends on revisions usually becomes greater and greater. Unfortunately, this is not always possible when one is taking a course. An academic term is relatively short, and the effectiveness of a course requires a high output of new material. Revision work cannot in most cases be given as much credit as new writing.

Working on your own or as a member of an informal writing group has one important advantage over taking a course: You can spend more time on each short story. If you are serious, you will soon find that a far greater percentage of your time and effort will go into the revisions than was spent on the original draft. You may get the feeling that writing fiction is like eating the dessert first—the initial draft being the fun part. Most professional writers spend from four to five times as much time on revisions as on the first draft.

Writing Groups as Support Systems

Once you are out of college, you may find it possible to join a writers' group or start one of your own. All it takes is three individuals who are serious about their work. There is a real benefit from receiving criticism of your own work, and the deadlines serve as great motivation.

Be careful, however, to consider carefully whether the other members are working with material that is like yours in intent if not in style. Some so-called writers' clubs are more social than literary, and others may be more commercial in motive than you wish to be. The best way to judge is to attend one or two meetings on a provisional basis before committing yourself.

Six Critical Questions

The six critical questions that follow can be used when you are reading a published story or novel. Or they can form the basis of a discussion in a class or informal writers' group. You should feel free to reproduce the headings without permission as long as credit is given and copies are not sold for profit.

In addition, you may want to use these critical questions when analyzing your own first draft. They echo the topics raised in the fiction section of this textbook, so you can always refer to the pertinent chapters if you need a quick review.

• First, *are the primary characters convincing or, in the case of satire, effective?* Stories which develop characters fully should give readers the feeling that they have actually met these people and have come to know them in some insightful way. Satiric fiction has a different goal since the characters being satirized usually represent types, not realistic individuals. In such cases the characters need not necessarily be convincing, but they should illustrate the type with some ingenuity. That is, they must be effective.

When discussing a fictional character in a class or an informal group, be careful not to get off on personal preferences about attitudes and personality types if this were a real person. Keep the focus on characterization—the ways in which character is being presented. How much do we find out about this character and how are we informed?

If a character does not seem to be developed properly, consider the possibility of changing the viewpoint. You may be too close to the character to maintain fictional control. Or in some cases a character you thought was central may not have as much fictional potential as another.

Secondary characters don't have to meet the same standards, but they still should have a purpose. As we have seen, minor characters sometimes offer commentary, serve as foils, or provide comic contrast. Or they may serve as a **catalyst**, a character who brings about a turn of events or a change in the attitude of another. The delinquent son in "Three Hearts," for example, is never developed fully, but his refusal or inability to help in an emergency has a dramatic effect on his mother.

• Second, *is the story constructed successfully?* It is often helpful to analyze just how many scenes there are before beginning to evaluate how they are handled. Once this is done, it is natural enough to discuss which scenes seem to be the most successful ones. Some may be too brief to provide the reader with a sense of being present; others may seem to drag. Frequently, a scattering of scenes may be combined to give the story a more solid base.

After discussing the scenes individually, examine the order: Is this the most effective sequence? If the opening is slow, for example, it might be worthwhile starting with a livelier scene and returning to the original situation at a later point in the story. If the order is complicated with a storyteller or with numerous flashbacks, consider whether the advantage of such a sequence is worth the risk of confusion and distraction. Keep in mind that while there is no "right" way for any one story, every approach has both advantages and disadvantages—and in different proportions. The critic's job is not to make pronouncements like, "You can't write a story that way," but, rather, to describe what seems to be successful from the reader's point of view and what is confusing or dull. Frequently, such reactions stem from the handling of the plot.

• Third, *does the story contain the types of tensions that keep fiction alive and interesting?* It is all too easy to say that a story is slow or that "It's just plain dull." But a critic who is helpful moves directly to the problem of determining what kinds of tensions might be established. In some cases it may be a matter of creating a conflict between the protagonist and another character or some other force. This could mean basic revisions in plot. In other cases the problem might be solved by adding some kind of dramatic question to arouse the curiosity of the reader.

• Fourth, *what is the theme, and is it sophisticated enough to be fresh and evocative?* You may have started with a clear idea of what your central concern was, but look at the finished story objectively to see if your aim has shifted. If your work is being discussed by a group, let them talk about what they see as the theme before you say anything. Ask them to be specific.

When dealing with theme, make sure that every scene and most of the small details contribute in some way to that central concern. Sometimes elements remain in a story merely because they were a part of the original experience or an earlier draft of the story. In those cases, careful cutting is needed.

• Fifth, *is the setting vivid, and does it contribute to the theme?* As we have seen, setting is not always a highly visible factor in fiction, but look closely at what you have and see if your setting does all you want it to. Could the same plot be moved to a place that would make more of an impression on the reader? If the setting is exotic, has it become an end in itself? Has a potentially interesting study of character become upstaged by theatrical special effects?

Although short-short stories are usually limited to a single setting, longer ones can easily afford two or more. Consider the possibility of contrasting two quite different settings, as was done in "Sausage and Beer" and "Man and Daughter in the Cold."

• Finally, *are the style and tone appropriate*? Is the story written in a manner that brings undue attention to the style? For example, have figurative language or blatant symbols made the work seem artificial or contrived? Or, on the other hand, does the story need greater implications?

What about the balance of modes? Is the story too talky? Perhaps it relies too heavily on dialogue. Is it breathlessly "action-packed"? An occasional change of pace might help. Is it too slow and introspective? Get your characters doing more and saying more.

The two greatest dangers in the area of tone are sentimentality and melodrama. In the first, the story appears to make an unjustified appeal to emotions such as pity or love. In the second, drama is pushed too far and becomes blatant and unconvincing. Group response is very helpful in determining whether you have moved in either of these directions. But if you have no critics available, you will have to make a special effort to read your own work as objectively as possible.

You may not always want to apply all six of these critical questions to every work you are analyzing. Keep them in mind, however, for these questions will serve to make you critically alert. They will help you when you are discussing the work of a colleague, reading published fiction, or evaluating your own work. The creative process and critical evaluation are two separate but equally important skills. Writers must be also be perceptive critics. It is through this dual role as creator and critic that we learn to develop our abilities on our own.

26
THEATER:
A LIVE PERFORMANCE

Drama as live performance. Special attributes of drama: dramatic impact, visual and auditory appeal, physically produced, continuous action, a spectator art. Getting started: A concept, primary characters, a plot outline.

The transition from writing fiction to writing plays is not as great as one might think. Both depend heavily on plot. Both reveal character through action and dialogue. Both are presented with a distinctive tone and are unified with some kind of central concern or theme.

The primary difference, however, is that a play is a live performance. It is produced physically in front of an audience and is performed by actors. This is theater's greatest asset and explains why it is flourishing today in spite of competition with film and television.

Ever since the first "talking movie," critics have predicted the end of legitimate theater. But not even the competition of television and then video have slowed the constant growth of new theaters. Many middle-sized cities have resident companies, and these are augmented with university theater programs of high quality.

Legitimate theater—live performance on a stage—continues to be popular in part *because* of television, not in spite of it. The economics of mass-audience television drama requires all but a few specially funded programs to reach for the widest possible audience. As a result, there is a certain uniformity in sitcom and action-drama scripts. Plotting, characterization, and theme are reduced to the simplest level and repeated with ritualistic regularity. Those who prefer subtlety and originality remain hungry for legitimate theater.

Every **genre** has its special attributes—qualities that distinguish it fundamentally from other forms of writing. It is a mistake to think of a play as fiction acted out on the stage or as a poem performed or as a low-budget version of film. It is none of these things. Before you begin writing your first play script, consider carefully what the special characteristics of the genre are.

The Special Attributes of Drama

The unique qualities of drama stem from the fact that the genre is intended to be a live performance. You will be able to find plays that do not contain one or two of the following characteristics, just as you can find some poems that make little use of rhythm and some stories without dialogue. Clearly these are not rules; they are recurring characteristics. Most playwrights consider them the assets of the genre.

• First, **drama** is by definition a *dramatic art*. That is, it generally has an emotional impact or force. In the case of comedy, we call it vitality. This is not just a tradition; it is a natural aspect of an art form that requires an audience to give its undivided attention for two-and-a-half to three hours.

This impact is often established early in a play with a **dramatic question** that seizes the attention of the audience long before the theme becomes evident. Dramatic questions are usually blunt and simple: Is this stranger a threat? Whom are they waiting for? Why do these characters hate each other? In most cases, these initial questions develop into specific conflicts. Although the need for tension like this is not as strong in very short plays and in comedies, it is usually greater in drama than in either fiction or poetry.

As in fiction, irony and satire often add to the dramatic aspect of a play. Still another device is the use of **shock**. Unusual or violent situations can explode when the audience least expects them.

Dramatic impact is hard to sustain, however. For this reason, most plays work up to a series of peaks, allowing the emotions of the audience to rest in between. This system of rising and falling action does not follow any prescribed pattern and is often intuitive on the part of the playwright—just as it is in the writing of short stories. But the need for such structure tends to make drama more sharply divided into scenes and acts—divisions that help to control the dramatic impact.

• Second, drama is a *visual art*. Action on the stage is usually a significant and organic part of the whole production. It is not enough in the twentieth century to have characters simply walk back and forth reciting poetry as they did in the highly stylized tradition of Greek theater. In most cases, the movement of characters on the stage is as important as the lines themselves.

And the visual concern extends beyond the characters. The set itself is often another important part of the production. Sophisticated lighting boards can convert the set from a static backdrop to a dynamic factor in developing the moods of each scene. The addition of projected images and even movie sequences—experiments in mixed media—offers one more appeal to the visual aspect of theater.

- Third, drama is an *auditory art*. It appeals to the ear. Except for stage directions, every word is **dialogue** and is intended to be spoken out loud. The sound of those lines becomes very important. In some respects, this brings playwrights closer to poets than to writers of fiction. Playwrights often read their lines out loud or have others read them, listening to the composition rather than studying it on the page.

This special attention to the sound of language applies as much to plays that are in the tradition of realism as to those that create the dreamlike distortions of expressionism. Not only are the sounds important, but the space between the lines can be utilized. In theater, silence can have as much dramatic impact as a shout.

- Fourth, drama is a *physically produced art*. This is sometimes difficult to remember for those who have been writing fiction. Since sets have to be constructed with wood and nails, there is not the freedom to shift from scene to scene the way one can in a short story. Scriptwriters should keep in mind just what kinds of demands they are placing on set designers and stage crews.

At first this may seem like a limitation, but there are compensating assets. Playwrights have an intense, almost personal contact with their audiences which is entirely different from the indirect connection fiction writers have with their readers. And the constraints of the stage often stimulate the imagination. For many playwrights these aspects outweigh any disadvantage.

- Fifth, drama is a *continuous art*. Members of the audience, unlike readers of fiction or poetry, must receive the play at whatever pace the playwright sets. They cannot linger on a sage observation or a moving episode. They cannot turn back a page or review an earlier scene. If you are shifting from writing fiction to drama, you can be more blatant with your themes and can, as we will see, make use of refrains to repeat your key themes.

As you get into play writing, you will find that the flow of drama is an aspect you can utilize. There is a momentum to a play that you can control. With practice you can make one portion of a scene move rapidly and another more slowly. Fiction writers can't maintain quite this kind of control over their readers.

The other side of this same coin is the concern a playwright must have about pacing. A slow scene that is extended just a bit too long can do real damage.

• Finally, and closely connected, is the fact that drama is a *spectator art*. Even more than with spectator sports, audience reaction is important. Poets are relatively far removed from such concerns. It is rare indeed for poets to change lines of their verse because of critical reviews or poor public response. Novelists are slightly more susceptible to "audience" reaction. Their circle of readers is potentially larger than a poet's, and authors tend to be aware of this. Many novelists will make fairly extensive revisions on the basis of their editors' suggestions. Usually, however, the publication of the work marks the end of the revision process.

Not so with plays. Playwrights often revise when their work is in rehearsal and after the opening-night reviews and even later if changes seem necessary. They frequently base their revisions on audience reaction—those awful moments when it laughs at the wrong moment or squirms with boredom.

This does not mean that dramatists are slaves to the reactions of audiences and critics. In most cases playwrights have a basic conception of the work which remains unalterable. But there is a direct and dynamic relationship between playwrights and their audiences. For many, this is one of the real pleasures in writing for the legitimate stage.

Getting Started

Poems frequently begin with an image; stories usually begin with a character in a situation. Plays more often begin with what is called a **concept**.

A dramatic concept includes a basic situation, some type of conflict or struggle, and an outcome, all in capsule form. You can, of course, start a play as tentatively as you might begin a story, hoping to shape and develop the plot as you work through the first draft. But such an approach is generally not as successful in play writing because so much depends on the whole dramatic structure.

Plays, like stories, often evolve from personal experience, but the need to create a dramatic situation involving conflict or struggle between two or more people often requires metamorphosing of the original episode from the start. Although this is a risky generalization, it is probably fair to say that plays tend to be less closely tied to direct personal experience than stories. In any case, you should feel free to explore newspaper stories and accounts told to you about individuals you have not met, as long as the situation is familiar enough for you to make it appear authentic.

If you keep a literary journal, jot down a number of possible concepts. If one seems to take shape in your mind, add the name and a brief description of one or two characters. Actually giving these characters names at the outset will help stimulate your imagination.

Next, try some sample dialogue. It helps if you can begin to hear two characters interact. See if you can create a little scene that at least roughly contributes to the concept you have in mind. Read the lines out loud. Imagine actors (male or female) saying those lines. Close your eyes and visualize the scene.

If you have done all this and you still feel that the concept has potential, begin to block out the action. That is, develop an outline in which each brief sequence of events is described in a telegraphic phrase or sentence. Such an outline might start this way:

1. Man alone on stage; talks to girl offstage.

2. Girl enters; they get to know each other.

3. Girl exits; man gives brief monologue.

Needless to say, there is no one right technique, and whatever works is fine; but the reason many playwrights block out the action before they actually write the dialogue has a good deal to do with the nature of the genre.

Even if you are writing a one-act play with a single set—which is a good pattern to start with—you will want to think in terms of **scenes**. I will have more to say about this in the chapter on plot (Chapter 28), but essentially a dramatic scene is a unit of action and dialogue that begins and ends with a character coming on stage or leaving. Some short plays have been written without these subtle yet important divisions, but they are rare. *Hello Out There*, which is presented as the next chapter, uses eight such scenes. When you read it, mark these divisions and see how they provide structure for the play.

As for the form of the script, follow the pattern used by the plays included in this volume. At first it may seem monotonous to repeat the name of each speaker, but it is the customary practice, one that actors depend on in rehearsal. If you are working with a computer, you may be able to program the name of each major character as a macro so that it will appear on the left margin with a simple two-stroke command.

Stage directions are written in italics. Italics in manuscript are still indicated by underlining even if your computer is capable of producing special type. Underlining is a traditional signal to the printer. Place directions in parentheses when they are short. It is helpful to include names of characters after the title, listing them in order of appearance.

There are two plays included in this section. The first is serious, realistic, and highly dramatic. The second is comic, often farcical, occasionally satiric, yet serious in its underlying themes. These two works are fundamentally different in tone and treatment and serve as a good indication of what an enormous latitude you have when writing drama.

To get started, begin with a good concept—not just an idea, but a situation. Then develop characters, fleshing them out with some samples of dialogue. Next, block out the action by outlining a plot scene by scene.

As you write, keep in mind that your script is more than something to be read on the page. You are creating a live performance for a live audience. Make their experience a memorable one.

27
A PLAY BY
WILLIAM SAROYAN

Hello Out There

for George Bernard Shaw

Characters
    A YOUNG MAN
    A GIRL
    A MAN
    TWO OTHER MEN
    A WOMAN

Scene
> *There is a fellow in a small-town prison cell, tapping slowly on the floor with a spoon. After tapping half a minute, as if he were trying to telegraph words, he gets up and begins walking around the cell. At last he stops, stands at the center of the cell, and doesn't move for a long time. He feels his head, as if it were wounded. Then he looks around. Then he calls out dramatically, kidding the world.*

YOUNG MAN: Hello—out there! (*Pause.*) Hello—out there! Hello—out there! (*Long pause.*) Nobody out there. (*Still more dramatically, but more comically, too.*) Hello—out there! Hello—out there!
    A GIRL'S VOICE *is heard, very sweet and soft.*
THE VOICE: Hello.

YOUNG MAN: Hello—out there.

THE VOICE: Hello.

YOUNG MAN: Is that you, Katey?

THE VOICE: No—this here is Emily.

YOUNG MAN: Who? (*Swiftly.*) Hello out there.

THE VOICE: Emily.

YOUNG MAN: Emily who? I don't know anybody named Emily. Are you that girl I met at Sam's in Salinas about three years ago?

THE VOICE: No—I'm the girl who cooks here. I'm the cook. I've never been in Salinas. I don't even know where it is.

YOUNG MAN: Hello out there. You say you cook here?

THE VOICE: Yes.

YOUNG MAN: Well, why don't you study up and learn to cook? How come I don't get no jello or anything good?

THE VOICE: I just cook what they tell me to. (*Pause.*) You lonesome?

YOUNG MAN: Lonesome as a coyote. Hear me hollering? Hello out there!

THE VOICE: Who you hollering to?

YOUNG MAN: Well—nobody, I guess. I been trying to think of somebody to write a letter to, but I can't think of anybody.

THE VOICE: What about Katey?

YOUNG MAN: I don't know anybody named Katey.

THE VOICE: Then why did you say, Is that you, Katey?

YOUNG MAN: Katey's a good name. I always did like a name like Katey. I never *knew* anybody named Katey, though.

THE VOICE: *I* did.

YOUNG MAN: Yeah? What was she like? Tall girl, or little one?

THE VOICE: Kind of medium.

YOUNG MAN: Hello out there. What sort of a looking girl are *you*?

THE VOICE: Oh, I don't know.

YOUNG MAN: Didn't anybody ever tell you? Didn't anybody ever talk to you that way?

THE VOICE: What way?

YOUNG MAN: You know. Didn't they?

THE VOICE: No, they didn't.

YOUNG MAN: Ah, the fools—they should have. I can tell from your voice you're O.K.

THE VOICE: Maybe I am and maybe I ain't.

YOUNG MAN: I never missed yet.

THE VOICE: Yeah, I know. That's why you're in jail.

YOUNG MAN: The whole thing was a mistake.

THE VOICE: They claim it was rape.

YOUNG MAN: No—it wasn't.

THE VOICE: That's what they claim it was.

YOUNG MAN: They're a lot of fools.

THE VOICE: Well, you sure are in trouble. Are you scared?

YOUNG MAN: Scared to death. (*Suddenly.*) Hello out there!

THE VOICE: What do you keep saying that for all the time?

YOUNG MAN: I'm lonesome. I'm as lonesome as a coyote. (*A long one.*) Hello—out there!

THE GIRL *appears, over to one side. She is a plain girl in plain clothes.*

THE GIRL: I'm kind of lonesome, too.

YOUNG MAN (*turning and looking at her*): Hey—No fooling? Are you?

THE GIRL: Yeah—I'm almost as lonesome as a coyote myself.

YOUNG MAN: Who *you* lonesome for?

THE GIRL: I don't know.

YOUNG MAN: It's the same with me. The minute they put you in a place like this you remember all the girls you ever knew, and all the girls you didn't get to know, and it sure gets lonesome.

THE GIRL: I bet it does.

YOUNG MAN: Ah, it's awful. (*Pause.*) You're a pretty kid, you know that?

THE GIRL: You're just talking.

YOUNG MAN: No, I'm not just talking—you *are* pretty. Any fool could see that. You're just about the prettiest kid in the whole world.

THE GIRL: I'm not—and you know it.

YOUNG MAN: No—you are. I never saw anyone prettier in all my born days, in all my travels. I knew Texas would bring me luck.

THE GIRL: Luck? You're in jail, aren't you? You've got a whole gang of people all worked up, haven't you?

YOUNG MAN: Ah, that's nothing. I'll get out of this.

THE GIRL: Maybe.

YOUNG MAN: No, I'll be all right—*now.*

THE GIRL: What do you mean—now?

YOUNG MAN: I mean after seeing you. I got something now. You know for a while there I didn't care one way or another. Tired. (*Pause.*) Tired of trying for the best all the time and never getting it. (*Suddenly.*) Hello out there!

THE GIRL: Who you calling now?

YOUNG MAN: You.

THE GIRL: Why, I'm right here.

YOUNG MAN: I know. (*Calling.*) Hello out there!

THE GIRL: Hello.

YOUNG MAN: Ah, you're sweet. (*Pause.*) I'm going to marry *you*. I'm going away with *you*. I'm going to take you to San Francisco or some place like that. I *am*, now. I'm going to win myself some real money, too. I'm going to study 'em real careful and pick myself some winners, and we're going to have a lot of money.

THE GIRL: Yeah?

YOUNG MAN: Yeah. Tell me your name and all that stuff.

THE GIRL: Emily.

YOUNG MAN: I know that. What's the rest of it? Where were you born? Come on, tell me the whole thing.

THE GIRL: Emily Smith.

YOUNG MAN: Honest to God?

THE GIRL: Honest. That's my name—Emily Smith.

YOUNG MAN: Ah, you're the sweetest girl in the whole world.

THE GIRL: Why?

YOUNG MAN: I don't know why, but you are, that's all. Where were you born?

THE GIRL: Matador, Texas.

YOUNG MAN: Where's that?

THE GIRL: Right here.

YOUNG MAN: Is this Matador, Texas?

THE GIRL: Yeah, it's Matador. They brought you here from Wheeling.

YOUNG MAN: Is that where I was—Wheeling?

THE GIRL: Didn't you even know what town you were in?

YOUNG MAN: All towns are alike. You don't go up and ask somebody what town you're in. It doesn't make any difference. How far away is Wheeling?

THE GIRL: Sixteen or seventeen miles. Didn't you know they moved you?

YOUNG MAN: How could I know, when I was out—cold? Somebody hit me over the head with a lead pipe or something. What'd they hit me for?

THE GIRL: Rape—that's what they *said*.

YOUNG MAN: Ah, that's a lie. (*Amazed, almost to himself.*) She wanted me to give her money.

THE GIRL: Money?

YOUNG MAN: Yeah, if I'd have known she was a woman like that—well, by God, I'd have gone on down the street and stretched out in a park somewhere and gone to sleep.

THE GIRL: Is that what she wanted—money?

YOUNG MAN: Yeah. A fellow like me hopping freights all over the country, trying to break his bad luck, going from one poor little town to another, trying to get in on something good somewhere, and she asks for money. I thought she was lonesome. She *said* she was.

THE GIRL: Maybe she was.

YOUNG MAN: She was *something*.

THE GIRL: I guess I'd never see you, if it didn't happen, though.

YOUNG MAN: Oh, I don't know—maybe I'd just mosey along this way and see you in this town somewhere. I'd recognize you, too.

THE GIRL: Recognize me?

YOUNG MAN: Sure, I'd recognize you the minute I laid eyes on you.

THE GIRL: Well, who would I be?

YOUNG MAN: Mine, that's who.

THE GIRL: Honest?

YOUNG MAN: Honest to God.

THE GIRL: You just say that because you're in jail.

YOUNG MAN: No, I mean it. You just pack up and wait for me. We'll high-roll the hell out of here to Frisco.

THE GIRL: You're just lonesome.

YOUNG MAN: I been lonesome all my life—there's no cure for that—but you and me—we can have a lot of fun hanging around together. You'll bring me luck. I know it.

THE GIRL: What are you looking for luck for all the time?

YOUNG MAN: I'm a gambler. I don't work. I've *got* to have luck, or I'm a bum. I haven't had any decent luck in years. Two whole years now—one place to another. Bad luck all the time. That's why I got in trouble back there in Wheeling too. That was no accident. That was my bad luck following me around. So here I am, with my head half busted. I guess it was her old man that did it.

THE GIRL: You mean her father?

YOUNG MAN: No, her husband. If I had an old lady like that, I'd throw her out.

THE GIRL: Do you think you'll have better luck, if I go with you?

YOUNG MAN: It's a cinch. I'm a good handicapper. All I need is somebody good like you with me. It's no good always walking around in the streets for anything that might be there at the time. You got to have somebody staying with you all the time—through winters when it's cold, and spring-time when it's pretty, and summertime when it's nice and hot and you can go swimming—through *all* the times—rain and snow and all the different kinds of weather a man's got to go through before he dies. You got to have somebody who's right. Somebody who knows you, from away back. You got to have somebody who even knows you're wrong but likes you just the same. I know I'm wrong, but I just don't want anything the hard way, working like a dog, or the *easy* way, working like a dog—working's the hard way and the easy way both. All I got to do is beat the price, always—and then, I don't feel lousy and don't hate anybody. If you go along with me, I'll be the finest guy anybody ever saw. I won't be wrong any more. You know when you get enough of that money, you *can't* be wrong any more—you're right because the money says so. I'll have a lot of money and you'll be just about the prettiest, most wonderful kid in the whole world. I'll be proud walking around Frisco with you on my arm and people turning around to look at us.

THE GIRL: Do you think they will?

YOUNG MAN: Sure they will. When I get back in some decent clothes, and you're on my arm—well, Katey, they'll turn around and look, and they'll see something, too.

THE GIRL: Katey?

YOUNG MAN: Yeah—that's your name from now on. You're the first girl I ever called Katey. I've been saving it for you O.K.?

THE GIRL: O.K.

YOUNG MAN: How long have I been here?

THE GIRL: Since last night. You didn't wake up until late this morning, though.

YOUNG MAN: What time is it now? About nine?

THE GIRL: About ten.

YOUNG MAN: Have you got the key to this lousy cell?

THE GIRL: No. They don't let me fool with any keys.

YOUNG MAN: Well, can you get it?

THE GIRL: No.

YOUNG MAN: Can you *try*?

THE GIRL: They wouldn't let me get near any keys. I cook for this jail, when they've got somebody in it. I clean up and things like that.

YOUNG MAN: Well, I want to get out of here. Don't you know the guy that runs this joint?

THE GIRL: I know him, but he wouldn't let you out. They were talking of taking you to another jail in another town.

YOUNG MAN: Yeah? Why?

THE GIRL: Because they're afraid.

YOUNG MAN: What are they afraid of?

THE GIRL: They're afraid these people from Wheeling will come over in the middle of the night and break in.

YOUNG MAN: Yeah? What do they want to do that for?

THE GIRL: Don't *you* know what they want to do it for?

YOUNG MAN: Yeah, I know all right.

THE GIRL: Are you scared?

YOUNG MAN: Sure I'm scared. Nothing scares a man more than ignorance. You can argue with people who ain't fools, but you can't argue with fools—they just go to work and do what they're set on doing. Get me out of here.

THE GIRL: How?

YOUNG MAN: Well, go get the guy with the key, and let me talk to him.

THE GIRL: He's gone home. Everybody's gone home.

YOUNG MAN: You mean I'm in this little jail all alone?

THE GIRL: Well—yeah—except me.

YOUNG MAN: Well, what's the big idea—doesn't anybody stay here all the time?

THE GIRL: No, they go home every night. I clean up and then I go, too. I hung around tonight.

YOUNG MAN: What made you do that?

THE GIRL: I wanted to talk to you.

YOUNG MAN: Honest? What did you want to talk about?

THE GIRL: Oh, I don't know. I took care of you last night. You were talking in your sleep. You liked me, too. I didn't think you'd like me when you woke up, though.

YOUNG MAN: Yeah? Why not?

THE GIRL: I don't know.

YOUNG MAN: Yeah? Well, you're wonderful, see?

THE GIRL: Nobody ever talked to me that way. All the fellows in town—(*Pause.*)

YOUNG MAN: What about 'em? (*Pause.*) Well, what about 'em? Come on—tell me.

THE GIRL: They laugh at me.

YOUNG MAN: Laugh at *you*? They're fools. What do they know about anything? You go get your things and come back here. I'll take you with me to Frisco. How old are you?

THE GIRL: Oh, I'm of age.

YOUNG MAN: How old are you?—Don't lie to me! Sixteen?

THE GIRL: I'm seventeen.

YOUNG MAN: Well, bring your father and mother. We'll get married before we go.

THE GIRL: They wouldn't let me go.

YOUNG MAN: Why not?

THE GIRL: I don't know, but they wouldn't. I know they wouldn't.

YOUNG MAN: You go tell your father not to be a fool, see? What is he, a farmer?

THE GIRL: No—nothing. He gets a little relief from the government because he's supposed to be hurt or something—his side hurts, he says. I don't know what it is.

YOUNG MAN: Ah, he's a liar. Well, I'm taking you with me, see?

THE GIRL: He takes the money I earn, too.

YOUNG MAN: He's got no right to do that.

THE GIRL: I know it, but he does it.

YOUNG MAN (*almost to himself*): This world stinks. You shouldn't have been born in this town, anyway, and you shouldn't have had a man like that for a father, either.

THE GIRL: Sometimes I feel sorry for him.

YOUNG MAN: Never mind feeling sorry for him. (*Pointing a finger.*) I'm going to talk to your father some day. I've got a few things to tell that guy.

THE GIRL: I know you have.

YOUNG MAN (*suddenly*): Hello—out there! See if you can get that fellow with the keys to come down and let me out.

THE GIRL: Oh, I couldn't.

YOUNG MAN: Why not?

THE GIRL: I'm nobody here—they give me fifty cents every day I work.

YOUNG MAN: How much?

THE GIRL: Fifty cents.

YOUNG MAN (*to the world*): You see? They ought to pay money to *look* at you. To breathe the *air* you breathe. I don't know. Sometimes I figure it never is going to make sense. Hello—out there! I'm scared. You try to get me out of here. I'm scared them fools are going to come here from Wheeling and go crazy, thinking they're heroes. Get me out of here, Katey.

THE GIRL: I don't know what to do. Maybe I could break the door down.

YOUNG MAN: No, you couldn't do that. Is there a hammer out there or anything?

THE GIRL: Only a broom. Maybe they've locked the broom up, too.

YOUNG MAN: Go see if you can find anything.

THE GIRL: All right. (*She goes.*)

YOUNG MAN: Hello—out there! Hello—out there! (*Pause.*) Hello—out there! Hello—out there! (*Pause.*) Putting me in jail. (*With contempt.*) Rape! Rape? *They* rape everything good that was ever born. His side hurts. They laugh at her. Fifty cents a day. Little punk people. Hurting the only good thing that ever came their way. (*Suddenly.*) Hello—out there!

THE GIRL (*returning*): There isn't a thing out there. They've locked everything up for the night.

YOUNG MAN: Any cigarettes?

THE GIRL: Everything's locked up—all the drawers of the desk, all the closet doors—everything.

YOUNG MAN: I ought to have a cigarette.

THE GIRL: I could get you a package maybe, somewhere. I guess the drug store's open. It's about a mile.

YOUNG MAN: A mile? I don't want to be alone that long.

THE GIRL: I could run all the way, and all the way back.

YOUNG MAN: You're the sweetest girl that ever lived.

THE GIRL: What kind do you want?

YOUNG MAN: Oh, any kind—Chesterfields or Camels or Lucky Strikes—any kind at all.

THE GIRL: I'll go get a package. (*She turns to go.*)

YOUNG MAN: What about the money?

THE GIRL: I've got some money. I've got a quarter I been saving. I'll run all the way. (*She is about to go.*)

YOUNG MAN: Come here.

THE GIRL (*going to him*): What?

YOUNG MAN: Give me your hand. (*He takes her hand and looks at it, smiling. He lifts it and kisses it.*) I'm scared to death.

THE GIRL: I am, too.

YOUNG MAN: I'm not lying—I don't care what happens to me, but I'm scared nobody will ever come out here to this Godforsaken broken-down town and find you. I'm scared you'll get used to it and not mind. I'm scared you'll never get to Frisco and have 'em all turning around to look at you. Listen—go get me a gun, because if they come, I'll kill 'em! They don't understand. Get me a gun!

THE GIRL: I could get my father's gun. I know where he hides it.

YOUNG MAN: Go get it. Never mind the cigarettes. Run all the way. (*Pause, smiling but seriously.*) Hello, Katey.

THE GIRL: Hello. What's *your* name?

YOUNG MAN: Photo-Finish is what they *call* me. My races are always photo-fin-ish races. You don't know what that means, but it means they're very close. So close the only way they can tell which horse wins is to look at a photograph after the race is over. Well, every race I bet turns out to be a photo-finish race, and my horse never wins. It's my bad luck, all the time. That's why they call me Photo-Finish. Say it before you go.

THE GIRL: Photo-Finish.

YOUNG MAN: Come here. (THE GIRL *moves close and he kisses her.*) Now, hurry. Run all the way.

THE GIRL: I'll run. (THE GIRL *turns and runs. The* YOUNG MAN *stands at the center of the cell a long time.* THE GIRL *comes running back in. Almost crying.*) I'm afraid. I'm afraid I won't see you again. If I come back and you're not here, I—

YOUNG MAN: Hello—out there!

THE GIRL: It's so lonely in this town. Nothing here but the lonesome wind all the time, lifting the dirt and blowing out to the prairie. I'll stay *here.* I won't *let* them take you away.

YOUNG MAN: Listen, Katey. Do what I tell you. Go get that gun and come back. Maybe they won't come tonight. Maybe they won't come at all. I'll hide the gun. When they let me out you can take it back and put it where you found it. And then we'll go away. But if they come, I'll kill 'em! Now, hurry—

THE GIRL: All right. (*Pause.*) I want to tell you something.

YOUNG MAN: O.K.

THE GIRL (*very softly*): If you're not here when I come back, well, I'll have the gun and I'll know what to do with it.

YOUNG MAN: You know how to handle a gun?

THE GIRL: I know how.

YOUNG MAN: Don't be a fool. (*Takes off his shoe, brings out some currency.*) Don't be a fool, see? Here's some money. Eighty dollars. Take it and go to Frisco. Look around and find somebody. Find somebody alive and halfway human, see? Promise me—if I'm not here when you come back, just throw the gun away and get the hell to Frisco. Look around and find somebody.

THE GIRL: I don't *want* to find anybody.

YOUNG MAN (*swiftly, desperately*): Listen, if I'm not here when you come back, how do you know I haven't gotten away? Now, do what I tell you. I'll meet you in Frisco. I've got a couple of dollars in my other shoe. I'll see you in San Francisco.

THE GIRL (*with wonder*): San Francisco?

YOUNG MAN: That's right—San Francisco. That's where you and me belong.

THE GIRL: I've always wanted to go to *some* place like San Francisco—but how could I go alone?

YOUNG MAN: Well, you're not alone any more, see?

THE GIRL: Tell me a little what it's like.

YOUNG MAN (*very swiftly, almost impatiently at first, but gradually slower and with remembrance, smiling, and* THE GIRL *moving closer to him as he speaks*): Well, it's on the Pacific to begin with—ocean water all around. Cool fog and seagulls. Ships from all over the world. It's got seven hills. The little streets go up and down, around and all over. Every night the fog-horns bawl. But they won't be bawling for you and me.

THE GIRL: What else?

YOUNG MAN: That's about all, I guess.

THE GIRL: Are people different in San Francisco?

YOUNG MAN: People are the same everywhere. They're different only when they love somebody. That's the only thing that makes 'em different. More people in Frisco love somebody, that's all.

THE GIRL: Nobody anywhere loves anybody as much as I love you.

YOUNG MAN (*shouting, as if to the world*): You see? Hearing you say that, a man could die and still be ahead of the game. Now, hurry. And don't forget, if I'm not here when you come back, get the hell to San Francisco where you'll have a chance. Do you hear me?

THE GIRL *stands a moment looking at him, then backs away, turns and runs. The* YOUNG MAN *stares after her, troubled and smiling. Then he turns away from the image of her and walks about like a lion in a cage. After a while he sits down suddenly and buries his head in his hands. From a distance the sound of several automobiles approaching is heard. He listens a moment, then ignores the implications of the sound, whatever they may be. Several automobile doors are slammed. He ignores this also. A wooden door is opened with a key and closed, and footsteps are heard in a hall. Walking easily, almost casually and yet arrogantly, a* MAN *comes in.*

YOUNG MAN (*jumps up suddenly and shouts at* THE MAN, *almost scaring him*): What the hell kind of jailkeeper are you, anyway? Why don't you attend to your business? You get paid for it, don't you? Now, get me out of here.

THE MAN: But I'm not the jailkeeper.

YOUNG MAN: Yeah? Well, who are you, then?

THE MAN: I'm the husband.

YOUNG MAN: What husband you talking about?

THE MAN: You know what husband.

YOUNG MAN: Hey! (*Pause, looking at* THE MAN.) Are you the guy that hit me over the head last night?

THE MAN: I am.

YOUNG MAN (*with righteous indignation*): What do you mean going around hitting people over the head?

THE MAN: Oh, I don't know. What do you *mean* going around—the way you do?

YOUNG MAN (*rubbing his head*): You hurt my head. You got no right to hit anybody over the head.

THE MAN (*suddenly angry, shouting*): Answer my question! What do you mean?

YOUNG MAN: Listen, you—don't be hollering at me just because I'm locked up.

THE MAN (*with contempt, slowly*): You're a dog!

YOUNG MAN: Yeah, well let me tell you something. You *think* you're the husband. You're the husband of nothing. (*Slowly.*) What's more, your wife—if you want to call her that—is a tramp. Why don't you throw her out in the street where she belongs?

THE MAN (*draws a pistol*): Shut up!

YOUNG MAN: Yeah? Go ahead, shoot—(*Softly.*) and spoil the fun. What'll your pals think? They'll be disappointed, won't they. What's the fun hanging a man who's already dead? (THE MAN *puts the gun away.*) That's right, because now you can have some fun yourself, telling me what you're going to do. That's what you came here for, isn't it? Well, you don't need to tell me. I *know* what you're going to do. I've read the papers and I know. They have fun. A mob of 'em fall on one man and beat him, don't they? They tear off his clothes and kick him, don't they? And women and little children stand around watching, don't they? Well, before you go on *this* picnic, I'm going to tell you a few things. Not that that's going to send you home with your pals—the other heroes. No. You've been outraged. A stranger has come to town and violated your women. Your pure, innocent, virtuous women. You fellows have got to set this thing right. You're men, not mice. You're homemakers, and you beat your children. (*Suddenly.*) Listen, you—I didn't know she was your wife. I didn't know she was anybody's wife.

THE MAN: You're a liar!

YOUNG MAN: Sometimes—when it'll do somebody some good—but not this time. Do you want to hear about it? (THE MAN *doesn't answer.*) All right, I'll tell you. I met her at a lunch counter. She came in and sat next to me. There was plenty of room, but she sat next to me. Somebody had put a nickel in the phonograph and a fellow was singing *New San Antonio Rose*. Well, she got to talking about the song. I thought she was talking to the waiter, but *he* didn't answer her, so after a while *I* answered her. That's how I met her. I didn't think anything of it. We left the place together and started walking. The first thing I knew she said, This is where I live.

THE MAN: You're a dirty liar!

YOUNG MAN: Do you want to hear it? Or not? (THE MAN *does not answer.*) O.K. She asked me to come in. Maybe she had something in mind, maybe she didn't. Didn't make any difference to me, one way or the other. If she was lonely, all right. If not, all right.

THE MAN: You're telling a lot of dirty lies!

YOUNG MAN: I'm telling the truth. Maybe your wife's out there with your pals. Well, call her in. I got nothing against her, or you—or any of you. Call her in, and ask her a few questions. Are you in love with her? (THE MAN *doesn't answer.*) Well, that's too bad.

THE MAN: What do you mean, too bad?

YOUNG MAN: I mean this may not be the first time something like this has happened.

THE MAN (*swiftly*): Shut up!

YOUNG MAN: Oh, you know it. You've always known it. You're afraid of your pals, that's all. She asked me for money. That's all she wanted. I wouldn't be here now if I had given her the money.

THE MAN (*slowly*): How much did she ask for?

YOUNG MAN: I didn't ask her how much. I told her I'd made a mistake. She said she would make trouble if I didn't give her money. Well, I don't like bargaining, and I don't like being threatened, either. I told her to get the hell away from me. The next thing I knew she'd run out of the house and was hollering. (*Pause.*) Now, why don't you go out there and tell 'em they took me to another jail—go home and pack up and leave her. You're a pretty good guy, you're just afraid of your pals.

THE MAN *draws his gun again. He is very frightened. He moves a step toward the* YOUNG MAN, *then fires three times. The* YOUNG MAN *falls to his knees.* THE MAN *turns and runs, horrified.*

YOUNG MAN: Hello—out there! (*He is bent forward.*)

THE GIRL *comes running in, and halts suddenly, looking at him.*

THE GIRL: There were some people in the street, men and women and kids—so I came in through the back, through a window. I couldn't find the gun. I looked all over but I couldn't find it. What's the matter?

YOUNG MAN: Nothing—nothing. Everything's all right. Listen. Listen, kid. Get the hell out of here. Go out the same way you came in and run—run like hell—run all night. Get to another town and get on a train. Do you hear me?

THE GIRL: What's happened?

YOUNG MAN: Get away—just get away from here. Take any train that's going—you can get to Frisco later.

THE GIRL (*almost sobbing*): I don't want to go any place without you.

YOUNG MAN: I can't go. Something's happened. (*He looks at her.*) But I'll be with you always—God damn it. Always!

He falls forward. THE GIRL *stands near him, then begins to sob softly, walking away. She stands over to one side, stops sobbing, and stares out. The excitement of the mob outside increases.* THE MAN, *with two of his pals, comes running in.* THE GIRL *watches, unseen.*

THE MAN: Here's the son of a bitch!

ANOTHER MAN: O.K. Open the cell, Harry.

The THIRD MAN *goes to the cell door, unlocks it, and swings it open. A* WOMAN *comes running in.*

THE WOMAN: Where is he? I want to see him. Is he dead? (*Looking down at him, as the* MEN *pick him up.*) There he is. (*Pause.*) Yeah, that's him.

Her husband looks at her with contempt, then at the dead man.

THE MAN (*trying to laugh*): All right—let's get it over with.

THIRD MAN: Right you are, George. Give me a hand, Harry.

They lift the body.

THE GIRL (*suddenly, fiercely*): Put him down!

THE MAN: What's this?

SECOND MAN: What are you doing here? Why aren't you out in the street?

THE GIRL: Put him down and go away.

She runs toward the MEN.

THE WOMAN *grabs her.*

THE WOMAN: Here—where do you think *you're* going?

THE GIRL: Let me go. You've no right to take him away.

THE WOMAN: Well, listen to her, will you? (*She slaps* THE GIRL *and pushes her to the floor.*) Listen to the little slut, will you?

They all go, carrying the YOUNG MAN's *body.* THE GIRL *gets up slowly, no longer sobbing. She looks around at everything, then looks straight out, and whispers.*

THE GIRL: Hello—out—there! Hello—out there!

CURTAIN

28
THE DRAMATIC PLOT

**The importance of concept. The scene as the basic unit of drama.
Providing dramatic questions throughout the play. Controlling the pace
through rising and falling action. The value of subplots.**

A good dramatic plot starts with a good concept. As I explained in Chapter
26, a **concept** is a very brief description that includes a basic situation, some
type of conflict or struggle, and an outcome.

A concept is not the same as a theme. The **theme**, which we will examine
in Chapter 34, is that portion of a play that comments on the human condition.
It is far more abstract. The *theme* of Shakespeare's *Othello*, for example, suggests that when blind trust in another person is combined with a poor ability
to judge character, the result can be total disaster. The *concept*, on the other
hand, is more specific: A kind-hearted nobleman places his trust in a scheming
and evil underling and is driven to murder the woman he loves.

Think of a concept as a complete sentence that will convince anyone that
your play is well worth reading or seeing. Here are some concepts that are
distinctly unpromising, and ways they could be improved:

- "It's a play about jealousy."

Who is jealous of whom? Why? And what is the outcome? Contrast that
with "Because Estelle could never forget her unfaithful father, she couldn't
trust her husband until she confronted her past."

- "War is hell."

This is a truism that has been repeated so often it no longer has impact. To become meaningful, it would have to be presented through specific characters. Here is one possibility: "For years the family revered the memory of Frank who had been killed in the Vietnam War, but only belatedly did they realize how seriously his younger brother had been psychologically damaged in the same war."

- "A play about a college student getting a summer job."

Yawn! We need specifics and some assurance that this is going to be a fresh treatment of a frequently used situation. For example: "Kathleen is delighted to be hired as a mechanic at an auto repair shop but faces a moral dilemma when she discovers that her newfound friends are reconditioning stolen cars."

These concepts are fairly blunt appeals to a potential audience, but they all serve to assure the playwright that the basic situation is one which will keep people in a theater. It is important to begin with a concrete situation charged with conflict because drama, even more than fiction, depends on tension and on events.

We can be fairly certain, for example, that in *Hello Out There*, William Saroyan did not start out with a determination to reveal aspects of hypocrisy in society and the fundamental need for individuals to make contact with one another. More likely he began with a concept that might be described like this: "A drifter is held in a small-town jail on a false rape charge. He almost manages to escape with the help of a young woman who is as lonely as he, but a mob, filled with a hypocritical sense of justice, reaches him first and kills him."

Turning from concept to the characters, brief descriptions might read like this: "Young man is a drifter and is genuinely lonely. Has always taken chances (named Photo-Finish). Appears to take advantage of girl to get out of jail, but is sincerely concerned about her plight as well. Does his best to get her to leave town before he is killed."

These are the raw materials of a play. Once you have them down on paper, you are ready to start outlining the plot.

The Scene as Basic Unit

In full-length plays the word **scene** is generally used to describe subdivisions of *acts*. Often they are written into the program notes and may involve a lapse of time or even a change of setting. In some cases they replace acts altogether.

For dramatists, however, the word *scene* also refers to each unit of action that begins with an entrance or an exit and ends with the next shift of characters on the stage. To avoid confusion, think of these as *secondary scenes*. They are the essential and basic units of action for the playwright, the actors, and the director as well.

Occasionally, a secondary scene may have a strong dramatic unity. It may build to a climax that is dramatically punctuated by the departure of one or more characters. Often, the unity is more subtle. It establishes the almost unnoticed rise and fall of action that distinguishes the play which is "dramatic" from the play that appears to be "flat" or "dull."

Hello Out There is an excellent example. It is a one-act play presented in one primary scene. There is one stage set and one apparently uninterrupted flow of action. But from a playwright's point of view, the work is divided into eight secondary scenes. Each of these is marked by an exit or entrance, and each has an influence on the rise and fall of dramatic impact.

Here are the scenes listed in the kind of outline some playwrights find helpful when planning a new play. The word *girl* is used rather than the more contemporary *young woman* simply to conform with Saroyan's script.

1. Man alone on stage; talks to girl offstage
2. Girl enters; they get to know each other
3. Girl exits; man gives brief monologue
4. Girl returns; they make pact
5. Girl exits; husband enters, argues, shoots
6. Husband exits, girl returns
7. Husband and pals return, drag body out
8. Girl alone on stage; repeats refrain

This sparse outline demonstrates how many separate units will be involved, but it doesn't indicate which are major scenes and which are minor, which are highly dramatic and which merely develop relationships. Each of these secondary scenes deserves a closer look.

Although the opening scene has only one actor on the stage, it is far from static. Notice that the man is neither musing philosophically to himself nor addressing the audience. His first lines call out for contact with someone else, and then almost at once he is interacting with the young woman, even before she is on stage. This is no prologue. Psychologically, the play begins as soon as these two characters are in voice contact.

The second scene begins when the young woman actually appears. If one merely reads the script on the page as if it were fiction, her entrance may not seem significant. But a playwright always keeps the visual aspect in mind, imagining the action from the audience's point of view. In production, her arrival on stage is the psychological start of a new scene.

This second scene is the longest in the play. Saroyan has to fill in a great deal of background and, in addition, draw these two strangers together convincingly. It would have been possible to have Emily on stage from the start, but postponing her entrance helps to keep that long second scene from becoming even longer.

The third scene is very brief. She goes out to look for tools, and he is left on the stage alone. But it is important because it allows him to lash out vehemently against what he sees as injustice. The fact that he is alone on the stage indicates to the audience that he is speaking his inner conviction. Were it not for this little scene, we might feel that he was cynically lying to the girl simply to save himself.

The fourth scene is one in which Emily and Photo-Finish make the pact to meet in San Francisco. Notice that their relationship has grown with surprising speed. In a story, one might be tempted to spread the action out over the course of a day or so; but Saroyan's dramatic sense leads him to keep the action continuous.

Emily leaves, ending the fourth scene, and there is only a moment of sound effects before a new character suddenly appears on the stage. The tension mounts as we learn that this is the angered husband. An argument pushes the dramatic impact to new levels, and the husband draws his gun. The scene culminates with three shots.

In the sixth scene the husband has fled and Emily returns. The dying hero and heroine are alone on the stage. If this were opera, it would be the point where the final duet is sung. As realistic drama, it is a brief, terse, yet tender moment.

But a problem arises here. How is the playwright going to maintain dramatic interest in that brief yet important section which follows the death of the protagonist? Once again, a new secondary scene is prepared for—the seventh. First the audience hears activity building off stage. Saroyan is careful to include this in his stage directions: "The excitement of the mob outside increases." The husband, two friends, and then the wife all burst on the stage. Emily demands that they put the body down—what we can assume is the first dramatically assertive act of her life. She is slapped and pushed to the floor.

The last of these secondary scenes is so brief that it consists of only one line. But to understand just how powerful the device is, imagine the girl delivering that last line with the other characters still on stage, struggling to drag the body off. Emily would be literally upstaged. In addition, her line would be a mere continuation of the preceding dialogue. Having her alone on the stage, probably with a single beam of light on her, isolates the final words. Her plight—now matching that of Photo-Finish at the very beginning of the play—becomes the focal point of the play.

When one first reads a play like this, it is easy to assume that it is one continual flow of action from beginning to end. Such an approach would, of course, be possible. But it would be far more difficult to hold the audience's emotional involvement for that length of time. Exits and entrances in this play provide the basic organizational structure with which the dramatic impact is heightened and lowered and then heightened again in regular succession, holding the audience from beginning to end.

Because most of us have seen more films than plays, it is easy to be influenced by the rapid pace of their scenes. The camera not only can blend extremely brief units of action into an apparently smooth flow, it can shift setting without a break. Changing the set on the stage is time-consuming and tends to break the illusion of reality. For this reason, many full-length plays and almost all one-act plays maintain a single set. In addition, very short scenes such as the ones Saroyan uses to reveal Photo-Finish alone on the stage are kept to a minimum.

In judging the length of your secondary scenes, keep imagining the effect on your audience. Too many short scenes will make the action seem choppy; lengthy scenes may create monotony and slow the pace. You can make these decisions more easily if you have a chance to hear your script read aloud or, best of all, to see it in production.

Providing Dramatic Questions

How are you going to hold your audience in their seats? When you write fiction, this is less of a problem. A story or novel can be read in installments. But when you produce a play you are asking an audience to give it their uninterrupted attention—often while sitting on uncomfortable seats.

Because of this, most plays are energized with a series of **dramatic questions**. These are like lures to hold the interest of the audience. We have already seen how fiction also makes use of dramatic questions (Where are we going? What will this stranger be like?), but plays depend on them to a far greater degree.

Looking at the full range of drama from Sophocles to our own decade, there are certain dramatic questions that recur frequently. This does not make the plays redundant; one hardly notices the similarity. But their widespread use does suggest just how important the dramatic question is.

1. *Will he come?* Shakespeare charged the first act of *Hamlet* with this question, applying it to the ghost. More recently, it has been broadened to cover the full length of plays. Clifford Odets' *Waiting for Lefty*, written in the thirties, Samuel Beckett's *Waiting for Godot*, and Harold Pinter's *The Dumb Waiter* all rely heavily on anticipation of a character who never appears. And to some degree, the question is a factor in *Hello Out There* as soon as the threat of a lynching is raised.

2. *Who did it?* This is, of course, the literary version of "Whodunit?" We find it running the full length of drama from *Oedipus Rex* to Tennessee Williams' *Suddenly Last Summer*. The trial scenes in *The Caine Mutiny Court Martial* and, in a loose sense, *Tea and Sympathy* and *The Crucible* are simply variations of this. In many cases the audience knows who is guilty; the dramatic question arises out of the attempt on the part of the *characters* to determine guilt. It is a highly variable device, though the trial scene has become overused.

3. *Will he or she succeed?* This is by far the most used of all dramatic questions. It has been applied to noble and evil characters alike.

4. *Will he or she discover what we know?* The classic example is *Oedipus Rex*, in which the audience is held by the drama of a character gradually discovering terrible truths about himself. It is also a factor in *Othello*. And it has more recently been adapted in plays of psychological self-discovery such as Arthur Miller's *Death of a Salesman*.

5. *Will a compromise be found?* This question has held audiences in such varied plays as Sophocles' *Antigone*, John Galsworthy's *Strife*, and more subtly in Tennessee Williams' *A Streetcar Named Desire*. In all three of these examples, by the way, the dramatic question is merged with the theme itself—a connection none of the other questions have.

6. *Will this episode end in violence?* This is frequently used in contemporary drama. In fact, it is one of the final questions in *Hello Out There*. Even though almost every indication points to a tragic ending, we are still deeply concerned.

7. *What's happening?* This is the question most frequently asked of plays in the absurdist tradition. Like dream fiction, these works plunge the audience into a confusing, often inexplicable environment. Playwrights like Pinter, Beckett, Ionesco, and occasionally Albee utilize ambiguity as a dramatic question. This is, however, a risky device for the novice. Like free verse, it seems easy at first but often slides into meaninglessness. It requires wit or ingenuity of thematic suggestion to keep the play alive. In short, a dull play is not improved by making it an obscurely dull play.

The opening dramatic question is often referred to as the **hook**. It arouses interest from the start. But most plays move from one dramatic question to the next so that the audience is kept wondering about immediate outcomes as well as about what the ultimate resolution will be. *Hello Out There* is a good example of how the playwright can create a new question just as an old one has been resolved.

The play begins with a man in jail, and the audience immediately wonders why he is there. What did he do? Should we sympathize with him? Through the girl we begin to get answers to these questions, but at the same time a new cluster of dramatic questions is forming: Will she help him? And if she does, will they succeed? Toward the end of the play, we have a sense of foreboding: It is not likely that the outcome will be happy. But as in all tragedies, we still concern ourselves with the survival of the protagonist. There is for most members of the audience a lingering hope that he will live up to his nickname and win by a photo-finish.

Don't confuse these questions with the theme. Saroyan's thematic concern is with the loneliness of individuals; he is comparing life in a small and hostile town with being in jail. I will return to various aspects of theme in later chapters. My concern here is for the basic technique of generating dramatic questions. They are truly theatrical devices and are essential if a play is to hold the attention of the audience.

Controlling the Pace

Pace is all-important in a play. Scenes that appear to drag are revised well into production. Although one rarely hears about a play in which the pace is too rapid, it is possible to race too quickly through scenes that should unfold character or clarify aspects of the plot. And too much dramatic voltage at the beginning of a play can create a slump later on.

Traditional terms are helpful if we remember that they apply mainly to the plots of traditional plays. **Rising action**, for example, accurately describes the mounting complications with which many plays from all historical periods are begun. In full-length dramas, problems may be compounded with subplots involving secondary characters acting as **foils** to highlight or set off the major characters. The crisis is not the very end but the turning point at which the protagonist's fortunes begin to fail. From there on we have **falling action**, which in tragedies results in a **catastrophe**—often the death of the hero.

Sound old-fashioned? True, Aristotle described drama in those terms. True, they apply to Greek and Elizabethan tragedies. But they also apply to many modern works by such playwrights as Eugene O'Neill, Arthur Miller, and Tennessee Williams. In condensed form, they can be seen in William Saroyan's *Hello Out There* as well.

The rising action involves the young man meeting an ally and planning an escape. The crisis occurs when the enraged husband returns. From there on it is falling action through to the death of the protagonist. Although the play is brief and in one act, the plot structure is similar to that of a traditional three-act play or an Elizabethan tragedy of five acts.

This plot form continues to be popular not because playwrights who use it are imitative but because it is good theater. It lends itself to a variety of situations and it holds audiences.

This is, however, only one way to handle the pacing of a dramatic plot. Another method focuses on characterization and is sometimes referred to as the onion approach: A series of scenes exposes the inner life of a character or a couple like peeling the layers of an onion. Eugene O'Neill's *The Iceman Cometh* reveals a single character this way; Edward Albee's *Who's Afraid of Virginia Woolf?* exposes the illusions of a couple with equal intensity.

Another type of loose plotting is sometimes called the *Grand Hotel* pattern, though the title refers to a novel by Vicki Baum, not a play. The novel brings together a number of different characters to portray European society in the 1920s. This approach weaves together many parallel plots and lends itself to longer plays. A good contemporary example is *The Hot l Baltimore* by Lanford Wilson. Once again a hotel (this one not so grand) is used to link characters, and the plot is episodic. Arthur Miller's relatively short *A Memory of Two Mondays* deals with the men who work in the shipping room of an auto-parts warehouse. It is concerned almost equally with all the characters. The pace in plays like this is controlled not by the rise and fall of a protagonist, but by a series of dramatic questions based on the problems faced by a number of different characters.

In the case of comedy and farce, which we will examine in more detail in Chapter 35, pace is often controlled by increasing the intensity. In satire, this means increasing the degree of exaggeration. That is, the opening scenes are presented as relatively mild satire; but as the play builds, so does the intensity of the satire. As we will see, Louis Phillips' play *Goin' West* (Chapter 31) starts with a well-meaning family heading west for the best of reasons, builds to scenes involving a man who would sell his wife to get ahead in films, and concludes with disaster for the entire state of California. What seems at first like a series of skits is in fact a carefully controlled series of steps in which the pace and the degree of satire accelerate throughout the work.

As we examine the variety of approaches available, it becomes clear that we cannot talk about "rules" for constructing plots. You are free to make good use of certain traditional patterns, and you are also free to strike out with a new approach. But this doesn't mean that anything goes. You must control the pacing in some way. If you don't make use of rising and falling action, consider some type of unfolding to replace it. Low-key scenes must be alternated with dramatic ones effectively enough to maintain interest. If you ignore these basic requirements of pacing, your audience will be quick to let you know.

The Resonance of Subplots

The term *one-act play* is often used rather loosely to describe those works that run less than 30 minutes or so. Both of the plays in this volume are one-acts even though each is presented through a series of distinct scenes. One-acts are the best form to work with when you first begin writing plays, just as the short-short story is the best form for those beginning to write fiction.

In most cases, a one-act play is not long enough to support a subplot. But the technique is so important in longer plays that it is worth examining here.

A **subplot**, as the name implies, is a sequence of actions involving secondary characters. If, for example, the main plot deals with a relationship between a man and a woman, a subplot might develop a second couple. Or the subplot might focus on the activities of a single individual.

One common use of the subplot is to echo the serious plot with one that is similar but either lighter or actually comic. This provides a tonal contrast, a kind of counterpoint to the main plot. It also is a natural way to introduce **comic relief**, a technique of easing tension that I will discuss in more detail in Chapter 35.

A second use of the subplot is to dramatize a different approach to the problems faced by the protagonist. If, for example, the major character is about to lose his job because he is careless, disorganized, and unrealistically optimistic, a secondary character may serve as contrast by being highly organized and efficient to the point of endangering his marriage. Although the two characters interact, each has his own set of problems and each works toward a different resolution.

Frequently the subplot echoes the pattern of rising and falling action, though it is usually resolved before the conclusion of the main plot so as not to interfere. Be careful not to allow the subplot to dominate the play. If it begins to compete with the main plot in intensity, the play will seem to lack a focus. The only exception to this is in the case of what we have been calling the Grand-Hotel pattern in which there are many equally important plots. These are not, however, true subplots since they are parallel and relatively equal.

It is difficult to establish a subplot in a one-act play because of the time it takes to develop the secondary characters. But study the technique when you read full-length plays, and consider it when you begin a longer work. A subplot can often bring needed resonance to a play that would otherwise have seemed tonally monotonous or narratively simple.

Plot exists in narrative poetry; it is important in fiction; but it is crucial in drama. While a story can afford to suspend the flow of action for passages of reflection or description, a play must be an intense experience for an audience. It must hold everyone's full attention without interruption. And it must be done with action and dialogue alone.

This is a challenge, but it has its positive side. A dramatic plot gives you as playwright an opportunity to attract and hold the attention of an audience with a sustained intensity rarely generated by the printed page. This direct and charged contact between artist and viewer is one of the special rewards for the playwright.

29
CONFLICT

The limitation of simple conflicts. Creating multiple conflicts. Revealing inner conflict. Triangular conflicts. The individual against society. Making conflict visual.

Simple dramas have simple conflicts. Such conflicts usually erode characterization, reducing the work to a combat between good and bad. In such plays, the loyalties of the audience are fixed from start to finish. It's our team versus theirs. We see this pattern so often in popular film and television dramas that we sometimes discount the real potential of conflict.

Conflict is, however, the primary energizing force in drama. When we say that a work is "dramatic" or "powerful," we are implying that **dramatic conflict** has been used convincingly. Dramatic questions, described in the previous chapter, arouse curiosity. Conflict evokes fear, excitement, anger, commitment. It pumps adrenalin.

There are ways to use conflict without turning your play into a simple slugfest. The best approach is to create a network of related conflicts. One should also consider inner struggles, triangles, and conflicts with society. We can examine these in the abstract, but remember that selecting a type of conflict is not a good way to start a new play. As I have suggested before, start with a specific character or group of characters already involved in an ongoing situation. Once you have that as a base, consider what types of conflict arise naturally from that situation and which of these might be developed.

Multiple Conflicts

At first glance, the conflict in many plays—even highly sophisticated works—appears to be a basic struggle between two characters. It is easy enough in most cases to pick out the **protagonist** (central character) and the **antagonist** (his or her opponent). But if there are more than two characters, this struggle may well be a part of what is really a system of interrelated conflicts.

In full-length plays this pattern of conflict may be dramatized through one or more **subplots** involving secondary characters who echo, amplify, or contrast the conflicts of the main plot. Although there is rarely time to construct a subplot in a one-act play, you can still develop a cluster of conflicts rather than relying entirely on a single struggle.

Hello Out There is a good example. When the play opens, there is no antagonist in sight. The first major conflict to be developed is a man against a hostile town. The enemy is "they"—a vague notion of forces outside that jail. This conflict, man against society, is highlighted when we learn that the name of the town is Matador. He is the bull in the arena.

We soon see that Emily is also pitted against this town. Her life is not threatened, but her spirit is. She is not just lonesome, she is alienated. The men in town, she reports, laugh at her. Her father takes what little money she earns. She is willing to take great risks to escape.

Their shared conflict with this oppressive town continues throughout the play, but our attention is soon focused on the direct confrontation between Photo-Finish and the outraged husband. This isn't some vague possibility, it is immediate, direct, and physical.

But the husband is more than some simple comic-strip villain. It is soon apparent that he is dealing with a second conflict, one with his friends. We are told in the stage directions that he is "very frightened," and a good actor would show this in his behavior. In spite of this, he is driven by the other men to behave in a harsh and brutal manner. "You're a pretty good guy," Photo-Finish says, "you're just afraid of your pals." Even though the killing takes the outward form of a simple television drama, the play is not simply an all-good hero pitted against an evil antagonist. The killing is a tragic result of a network of conflicts.

In a longer play, it would be possible to increase the complexity of the situation by establishing an initial conflict between Photo-Finish and the young woman. It would be natural enough to have her go through a period of hostility toward him, a conflict that might be resolved as they face a common enemy. This might make the situation more realistic, but it would have the disadvantage of adding more scenes without much action.

It may seem difficult at first to generate a multiplicity of conflicts in the very limited time frame of a short one-act play. But if you have well-rounded characters, the problem often solves itself. I will return to characterization in Chapter 30, but it is worth pointing out here that plays which depend too heavily on a single, simple conflict almost always suffer from characterization that is also simple.

Inner Conflict

Inner conflicts are another effective method of achieving subtlety. The very phrases with which we describe such indecision suggest dramatic tension: A character is "of two minds," "struggling with himself," or even "at war with herself." Such individuals are torn between love and fear, courage and timidity, anger and affection. Or they may be attracted to two different people, two opposing ethical positions, two sexual identities. Inner conflict is a part of the human condition.

But how is one to reveal what goes on in the mind of a character in a genre that depends almost entirely on dialogue and actions? If you have been writing fiction, your first inclination may be to consider monologues. After all, Shakespeare used them. The soliloquies of Hamlet and Lady Macbeth are among the most quoted dramatic lines in the language. But remember that those monologues were embedded in five-act plays. If we hadn't heard them so often and studied them so carefully out of context they would blend into the work as a whole. In addition, Elizabethan drama accepted the convention of major characters expressing their inner conflicts eloquently in blank verse. In a contemporary, realistic play that is intended to reflect more closely the behavior and speech of daily life, the inner debate expressed through a monologue may seem artificial.

In spite of these risks, monologues are used from time to time in contemporary drama. Saroyan's first scene begins with a brief one, and he repeats the device by having Photo-Finish alone on the stage in the abbreviated third scene. This second monologue is particularly important because it is the only hard evidence the audience has that Photo-Finish really is fond of Emily and is not just using her for escape. Although Emily's two lines at the very end of the play take only a moment, they effectively reveal her inner lament.

During the 1960s and '70s there was a certain vogue for long monologues among playwrights of the absurdist school. Their plays were often dreamlike, philosophical, and talky. They frequently contained lengthy pronouncements. The best of them held interest through flashes of insight and wit, but the approach was short-lived. It takes remarkable skill on the part of both playwright and actor to maintain the interest of an audience with thought alone.

To avoid the static quality of monologues, consider the possibility of providing your protagonist with a confidant—a personal friend who is not quite central to the action. In some cases, this may turn out to be a **foil**—a character who sets off some of the characteristics of your protagonist by contrast. If you are working with two couples, the two women or the two men can sometimes reveal to each other inner conflicts that they are reluctant to share with their partners.

Another approach is using action. People often reveal their inner conflicts through the way they behave—often quite unconsciously. It is not difficult to have your characters do the same. There is a small example in *Hello Out There* which is easily missed, but it represents a well-used device. Emily is struggling between the desire to do whatever she can for Photo-Finish and, on the other hand, the fear of leaving him for a minute. When he asks her to go and look for cigarettes, she leaves, running, and then comes running back without the cigarettes almost at once. Alternating behavior like this can be used in more significant scenes as well. A character starts to do one thing, then abruptly does another. Often no lines are needed to spell out the inner conflict.

Inner conflicts or debates with oneself are almost always linked in some way to outer conflicts. Such indecision is one of the best ways of keeping your major conflict from becoming wooden and unconvincing.

Triangular Conflicts

To this point we have been examining conflicts that pit a single element against another. Triangles provide an additional dimension.

The first pattern that comes to mind is the couple threatened by a third party. It has a venerable tradition. Medea's betrayal by her husband, Jason, who fell in love with another woman has been told and retold from the tragedy of Euripides to the modern verse play of Robinson Jeffers. The same pattern of betrayal and revenge is repeated endlessly in contemporary play and film scripts, both on serious and comic levels. Sometimes the malevolent agent is not another lover but simply an evil force, as in the case of Iago in Shakespeare's *Othello*.

If you consider a love triangle as the basis of conflict in a one-act play, you will have to work hard to achieve originality. The sexy baby-sitter and the obliging secretary are stereotypes. But triangles do continue to exist in life, and in some cases the unique circumstances of an actual case will suggest a fresh dramatic situation.

Remember too that not all triangles involve a third person. Both husbands and wives have been known to become seduced by professional commitments. A married person's involvement with a political cause, a new religious faith, or a physically disabled child can have the impact of an infidelity. Here too there are situations that have been overdone. The marriage that is threatened by a husband's preoccupation with his business can, if not done in a fresh manner, become as hackneyed in drama as in fiction. As I mentioned in the fiction section, merely reversing the sexes doesn't add much if the characters are still cardboard. And there should be a moratorium on drama plots based on painters who wreck their marriages for the sake of art. But even setting these aside, there are enough triangulations left to serve future dramatists for some time to come.

It is not enough merely to select or invent a triangular pattern of conflict and fill in the blanks. Remember that if you are writing serious drama you are dealing with people in pain. If you consider the situation carefully, you will see inner conflicts as well as the more obvious outer ones. In short, the triangle is only a frame. The worth of your play will depend on how successfully you can humanize that structure with credible characters.

The Individual Against Society

Conflict between individuals is often given greater resonance when it is played against a larger struggle with society. The confrontation between a small-time gambler and an irate husband in a backwater town does not in itself seem very promising. But Saroyan raises the play above the level of a minor news item by using that incident to dramatize and personalize a conflict between the individual and society as a whole.

In that broader conflict, Saroyan unmistakably takes sides. On the one hand, all the characters are treated with some compassion—even the worst of them. The husband who does the killing is described in the lines quoted earlier as a frightened man who is mainly motivated by what others expect of him. And although the wife is seen as hard and brutal when in the company of the men at the end, she is earlier described as more pathetic than evil. Society, on the other hand, is pictured as the real culprit. Photo-Finish, musing to himself, says "This world stinks." Later, outraged at the charge of rape and also at how the town has treated Emily, he says, "Rape? *They* rape everything good that was ever born." When there is still hope of escape, Emily asks, "Are people different in San Francisco?" "People are the same everywhere," he says. "They're different only when they love somebody. More people in Frisco love somebody, that's all." In the conflict between the individual and society as a whole, Saroyan clearly sides with the individual.

Society for Saroyan is a fairly general concept. But it can be viewed in much more specific terms. Some playwrights see society as made up of the rich and powerful. Their work takes a political stance. For many black playwrights, society is the white world. I will have more to say about socially conscious drama and themes of protest in Chapter 34, "Dramatic Themes." What concerns us here is the way in which society can be seen as the opposing force, creating a conflict that is almost always repeated in the form of individual against individual.

The dramatic impact that can be generated by pitting the individual against society is enormous. If you take that route, however, be careful not to let your play turn into a sermon. Sermons have their place, but they make poor drama—except for those who already agree. The most successful plays dealing with society are the ones that can translate those relatively abstract convictions into person-to-person conflict. Even when social statement is the primary concern of the playwright, it is personal conflict between credible characters that has immediate impact.

Making Conflict Visual

For most of our childhood we have been told not to shout, not to cry, not to hit our classmates or break windows. In short, the message was to hide our emotions. This is necessary, no doubt, if humans are to live together in school or in the world at large. But when it comes to writing a play, we have to do all of these and more.

It is not enough for a character in a play to talk about how she hates her brother. It isn't sufficient for a father to confess that he resents his son or for a woman to admit that she hates strangers or for a couple to tell a counselor that they feel like killing each other. All these have to be shown. They have to be shown repeatedly and in different ways. Emotions have to be translated into action.

A good actor or actress will provide appropriate facial expressions and gestures. And a director may add actions that will augment what is in the script. Lovers touch, antagonists gesture threateningly, a character struggling with inner conflict may pace or even pound the wall. But don't rely on actors or directors to do it all. Give them something to work with. You as playwright have to provide dramatic ways for the audience to see the conflict.

Saroyan gives us many visual cues. I have already pointed out how Emily dramatizes her inner conflict by running off to get her father's gun and just as quickly running back for fear of not seeing Photo-Finish again. And later when Photo-Finish is alone on the stage, his sense of entrapment and rage against his captors is dramatized with the stage directions, "He...walks about like a lion in a cage."

When the husband appears onstage, the visual cues of hostility are appropriately more apparent. He draws a gun. But when Photo-Finish begins to talk reasonably with the man (the stage directions say "softly"), the husband puts the gun away. At the height of the exchange, the gun comes out again.

At the end of the play, the contempt of the scheming wife toward Emily is dramatized not just with the line, "the little slut," but also by a slap.

Two words of caution. First, be careful about the standard cues—the fistfight, the shooting, the suicide. If you don't prepare for them carefully, they will make your play seem like a rerun of an old Western film. Much depends on whether you, like Saroyan, have created credible characters. But even then, consider fresh and original ways of demonstrating inner and outer conflict.

Second, remember pacing. If you start your play with highly visual displays of violent conflict and sustain them, the effectiveness will decrease simply through repetition. If a serious play even faintly echoes the Three Stooges, it is in deep trouble.

One way to test whether conflict is being communicated visually is to imagine a scene without the dialogue. The last third of *Hello Out There*, for example, is visually communicated step by step through to the concluding tragedy almost as if it were a ballet.

When we use the word *dramatic*, we imply conflict. Plays that lack conflict are often described as slow, talky, tedious, lacking in vitality, or just plain dull. Fiction can afford reflective or descriptive passages if they are occasionally revitalized by a forward movement of the plot. But a play thrives on energy, and energy is generated through conflict.

30
DRAMATIC
CHARACTERIZATION

The need for vividness. The importance of first impressions. Creating depth of character. Characters in flux: shifts in attitude, in fortune, and in audience perception. Using minor characters effectively.

On a literal level, the title of this chapter refers to the special ways in which characters in plays are developed. It also suggests quite correctly that such characters are often more *dramatic* than those in fiction in the sense of being vivid and slightly exaggerated. What we think of as "realism" on the stage is usually on close examination an intensification of what we expect in life. While this is not true in every case, it is a general characteristic and applies to both the plays included in this text.

This special vividness of characters on the stage is due partly to the nature of the genre. As I pointed out earlier, drama is a continuous art. Unlike fiction, it is presented at a single sitting and at a regular rate. There is no going back to review a passage that introduced a character or to fill in some missing detail. Imagine novelists insisting that their work be read nonstop from cover to cover in a public place miles from home in the company of total strangers. It's no wonder playwrights tend to paint in bold colors!

There is a second factor that tends to make characters on the stage just a bit stagy. Writers of fiction have at their disposal a whole array of techniques with which they can develop characters. They can quote thoughts naturally and frequently without slowing the action; they can thrust a reader into a flashback at any moment; they can even comment on a character in their own voice if they wish. Not so for playwrights. Essentially they are limited to what a character says and does. True, there are ways of extending these limitations—techniques I will turn to shortly. But the basic restriction is there. Because drama relies so heavily on action and dialogue, playwrights tend to use them more boldly.

The Importance of First Impressions

When the protagonist of a play enters for the first time, what he or she does and says provides an initial impression that will linger for the length of the play. Those first few lines have a crucial influence on the audience's judgment of a character.

In the case of *Hello Out There*, Saroyan is faced with a particularly difficult challenge. How can he induce an audience to look favorably and sympathetically at a small-time gambler and drifter who has been jailed for rape? With this question in mind, take a close look at the way Saroyan handles those very first lines:

> YOUNG MAN: Hello—out there! (*Pause.*) Hello—out there! (*Long pause.*) Nobody out there. (*Still more dramatically, but more comically, too.*) Hello—out there! Hello—out there!

Normally, playwrights don't provide so many stage directions, since both directors and actors like to have more leeway. But in this case Saroyan is clearly concerned with creating just the right initial impression. He keeps his protagonist alone on the stage and gives him lines that establish his mood and character before revealing the actual situation.

Those very first lines are hesitant, nonthreatening, appealing. They focus on loneliness and reach out for sympathy as much as for companionship. His tone is insistent—we are encouraged to take him seriously—yet also comic. And those same qualities dominate that entire initial scene. Why is this so important? Because if the audience is not won over in the first few minutes, it will not believe him when he claims that the charge of rape is false. Deciding whether to accept as true what strangers say is based entirely on a quick judgment of character. The fact that the audiences for this play believe Photo-Finish's claim of innocence just as quickly as Emily does is a dramatic illustration of how rapidly a good playwright can establish character.

For some, there are lingering doubts about his actual feelings toward Emily. He is, after all, a streetwise character in a life-and-death situation, and Emily is naive. Does he really feel love for her? Or does he see her as the last chance of escape? If we read the play script as if it were a story, his protestations of love seem preposterously rapid—far too sudden to be taken seriously. But the play insists that you believe it. As I have pointed out before, we know that he is presenting his inner thoughts honestly in the little monologue that forms the third scene because he is speaking to himself. He refers to her as "the only good thing that ever came their way." And later when he realizes that there is practically no chance of escape, he gives her his last eighty dollars so that she can escape her own imprisonment in that town and get to San Francisco. There can be no ulterior motive in this offer. So both in lines of dialogue and in action we are assured that his love for her is genuine.

How can an aspect of character that would be hard to believe in fiction somehow work in drama? The answer lies in one of the more subtle distinctions between the two genres. As I mentioned at the beginning of this chapter, characters tend to be slightly exaggerated in drama, and their emotions are allowed to develop and shift at a faster rate. Certain aspects of character and especially changes in attitude that would be unconvincing if read on the page become credible when viewed in production.

In a sense, when you read a script you are not reading a play; you are reading lines of dialogue and a few stage directions—merely two ingredients of a full production. The rest is provided by the actors, director, set designer, costume designer—an entire team. How, then, can a writer learn to create effective dramatic characterization in a script when what appears in production is influenced by so many others? Mainly by seeing as many plays as possible in production and studying the scripts. With experience one begins to judge what is possible and how to go about creating it. Saroyan, for example, knew that he could convince an audience that a man like Photo-Finish could sincerely fall in love in what by real-life standards is only minutes because he had a sense of what works on the stage. And the continuing popularity of this play (it has become a kind of classic) demonstrates that he was right.

Important as your protagonist's first lines are, don't spend hours getting that introduction just right in your first draft. Once you have your opening scene in mind, plunge in and get it down on paper. After you have completed the first draft, however, take a second look at that opening. Have you done all you can to give your audience a "handle" on your protagonist? Read the first two minutes of dialogue and ask yourself whether that character has been individualized. With your first draft safely down on paper, you will have a clear idea of how that character is developed later, and you can then make sure that the audience has started off with just the right impression.

Creating Depth of Character

The central characters in serious, realistic drama are usually well rounded and carefully delineated. Achieving this effect in a short one-act play is a challenge, but it can be done. Saroyan manages to tell us a good deal about Photo-Finish in only a few minutes of playing time. He is lonely but not a whiner. He has a whimsical sense of humor yet can be serious, not only about practical things but about broader concerns like what makes people so mean. There is a merry quality to the way he treats Emily, but we know almost from the start that he is genuinely scared about his position. These contrasts provide a range of characteristics and attitudes, and it is this range that gives us a sense of knowing him as an individual.

Characterization in this play is particularly important because so much depends on the audience's feeling sympathy for this unsuccessful gambler and born loser. Only if we take him seriously will we respond to the theme of the play—the capacity of love to transform "little punk people" to something fine.

Achieving depth of character in a play is somewhat similar to the technique in fiction except that it has to be presented more rapidly. The goal is to balance consistency with variation. Consistency requires that the character never behave in a way that seems implausible. A line of dialogue or a particular action may seem surprising to the audience at first, but it must ultimately be explained.

On the other hand, excessive consistency makes the character overly predictable. So every major character should have a variety of characteristics. Photo-Finish, for example, is not a naive college sophomore on spring vacation. He is a small-time hustler who has been living precariously on the fringes of the racetrack world. His ability to see the good qualities in a young woman like Emily and even to appreciate the conflicts in the outraged husband are in sharp contrast with what we might expect. That contrast is important, but equally important is the fact that for most viewers it is credible. If he were a convicted mass murderer on the run and ended up marrying Emily and going to medical school, the audience would tiptoe to the exits.

Notice, too, that there is nothing in the play to suggest that Emily is tall, beautiful, or sophisticated. Yet she is elevated in stature at the very end, and we take her cry of "Hello out there!" seriously.

One way to achieve both consistency and some measure of contrast in your characters is to take the time to write out a character sketch. Put down more than you will ever need: What their parents were like, whether they had sisters or brothers, where they went to school, what they were good at, and what their weaknesses are. Determine some traits that suggest consistency ("gentle temperament; almost never loses her temper") and some contrasting trait ("can't stand messy people or a disorderly house").

If you have trouble writing more than a few sentences, try basing your description on a friend or member of your family. Be sure to **metaphorphose** some aspect of the character—that is, alter a basic element like age, sex, or appearance—so that you don't lose friends or, worse, hinder the creative process. The goal is to create a new and interesting character who is generally consistent in outlook and nature and yet who occasionally demonstrates certain contrasting traits as well.

Major Characters in Flux

Major characters almost always go through some type of significant transformation. Such development is at the very heart of drama.

The term we use is "character change." It's a handy phrase, but it is also a bit misleading. Characters in plays rarely go through a basic personality change any more than people do in life. Only in comedies do villains finally see the light, go through a complete character transformation, and undo the damage they have done.

There are, however, three types of character change that are well worth considering. One is when a character's *attitude* changes. Such occurrences are almost never radical transformations of personality, but they can be dramatic or even catastrophic. In plays as in life, people are occasionally stricken with remorse, given new hope, shattered by a crisis or strengthened by it. Friendships form between unlikely pairs, and "ideal" couples become alienated. Quite often a naive character is suddenly made aware of life's complexity; occasionally a sophisticated character is taught how to appreciate some simple truth.

All this is fairly abstract, and plays, as I have pointed out before, are not created out of abstractions. But keep your eyes open for situations in which individuals have gone through a significant shift in attitude. Plays are less often rooted in life experience than are stories, and this may be due to the fact that for playwrights a dramatic concept is more important than the fine nuances of personal experience. But it is worth noting dramatic changes in attitude when they occur in people you know or even in public figures whose names appear in the newspaper. Former supporters of a particular war may later have a radical and public change of heart; criminal types occasionally have genuine religious conversions; and, sadly, men and women of high principle sometimes become obsessed with some form of corruption.

As a playwright, you have to be careful not to oversimplify some major transformation such as this. If you have seen it done in television, you run the risk of imitating the TV script rather than developing more subtle aspects on your own. Remember too that if you are writing a short one-act play, you may have to tone down the degree of transformation to make it credible. Still, such shifts can generate a fruitful dramatic concept.

The second type of character change is a shift in fortune. Traditionally, tragedies dealt with men and, less often, women of power who are brought low by the lust for more power (Macbeth, Julius Caesar), by poor judgment (King Lear, Othello), by turns of fate (Oedipus), or by treachery (Medea). In recent times, tragedies have dealt more frequently with average people like Willy Loman in *Death of a Salesman* who is brought down by the forces of society and self-delusion.

Hello Out There follows that pattern—the hero's change in status and his eventual death are due essentially to forces beyond his control. Remember, however, that he is presented as a chance-taker and as one who loses races by a nose. So losing this last race is a part of the pattern.

It is not at all necessary to bring a character to the point of death to dramatize a change in status. In fact, murders and suicides are risky outcomes in short plays. If you are tempted, carefully weigh the advantages of indicating personal failure in some less terminal way. Extreme violence is used so much on television it actually lacks impact unless prepared for carefully. The murder mystery, after all, has become ritualized family entertainment free from any true sense of tragedy. In addition, you should be careful to avoid the risk of melodrama. Melodrama pushes drama to the point where it no longer seems credible and the audience loses its sense of involvement. You can charge a short play with more voltage than a story of the same length, and *Hello Out There* is a good example. But to continue that metaphor, melodrama overloads the system. How can you tell when you have pushed dramatic intensity too far? Read the play to an audience of three or more, and if one of them giggles you have some rewriting to do.

The third type of character change is quite different. Here the character actually remains the same but audience perception of that character changes. This is a standard device of simple murder mysteries in which the character who seems least likely to be the killer is revealed in the end to be just that. In such plays, however, characterization is often reduced to a kind of shorthand. The same technique can be used in much more sophisticated dramas.

One of the best-known examples in full-length plays appears in *The Country Girl* by Clifford Odets. This play concerns the efforts of an older actor to make a comeback. For much of the play the audience is convinced that he is doing his best to cope with a very difficult wife. But it turns out that he is an alcoholic and that she has been heroically trying to cover for him. The audience has been as thoroughly misled as have the other characters, and the revelation has genuine dramatic impact.

There are all kinds of deceits of this sort that can be used. Some may take the form of conscious scheming on the part of the character as in the Odets play; others may develop from self-deception. If you are working with this type of reversal, remember to drop small hints along the way so that when the correct view is revealed the audience will have that special sense of, "Oh, I should have seen it."

Using Minor Characters Effectively

E. M. Forster's distinction between "round" and "flat" characters in fiction applies just as well to drama. Although "flat" characters are seen in one dimension like cardboard cutouts and rarely change or develop, they can be essential elements of a play. In comedy, for example, all of the characters are relatively "flat." Yet, as you will see in *Goin' West,* which appears as the next chapter, these characters create the satire that is at the heart of that play. Like a cartoon, satiric figures are exaggerations of particular traits. And in highly didactic plays committed to a particular political or social thesis, characters are also drawn in a bold, exaggerated manner without depth.

Even in realistic plays that develop the major characters fully, the minor characters are usually "flat." They may serve as **catalysts**—necessary elements for the advancement of plot or for the development of a major character without themselves changing.

The two men who accompany the husband in *Hello Out There*, for example, are extremely important since their presence just outside the jail room drives the husband to the point of murder. In that respect, they are far from "minor." They are essential elements. But as individuals, they are faceless, even inter-changeable, and completely unchanging.

There is a tendency to become careless with minor characters, creating them to perform trivial tasks that are not truly essential. Anyone who has been active in professional theater companies, however, can tell you that produc-tion costs place a premium on plays that can be presented with a minimum of actors. And entirely aside from those practical considerations, there is an aesthetic value to economy. A play is apt to have more power if a lot is suggested by a few carefully developed characters as opposed to a more diffuse theme cluttered with too many characters.

There are two questions to ask about any minor character: What signifi-cant function does this character serve, and exactly what would happen if we removed him or her? If we apply those questions to the pair of unnamed men in the Saroyan play, we can see why they are so important. The men serve the function of a mob; without them, the play would suggest that the husband was driven to murder by an unquestioning sense of revenge rather than by being driven in part by "trying to look good" in the eyes of other men.

Minor characters are generally as static as stage props, but they can serve significant functions. Don't add them the way you add a couch or a chair to the set. Use them as essential elements or drop them from your script.

Characterization is a continuing concern at every stage of writing a play. In the case of static or "flat" characters, consider exactly what their function is to be. With major characters, work to make them vivid yet credible. To do this you should consider both consistency and variation. Sophisticated drama is, among other things, the illusion of getting to know total strangers surprisingly well in a very short amount of time.

31
A Play by
Louis Phillips

Goin' West

Characters

    VOICE OF "THE OREGON TRAIL"
    ARCHIBALD MONTH
    AMY MONTH
    APRIL MONTH
    CAMERAMAN (HENRI CHATILLON)
    PREACHER
    CAPTAIN
    SHAW
    SCRIPT GIRL
    INDIAN
    DESLAURIERS
    ROGERS
    ALFRED MONTAIGNE
    MAY MONTAIGNE
    AMY MONTAIGNE
    STRANGER (FREDERICK JACKSON TURNER)
    NEWSPAPER GIRL
    MAN WITH MICROPHONE
    EXTRAS: PIONEERS, INDIANS, VAGRANTS, MOVIEGOERS

Setting

> The stage consists of a single wooden table. The table will be used to represent, at various stages of the journey goin' west, a raft, a small wagon, a steamship or whatever is needed to transport the Month family from east to west.
>
> In the dark we hear a voice reading the opening paragraph of Francis Parkman's The Oregon Trail.

VOICE: "Late spring, 1846, was a busy season in the city of St. Louis. Not only were emigrants from every part of the country preparing for the journey to Oregon and California, but an unusual number of traders were making ready their wagons and outfits for Santa Fe. The hotels were crowded, and the gunsmiths and saddlers were kept constantly at work in providing arms and equipment for the different parties of travellers. Steamboats were leaving the levee and passing up the Missouri, crowded with passengers on their way to the frontier."

(As the lights come up we see a man, a woman, a young child holding a rag doll, and a young man in the dress of the early 1900's trying to set up a very crude motion picture camera mounted upon a tripod. The man, Archibald Month, is dressed in buckskins; his wife, Amy, is dressed in homespun calico, as is the daughter, April. The daughter is about eight years old, with her hair in braids.

We hear the sound of swirling water. The man holds a long pole and struggles heroically as he tries to get the tiny raft down the river)

AMY: We're going to capsize!

ARCHIBALD: No, we ain't. No, we ain't.

CAMERAMAN: Gonna make a wonderful movie, Mrs. Month.

ARCHIBALD: No, it ain't. No, it ain't.

CAMERAMAN: Sure, it will. The raft capsizing and all of us falling into the water.

APRIL: *(To Doll)* Don't you worry, Marzipan. I know how to swim.

ARCHIBALD: We ain't goin' to fall into no river. Get that out of your mind.

CAMERAMAN: Make a wonderful movie for my Uncle Cecil. We'll sell it and make a lot of money.

AMY: I don't want my daughter and me to fall into the water just to make you a lot of money.

CAMERAMAN: Of course you do. Of course you do. Why else would any normal person want to go West. Especially to California.

APRIL: *(To Doll)* Don't listen to him, Marzipan. We ain't goin' into that nasty river.

(Sound of waterfalls)

AMY: What's that sound, Archibald.

CAMERAMAN: Why, that's Death's-Head Falls.

(Cameraman cranks his camera furiously)

ARCHIBALD: No, it ain't. No it ain't.

CAMERAMAN: *(Produces a map)* Sure it is. It was marked right out on this map.

ARCHIBALD: Why didn't you mention it before?

CAMERAMAN: I just thought it would make a wonderful picture.

ARCHIBALD: Don't seem fair to me. To spring a surprise like that. You said this river was as gentle as a baby's breath.

APRIL: Marzipan and I always wanted to see waterfalls.

CAMERAMAN: No one's ever gone over these falls and lived.

(April stands up)

AMY: April, you sit down. There's nothing to be gained by dying standing up.

CAMERAMAN: Thank you, Lord!

APRIL: What are you thanking God for?

CAMERAMAN: Because God has reached into his hip pocket and pulled out my big chance. When we go over Death's-Head Falls, Documentary Photography is going to come of age!

ARCHIBALD: Put down that camera, and pole, you bastard!

APRIL: Look how white the water is.

(Roar of the falls drowns out further human sounds. Lights out. In the darkness we hear the sound of a man's voice. As the lights come up we see a scarecrow of a travelling preacher standing with his head bowed, his large black hat at his side. Under the table are three white wooden crosses. On the table is Marzipan the doll. Standing next to the preacher is the Cameraman. He takes films of the ceremony in progress)

PREACHER: Dearly beloved…*(He looks around; then to Cameraman)* I guess that means you…We are gathered here today to bury the bodies of the Month family—Archibald, Amy, and April. Some say April is the cruelest Month, but, being that she is so young, I doubt that it is so…They were goin' West, Lord, and their journey was swift. The river was goin' West, and its journey was swifter. For as it saith in the book of Isaiah, "For as a young man marrieth a virgin, so shall thy sons marry thee; and as the bridegroom rejoiceth over the bride, so shall thy God rejoice over thee." Amen.

CAMERAMAN: Preacher, I don't know how that verse of yours about the bridegroom rejoicing over his bride was appropriate to the occasion.

PREACHER: *(Puts on his hat)* It's got to be…It's the only one I know.

CAMERAMAN: Maybe you should have read from the Bible. Something like "Dust to dust…"

PREACHER: Can't. Can't read. Can't write. I'm only fit to be two things—a preacher or a movie producer…

(Sounds of a coyote howling in the distance)

CAMERAMAN: If you loan me your *Bible*, I could read something over them.

PREACHER: Traded my *Bible*.

CAMERAMAN: Traded your *Bible*?

PREACHER: Traded it for a picture of Betty Grable. I mean *Bible* is *Bible*, but legs is legs.

CAMERAMAN: Nobody can dispute with you on that.

PREACHER: *(Spits)* Nope.

(Sound of a coyote howling)

CAMERAMAN: You goin' West, too?

PREACHER: Yep. Everybody goes West. Nothing in the East. They don't even make TV shows there.

CAMERAMAN: Maybe our paths will be crossing then.

PREACHER: Paths are crossing all the time.

(*Preacher holds out his hand. The Cameraman puts a silver dollar into it. The Preacher bites it*)

PREACHER: Lots of counterfeiting going on lately. Don't know who to trust.

(*Preacher exits. The cameraman discovers Marzipan, and props the doll against the smallest of the three white crosses*)

CAMERAMAN: I guess we should have buried the doll with you, child. But now it will just have to stand guard. Lord, let it guard all these lives. All these lives lost goin' West. And the wind will come and the dust. Then maybe somebody will find you, and they'll know. (*He picks up his camera and exits. Lights down*)

VOICE: "One day, after a protracted morning's ride, we stopped to rest at noon upon the open prairie. No trees were in sight; but close at hand a little dribbling brook was twisting side to side through a hollow...Henri Chatillon, before lying down, was looking for signs of snakes, the only living things he feared, and uttered various ejaculations of disgust at finding several suspicious-looking holes close to the carts."

(*When the lights come up, we see two men lying underneath the table—Shaw and the Cameraman. Henri Chatillon is looking for snakes*)

CAMERAMAN: If there's one thing I can't stand it's snakes.

SHAW: You'll love California then.

(*A man in a cavalry uniform enters. Scene from the Oregon Trail.*)

CAMERAMAN: 'Lo...Here comes the Captain!

CAPTAIN: See that horse!...There! By Jove, he's off. That's your big horse, Shaw.

SHAW: Hey, that's my horse!

CAPTAIN: Go catch your horse, if you don't want to lose him.

(*Shaw bolts off, trying to buckle his trousers and run at the same time*)

CAPTAIN: I tell you what it is, this will never do at all. We shall lose every horse in the band some day or other, and then a pretty plight we'll be in. Now I am convinced that the only way for us is to have every man in camp stand horse-guard in rotation whenever we stop. Supposing a hundred Pawnees should jump up out of that ravine, all yelling and flapping their buffalo robes in the way they do! Why, in two minutes, not a hoof would be in sight.

CAMERAMAN: If a couple hundred Pawnees jump out of a ditch, a few horse guards ain't goin' to stop them.

CAPTAIN: At any rate, our whole system is wrong; I'm convinced of it; it is totally unmilitary. Why, the way we travel, strung out over the prairie for a mile, an enemy might attack the foremost men, and cut them off before the rest could come up.

CAMERAMAN: We're not in enemy country yet. When we are, we'll travel together.

CAPTAIN: Goin' West, ain't we?

CAMERAMAN: I'm goin' West. That's for certain.

CAPTAIN: Then we're in enemy country. They're the god-damndest Philistines out there. Just as you think you've got it made in the shade, you get attacked in your camp. We've no sentinels. We camp in disorder; no precautions at all against surprise. My own convictions are that we ought to camp in a hollow square with the fires in the centre, and have sentinels and a regular password appointed every night. Besides, there should be vedettes, riding in advance...

CAMERAMAN: Vedettes?

CAPTAIN: I don't write it. I just read it.

CAMERAMAN: Who in the hell knows what vedettes are?

CAPTAIN: Script girl!

(*Script Girl enters*)

SCRIPT GIRL: Please! Let's not have any more arguments about the script. We've got to shoot the scene before we lose the light.

CAPTAIN: Light! That's what we're always losing around here! That's all we ever lose. I want to live someplace where I can lose something else beside light!

CAMERAMAN: Nobody knows what vedettes are.

SCRIPT GIRL: Shall I ask the writer?

CAPTAIN: He don't know. He just puts them in because it sounds good. Big long word like that.

SCRIPT GIRL: It's only eight letters.

CAPTAIN: Shouldn't be no words in a Western. A Western is action. It's shoot 'em up, bang, bang. The good guys chasing the bad guys all over the landscape and roundin' 'em up. But no, playwrights have got to have us stand around and talk.

(*During the above a savage Indian has snuck up on the crew. He lets out a savage cry and leaps. The Captain pulls out his pistol and shoots. He catches the savage in mid-air, the Indian falls dead in a heap*)

CAPTAIN: Now that's what people pay to see. That's what a Western is. If movies are goin' to survive, it's got to have more action in them than in real life. In the East, people ride about in little vehicles; in the West we stand free and unafraid. We move. We revel in action. We take meetings!

(*The Cameraman walks to the savage and kicks him*)

CAMERAMAN: You know what I think?...I think we're runnin' out of Injuns.

(*Lights out. In the dark we hear the song "She Wore a Yellow Ribbon." The song fades. We hear a voice in the dark*)

VOICE: "On the next morning we had gone but a mile or two when we came to an extensive belt of woods, through the midst of which ran a stream, wide, deep, and of an appearance particularly muddy and treacherous. Deslauriers was in advance with his cart...In plunged the cart, but mid-

way it stuck fast."
(*Lights up. A French Canadian stands on the table with a whip. Behind the wagon,
two other men are trying to use poles to help the cart out of the mud*)
DESLAURIERS: Sacré...
ROGERS: Drive on! Drive on!
CAPTAIN: My advice is that we unload; for I'll bet any man five pounds that if
   we try to go through we shall stick fast.
DESLAURIERS: Mud! That's all this country is...from one end to the other. Mud.
ROGERS: Drive on! Drive on!
CAPTAIN: Well, I can only give my advice, and if people won't be reasonable,
   why, they won't, that's all.
DESLAURIERS: Mud...What good is mud?
CAPTAIN: Mud.
ROGERS: Drive on! Drive on!
DESLAURIERS: Can't you say nothin' else?
ROGERS: I don't write it. I just read it.
CAPTAIN: That's the attitude that's going to make you a star, boy!...Look at this
   mud. You know what I predict? I predict that someday there's goin' to be
   a great motion picture palace, and in front of it there's goin' to be lots of
   mud. Tons and tons of mud, and people are goin' to lie down in the
   mud...They're goin' to stick their noses and legs and faces and moustaches
   right into it...It'll be the biggest thing to hit the West since the Buffalo.
ROGERS: Sounds like a great idea, Captain.
   (*Enter the Cameraman, carrying a motion picture screen*)
CAPTAIN: What's that blockhead bringin' with him now?
CAMERAMAN: I've got this idea. We're goin' to line up all the covered wagons
   around this movie screen and we'll show movies under the stars. It will
   change our whole attitude how we look at movies.
   (*Sound of Indians*)
ROGERS: Sounds like the Pawnees, Captain.
CAPTAIN: Deslauriers, would you run away if the Pawnees should fire at us?
DESLAURIERS: Ah! Oui, oui, monsieur.
CAPTAIN: Good. If there is one thing disastrous to the human race, it's reckless
   courage.
ROGERS: They're comin' over the ridge, Capt'n.
CAPTAIN: Men, prepare to fire.
   (*Sound of an Indian attack. Rifle shots. Lights out. Lights up on the Captain who
   stands alone in a circle of light*)
CAPTAIN: Four or five horsemen soon entered the river, and in ten minutes had
   waded across and clambered up the loose sandbank. They were ill-looking
   fellows, thin and swarthy, with careworn anxious faces, and lips rigidly
   compressed. They had good cause for anxiety; it was three days since they
   first encamped here, and on the night of their arrival they had lost a
   hundred and twenty-three of their best cattle, driven off by wolves,

through the neglect of the man on guard. This discouraging and alarming calamity was not the first that had overtaken them. Since leaving the settlements, they had met with nothing but misfortune. Some of their party had died; one man had been killed by the Pawnees; and about a week before they had been plundered by the Dakotahs of all their best horses, the wretched animals on which our visitors were mounted being the only ones that were left. They had encamped, they told us, near sunset, by the side of the Platte, and their oxen were scattered over the meadow, while the horses were feeding a little farther off. Suddenly the ridges of the hills were alive with a swarm of mounted Indians, at least six hundred in number, who came pouring with a yell down towards the camp, rushing up within a few rods, to the great terror of the emigrants; when, suddenly wheeling, they swept around the band of horses, and in five minutes disappeared with their prey through the openings of the hills.

(*Lights down. Lights up on a family in their wagon goin' West—a man, a woman, and a young child. They should remind us of the family we met in the opening scene. The man—Alfred Montaigne—is dressed in buckskins. His wife, Amy, is dressed in homespun calico, as is their eight year old daughter, May. They are singing the children's song, "The Tailor and the Mouse," their voices lifting high and carrying over the wide expanse of prairie*)

MONTAIGNE FAMILY: (Singing)
"There was a tailor had a mouse,
Hi-diddle dum cum feed-a.
They lived together in one house.
Hi diddle dum cum feed-a,
Hi diddle dum, cum tin-trum, tantram,
Through the town of Ramsey,
Hi diddle dum, come over the lea,
Hi diddle dum cum feed-a."

ALFRED: Onward, Old Paint. We have to go to California. That's where the money is. Heaps and heaps of it, piled all the way up to the sky. All you have to do is sell your life story to the movies and you're on easy street forever. Onward, Old Paint. To Beverly Hills and Rodeo Drive.

MAY: I don't like the way you call the horse "Old Paint," Poppa. Can't we call him something else?

AMY: Hush, dear. Don't talk while Daddy is driving.

ALFRED: Look at it, Amy. The whole prairie is clogged with covered wagons.

AMY: I guess everybody's got the same idea we've got.

ALFRED: Goin' West. Everybody and their uncle goin' West. Because the West is a dream, and we're pushing our horses hard, and our families hard, and ourselves hard to get a piece of it. If you get up on that silver screen, it's immortality. Onward, Old Paint!

AMY: I want to call him something else, Poppa.

ALFRED: Anything you want, my darlin'. Anything you want, my dear. Why do you think we're risking starvation, risking sandstorms, risking mud, risking Indian attacks—so my little girl can grow up in Hollywood.

AMY: All right, May. You go ahead. What do you want to name the horse?

MAY: Can we call him "Giddy-up" ?

ALFRED: Can't call a horse "Giddy-up."

MAY: Why not, Poppa?

ALFRED: Well, suppose I want it to "Whoa" and I have to say, "Whoa, Giddy-up." Now "Whoa, Giddy-up" is goin' to be pretty confusin' to a horse. Old Paint won't know whether to stop or to plunge forward. The poor horse will have a nervous breakdown, and it's not easy to find a good animal psychiatrist out on this freeway.

AMY: Lot of animal psychiatrists in Los Angeles.

ALFRED: I know, but we ain't there yet.

MAY: Then let's call him something else.

ALFRED: OK, giddy-up, Something Else.

MAY: I gotta go to the bathroom.

AMY: We just left Fort Leavenworth.

ALFRED: All right. But make it quick. And be on the lookout for snakes.

(*The wagon stops. May hops off and goes offstage. A man appears. He is Frederick Jackson Turner, author of* The Frontier in American History. *He is dressed in simple black and wears spectacles. He carries with him a satchel filled to overflowing with notes and papers and books*)

AMY: Look, Alfred. There's a man standing there!

(*Alfred Montaigne reaches for his rifle*)

ALFRED: Howdy, stranger!

STRANGER: Howdy.

ALFRED: What are you doin' out here on foot? Shank's mare is no way to travel, especially if you're goin' West. You've got to enter California first class, or they don't pay no attention to you at all.

STRANGER: My horse was stolen by the Pawnees, so I'm hoping some West-goin' family will offer me friendly transportation.

ALFRED: Well, we're right friendly enough. I'm Alfred Montaigne, this is my wife, Amy...Our little girl, May, has gone off into the bushes.

STRANGER: Pleased to meet you all. I'm Frederick Jackson Turner.

ALFRED: You're not dressed to be a frontier scout, Mr. Turner.

TURNER: Well, I am a frontier scout in a way.

(*He climbs onto the wagon table*)

TURNER: You see I'm doing a study of the "Significance of the Frontier in American History."

ALFRED: A professor, uh. Now ain't that interesting...Ain't that interesting, Amy?

AMY: Our family don't know much about book larnin'.

TURNER: It's my thesis, ma'am, that "...the frontier is the outer edge of the wave—the meeting point between savagery and civilization."

AMY: What do you mean by savagery, Mr. Turner?

TURNER: Savagery? Oh, I suppose, killing, looting, violence, and, pardon me, ma'am, rape, in a savage sort of way.

(*Alfred Montaigne takes up a jug of corn liquor*)

ALFRED: And civilization?

TURNER: Civilization? Oh, I suppose, killing, looting, violence, and, pardon me, ma'am, rape, in a civilized sort of way.

AMY: What's taking that girl so long... (*She stands up and calls*) May!

ALFRED: It's refreshing to talk to a man of ideas, Professor, because that's all our great country is, a land of ideas from one coast to the other. Ideas piled up like boulders, like rocks, like mountains, and we got to dynamite our way through.

AMY: May! You answer me! You hear me, girl?

TURNER: I agree with you, Mr. Montaigne. "The most important effect of the frontier has been the promotion of democracy here and in Europe." The frontier produces individuals.

AMY: May!

ALFRED: I'll go fetch her. I guess she's playing games with us again.

TURNER: Can I be of any help?

ALFRED: (*Jumping down*) You just sit here, Professor, and think your great thoughts. Our daughter's just angry with us because I wouldn't let her change the name of the horse.

(*Alfred goes off*)

AMY: I should have gone with her.

TURNER: Oh, it's a great opportunity goin' West, ma'am. We're goin' to expand westward and develop all sorts of new opportunities...Whatever pressures build up in the East, we've got the West...It's a safety valve. We blow off steam by movin' West.

(*Alfred emerges from the undergrowth. He carries his dead daughter in his arms. An arrow sticks from her breast*)

AMY: (*Horror stricken*) May!

ALFRED: Savages!

(*Lights out. In the darkness we can hear the melancholy song of a lone harmonica. As the lights come up, we see Alfred and Amy standing beside a small white cross. With the man and wife is the scarecrow of the travelling Preacher, and the Professor with his satchel of papers by his side*)

PREACHER: "For as a young man marrieth a virgin, so shall thy sons marry thee: and as the bridegroom rejoiceth over the bride, so shall thy God rejoice over thee." Amen.

OTHERS: Amen.

(*Preacher holds out his hat and takes up a collection. One by one, he pulls out the coins and tests them with his teeth*)

PREACHER: Sorry it couldn't be more elaborate...but you know how it is. All this dying hardly gives a man time to prepare. It's hard to see the significance of it all when there's so much space to traipse around in...Too much space for the eye to behold, and it all comes down to a few feet of earth. (*Preacher exits*)

TURNER: The wilderness masters the colonist. It finds him a European in dress, industries, tools, modes of travel, and thought. It takes him from the railroad car and puts him in the birch canoe. It strips off the garments of civilization and arrays him in the hunting shirt and the moccasin. It puts him in the log cabin of the Cherokee and Iroquois.

ALFRED: Will you shut off your yap...

AMY: Alfred!

ALFRED: Goin' West ain't no theory...it's no big words from educated men...Oh no, Goin' West is living and dyin' and scrapin'. It's holdin' your family together by the sweat of your brow...

AMY: (*To Turner*) Don't mind him. He's out of his head with grief.

ALFRED: Out of my head with grief! Well, let me tell you somethin'. When you look at that horse there, you call him 'Giddy-up' and nothing else...Because that's what its name is, for now and forever! Amen and Giddy-up! (*Lights out. Sound of people singing "Shall We Gather by the River." When the lights come up we see Alfred Montaigne standing on the table with his wife, Amy. Around Amy's neck is a halter of rope. Alfred holds the end of the rope. A crude sign reads:* AUCTION THIS MORNIN'. *A few people, including the Cameraman [Henri Chatillon] stand lazily about*)

ALFRED: Sure, she's got a few lines on her...

(*The Captain crosses to Henri Chatillon*)

CAPTAIN: What's goin' on, Henri?

ALFRED: A few miles on the old speedometer, but that don't mean she don't have some good years left.

CAPTAIN: Another one of your publicity stunts?

ALFRED: She may not give you any more children, but what are you goin' to do with children anyway? They aren't writin' movies for children.

CAMERAMAN: Auctioning off his wife.

ALFRED: How about an openin' bid of a hundred dollars?

CAPTAIN: You kiddin' me, Henri?

CAMERAMAN: Nope.

ALFRED: One hundred dollars, and you take this woman home with you.

CROWD MEMBER: How about a thirty-day guarantee?

(*Laughter*)

CROWD MEMBER: If we take her off your hands and it don't work out, can we return her to you?

ALFRED: Guarantee? Why, I'm givin' this woman the highest recommendation a lovin' husband can give...When you snore or come to bed without washing the mud off your boots, she don't make no piss and moan about it.

CROWD MEMBER: Seventy-five and a bottle of hootch.

ALFRED: One hundred or nothing. This old lady loves the hanky-pank so much, she's worth her weight in gold. In fact that's what I should be asking—her weight in gold.

CROWD MEMBER: What do you need all this money for, friend?

ALFRED: I won't lie to you. I need the money to start my own movie company. I've got a blockbuster of a film deal cooking with 20th Century Coyote. So there's got to be a little trade-off involved. Look at me, ladies and gents. I ain't done much in my life, so don't let this big chance pass me by just because you got a few twinges of conscience. When it comes to goin' West, conscience can have nothin' to do with it. It's a once in a lifetime deal. A chance to rub elbows with Eddie Polo and all the big name movie stars. If you don't bid on this woman, I'm goin' to kill myself, because I was born to make movies, I was born to take meetings and to talk deals. When I was born, The Good Fairy of the Expense Account was hovering over my cradle. It's her wand that has touched me.

CROWD MEMBER: Touched you in the head, you mean.

ALFRED: Oh, no, friend, we're all in the same boat. We wanna talk money. We don't wanna talk buffalo dung, that's for sure. I wanna talk money in seven figures. I wanna plaster dreams up where everybody can see 'em. Everybody stands in line waiting for the big dream, the beautiful bodies to be flashed.

CROWD MEMBER: Flash us some of those beautiful bodies, and maybe you've got yourself a deal.

ALFRED: A beautiful body don't bring you no peace of mind the way this woman brings you peace of mind...It's getting late. The Decline of the West is setting in. What are we goin' to do?

CROWD MEMBER: I bid one hundred pound sterling!

ALFRED: Let me tell you this. Whoever buys this woman here...when I go on the Academy Awards show, and everybody in the whole world is watching, I will speak that person's name...speak that person's name in front of the whole world, thanking that person for making my great success possible. How about that?

(*The bidding increases*)

CROWD MEMBER: One hundred twenty-five.

ALFRED: I hear one hundred twenty-five pound sterling.

CROWD MEMBER: One hundred and fifty.

CROWD MEMBER: One hundred and sixty.

CROWD MEMBER: One hundred and seventy.

ALFRED: One hundred and seventy, once...How about her weight in gold?

CROWD MEMBER: One hundred and eighty.

CROWD MEMBER: Gol' durn it. Let's stop this pussy-footin' around. (*He tosses up some bags of gold dust*) I offer her weight in gold.

ALFRED: Gents. Anyone want to beat that offer?...Going once, twice, gone. Sold! I tell you, sir, you've made a wise decision...Now I can start my search for a new Rhett Butler and a new Scarlett O'Hara.

(*Winner jumps to the table and grabs the woman, lifting the woman's dress*)

CROWD MEMBER: (*Winning bidder*) Come here, woman. Let's get down to the hanky-pank.

(*Lights out. We hear the voices of whippoorwills and the voices of quail. And then the flash of lightning. The sound of rain*)

VOICE: "But all our hopes were delusive. Scarcely had night set in when the tumult broke forth anew. The thunder here is not like the tame thunder of the Atlantic coast. Bursting with a terrific crash directly above our heads, it roared over the boundless waste of prairie, seeming to roll around the whole circle of the firmament with a peculiar and awful reverberation. The lightning flashed all night, playing its livid glare upon the neighboring trees, revealing the vast expanse of the plain, and then leaving us shut in as if by a palpable wall of darkness."

VOICE #2: How are ye, boys? Are ye for Oregon or California?

VOICE #3: California.

VOICE #4: California.

VOICE #5: California.

VOICE #2: Everybody in the whole world is goin' West, headin' to California!

(*Music—"California, Here I Come." Lights up. A Newspaper Girl stands on the table, hawking her wares*)

NEWSPAPER GIRL: Extra, extra, read all about it! California sinks into the ocean!…Extra, Extra, read all about it! California sinks into the ocean!

(*Man with a microphone appears*)

MAN WITH MICROPHONE: This is Burt Ellis from Station KLO reporting on the events of the day.

NEWSPAPER GIRL: Movie studios destroyed. Economists predict great depression.

MAN WITH MICROPHONE: The stock market plunged today when news reached the East Coast about the apparent demise of California. It seemed that four billion persons of all nations, weights, and sizes, descended upon California today to take part in the worldwide search for the new Rhett Butler and Scarlett O'Hara. Early reports suggest that the combined weight of all the hopefuls was just too much for the state to bear. The entire United States shifted toward the West, and California simply broke off and sunk into the Pacific. It is too early to say whether there are any survivors.

NEWSPAPER GIRL: Read all about it! "California Sinks Into the Ocean." No more movies to be made.

MAN WITH MICROPHONE: Stay tuned, ladies and gentlemen. We'll bring you an update as soon as we get it, and now back to our studios for a little mood music.

(*Lights down. Mood music is the "Hallellujah Chorus." When the lights come back up, the table now holds a life-sized cutout of the woman, Amy Montaigne, who had been auctioned off. She is dressed in sexy lingerie and strikes a suggestive pose. Next to the cutout is a movie poster that reads: "Today only. Hollywood's*

Final Film—May Montaigne in *The Palpable Wall of Darkness.*" *We hear the rain. The lightning flashes. Two patrons of the movies enter. They check the skies and hoist their umbrellas.*

Under the table are vagrants, bums, the down-and-out. All members of the cast are there dressed in rags. They warm their hands by a small fire. They cook soup in cans)

MOVIEGOER #1: How did you like the movie, darling?

MOVIEGOER #2: I'm tired of Westerns, Alfred. They're all the same. Shoot 'em up, bang, bang.

BEGGAR: *(Henri Chatillon)* Take your picture for a quarter?

MOVIEGOER #1: Go away.

MOVIEGOER #2: The good guys chasing the bad guys all over the landscape. It's always the same.

VAGRANT: *(To his daughter)* Get up there, daughter, and sing for the nice people.

MOVIEGOER #2: You would think the last movie would have had more imagination...

VAGRANT GIRL: *(Sings)*
"There was a tailor had a mouse,
Hi diddle dum cum feed-a.
They lived together in one house,
Hi diddle dum cum feed-a."

MOVIEGOER #1: Didn't you like the part about the family goin' over Death's-Head Falls?

MOVIEGOER #2: Too sad. Movies should let us forget our troubles...(*Pauses in front of the life-sized cutout*) I don't know why they never once let May Montaigne make any comedies. I bet there was a secret sadness to her life, something the fan magazines were afraid to reveal.

VAGRANT: *(To his daughter)* Do a little dance for the nice people, darling.

MOVIEGOER #1: You know what I was thinking about when I saw that family go over Death's-Head Falls?

MOVIEGOER #2: What?

MOVIEGOER #1: I was thinking Documentary Photography had finally come of age...Too bad California had to fall off into the ocean.

(One of the beggars removes a harmonica and starts to play a melancholy tune. As the Moviegoers exit, the man with the daughter turns and calls to them)

VAGRANT: If things had been different, my daughter could have been another Shirley Temple! Yes, she could! Another Shirley Temple!

(The Moviegoers exit)

VAGRANT GIRL:
"Hi diddle dum, cum tin-trum, tantram,
Through the town of Ramsey...
(Lights out)

The End

32
REALISTIC
AND NONREALISTIC
APPROACHES

**Realistic versus nonrealistic drama. Significant differences in plot.
Realistic and nonrealistic characterization. Contrasting use of setting.
Cross-fertilization of techniques. The heritage of nonrealistic drama.
Risks and advantages of each approach.**

Realistic drama creates an illusion that reflects the world about us. The plot is a logical sequence of events, characters behave in ways we understand, and the setting is identifiable.

Nonrealistic drama, on the other hand, is an illusion that in some ways echoes a dream. It *seems* real just as a dream usually does, but the plot may be an illogical sequence of events in which time is distorted, characters behave in ways that lack motivation, and the setting is either unidentified or a satiric exaggeration of some vaguely familiar place.

At first glance, these two approaches appear to be entirely different. Actually they have much in common and frequently borrow techniques from each other. I will begin by describing their differences, but keep in mind that there is no sharp line between them.

Significant Differences in Plot

A prominent characteristic of realistic drama is a logical plot. The sequence of events may be startling or unusual, but it resembles the way things happen in everyday life.

In Saroyan's *Hello Out There*, for example, the plot is as logical as a newspaper account would be. We learn why the protagonist is in jail, and we soon discover why this is unjust. We are told why the young woman happens to be there. We understand why it is difficult for her to obtain the key and just how long it would take her to go home and get her father's gun. We are very much aware of the passage of time as the situation becomes increasingly threatening. When Photo-Finish is shot, we realize that he has exhausted all his possibilities of escape. A series of interlocking events has resulted in the final tragedy.

Contrast this with what could occur if this were written as a nonrealistic play. The two major characters might discover that they are trapped in that jail for eternity, that they are quite literally in hell. Absurd? This is essentially the plot of a highly successful play called *No Exit* by Jean-Paul Sartre. (The play is available in most libraries and is an excellent example of nonrealistic drama.) Or imagine a final scene in which a chariot drawn by dragons sweeps down and carries Emily off to a better world. Wild as that may seem, it is the dramatic conclusion to Euripides' *Medea*, a play that has gripped audiences for over 2,000 years.

These nonrealistic scenes seem preposterous in a play like *Hello Out There*, yet they are entirely acceptable when used in other plays. Why? Because the kind of imagination that will be used in a play is communicated to the audience almost at the outset. Theatergoers are assured within the first few minutes of *Hello Out There* that events will probably occur in a logical manner. I will return to the ways in which an audience is cued to the type of imagination that will be used in a play, but for now think of it simply as establishing the rules of the game that will probably apply for the length of the work.

Just as the plot moves logically, so also does time. A realistic play is usually quite specific about the time of day and often the season. If it is a period piece, we are informed about the historical period as well. Full-length plays often include a statement in the program indicating, for example, "An August afternoon, 1945," or will signal a change in subsequent acts with an announcement like "Later that week."

In one-act plays the time is frequently unbroken, but we have the feeling that we are living through a particular morning, afternoon, or evening. In *Hello Out There*, for example, we are not informed as to what time of day it is at first, but eventually we learn that the time is about ten in the morning and that Photo-Finish was brought in the preceding night. The play moves without a break through to the end. Notice how carefully Saroyan accounts for each step of his plot. In fact, the stress on time is the way he achieves suspense. Emily knows where her father's gun is, but there isn't time to get it. She has mentioned that a gang might try to get Photo-Finish, and sure enough the husband shows up with his friends close behind. We keep hoping that the two principals will be able to escape, but time rapidly runs out. The pace is relentless, and time is accounted for at every stage.

Compare this with the sequences in *Goin' West*. At first we assume that the action of the play is "late spring, 1846." This is stated as clearly as it would be in any documentary. But then we see a man with an early motion picture camera that suggests that perhaps the historical period is around 1900.

Although the voice of the narrator keeps returning us to 1846, we are not entirely surprised to hear the characters talking about whether the horse will have a nervous breakdown. Alfred says, "It's not easy to find a good animal psychiatrist out on this freeway." Amy assures him, "Lot of animal psychiatrists in Los Angeles." And as the play approaches its climax, we hear an announcer from "Station KLO reporting on the events of the day." All the movie studios have been destroyed. Although the time sequence is completely illogical from a realistic point of view, there is a logic when we view the play thematically. The drive to head west is being satirized in many different aspects and across several time periods—the earnest frontiersmen and their families, the early historians and journalists, the hucksters and con men, and ultimately the movie-crazed hustlers.

Time in nonrealistic plays is often distorted like this or left entirely vague because the sequence of events is linked to ideas rather than to the illusion of a literal episode.

Realistic and Nonrealistic Characterization

In Chapter 30 we examined ways in which characters can be made credible and convincing. I pointed out how primary characters are usually presented with depth and how important it is to give them different traits and to show them developing in some way. Photo-Finish, for example, has been a loser all his life, but he has an underlying sense of decency that shows through. Although he is killed at the end of the play, he has risen in stature. We are moved by the event not because of the abstract idea that poor, unsuccessful people are capable of dignity under stress but because we have come to take him seriously as a person. Theme is important in this play, but our emotional commitment is primarily with the character, not with the ideas he may suggest.

The same is true of Emily. She risks her life because she has fallen in love. If audiences remained unconvinced that she could fall in love that quickly with a character like Photo-Finish, the play would be judged a failure. Success in a realistic play is measured in part by the degree to which motivation is convincing.

Even secondary characters who remain "flat" and undeveloped act in ways that are comprehensible. Why does the husband kill? He is torn between the suspicion that his wife really was lying and the pressure from his friends who are just outside. He is weak, so he does what is expected of him—the ultimate in peer-group pressure. We don't get to know him well, but his motivation is carefully accounted for.

Not so in nonrealistic dramas. The cameraman in *Goin' West* deliberately misleads Archibald about the river, leading him and his family over the falls that no one has survived. Why? Because "God has reached into his hip pocket and pulled out my big chance." Documentary photography, he tells them, is "going to come of age." Are we bothered by the fact that an entire family is being killed due to his duplicity? Not seriously. And are we surprised when the cameraman appears in the next scene, recording the funeral of the family he has just wiped out? Not at all. Our concern is not focused on these characters as if they were people but, rather, on the ideas they represent. The cameraman is the objective, uncaring reporter in every age, the one for whom recording history and making a film mean more than life itself. In short, he is an *idea* presented as a character, not a realistic character who may in some secondary way suggest an idea. This is just the opposite from the technique in *Hello Out There* in which our sense of having been introduced to a "real" person outweighs what we later piece together as the thematic elements.

Our indifference to death in nonrealistic plays is a clear indication that our attention is not on the character as a character but, rather, on a character as a representative of an idea. In a play called *The Lesson* by Eugene Ionesco a raving professor berates his young students in a manner that by realistic standards we would classify as child abuse. Eventually he kills them for no apparent reason. If we made the mistake of viewing this play as an attempt at realism, we would find it an appalling act of violence without credible motivation. On that basis, the play would be a total failure. But the playwright is not concerned with psychological motivation or even with characterization. His theme has to do with the nature of authority and the abuses of absolute power. He has, in effect, drawn a savage cartoon to illustrate his point. Cartoons have the power to argue, even shock, but they deal with ideas, not with people as people.

This fundamental difference in the use of characters also affects how much background information the playwright has to provide. As I pointed out earlier, major characters in realistic drama are usually provided with a past so that we know where they came from. We have at least a rough idea, for example, how Photo-Finish has been trying to make a living and how he landed in jail.

Because characters in nonrealistic plays are usually satiric representations of abstractions like the professor in *The Lesson* or types like the self-centered cameraman in *Goin' West*, they simply appear as if from nowhere.

In some cases there is no way to fill in a past. Take Alfred, for example—the man who tries to sell his own wife so he can "start my own movie company." As he explains, he has "a blockbuster of a film deal cooking with 20th Century Coyote." To some degree, he is every twentieth-century hard-driving film producer who lives without a conscience; but he is also a nineteenth-century hard-driving entrepreneur who will do anything in the name of success. As he himself puts it, "When it comes to goin' West, conscience can have nothin' to do with it." Since he is a type who unfortunately appeared among the earliest settlers as well as among the latest arrivals, there is no way to present him with a detailed background. As a character, he is a type, not a person.

This does not mean that nonrealistic characters are more easily created, however. When you work in this vein you have to make sure that the audience understands your intent. If you are too obvious, the play may turn into a simple skit, but if you are not clear enough the audience will be too baffled to applaud.

Contrasting Use of Setting

In addition to plot and characterization, the sense of place is usually handled quite differently in realistic drama than it is in nonrealistic plays. Realistic drama is frequently "grounded" in a particular place. The script for *Hello Out There*, for example, states that the action takes place "in a small-town prison cell." That's fairly specific to start with, and the dialogue tells us even more. From Emily we learn that this is a town called Matador in Texas. These details give us a lot of associations to work with.

There is a long tradition for this. Shakespeare, whose audiences didn't have written programs to read, identified his many scene changes in his tragedies and especially in his history plays through cues in the dialogue itself. These cues are often worked in so subtly that we who read the play with the setting identified hardly notice.

In nonrealistic plays, on the other hand, the setting is either detached from place and time or, as in *Goin' West*, is in constant flux. Some plays are placed in a realistically designed room that is not identified with any community, country, or even historical period. Others are more fanciful—and more symbolic. Ionesco's play *The Chairs*, for example, takes place in a castle in the middle of the sea. He calls for the realistic sound of boats moving through the water as guests arrive, but we have no idea where the guests are coming from. The audience does not concern itself with questions of where the action is taking place; it accepts this dreamlike setting just as it accepts the raging torrent in *Goin' West* or the dreamlike auction of Amy, which is not even fixed in a particular century.

The Rich Heritage of Nonrealistic Drama

When one first approaches nonrealistic drama, it sometimes appears to be literary anarchy without limits or traditions. Actually it draws from two specific sources. Although the focus of this text is on the process of writing, not on literary history, a brief introduction to these two dramatic schools is an excellent way to explore the potential of nonrealistic drama.

The first of these traditions is **expressionism**. This movement included painting, fiction, and poetry at the turn of the century and continued through the 1920s. Early examples in drama are seen in the plays of August Strindberg, a Swedish playwright. Plays like *The Dance of Death* and *The Dream Play* are readily available in translation and provide vivid contrasts with the realistic drama of the time by such playwrights as Henrik Ibsen. Strindberg's plots were frequently dreamlike, his characters symbolic rather than psychologically comprehensible, and his tone frequently dark and pessimistic.

Another excellent example of early expressionism is the work of the Czech dramatist Karel Capek. His nightmarish vision of the future, *R.U.R.*, was written in 1920. It is an early example of science fiction, complete with robots who revolt against their masters. More thematically comprehensible than many of Strindberg's more dreamlike works, *R.U.R.* has a strong element of social protest.

For a good example of American expressionism, I would recommend Elmer Rice's *The Adding Machine* in which the protagonist, a cipher in a highly mechanical society, is named Mr. Zero. He lives in a room surrounded by numbers. His associates are also known by numbers—all higher than his, of course. Costumes, set, action, and dialogue are all distorted as they are in dreams, but also as in dreams there is an internal consistency that allows us to make sense of it all. We have all had occasions when we felt as if we had been treated like a mere number.

Another excellent example is seen in Eugene O'Neill's *The Emperor Jones*, a symbolic study of a deposed black leader in the Caribbean whose world is crumbling about him. The play focuses less on external events than on his inner fantasies and fears as he tries to escape through the jungle.

Varied as expressionistic plays are, they reject situations and characters that reflect in a literal way the world that we see. Instead, they explore the world we feel. They do this through symbolic representation. In addition, they often share a critical or even angry view of society as a whole. The individual is frequently seen as victim.

In the 1950s and 1960s there was a new surge of interest in nonrealistic drama. This school of drama became known as **theater of the absurd** because many of the playwrights shared the existential notion that life is absurd in the sense of being without ultimate meaning. Oddly, few of them recognized the other important aspect of existential thought: that we create meaning and values by the way we act. As a result, **absurdist** plays tend to be pessimistic and often cynical.

The school is best represented by the works of Eugene Ionesco, whose plays The Lesson and The Chairs I have already described. Other absurdist playwrights include Samuel Beckett, Harold Pinter, and occasionally Edward Albee.

Cross-fertilization of Techniques

Until now I have been describing realistic and nonrealistic approaches as if they were mutually exclusive. This is handy for analysis, but it is important to remember that they are both illusions and that each approach has enriched the other in many ways.

We are so used to the conventions of drama that we are hardly aware of the ways in which even the most realistic play is unrealistic. We look in on a room that has only three sides, for example. Some basically realistic plays have a set that calls for a downstairs and an upstairs room, both open to the audience; and others, as we will see in the next chapter, divide the stage into different settings. All this under the heading of "realism."

It is no wonder, then, that techniques we associate with nonrealistic drama can be used in an otherwise realistic play, and that some dreamlike plays rely heavily on some of the traditions we associate with realism.

Arthur Miller's *Death of a Salesman*, for example, is essentially a realistic play, but it makes use of an imaginary character who appears onstage. This is a nonrealistic detail that is based on the inner perceptions of the protagonist. In a play entitled *After the Fall*, Miller presents a realistic protagonist but handles the plot in a highly nonrealistic way. What the audience sees is a series of nonchronological scenes presented as if they were memories running through the mind of the protagonist.

Edward Albee is one of the few playwrights whose work ranges from fully realistic plays (*Who's Afraid of Virginia Woolf?*) to highly nonrealistic (*Tiny Alice*) and gradations between (*The Sandbox*). His work is well worth careful study if you want to explore further the ways in which realistic and nonrealistic approaches can be used to enrich each other.

Risks and Advantages of Each Approach

The decision as to how realistic or nonrealistic to make a play is never simple. The matter will be decided by your own preferences, by the plays you have seen and read, and by the needs of the particular dramatic concept you have in mind.

Since there are no guidelines, much will depend on your experience as a reader of plays. How many plays should you read? Four is better than two, and forty is better than four. To be reasonable, though, if you are starting out and are taking a course, you will only be able to read a few additional short plays. But if you are at the point of writing drama with more than an exploratory concern, it is essential that you read and see as many plays as time and funds will permit. No matter what your preferences may be, however, do consider both the risks and the special advantages of each approach before you make a decision.

The greatest danger when working with realistic drama is making use of stock characters, hackneyed dialogue, and conventional situations. Many of the clichés I warned against in the section on fiction appear in drama as well. Be consciously aware of all those worn-out television plots that may be floating around in the back of your mind.

The advantage of realistic drama, on the other hand, is that it is rooted in character. The audience comes to believe in a carefully developed character more fully than is possible in nonrealistic plays. And the plot—whether serious or gently humorous—can hold the audience as deeply as an important episode in life itself. This emotive potential is extraordinary.

There are three risky areas when working with nonrealistic drama. The first is the danger of excessive fragmentation. If your audience can't see any coherent pattern, it will simply lose interest. You can't depend on novelty value alone. And you can't draw on the emotional appeal of characterization the way realistic drama often does because your approach is necessarily idea-oriented. For these reasons you should be sure that the ideas you are working with hold together and make a statement that is both logical and compelling.

Martin Esslin puts it this way in *The Theatre of the Absurd*:

> Mere combinations of incongruities produce mere banality. Anyone attempting to work in this medium simply by writing down what comes into his mind will find that the supposed flights of spontaneous invention have never left the ground, that they consist of incoherent fragments of reality that have not been transposed into a valid imaginative whole.

The second risk is that of unrelieved seriousness. The dead weight of an unpleasant dream is often hard to take. Imagine a nonrealistic play about pioneers that dwells exclusively on treachery and greed. If you hit the same harsh note often enough, you leave the audience too numb to applaud. Louis Phillips is certainly concerned with the darker qualities of those who headed west at various points in our history, but rather than preaching he holds the audience with bitter satire.

True, some nonrealistic plays are essentially humorless, but they are exceptions and are less frequently produced today for that reason. Many nonrealistic plays are less farcical than *Goin' West*, but most contain some element of satire. This isn't simply coincidence. Remember that because nonrealistic drama tends to reduce the pulling power of a dramatic plot and a realistic situation, the play must provide some other attraction for the audience. Shock is one alternative and was used a good deal in the 1970s, but it has a limited appeal and is difficult to sustain. Wit—even if caustic—is a natural leavening for nonrealistic drama.

The third special concern in the writing of nonrealistic drama is the need to cue the audience fairly early in the play regarding the type of imagination you will be using. In most plays, the audience is informed as to whether the play is going to be realistic or nonrealistic within the first few minutes of playing time.

The audience of *Hello Out There* may be puzzled when they hear someone tap on the floor with a spoon for a half minute and then begin to repeat the phrase of the title. That *could* be the opening of a nonrealistic play. But that is a very short scene. Notice that as soon as Emily appears she establishes the scene in precisely realistic terms. She soon informs us that the protagonist is in jail, that there is "a whole gang of people all worked up," and, soon, that he is in Matador, Texas. The audience is assured that this play is going to be realistic—even if the action is somewhat truncated.

Goin' West, on the other hand, starts as if it is going to be realistic. The voice offstage reads a factual description from Francis Parkman's *The Oregon Trail*, and even if we are not familiar with it, the material sounds historically accurate. The year is 1846, and the play is going to deal with emigrants heading for Oregon and California. Even the relatively bare stage doesn't suggest a fantasy. Realistic dramas from the Elizabethan period to the present have been presented without stage sets.

But in less than a minute we are introduced to a man with a motion picture camera. The absurdity of a cameraman in 1846 suggests that the play is going to be an unrealistic farce—a highly exaggerated comedy. Later we begin to realize how serious the theme is, but establishing the type of imagination has been achieved almost from the start.

Failing to establish the type of imagination early in the work can lead members of the audience to wonder just what kind of play it is, and as soon as they do this they have lost the sense of illusion. Card games, sports, and drama all share the need for establishing the rules early in the game.

In spite of these risks, however, there are distinct assets to nonrealistic drama. It is a particularly tempting approach if your theme is more important to you than your characters. You can cut through to the heart of your statement in a bold and imaginative manner without having to create credible characters or construct a plausible plot. You are working with a medium that, like the political cartoon and the poster, lends itself to strong statements. As for form, you can let your imagination take flight. Like free verse, nonrealistic drama offers freedoms and also the obligation to find new and effective structures.

You probably already have strong feelings about these two approaches. Most playwrights do. But in deciding which basic route to take, keep an open mind. Consider the special nature of your projected play. Determine whether it would be best served by a logical plot and in-depth characterization or whether it is idea-based and deserves a more innovative and possibly satiric presentation.

33
VISUAL IMPACT

The realistic set, with distortions for greater realism. The symbolic set. The bare stage. Lighting for effect. Costumes: symbolic, conventional, and satiric. Action used to define scenes and dramatize conflict. Visualizing the scene as you write.

The visual aspects of a play can have a major impact on the audience. When we read play scripts we can easily forget that words on the page are only a small portion of the total dramatic experience. The degree to which drama depends on visual elements is reflected in the way we describe a theatrical experience: "I *saw* a good play," we say, whereas we are more apt to say, "I *went* to the opera."

What the audience sees is made up of several different elements. There is the physical set, the lighting, the costumes, and the action of actors. Although directors, set designers, and actors all need some latitude, they need a play that gives them the opportunity for visual impact. This chapter has one urgent message that I will repeat several times: When you write any type of play script, maintain a mental picture of what your stage looks like scene by scene, moment by moment.

The Realistic Set

The term **set** includes everything the audience sees except for the actors themselves. Although each set designer will approach a play slightly differently, playwrights usually specify what the locale is and which properties are essential. These general suggestions often classify the set as falling into one of three loosely defined types: realistic, symbolic, or bare.

The realistic set is so common today that we tend to think of it as the traditional approach. Actually it is a fairly recent development—less than 200 years out of the 2,500-year-old tradition of Western drama. In large degree, highly realistic details on the stage had to wait until the introduction of electric lights. When Ibsen's plays were first introduced to England in the late nineteenth century, audiences gasped with amazement at the sight of a perfectly reproduced living-room scene complete with real books in bookcases, portraits on the walls, and doors that opened and shut. Soon the stage directions for the plays of Barrie and Shaw began to reflect this new realism by including the most minute descriptions—even to the title of a book left "carelessly" on a coffee table.

We can no longer depend on that kind of naive wonder, of course. Film and television have made realism commonplace. But when a realistic set is constructed with skill and imagination, it still has enormous impact. Even today, highly effective sets presented on traditional stages are occasionally greeted with applause even before the first character appears onstage.

How much detail should a script include? There is no standard policy, but the tendency now is to be brief. One reason is that there is such a variety of stages today that playwrights can no longer be sure of just how their work will be presented. The traditional stage has what is known as a proscenium arch, which forms a picture frame for the action, and a curtain, which signals the beginning and closing of the dramatic illusion. But an increasing number of stages now have no arch and no single-picture effect because they are open on three sides. The design allows more of the audience to sit close to the action. In such theaters, the use of lights replaces the curtain. **Theater in the round**, or **arena stage**, extends this concept further by having the audience encircle the playing area as it does in a circus tent. The playwright's description of the set in the script should be flexible enough to allow set designers to adapt to a wide variety of stages.

In *Hello Out There*, for example, Saroyan merely states that this is to be "a small-town prison cell." On a traditional stage, this might be handled quite literally. But on a stage that is surrounded on all sides by the audience, the cell will more likely be suggested by a few bars. A good deal will have to be left to the imagination of the audience.

Remember that even the most highly realistic and detailed set is an illusion. A living room on the stage, for example, has no third wall. In a play called *Period of Adjustment* by Tennessee Williams the focal object is a television set. Because it is often on, it is placed with its back to the audience upstage center. The set in the Broadway production was meticulously realistic, yet from a literal point of view the audience was impossibly wedged between the back of the television set and where the wall should be. In other plays, the audience finds itself behind fireplaces. Oddly, this kind of distortion in no way detracts from the notion that the set is "realistic."

The significance of this for playwrights is that one can use a high degree of distortion to achieve a realistic effect. Audiences are used to these tricks and are willing to exercise their imaginations. This is particularly helpful in plays that include both indoor and outdoor scenes. A yard may be separated from the interior of, say, a kitchen by a low board; a door may be used to suggest the division between two areas without adjoining walls. The same applies to the second story of a house suggested only by a flight of stairs. If the actors treat these divisions as real, the audience will perceive them this way too.

In Arthur Miller's *Death of a Salesman*, for example, the script calls for an upstairs room, two rooms downstairs, and a portion of the yard outside. It is realistic in that the entire set is treated as if it were a real house and yard, yet it requires an act of imagination to separate what is outside from what is inside. An *actor* in the kitchen can obviously see what another actor is doing outside; but it is soon made clear that a *character* must open the door in order to see. This is not as extraordinary as it seems when you recall how children at the beach can create the same sort of illusion playing house with various rooms merely marked in the sand. It's no accident that we call drama a *play*.

Another ingenious use of realistic design is seen in William Ritman's set for Harold Pinter's *The Collection*. Working closely with the director and the playwright, Ritman managed to present the illusion of three entirely unconnected separate settings on the relatively small stage of the Cherry Lane Theatre in New York. The set has been duplicated on larger stages since then. As the action shifts from one area to the next, the lights on the other two are dimmed. Illustrations of the set (drawn by Richard Tuttle) appear on pages 321–322. Look at them now and notice how the illusion of where the action is taking place shifts in each case.

The great advantage of a set like this is that the playwright does not have to stop the action in order to change a set. As I have mentioned before, dropping the curtain or even dimming the lights breaks the illusion and returns the audience to the theater itself. If in addition you ask a stage crew to scurry about in the dark and change a set, that break becomes even lengthier and more distracting. A set divided into different playing areas allows a playwright to maintain a steady flow of action.

A word of warning, however. If you, like most people, have watched more television shows and films than plays, you may unwittingly suggest an impossibly complex set. Remember that whatever you call for in the script will have to be built with wood and held together with nails. The set I described for *Death of a Salesman* is about as complex as you can get even on a big stage. It is a serious challenge in a small space. The three-part set for *The Collection* has the advantage of being on one level, but on a small stage it is about as many separate playing areas as you can manage.

The Collection, showing emphasis on the modern apartment, with the other areas dark.

The Collection, showing emphasis on the telephone booth, which is, in the play, some distance from either home.

The Collection, showing emphasis on the ornate apartment, with the other areas dark.

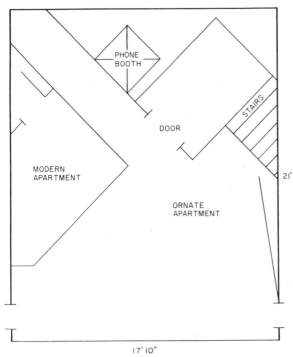

The Collection: a diagram of the stage, showing the technique of representing three entirely different scenes simply by shifts in lighting. Note how the unusual angles add both variety and depth even on a small stage.

It may seem strange that with so much distortion these sets are still described as realistic. In each case, however, the goal is to picture some aspect of the world as we know it. Walls may be only suggested, but in the imagination of the audience they are solid. And they remain so.

The Symbolic Set

The symbolic approach is fundamentally different in that it usually presents ideas rather than lifelike scenes. As I pointed out in the last chapter, the action of a play can take place without any clear sense of location as in the open, undefined landscape of *Waiting for Godot* by Samuel Beckett or the castle in the middle of the sea in Ionesco's *The Chairs*. Such sets may have a tree or fields or may consist of some highly imaginary room, but they are not intended to put the audience in a space that can be identified geographically or even in time.

Symbolic sets do not have to be vague, however. In the last chapter I described Elmer Rice's play *The Adding Machine* as a good example of expressionism. It is also a good example of how a symbolic set can be very precise in the same way that dreams can be specific. Most of the action takes place in Mr. Zero's bedroom, and the play would be perfectly comprehensible if the set were routinely realistic. But Rice chose to use a symbolic set. His script specifies that Zero's room be wallpapered with a vast collection of numbers ready for addition, subtraction, or division. Even the lampshade is decorated in that way. The set is not intended to place the audience in a room we can recognize; it is intended to make a statement about the kind of anonymous life Mr. Zero leads. The phrase "I feel like just a number" is dramatized symbolically through the set itself.

The Bare Stage

This third approach can be used in either realistic or nonrealistic plays. The set in *Goin' West* is essentially bare. The only stage prop is a single wooden table. The script tells us that this is to be used to represent "a raft, a small wagon, a steamship or whatever is needed...." The audience shifts its perception repeatedly, cued by the script itself. This gives the playwright great flexibility. What is a wagon trail one moment becomes a modern freeway the next.

Thornton Wilder's play *Our Town* is an earlier example of a bare-stage play, though it too has some minimum props that are used imaginatively. The script calls for a couple of folding chairs, two stepladders, and a plank that is often laid between them. Unlike *Goin' West*, the play is in many respects realistic and serious in tone, yet the use of the bare stage is similar.

When *Our Town* was first produced in 1938, presenting a major production without an elaborate set was considered innovative. Yet no one was confused. Like many daring experiments in theater, it was based on an old tradition. Elizabethan audiences were required to use their imaginations to visualize the rapid succession of scenes in Shakespearean plays. If this approach interests you, examine closely how Shakespeare ingeniously identifies the setting at the beginning of each new scene.

Although you will not want to spend more than a paragraph or so describing your set, you should have it clearly in your own mind as you write. This is the space your characters will inhabit, and it is also the space within which your imagination should flourish.

Here are some suggestions for making the best use of your set:

- Regardless of whether your play will be realistic or nonrealistic, determine whether it will be best served by a set that is realistic, symbolic, or essentially bare.

- Consider ways in which the set can have an impact right from the start. Think twice before you place a new play in that standard living room set with the stairs on one side and the front door on the other—this is the set of endless sitcom television programs.

- Be practical. Remember that some stages are small and there are limits to what one can build. You don't have to tell the set designers precisely how to proceed, but don't make impossible demands.

- Above all, keep your set in mind as you write. Make sure you know where your characters are. Make use of your stage properties.

Lighting for Effect

Lighting is the newest of all dramatic techniques. The Greeks depended on the sun, as did the Elizabethans. And from the time of the first enclosed theaters in the late sixteenth century until 1914, lighting consisted of a row of footlights designed simply to illuminate actors.

In 1914 the first spotlights were hung on the balcony rail of Wallack's Theater in New York. That was a radical improvement. But the progress made in the past twenty years with modern lighting boards is a quantum leap forward for drama. Although some playwrights leave lighting cues entirely to the director, others see lighting as an integral part of the whole effect and write basic instructions into the script.

The most obvious use of lighting is to suggest the time of day. It is natural enough to have the lights rise in the early morning or slowly dim as the sun sets. If the fading light also echoes an increasingly somber mood of the scene, the lighting will be additionally effective.

Much more often, lights are used simply to reflect the tone of the scene—whether inside or out. Quiet, low-key, or intimate scenes are enhanced with lowered lights; and conversely, scenes that are lively or dramatic can be charged with brighter lights. Techniques like these can be effective with any type of drama, but they are more frequently associated with nonrealistic plays.

In addition to influencing the overall tone of a scene, lights can be used to highlight a particular portion of the set while leaving other areas dark. As you can see from the illustrations of the three-part setting for *The Collection*, lighting effectively directs the audience's attention from one portion of the stage to another. In effect, selective lighting has the power to change the set.

Costumes

Like the lighting, the costumes create a visual effect that in some cases is left to the director but in other cases is written into the stage directions. In realistic plays with a contemporary setting there usually is no mention of costumes in the script. But if a play is nonrealistic, costumes may take on a symbolic significance. In such cases, playwrights sometimes become very specific.

In *A Lesson in Dead Language* by Adrienne Kennedy, a short and bitter play set in a school classroom, the pupils are all in "white organdy dresses"—a gentle symbolic suggestion of their conformity and innocence. The real distortion is the teacher who is costumed as an enormous white dog. Kennedy is working in dead earnest with both religious and racial themes in this play, and the result is a grotesque, relentless fantasy in which the costumes play an important role.

In *Goin' West*, the costuming is conventional but, like the play itself, a mix of periods. In the opening scene Archibald Month is specifically described as being dressed in buckskins to reflect the statement by the announcer that this is 1846. With equal specificity, the cameraman in that same opening scene is described as being "in the dress of the early 1900s." The illogical contrast is a visual confirmation of the farcical nature of the play. We are shown visually what we are learning from the dialogue—that this will be a farcical collage of different historical periods.

Sometimes highly conventional dress can be made a part of the satire in a nonrealistic play. In *The Bald Soprano* by Eugene Ionesco, for example, the hero is described with comically realistic detail as "an Englishman, seated in his English armchair and wearing English slippers, is smoking his English pipe and reading an English newspaper, near an English fire."

It is not necessary to specify costuming any more than it is required to give stage directions regarding the lighting. Both will be left to the director if the script doesn't refer to them. They are valuable options, however, especially if you are reaching for special visual effects.

The Visual Impact of Action

As I described in the chapter on plot, most plays are divided into a number of secondary scenes. Those units are begun and ended by entrances and exits. On this basic level, then, the very structure of a play depends on action.

For this reason, most playwrights outline their plays by scene and think of the whole drama in terms of these relatively short units. If a scene goes on too long, it may lose visual impact and appear to sag. It can either be cut a bit or it can be broken into two scenes by having another entrance or exit.

The action you provide within each scene is equally important. To some degree, good directors can enliven a static scene by adding "stage business"— minor activity like crossing the stage, opening a window, pacing up and down. But there are limits to this. And occasionally you may find that you have made matters even more difficult for the director by specifying that your characters sit while they talk.

Once again, it is essential that you visualize what is happening on the stage while you write. What is the speaker doing as he or she speaks, and what are the others doing as they listen? If you prefer to give only minimal stage directions, make sure your actors are not trapped into immobility. Saroyan, for example, provides only brief directions to the actors in *Hello Out There* and those only during periods when there is no dialogue ("...he turns away from the image of her and walks about like a lion in a cage"). But one can visualize the action in each scene—moving to the bars of the jail, backing off, turning to shout "Hello out there," drawing together again. Those two characters are never static. There is a restless energy in the play from beginning to end.

There is a different rhythm in *Goin' West*. The play consists of a series of short skits, each with a different cast of characters and generally with a different setting. There is no scene as long as the opening of *Hello Out There*.

In terms of action, there is a very good reason for this more rapid pace. A farce cannot depend on the gradually rising tension of a realistic tragedy. Each scene must sustain its own energy. For this reason, Phillips' play jumps from one lively scene to the next, never dwelling on any one long enough to lose the audience.

Each of Phillips' scenes focuses on a highly visual bit of action: a boat going over the falls, a funeral, a shooting, an attempt to get a wagon out of the mud, and so forth right through to the catastrophic sinking of California. Most of the action is exaggerated partly for laughter but also to intensify the theme, a concern we will turn to in the next chapter. As the Captain says, "A Western is action." While this play has a far more sophisticated theme than most Westerns, it is also a highly visual play.

Plays that have strong conflicts frequently dramatize them with a burst of violence toward the end. Audiences will accept intense dramatic action, but if it is not well motivated, it will seem hackneyed and melodramatic. The confrontation between Photo-Finish and the husband in *Hello Out There* comes close to the mob-versus-individual fights we have seen in standard television fare, but it is given stature partly by the character of the victim and partly by the mixed motives shown in the murderer.

Goin' West ends with an even more violent conclusion: the total destruction of the state of California. But there is no chance of this being taken as a melodrama because of the tone. Comedy deflates melodrama by laughing at it. As we will see, the *theme* of this play is just as serious as Saroyan's, but the violent action is kept in balance through the tone.

If your play is short and concludes with a highly dramatic scene that is too strong, remember that any confrontation can be muted a bit. Murders can become nonlethal fights, fights themselves can be downgraded. Action is essential, but don't forget that action without convincing characterization and credible motivation can easily turn the audience off. The other way to avoid having the action take over the play is to present it through satire as Louis Phillips does.

Occasionally the problem with an early draft is just the opposite: not enough action to keep the play moving. One way to test whether your script is static is to write a description of each scene without quoting any of the dialogue. If you can summarize certain scenes with bland statements like "They sit on the couch and blame each other for the state of their marriage," you may have some rewriting to do.

Seeing the Scene As You Write

If you have been writing fiction and are turning to drama for the first time, it may take a while to visualize the action as you work on a script. Keep in mind, however, that a reader of fiction moves at five times the speed at which the audience will observe your play. In fiction, three pages of an argument will flash by in two minutes; the same scene spoken out loud by characters sitting in two chairs may seem to take forever. If you are visualizing the action as you write, you might consider having the characters move about, throw things, or wake the neighbors, whose entrance immediately initiates a new scene.

If you are serious about drama and have a chance to see plays in production, you will find it helpful to see a play twice. To avoid the high cost, consider student productions. The first time, you may be too caught up with the characters and the plot to be analytical. But if you see the same play the following night, you can analyze aspects like scene construction, entrances and exits, and stage business. Some of this can be observed in the written script, but a good deal of the action within a scene will have been devised by the director or the actors themselves. Try to judge whether there is enough, whether it is effective, and how you would have done it differently. In this second viewing, whether you like the play or not is less important than what you can learn from it.

When we say a play is talky, slow, or lacks punch, we usually mean that there was not enough going on to catch the eye. A good play maintains vitality through its visual impact.

34
DRAMATIC THEMES

Theme as the central concern. Themes in *Hello Out There*. Themes in
Goin' West. Highlighting thematic concerns through repetition of lines,
visual repetition, and symbolic names. Social and political themes in
black theater and plays by women. Finding your own themes.

At the heart of most plays there is a *theme* or central concern. The **theme** is the
portion of a drama that comments on some aspect of the human condition.
This is similar to a theme in fiction except that frequently it is presented in
ways that are bolder and more vivid—that is, more dramatic.

As in fiction, what appears at first to be a single theme is often made up
of a number of different but closely related concerns. The longer and more
intricate a play, the more thematic suggestions it may contain. But as we will
see, even short plays can contain several concerns.

Themes do not generally provide answers to the questions a play raises.
Hamlet doesn't tell you precisely how to deal with stepfathers, and *Hello Out
There* hardly gives good advice on how to deal with a lynch mob. Although
there are plays that do take very specific positions on political and social issues,
these are said to present **theses**—that is, specific arguments—rather than
dealing with themes. The function of such plays is to persuade or convert, not
to explore. I will return to that approach later in this chapter.

Both the plays included in this text deal with a cluster of related themes.
The plays are helpful models for your own work because they manage to
suggest a good deal in a very short space. As we examine them, however, keep
in mind that the complexity of thematic suggestion that you see in a published

play is not usually what came to the playwright in the first draft. Themes often develop slowly as the writer moves through successive drafts.

Thematic Suggestion in *Hello Out There*

This play is remembered by theatergoers mainly for its dramatic impact. But if it had nothing more to offer than that, it would be a melodrama. The terror of an individual facing a lynch mob has been repeated frequently in film and television dramas. The elevation of the play above the level of a simple thriller is partly achieved through characterization; but the real complexity lies in its thematic suggestion.

Even a rapid reading of the play suggests that the theme deals with the loneliness of individuals and the need to reach out in friendship or love. The protagonist is held in jail, and the girl is trapped in a small town which seems to be no better than a jail. It appears that they might escape together; but in the end his luck runs out. The girl may still have a chance.

Perhaps that is all the casual reader will ever know about the play. But a writer has to examine the technique more closely. Saroyan has used three devices in this play to dramatize his thematic concerns to the point where they are unmistakable: repetition of certain key words throughout the length of the play like refrains, reiteration of the same words in "runs" or clusters, and the use of symbolic names.

The most pronounced use of the refrain is "hello out there." No one could miss the fact that this key phrase is used in the title, at the opening, and again at the closing of the play. More significant, however, is the fact that it is repeated a total of twenty-five times!

This is no accident. If you check the first twelve uses (all of which occur before the girl appears on stage), you will see how Saroyan has established the refrain early with a "run" or cluster of three and then spaced them increasingly farther apart. After the girl appears, they occur only occasionally. The next "run" occurs when the man is left alone in the cell again. He repeats it five times in the course of one short monologue. Once again the phrase is used sparingly until the very end when the girl, trapped and alone, repeats it twice as the curtain descends.

A second series is made up of the two words "scared" and "afraid." They are used interchangeably. They are repeated sixteen times and are used to apply not only to the young couple but to the men in the town and to the husband who eventually kills Photo-Finish. Notice the redundancy in the following "run":

> THE GIRL: ...They were talking of taking you to another jail in
> another town.
> YOUNG MAN: Yeah? Why?

> THE GIRL: Because they're afraid.
> YOUNG MAN: What are they afraid of?
> THE GIRL: They're afraid these people from Wheeling will come over
>   in the middle of the night and break in.
> YOUNG MAN: Yeah? What do they want to do that for?
> THE GIRL: Don't *you* know what they want to do it for?
> YOUNG MAN: Yeah, I know all right.
> THE GIRL: Are you scared?
> YOUNG MAN: Sure I'm scared. Nothing scares a man more than
>   ignorance.

First he uses "afraid" in a string of three successive lines, and then he uses "scared" three times in an almost poetic sequence.

There are two other refrains in this play which, though they are not as pronounced, still serve to dramatize the thematic concerns. One is "lonesome." It is used a total of twelve times, six of which occur in a "run" just before and just after the girl appears for the first time. Finally, there is "luck," which turns up ten times, six of which are in a cluster in about as many consecutive lines.

These, then, are five phrases or words that are repeated throughout the play and also bunched in clusters: "hello out there," "scared/afraid," "lonesome," and "luck." They also lie at the heart of what the playwright is working with: the loneliness and fear we all experience, the reaching out, and the element of luck with which we must always deal. All these are aspects of the human condition.

How does Saroyan get away with so much redundancy? He has, after all, violated a basic "rule" that is still generally honored in the writing of exposition and most fiction. This shows how far the technique of playwriting is from other types of prose.

Saroyan's approach here borrows from free verse. The use of repeated words and phrases either scattered or in clusters is, as I pointed out in Chapter 7, one of the characteristics found in the Bible, in the works of Walt Whitman, and more recently in the poetry of Allen Ginsberg, Lucille Clifton, and others.

A second device found in *Hello Out There* is the rather direct use of symbolic names. The town where the protagonist is about to meet his death is called "Matador." And the town from which the freewheeling, irresponsible men come is "Wheeling." Saroyan makes sure that the audience does not miss these names by repeating each one twice—a recognition of the fact that drama is a "continuous art form" that does not permit any hesitation.

He puts the same care into the young man's nickname, "Photo-Finish." Through the character's own dialogue we learn exactly what it means and how it is linked with the central theme of luck.

More subtle than the name is the symbolic action. The play begins with an isolated, frightened individual crying out for contact with someone—

anyone. It turns out that this same longing for companionship was what got him into this spot in the first place. Ironically, it is fear rather than rage that leads the husband to commit murder. And in the end, the girl has taken the role of the isolated, frightened individual crying out for contact with someone—anyone.

When one looks closely at these devices of repetition and symbolic details, they appear extraordinarily blatant. This is often true of drama. Remember that what one is analyzing here line by line is the written version of a performance that will slide through the consciousness of an audience in about twenty-eight uninterrupted minutes. For this reason, playwrights often repeat key phrases; and when they develop a symbol, they return to it at least once and at times frequently. Drama, more than any other genre, thrives on reiteration.

Thematic Suggestion in *Goin' West*

The themes in *Goin' West* are just as serious as those in *Hello Out There*, but because they are presented satirically it is possible to read or see the play without fully understanding just how strong a statement the play really is.

Satire ridicules by exaggeration. Good satire defines its target carefully, aiming not just for laughs (though that's an important element) but for criticism. Because satire is funny, one hardly notices that it is almost always a moral statement. Even the silliest satire on television attacks people (usually public figures), types (particularly the pompous and hypocritical), or institutions (the bigger the better). More sophisticated satire aimed, as plays are, at a smaller audience can be provocative. It is no accident that totalitarian regimes maintain tight control of theaters and playwrights.

When we first read *Goin' West* it seems as if the play is simply attacking many different selfish and hypocritical types involved in the westward movement. As such, the play becomes a kind of anti-Western farce. Documentary filmmakers, for example, are attacked for their cold-blooded indifference to their subject. Next comes the cynical and uneducated preacher who can't read or write or provide a decent funeral. He has even traded his Bible for a photo of a movie actress. He describes himself as "only fit to be two things—a preacher or a movie producer."

The military is also ridiculed through the character known as the Captain. He's a pompous windbag who represents the worst of the prejudices against Native Americans. He keeps talking about how the pioneers should have *vedettes*, which is an unwitting play on words. Vedettes were originally mounted sentinels posed in advance of a military column, but now the word refers to celebrities. He is a blend of the old military aggressive style and the more recent aggressiveness in show business.

As the play develops, the satire becomes even more pointed. Alfred

Montaigne is described as similar to Archibald Month, the man in the opening scene. Indeed, he has the same initials, also has a wife named Amy, and has a daughter named for a month in spring. But while Archibald is a simple frontiersman struggling to head west, Alfred is a self-seeking, hard-driving movie producer who is willing to sell his wife to get ahead in the film business. As he puts it, "I need the money to start my own movie company....When it comes to goin' West, conscience can have nothin' to do with it." When the crowd protests, he says "We wanna talk money." When they stall in the bidding, he urges them to hurry, pointing out that "It's getting late. The Decline of the West is setting in."

This is a prophetic statement, since shortly after that the entire state of California starts sliding into the sea. The playwright has one parting shot, this one at the news media. They cheerfully announce the grand disaster as a brief news bit and then turn "back to our studios for a little mood music."

With such a vast collection of targets, where is the center? What unifies the theme? True, they all have to do with the westward movement from the 1840s to the present, but that is plot, not theme. Oddly, the central theme is stated directly by one of the least reprehensible of this huge cast of characters. Frederick Jackson Turner is introduced as the author of *The Frontier in American History* and is portrayed as the foolish, naive professor (a frequent victim of satire). But he is the one who states that "the frontier is the outer edge of the wave—the meeting point between savagery and civilization." Questioned about what he means by savagery, he says "I suppose, killing, looting, violence, and...rape...." When he is then asked to define civilization, he uses exactly the same words. Anyone who has listened to local evening news in any large city will know what he means.

The theme of the play suggests that the development of the West was marked by a ruthless and often self-centered energy and more specifically that what we like to call civilization is not so different from what we call savagery.

Highlighting Thematic Concerns

Because drama is continuous, flowing past the audience without pausing to allow for reflection, themes have to be stressed. There are certain techniques for doing this that lend themselves particularly well to drama.

The first of these is repetition. As we have already seen, the phrase "hello out there" is used as a recurring refrain in Saroyan's play—from the title to the concluding lines. It reminds the audience repeatedly of the central theme, dealing with the need people have for other people. Repetition of the words "afraid" and "scared" is less noticeable, but it too works thematically to reinforce the suggestion of how fear influences us. As you remember, even the killer is described as being scared.

Repeating a visual pattern works the same way. The opening and closing scenes of *Hello Out There* provide a classic example—the plight of those two individuals compared not just in dialogue but in the way they stand alone on the stage staring out at the audience. It is the kind of visual repetition one sees frequently in ballet.

I have already pointed out how Phillips uses repetition in *Goin' West* by having Alfred Montaigne and his family so closely resemble Archibald Month and his wife and daughter. What may seem like a purely comic device actually serves two functions. First, it helps to bind together a play that might otherwise seem like a succession of almost unrelated themes. In addition, it shows the deterioration in moral outlook as the family approaches its goal.

Using symbolic names of characters and places is another device for highlighting thematic elements. Be careful, however, not to make them so obvious that the audience senses the heavy hand of the playwright at work. If the last name of a character is unmistakably symbolic, the play will lose verisimilitude. Suppose, for example, the protagonist of *Hello Out There* was called *Hy Risk*. That's clearly too obvious for a realistic play. But you can get away with a good deal by using nicknames, since they are knowingly selected to describe some aspect of the character. Photo-Finish explains why he is called this and we accept it as entirely plausible.

Watch out for Adams and Newman for characters who are in some way living in an Eden or starting new lives. But it is possible to find names that are thematically suggestive without hitting the audience with the implication. Many people have read or seen Miller's *Death of a Salesman* without noticing that the protagonist, a man who is low in the social order, is appropriately named Willy *Loman*.

Phillips also uses symbolic names of characters to highlight his themes, but his approach is to borrow the names of actual historical figures. The first voice we hear is a quotation from Francis Parkman's historical study, *The Oregon Trail*. And the character whose statement actually suggests a central theme of the work is Frederick Jackson Turner, the American historian and Pulitzer Prize winner who developed the notion that American society has been shaped more by the Western frontier than by European influence. The play's serious theme is filtered through these historical figures, but the tone is kept from sounding didactic by treating these characters satirically. This use of historical figures is also becoming popular in fiction and poetry.

As you read other plays, look for ways in which dramatists repeat key lines or significant action or employ symbolic names. In many cases, these theatrical devices will not be easy to spot when a play is first seen in performance, but if you read the script analytically you will be able to identify the techniques and learn from them.

Social and Political Themes

Drama has always been associated with social statement and political protest. Medieval miracle plays were originally intended to teach Biblical stories to illiterate peasants, but some became vehicles for satire. Vehement political statements were made through plays in the 1930s, and the Vietnam War continues to be a charged issue.

Today, **black theater** is a dynamic force in drama. Some plays develop themes of black identity, sharing the black experience with the whole society. Others present a specific thesis—a protest and a demand for reform.

The development of black theater is relatively recent. With a few rare exceptions, theater was a white art form until well into the 1960s. Black playwrights like Langston Hughes, Ossie Davis, and Lorraine Hansberry are known to most for one successful play each, but few white theatergoers can name the others they wrote. Langston Hughes alone turned out more than 20 plays. As a result, black playwrights, as well as black directors and actors, have been deprived of audiences and of the training that comes from regular production. This backlog of artistic frustration amplifies a deep sense of social injustice, to produce themes of bitter denunciation.

The harshest of these are written consciously and directly to a white audience. Plays like *The Toilet* by Amiri Baraka (LeRoi Jones) are intentionally designed to shock white, middle-class theatergoers. Rather than themes, these plays present theses—strong statements that often recommend specific social action.

Conscious appeal to a white audience is also found in plays that are thematic and less accusatory. In Charles Gordone's *No Place to Be Somebody*, for example, the plot of the play is stopped twice for lengthy monologues delivered like prose poems from the center of the stage. One of these is formally titled "There's More to Being Black than Meets the Eye." The other is a verse narrative of what it is like for a black to try living like white suburbanites, suffering the scorn of both urban blacks and white neighbors.

Other plays address themselves more specifically to black audiences. The seven plays selected originally by the Free Southern Theater group for their pilot program are good examples: *Purlie Victorious* by Ossie Davis, and *Do You Want to Be Free?* by Langston Hughes among others. Another important play of the period is Martin Duberman's *In White America*.

More recently, Athol Fugard has won wide audiences and much acclaim for such plays as *A Lesson from Aloes* and *Master Harold and the Boys*. These works touch on deep concerns that cut across racial lines as well as presenting immediate social issues. August Wilson has also achieved wide critical acclaim.

Women have also had a significant impact on drama in the past decade. As with black drama, plays by women vary from those that explore the woman's experience to those that make strong social or political statements.

The works of Wendy Wasserstein and Marsha Norman are excellent examples. One of the more innovative playwrights is Ursule Molinaro, whose works vary from brief, nonrealistic plays in the absurdist tradition to full-length works. In one, *Breakfast Past Noon*, a mother and daughter have a series of arguments without ever addressing each other directly. They refer to each other consistently in the third person. The effect is like two antagonists who refuse to make eye contact. The play is a highly effective dramatization of a hopelessly alienated relationship.

This play and others by women have been collected in an anthology called *The New Women's Theatre*, edited by Honor Moore. For a retrospective collection that gives historical perspective I would recommend *Plays By and About Women*, edited by Victoria Sullivan and James Hatch.

Finding Your Own Themes

If the thematic core of your play does not genuinely reflect your convictions, the play will probably not ring true. Further, you may find that this occasionally unconscious insincerity will result in characters that are stereotypes and situations that are hackneyed.

On the other hand, don't feel that if you do not have a social cause to defend you should turn to another genre. What you need is a situation that is potentially dramatic and involves characters whose lives are somewhat like the lives of people you know.

In some respects, your search will be similar to finding material for fiction, but the themes tend to be broader. It may strike you that Thornton Wilder's *Our Town* is a very mild piece of drama. The lives of reasonable and kindly people are depicted in episodic fashion. But there is drama in the way the tragedy of death in childbirth is finally resolved as a part of a universal harmony. Domestic situations make good plays if you can find a way of drawing a larger truth from them in a fresh and convincing way.

Don't forget your own roots. If you have a distinctive racial or national background, there will be tensions and perhaps successes and defeats associated with it. If your own life has been secure, what of your parents' lives?

Your life-style is also a source. Whether you live in a city apartment or on a farm, your experiences are in some ways unique. Do they have dramatic potential? Even if you see your environment as a "typical American suburban home," look again. When it comes to specific families (or individuals), there is no such thing as "typical." Each is individual.

Finally, draw on drama itself. What you read and what you see in production will suggest themes. And the play does not have to be contemporary. *Oedipus Rex* is about sons and parents in any age; *Antigone* is about the conflict between a woman's personal values and the laws of society; *Othello* raises questions of trust and honesty in those who mean the most to us; *Hamlet* explores, among other things, the uneasy relationship between young men and their stepfathers.

Costumes change. Language changes. Theatrical conventions change. But themes remain so constant that we still feel emotionally involved with works written more than 2,000 years ago. Whenever you feel this emotional pull, stop and ask what that play has revealed about your own situation, your own life, and your own society. You won't be borrowing a theme; you will be allowing another work of art to stimulate your own artistic imagination.

35
THE VOICES OF COMEDY

Humor versus wit and satire. Comedy of situation versus comedy of character. The degrees of satire from mild to biting. Comic relief. The pitfalls of comedy. Developing a comic sense.

It may seem odd to analyze comedy. We think of it as springing from an intuitive ability. The test of success is often thought of a simply a matter of audience reaction: If they don't laugh, the play has failed. It is true that a sense of humor is not something that can be taught. But almost no one is totally humorless. And if we don't as writers understand some of the underlying principles of comedy, we have no way of doctoring a script that doesn't work well. Or to put it more positively, understanding what makes us laugh helps us to create a successful script in the first place.

When we speak of **comedy**, we are actually referring to a wide range of approaches. The differences are more fundamental than just a matter of tone. The very intent of gentle comedy is different from, say, bitter satire. You can avoid a great deal of rewriting if you determine what type of comedy is appropriate for your particular play before you even outline the plot.

Humor versus Wit and Satire

Although the terms humor, wit, and satire are often used almost interchangeably, they refer to significantly different approaches. Humor tends to be gentle and supportive. It shares with an audience foibles that they have experienced or are familiar with like the awkwardness of young people in love, the tensions associated with a ritual like a job interview or a wedding, the anxieties, frustrations, and misunderstandings parents face in dealing with their children, and, conversely, the anxiety children experience in dealing with their parents.

Humor is often based on incongruities—the priest at a beer party, the gang member at an art opening, a man married to a woman half his age or the reverse. Some of these situations have been overused in the endless stream of situation comedies for television, but anyone who is observant can see new incongruities in daily live.

Wit, on the other hand, is often based less on the human condition than on verbal tricks—puns, plays on words. Or it may consist of a surprising turn of plot or a sudden revelation about character. Tonally, wit is often sharp, clever, surprising compared with the softer approach of humor. **Satire** is a form of wit with a specific purpose: to ridicule a person, a type, or an institution through exaggeration. It usually has the tonal sharpness of wit because its purpose is to criticize.

Although most of *Goin' West* is rooted in wit and satire, there are also small examples of humor. Because they are gentle, they are apt to be missed on first reading. In the first scene, for example, the young girl called April has a touching and humorous relationship with her doll Marzipan. April reassures Marzipan, telling her not to worry—an echo of the way we reassure others when in fact trying to calm our own anxieties. This is not satire because it is not ridiculing or even criticizing. It is simply a small example of an illogical but understandable reaction, one that we all recognize. It's not surprising that her counterpart, called May, is also treated with humor rather than satire. Her family is crossing the prairie in a covered wagon and she has to stop the whole procession to go to the bathroom. Her mother's reaction, echoing that of parents on every long motor trip: "We just left Fort Leavenworth."

These small examples show how the tone of humor differs from the wit and satire that dominate the play. The notion of California sliding into the sea is funny (unless you live in California) because it is a grotesquely bizarre cartoon of a state weighed down by population growth. It is also a darkly comic play on words illustrating literally the phrase "the decline of the West." It is a sharp, strident, rather cynical metaphor.

Witty as it is, the catastrophe itself is not true satire in that nothing is being attacked. The state of California is simply a victim. Contrast this with Alfred, the character who tries to auction off his wife to get ahead in the film business. This is clear and biting criticism of an aggressive male in a highly competitive field. Satire in this play is directed at specific types of people.

Comedy of Situation versus Comedy of Character

If you have an idea for a comedy, ask yourself whether the concept you have in mind is rooted in the situation or in character. That is, when you describe it to someone in a sentence or two, do you find yourself talking about what happens or who is involved?

Suppose, for example, you are exploring the possibility of a comedy in which a young husband and wife hope to move out of their apartment and are doing everything possible to induce the landlord to break the lease. They pretend they are keeping a dog, but the landlord loves animals; they paint the place black, but he is delighted; they pose as drug dealers, but all he wants is a cut of the profits. This is clearly a comedy in which the invention of original incidents is essential. Characterization is also important in that you want to develop differences between the husband and the wife (one, for example, may be more brazen in thinking up schemes and the other more cautious), but the focus of your efforts will be on plot and on some kind of unexpected resolution.

If, on the other hand, you are working with a man or woman who has, say, come to work at a newspaper office as an investigative journalist and gradually is revealed as a pathological liar with considerable guile and ingenuity, you have a play that is centered on character. Plot is important, as it always is, but your primary task is to convince the audience that this character can be both charming and convincing while at the same time psychologically incapable of telling the truth in conversation or in reporting.

Although these two approaches to comedy overlap, they represent an important distinction because they will determine where your primary attention must be placed right from the start. In the case of situational comedy, you will want to pay particular attention to pacing. The sequence of events will have to move from mild to extreme, each topping the previous one. You may have to mute some scenes toward the beginning in order to keep them from "upstaging" those toward the end. More likely, you will have to devise ways of intensifying those close to the climax so that the audience will sense the development.

Although pacing is also important in comedies based on character, more attention will have to be paid to creating a protagonist who will be truly memorable. The depth of characterization may not be as great as it has to be in serious drama, but vividness is essential. It may help to write out a character sketch for your own use, giving some range of personality so that you can avoid the limitations of a flat character.

The Degrees of Satire

Satire covers a wide spectrum from the gentlest sort of friendly gibe to the most vitriolic attack. In every case, however, there is some degree of exaggeration and some form of criticism.

In the last chapter I reviewed many satiric details in *Goin' West* as they related to the theme. The play also serves as a catalogue of the varying degrees of satire that are possible. About the mildest form is illustrated in the treatment of Archibald Month, the first pioneer to be introduced. What makes him a caricature is his absolute refusal to believe that his family is in trouble. Because of this refusal, he leads them all to their deaths. But he really is not reprehensible. Compare the satire of this character with that of the camera-man who knowingly gives false information about the falls just so he can get a good shot.

The preacher is an interesting case because although he is attacked as ignorant (he can't read or write), mercenary (he tests each coin), and indifferent to ritual (he uses a wedding parable at a funeral), he is also rather charmingly aware of his shortcomings. The playwright softens his tone a bit when he has his character admit that he's "only fit to be...a preacher or a movie producer." Characters who are aware of their own faults do not seem as reprehensible as those who are absolutely sure of themselves. Compare our attitude toward the preacher, for example, with our judgment of Alfred when he attempts to sell his wife without apology.

Strong as Phillips' satire is, it never gets really bitter or nasty. Notice how he softens the entire play with the two moviegoers at the end. In a sense, the playwright is smiling at his own play when he has them comment on the movie they have just seen. "The good guys chasing the bad guys all over the landscape," one of them says. "It's always the same." Even the catastrophic destruction of California turns into a film idea. "Too bad California had to fall off into the ocean"—the kind of comment we are apt to hear in the lobby when leaving even the most gripping film.

Phillips has adopted a level of satire that is highly critical without being bitter. Compare his tone with a play that ends with almost every character being swept into the sea while the cameraman wildly records the event shouting, "At last, the perfect epic film!" Far less subtle, far less forgiving, but it illustrates how wide the range is from gentle satire to a bitter attack.

Comic Relief

To this point, we have been treating comedy as if it were totally distinct from serious drama. Actually, the two are frequently blended. In fact, one of the most common weaknesses in student-written plays is a failure to employ **comic relief** in plays that are heavily dramatic.

Most of us were introduced to the technique of comic relief when we first read a Shakespearean tragedy or history play. Shakespeare had a talent for judging just how much heavy drama the audience could take and when to relieve the pressure with some kind of wit or satire.

His clowns (as in *King Lear*) specialize in wit—jokes, puns, and clever phrasing often commenting on the more serious aspects of the play in ironic terms. In the history plays like *Henry IV: Parts I and II* and more briefly in *Henry*

V, he employs satire in the form of Sir John Falstaff, a loudmouth liar and reveler who, almost because of his faults, becomes engaging and memorable.

Even Shakespeare, however, had to *learn* the technique. An early play, *Titus Andronicus*, is unrelieved and heavy-handed drama ending with a hideous bloodbath. The lack of comic relief turns it into a melodrama that few find moving. For good reason it is rarely produced, but it serves as a most important reminder that no matter how much talent we may possess, we all go through a learning stage.

Contemporary drama almost always contains some form of comic relief. In fact, the comic sections may almost match those portions that are serious. After all these years, comic relief still takes the two forms Shakespeare found effective: a witty minor character who can comment on the action or even kid the protagonist without being centrally involved, and a character who is presented in satiric form. Sometimes these characters appear frequently throughout the play; in other cases they are introduced only briefly and apparently casually. But there is nothing casual about when they appear. The playwright must decide when the audience will start squirming in their seats, and must take the pressure off just long enough to prevent this.

The Pitfalls of Comedy

Comedies are such fun to read and to watch we forget that they require just as much work as serious drama. No checklist is going to guard against all the potential problems of comedy, but there are four areas in which many student plays (and some professional plays as well) founder. Consider them carefully.

• **Poor pacing.** I have already pointed out that **pacing** is particularly important in comedies that are based on the buildup of a particular situation. But pacing is a concern in any comedy. If you open a play with the liveliest action or the strongest satire, you have nowhere to go but down. More often, problems in pacing involve the last half. Try to work the pace up as the play progresses. Longer plays can absorb a slow scene from time to time, but a one-act play that takes less than a half hour in playing time is like a hundred-yard dash—it's a mistake to pause along the way.

• **Fragmentation.** Sometimes writing a satire becomes good fun in itself and one forgets what the original aim was. Ask yourself just what the target is—as we did when analyzing *Goin' West*. Be careful not to stray too far. Drama, even satiric drama, has to have more structure than the routine of a stand-up comic or a night of improvisation. Fragmented satire may receive laughs, but it is not going to be repeated unless it is structured with considerable care and given a unifying central concern.

- **Imitation.** No form of writing in any genre is more subject to being imitative than comic drama. The reason is that television writers pump an endless stream of popular and largely forgettable comic drama into the American consciousness 365 days a year. Memories of these plots and characters are apt to lie like sludge in the recesses of our memories. It is all too easy to recycle them.

Television is forever imitating television, looting last year's sitcoms shamelessly. The writers know they are not working for the ages; like managers of fast-food chains, they are meeting a commercial demand. But when one writes for the stage, one hopes to create something a little more enduring. Check to make sure that both your characters and your plot are fresh. Don't be content just reaching for laughs; give your audience some nutriment as well.

- **Slapstick.** This term from vaudeville comes from the stick designed to make a loud whack! when actors hit each other. Vaudeville died, but the Three Stooges maintained the tradition in every detail except for sexual innuendo. Slapstick humor has its following just as comic strips do, and there is no harm in it. But it is also possible to write comic drama with some degree of sophistication. Shakespeare's Falstaff often appeared to be a precursor of slapstick, but when you see how that comic character was used to dramatize the development of Henry V from his drinking days to maturity, and when you review the way Falstaff the wastrel faces his own inevitable death, you understand how complex and insightful comedy can be.

The term "serious drama" is deceptive. Most sophisticated comedy has serious implications, just as most successfully serious tragedy has comic moments. Each supplements the other.

Developing a Comic Sense

If you are interested in writing comedy, there are two essential activities: read as many comic plays as you have time for, and see as many as you can afford. Never mind what century. You can learn from the few samples of Greek comedies just as you can from the Elizabethan period and from contemporary works.

One advantage to reading plays is that you can finish one in a single sitting. Granted, Elizabethan English slows you down, but start with one you have read before and you will see how much more rewarding the second experience is.

As with any group of works, you will find some you feel are totally unsuccessful. Be careful, however, not to shrug these off. You can learn as much from a play that strikes you as a failure as you can from one that is successful.

When you attend a performance, try to read the script in advance. Compare that experience with the audience reaction. Every evening is different, surprising even the actors on occasion. You will soon acquire a sense of what aspects of comedy work well on the stage.

If possible, talk with the actors about which parts seemed to work and which did not from their point of view. An actor can sense when he or she has the audience responding fully, and that insight can provide an understanding about what works and what does not work in comedy that one can never learn from the printed page.

Working with a summer stock company can also be a valuable experience. Summer companies tend to produce comedies, and even if you are a stagehand or have nothing but a walk-on part, you will have a chance to hear the same play presented repeatedly. If you keep listening as a writer, you can learn a good deal about the technique of making comedy work.

In essence, the task is to immerse yourself in comedies of all sorts. Learn from the work itself in production.

36
WRITING PLAYS
ON YOUR OWN

Evaluating your own work through a silent reading, a spoken delivery, and a group reading. Five core questions concerning dramatic impact, plot, characterization, themes, and degree of originality. The importance of embracing the medium.

The preceding chapters on drama should increase your ability to read plays and to watch productions critically. They should help you to avoid certain pitfalls and to strike out on your own with some measure of confidence. But this is just the beginning. The actual growth process will depend on how well you learn to evaluate your own work and, on a broader level, how successfully you can learn from studying professional work.

Evaluating Your Own Work

The opinions of friends may be helpful in evaluating the strengths and weaknesses of your work—possibly even more than with poetry because drama is usually intended for a wider audience. And the advice you receive from teachers and from professionals at conferences may prove to be invaluable. But ultimately *you* are the one who has to decide what revisions to make. When making these decisions, you are on your own.

Begin with a silent reading. You have been doing that in the process of writing, of course; but this reading is different. Give the script your undivided attention and don't stop to make corrections or notes.

As you read, picture all the action. Visualize each scene. Try to hear the lines as they would be spoken by actors and actresses. Don't analyze; just experience. Then, when you are through, imagine yourself the director at the end of the first dress rehearsal and write an objective critique.

That's the first step. The second is reading the script out loud. One mechanical purpose for this is timing. The total playing time can be estimated fairly accurately if you allow for action that occurs without lines. If it is a play divided into acts and scenes, it will be important to know how long they are. You will need this information when deciding where to cut and expand. It is also important to know the total playing time. This information is often asked for when a play is submitted to a contest.

In addition to these mechanical concerns, the spoken reading is an effective way for you to judge the quality of your dialogue before anyone else hears it. Lines that looked satisfactory on the page may sound awkward or out of character. Long speeches that seemed effective when read silently sometimes seem ponderous when read out loud.

After making corrections and revisions, you are ready for the third step, an informal group reading. Your readers should be familiar with the script, but there is no need for them to memorize the lines. If possible, the reading should be taped for further study. Naturally, some of the parts will appear better or worse depending on the skills of your readers, but no matter how informal the performance may be, it will give you your first real notion of what the play might be like in full production.

It is helpful to have a small audience of friends in addition to your readers. Encourage them to take notes about their reactions during the reading. They can do this in far more detail than your participants.

Try to allow time after the reading for a discussion of the play's dramatic impact, its theme, or any of the five critical questions suggested below. Aspects may be raised in discussion that never appeared in the written critiques. This also is the time for the participants to speak up.

One note of caution: Be careful not to let such sessions deteriorate into general conversations about the issues suggested by the play. Remind your critics that the subject is the play or script itself. You may wish to reproduce the following five questions (giving credit, of course) and to use them as guidelines for the discussion.

Five Core Questions

These five questions are central to the analysis of a dramatic script. They will help to keep the discussion from digressing. They should also serve as a way of looking at your own work in the early-draft stages.

1. *Does the play have dramatic impact?* Specifically, does it present some type of hook at the outset? Is this followed by dramatic questions strong enough to hold the interest of the audience? If wit and satire are used, do they work? Is the play really funny? Which characters and which specific scenes were successfully comic and which didn't come up to that standard? Precise comparisons are usually more useful than general pronouncements.

2. *Is the structure of the plot effective?* Even if your critics are not sure what improvements to suggest, you will learn a good deal if you ask them where the high points were. If they are unable to describe the work in terms of rising action and periodic climaxes, you should take a second look at the structure of your plot.

3. *Are the characters convincing and interesting?* Since characterization depends on dialogue and action, this question will necessarily include the effectiveness of the lines and the appropriateness of what each character does. As playwright, you may have to discourage such subjective comments as "I really didn't like that character." What you have to find out is whether it was the *characterization* that failed in some way.

   The group should understand that we don't make the same demands about secondary characters or those presented for comic relief or as satiric sketches. These may not be "convincing" as fully developed characters are, but they still must serve some function and in most cases provide interest.

4. *What themes are being explored and how are they developed?* It is important to find out just which themes reached your audience. Sometimes their views will differ from what you thought was clearly suggested. In such cases, don't be too quick to explain what your intent was. Encourage your critics to explain the play as they understood it. This will help you to see it objectively.

   If your themes were too subtle, the play is not going to be improved by convincing your critics that they should have seen what you had in mind. Try to work out actual approaches to revision that would highlight the ideas that didn't come through before. If, on the other hand, the group feels that the themes were too obvious, find out if the main ideas appeared to them hackneyed or preachy or just commonplace. Again, the most profitable approach you can take is not one of defense but of exploration.

5. *Does the play show originality?* There is nothing wrong in having your piece reflect the work of some playwright you admire. But your treatment should be fresh. Much will depend on characterization and how you shape your thematic concerns; yet originality goes beyond that. What you hope to hear is the feeling that this is a memorable script, one that is new and convincing. But if you don't get quite that sort of support, find out which elements of the play were too familiar to hold full interest and which were like a new experience for your audience.

Embracing the Medium

Writing a play can be a valuable experience. Even if you never attempt to write another, you will learn a good deal about the medium and will increase your enjoyment of performances. But if you want to go on from there and develop as a playwright on your own, you will have to immerse yourself in the medium.

This process must involve both reading and viewing, and if possible it should include participation in a production. The advantage of reading play scripts is that it offers you breadth. If you read a play a night five times a week, you will have read 260 plays in a year, and the chances are that not one of them was offered in production in your area during that period.

Every library has collections of "best plays" for particular years, and these will give you a wide variety. When you find a playwright whose work you admire, seek out his or her plays. And don't limit yourself to recent work. You can learn a lot from the way Shakespeare presents a dramatic question early in his tragedies or sets the scene in a history play or balances heavy drama with comic relief. If you are interested in strong themes, the plays of George Bernard Shaw will show you ways of masking highly didactic notions with wit and satire. Reading plays from all periods will be more profitable for you than any number of "how to" books on technique.

As much as possible, supplement your reading with seeing performances. Take in whatever is available—student and amateur productions as well as those presented by professional companies. If you are in college and cost is a factor, remember that you may be able to get special rates just before opening night. Since it is the play itself that concerns you and not the level of performance, a missed line or two won't bother you.

The third aspect of embracing the medium is getting involved in a production. Even if acting is not your primary concern, a bit part will help you to understand the dynamics of putting on a play. Or you might consider volunteering for the stage crew. Working with hammer and saw gives you a respect for both the limits and the opportunities of a stage set. If you are not at a college or university, consider working with a summer stock company. The mechanics of producing a play should be a part of any playwright's education.

Poets and writers of fiction have the option of living in relative isolation. Books and magazines serve as their connection with other writers. Playwrights, on the other hand, really thrive on being where the action is. Because the production—acting and the whole range of support activities—is a physical act of cooperation, the development of a script becomes more of a shared art. Make an effort to take part in some way.

Above all, however, is the need to know what other dramatists have done. You have at your disposal a host of playwrights covering a span of 2,500 years as your teachers. They have faced the same problems you will, considered some of the same options you will. Let them be your guide to the potential of the genre. Then you will be equipped to apply your own individual vision and your particular voice to a script that is uniquely yours.

A

SUBMISSION OF MATERIAL FOR PUBLICATION

Myths about publishing. Testing whether one is ready to submit material. Mechanical considerations: the manuscript, keeping records, computers. What to submit. Where to submit: listings, agents, small presses, double submissions. Marketing plays. A planned approach to publication.

The number of novice writers who submit material long before there is any chance of publication is matched by the number of those who are reluctant to submit even when they should enter the public market. This is because there are so many writers who have only a hazy notion about the whole area of marketing their work.

First, let's clear away a number of unfounded myths about publishing. One hears, for example, that nothing is published without "pull," that neither fiction nor drama can succeed without sex, that poetry must be obscure, that agents are unreliable, that book publishers are only interested in the bottom line, and that you have to live in New York to publish a play. Equally fanciful is the claim that if a piece of writing is really good it will be published without any effort on the part of the writer.

There are two essential facts to remember: First, publication is no more fair than life itself; there will always be good works that are not accepted and thoroughly rotten material that is. Second, if talent, practice, and a practical system of submission are combined, one can alter the odds in one's favor.

The test of whether you are ready to submit material is twofold. First, you should have written in that particular genre for some time. So-called "first novels" usually have been preceded by considerable practice in short stories and quite frequently by one or two unpublished novels.

During this difficult period of apprenticeship you should also be reading a good deal and familiarizing yourself with the magazines or publishers that might be interested in your work. I have repeatedly stressed the need to read carefully and regularly in the genre of your choice. Writers who do not do this are at such a great disadvantage that they eventually quit. Those who actively study their genre become perpetual students. They not only develop writing ability, they become increasingly familiar with the publications that may help them later.

If you have been writing for some time and have been an active, conscientious reader, you may be ready for the long and sometimes frustrating program of submitting material.

Mechanical Considerations

If you use a typewriter, the manuscript should be typed with a dark ribbon on a good grade of standard typewriter paper. Everything but your name and address should be double spaced. Be sure not to confuse this with the space-and-a-half available on some typewriters. Use pica type, 10 characters to the inch (standard on many typewriters), not elite or 12 cpi (characters per inch).

If you use a computer, follow the above specifications precisely (pica, 10 cpi). Resist the strong temptation to use fancy type, italics, gothic, or other decorative arts. As for the printer, laser and letter quality are best. "Near letter quality" (24 pin—each letter formed by 24 tiny dots) is acceptable. It looks even better if photocopied. Never use a dot matrix printer lower than 24 pin—editors have enough problems without being given headaches.

Place your name and address on the left, about two inches down from the top, and type "Fiction" or "A Poem" on the right. Some authors add the approximate length of the piece there, but this is no longer required.

The title is usually centered, in capital letters (not underlined or placed in quotation marks) about a third of the way down the page in this fashion:

```
Harley Q. Smith
205 Main St.                                    Fiction
Middletown, IL 62666

                    LOOKING FORWARD
```

The story begins two double line spaces below the title. Remember to double space it and indent the first line of each new paragraph three or five spaces. Never use separate title pages for stories or individual poems. Use them only for collections of poems, novels, or plays.

The pages (after the first) should be numbered in Arabic numerals along with your last name in the *upper right* corner: Smith 2, Smith 3, and so on.

Do not place the manuscript in a folder or binder and do not staple it. A simple paper clip will do. Novels should be sent loose in a box. Covering letters are not necessary with poetry or fiction unless you have something specific to say. If the editor has added a kind word to a previous rejection slip or has actually written a letter, be sure to remind him or her. In any case, be brief and factual. Never defend your own work.

If all this seems rather restrictive, remember that originality belongs in the art form itself, not in the manuscript or covering letter.

If you know no one on the staff, merely send the manuscript to the fiction or poetry editor at the address given in the magazine. But if you have met or corresponded with an editor of even a junior reader, send it to him or her.

For mailing, the envelope should be large enough so that the manuscript need not be folded. If one buys 9½" × 12½" envelopes for sending, one can include a self-addressed, stamped 9" × 12" envelope for its return. If this is too complicated, merely fold the second 9" × 12½" envelope so that it can be placed inside the first with the manuscript. In either case, be sure that your address and proper postage are on it. Failure to do this not only irritates the editor but increases your chances of never seeing it again.

Poems and stories are sent first class. Novels are wrapped or boxed and sent in padded mailers. Special Fourth Class is cheaper but slow and unreliable. First class is preferred. United Parcel rates vary by zone but are often almost as inexpensive as the Postal Service book rate.

In awaiting a reply, allow about four weeks for poetry and short stories and an agonizing three months for novels. Resist the temptation to inquire about work sent until at least twice the expected time has passed.

Keeping records is extremely important. It is impossible to remember what went out when and to which magazine if you do not keep a submissions notebook. In addition, it is invaluable to record not only which editors had a kind word or two, but which magazines sent specifically worded rejection slips. The lowest level of rejection slip is merely a printed statement saying that they appreciated receiving your work but were unable to use it. In addition, most magazines have one or two special slips with wording like "this was of particular interest to us" or "we hope to see more of your work." Take these seriously. Next on the scale is the penned comment on the bottom of the slip like "good dialogue" or "try us again." These are infuriatingly brief, but they are worth recording. Be careful, however, not to inundate a magazine with weekly submissions. An editor who has commented on one poem is not going to be impressed with a flood of inferior work. Treat such individuals as potential allies who deserve only your best efforts.

The highest point on this scale is the rejection *letter*. Even if brief, this is close to acceptance. If they suggest specific revisions that seem appropriate, revise and resubmit. If they don't, send your next really good piece. These are two situations in which you should definitely include a short covering letter.

Computers

Should you buy a computer? If you spend four or more hours a week writing prose or poetry and can afford the investment, the answer is probably yes.

In making this decision, don't be deluded into thinking that a computer will help you keep a checkbook balance, maintain a budget, or store recipes. They *can* do these things, but most people find electronic storage more cumbersome than paper and pencil. Your decision should be made primarily on the basis of how many hours a week you presently use a typewriter.

Most (but not all) serious writers of fiction and drama find a computer invaluable. Some poets too are beginning to be converted. The decision is essentially a personal one, but consider the advantages:

A computer allows you to see your work on a screen before it is committed to paper, to move blocks of material around, to break up and reform paragraphs, try different wording, compare different versions. It will also identify about half your spelling mistakes. Most important, you can return to a work weeks or months later and revise without having to retype the entire manuscript.

Surprisingly, a computer probably won't reduce the time you spend revising. Many recent converts find that they spend more time revising simply because the process is so much more pleasurable than it was when it involved the rather demeaning task of cutting and pasting.

There are four disadvantages that no computer magazine will warn you about. First, your typing accuracy will deteriorate. Corrections are so easy to make that you become permanently careless. Second, computers occasionally break down. Those failures are more complicated and more expensive than anything that happens to a typewriter. Breakdowns occur regardless of brand or price. Oddly, some machines will run flawlessly year after year, while others made by the same company will give trouble. Third, once in a long time a computer will simply wipe out a block of material or even its entire memory for no discernible reason. It is absolutely essential to make backup copies regularly. Finally, you will bore all your non-computing friends. Conversationally, computers are as addictive as baseball.

What kind to buy? That's a big topic, but here are some basic guidelines: Talk with friends about their own computer experiences. They will tell you more than you really want to hear. If your primary need is writing, don't spend extra money for capabilities required by business firms, chemical laboratories, and computer game freaks. Investing in a hard disk (rather than two floppies) is wise, but for a writer to get more than 10 MG (megabytes) is like an average driver investing in a 300-horsepower automobile. It is now probably wise to use a system that is IBM compatible so you can exchange diskettes or use another computer, and there are advantages to learning a widely accepted program such as WordPerfect for the same reasons. In general, stick to major brands that offer a full-year guarantee, and make sure it is in writing. Unlike automobiles, computers are just as likely to have major breakdowns in the first year as in the third.

As for printers, new designs are coming on the market all the time, but at present there are three basic types. Laser printers have the best resolution but are about ten times as expensive as a good dot matrix. True letter-quality printers (with a daisy wheel) produce the excellent appearance of a first-rate electric typewriter, but they are fast going out of style because of cost (well under a laser but twice as much as a good dot matrix) and lack of reliability. Dot matrix is the standard, but there are two types: "Near letter quality" has 24 pins and is acceptable for manuscripts. Less than 24 pins makes the machine cheaper but of little value for a writer since the print will give you a headache and most editors will wisely return your work unread.

What to Submit

This decision must rest ultimately with you. Although the advice of other serious writers can be helpful, don't be swayed by friends who do not know what you are doing. Classmates or neighbors who never read poetry are not going to be very helpful as critics.

This does not hold for play scripts, however. Since such work is designed to reach a larger audience, the advice of nonwriters may be of real value.

Poets should select a group of three or four poems. Writers of fiction should limit each submission to one story. Once the choice is made, send the work out repeatedly. A single editorial rejection means absolutely nothing. A manuscript is not "dead" until it has been turned down by at least ten magazines. The best approach is to send the work out on the very day it is returned—otherwise you are apt to lose courage. As a practical matter, just as many manuscripts are accepted after six or eight rejections as after only one. This is largely due to the fact that so many nonliterary factors go into selecting a work for publication, such as the number and kind of manuscripts on hand, the balance of a particular issue, and the personal preferences of the first reader.

There is no easy rule concerning what should be sent out; but once the decision is made, stand by it until you have cumulative proof that the work is unpublishable.

Where to Submit

As I have suggested in earlier chapters, the place to start studying publications is your nearest library. Read the little magazines and quarterlies and find out which ones are printing your kind of work. Keep a file on each publication with a brief description of the works you found successful so that you will remember them and will be able to look them up later.

You can find additional titles listed in *The International Directory of Little Magazines and Small Presses* (Dustbooks, Box 100, Paradise, CA 95967). This is by far the best directory of little magazines available. Other directories (listed in Appendix B) may prove helpful but tend to concentrate on more commercial markets.

Never submit material to a magazine on the basis of a listing alone. Always review at least one issue of the periodical and make sure that it would be interested in your kind of work. "Blind submissions"—those made without being familiar with the publication—not only waste your time and money, they are a terrible burden for the editors, who frequently work for little or no salary.

Mainstream novels—those aimed at a broad audience—should be circulated through a literary agent, a topic I will turn to shortly. You are on your own, however, with innovative or experimental novels, collections of stories, and book-length collections of poetry. Spend some time in one or two good bookstores identifying publishers who handle work that is somewhat similar to yours. Then look up the addresses and names of the publishers in *The International Directory of Little Magazines and Small Presses*. Major presses are listed in *Literary Market Place* (known as *LMP*). Make up a list and keep submitting your manuscript until you have been rejected by at least 13 or 14 publishers. This will take about three years—time enough for you to complete the next novel or collection.

Circulating novels and book-length collections of short works raises four questions which are asked at every writer's conference. First, what about vanity presses?

A vanity press is a publisher that charges the author a large fee for publication costs and sometimes for revisions. Many such organizations are perfectly honest, but it is rare indeed that a vanity press with its minimal system of distribution can do much for a novel that has been rejected by major publishers.

Don't confuse these commercially oriented vanity houses with small presses often run by individuals who love books and are willing to live a marginal economic life to work with them. Private and cooperative presses are used less for novels, but they are a growing outlet for collections of poems and stories. The author still has to pay, but the venture is a cooperative one.

Another question raised by those submitting book-length manuscripts is whether it is appropriate to make use of a personal contact at a publishing house. Yes, it most certainly is. Even if your acquaintance is not in the editorial department, submit through him or her. Using such a connection probably won't get a bad manuscript published, but it may bypass that first reader who has a great many manuscripts to review. In the case of rejections, the writer is apt to receive a lengthier comment if the reader has some personal interest. I can testify to the fact that such personal contact is not a prerequisite for having stories or novels accepted; but it is neither unethical nor a waste of time to make use of any interested reader or publisher.

Third, should you submit copies of the same work to different publishers at the same time? No, you should not. This applies to individual stories and poems as well. Such double submissions are acceptable only from novelists who have repeatedly been on the best-seller list and who have a high-powered agent who can referee what may resemble a kind of manuscript auction. For the rest of us, it's one at a time.

Publishers assume that if they accept a novel, they are investing in an author. Standard contracts usually insist on a first refusal on whatever book-length manuscript you may submit next. This does not apply to individual stories or poems you may be circulating at the same time, but it does mean that you should not have two copies of a book-length manuscript or even two different novels circulating at the same time.

This is frustrating and, to my mind, unfair to writers who have two novels they would like to keep in circulation. As for taking a chance, remember that the publishing world is small and closely connected. It is not worth trying to violate what editors call "publishers' ethics."

Finally, what about agents? Don't even consider using an agent if you write short stories intended primarily for little magazines or poetry of any sort. Placing material in literary quarterlies is an honor well worth struggling for, but they pay relatively little, and an agent's 10 percent of that hardly covers postage. Agents, unlike writers, cannot afford to work for love alone.

On the other hand, you *should* consider looking for an agent if you have completed a mainstream novel or if you have a group of five or six potentially publishable stories that might be considered by quality magazines (*The Atlantic, The New Yorker*), the women's magazines (*Redbook, McCalls, The Ladies' Home Journal*) or the men's magazines (*Playboy, Penthouse, Esquire*). Manuscripts submitted to such magazines through agencies usually receive more careful scrutiny by readers with more editorial authority.

Most reputable agents still charge a flat 10 percent of all material sold through them and make no other charges whatever, regardless of how much postage or time they spend. In return, they expect to handle *all* your work.

A few agents are now beginning to charge 15 percent, and some are requiring a "reading fee" for unpublished writers. Don't confuse this with a "criticism fee," for which you will receive a critical report. Watch out for those who charge "overhead"—additional fees. All this may become a growing trend, but the basic 10 percent contract is still the standard.

If you are unpublished, it will be difficult but not impossible to find an agent. Some writers try to place their first book and then secure an agent to handle the contract when it is offered by a publisher. Others send query letters to many different agents (addresses in *LMP*) describing the completed manuscript they hope to place. It is perfectly all right to send out many query letters at the same time. Be sure to ask them to recommend another agent if they cannot take on your work themselves. Often they will know of younger agents who are looking for new clients.

Marketing a play requires a somewhat different approach. There are four basic techniques which can be adopted separately or together:

- ENTER PLAY CONTESTS. The best listings are in the *Dramatists Sourcebook* (Theater Communications Group, 355 Lexington Ave., New York, NY 10017). This annual is fully revised each August. In addition, consider *Poets and Writers Magazine* (201 W. 54th St., New York, NY 10019).

- SUBMIT TO THEATERS. Again, use the *Dramatists Sourcebook*. Another listing appears in *Writer's Market* (Writer's Digest Books). Each theater has special needs, requirements, and deadlines, so read the fine print carefully.

- WORK WITH A THEATER GROUP. Any theater experience will be useful. In addition, you will meet people who will guide you. Even as a volunteer you will benefit.

- SUBMIT TO PUBLISHERS OF PLAYS. The two major publishers are Baker's Plays and Samuel French. Their addresses are in Appendix B. They accept many new plays (mostly mainstream) each year. If you are offered a contract, consider the terms carefully.

There is probably no other branch of the arts more committed to personal contact than drama. To put it bluntly, "pull" is extraordinarily valuable. If you know a producer, director, actor, or even a stagehand, write to him or her. This situation is not merely a matter of commercial corruption. The fact is that although book publishers come to know potential writers through little magazines (which they read with professional care), producers have little contact with the young playwright whose work has not yet appeared on the stage. This situation will continue until there are more little magazines willing to specialize in original plays and more low-budget stage companies in the smaller cities. Meanwhile, playwrights must struggle with the particularly difficult task of presenting their material.

If you are serious about your art, you must be realistic when considering publication. It is naive to assume that marketing your work is crass and demeaning. Publishers have no way of discovering you if you make no effort to circulate your work. On the other hand, a mania to publish at all costs can be damaging to the creative process. It often leads to imitative and conventional work and to feelings of hostility toward editors and publishers.

To avoid these most unrewarding extremes, begin with an honest evaluation of your own work. Then follow through with a planned, long-range program of submissions. There are, of course, writers who achieve wide recognition very suddenly; but this is rare and not always a blessing. Ideally, creative work is a way of life, and the effort to publish is an important though not a central portion of that life.

B
RESOURCES
FOR WRITERS

General Reference Books

The following four reference books are published annually and can be found in most libraries. The most complete listing of little magazines and quarterlies is found in *The International Directory of Little Magazines and Small Presses*. A specialized directory and information book for dramatists is described in the drama section of this appendix.

- *The International Directory of Little Magazines and Small Presses*, Dustbooks. This is by far the best listing of little magazines, quarterlies, literary journals, and small presses. It devotes a paragraph to each magazine, describing what it publishes and listing names of editors, payment scale, and the like. It gives cross-listings by subject, genre, and region. It does *not* list large-circulation magazines or major publishers. Dustbooks also offers *The Directory of Poetry Publishers*, which is handy for those working only with poetry.
- *Literary Market Place*, R.R. Bowker Co. *LMP* no longer lists magazines, but it remains the most authoritative list of book publishers, literary agents, writers' conferences, and addresses of those in publishing. It is entirely factual and does not contain articles on how to write or market your material. It is astonishingly expensive, but most libraries have it.
- *The Writer's Handbook*, The Writer, Inc. This annual is dominated by "how-to" articles on all aspects of writing, with an emphasis on commercial markets. There is also a list of magazines.

- *Writer's Market*, Writer's Digest Books. This has fewer articles than *Writer's Handbook* but more listings. Many are commercial (science, sports, travel) or technical journals (hardware, real estate, toys), but there is a small listing of literary journals. *Writer's Digest* also publishes *Poet's Market, Fiction Writer's Market,* and *Novel & Short Story Writer's Market.*

Informative Magazines

These magazines provide information and advice for writers, poets, and to a lesser degree, dramatists. They do not generally publish fiction or poetry. Consult library copies for current subscription rates.

- *AWP Chronicle*, Old Dominion University, Norfolk, VA 23529-0079. Published by Associated Writing Programs, this tabloid-form publication appears six times a year. It contains articles and news items about writers, poets, creative writing programs, contest winners, and the teaching of writing.
- *Poets and Writers Magazine,* 72 Spring St., New York, NY 10012. This nonprofit publication is a must for anyone who writes poetry or fiction. It is published six times a year. Its articles deal with problems faced by all literary writers: how to find time to write when teaching, how to arrange readings, publishing translations, dealing with small presses. It is also the best source of contest and grant application deadlines, dates of conferences and readings, and winners of awards.
- *Publishers Weekly*, 205 E. 42nd St., New York, NY 10017. Of particular interest to those in the business end of publishing, this magazine covers which books are about to be released, who is doing what in the field, author profiles, and future trends.
- *The Writer*, 8 Arlington St., Boston, MA 02116. This monthly focuses more on mass markets than does *Poets and Writers Magazine*. Articles give advice on writing and marketing a great variety of material from gothic novels to "confessionals" and from poetry to greeting-card verse.
- *Writer's Digest*, 1507 Dana Ave., Cincinnati, OH 45207. Fiction and verse outlets. Similar in emphasis to its competitor, *The Writer* (above).

Little Magazines

These magazines, also known as *quarterlies* (though they may appear from two to six times a year) and *literary journals*, publish fiction, poetry, and articles in varying proportions. The following list, a small sampling of the many fine literary journals being published today, has been selected especially for writers of fiction and poetry. They should all be available in your public or university library. (If not, urge your librarian to add the missing titles.) Most are quarterlies unless otherwise noted. Be sure to read at least one copy before submitting.

- *Agni*, Boston University, 236 Bay State Rd., Boston, MA 02215. Fiction, poetry, and excerpts from novels; two issues a year.
- *American Poetry Review*, 1721 Walnut St., Philadelphia, PA 19103. Mostly poetry and articles about poetry; some fiction, art, interviews. Six times a year in tabloid form; larger circulation than most little magazines.
- *Beloit Poetry Journal*, Box 154, RFD 2, Ellsworth, ME 04605. All poetry; a quarterly established in 1950.
- *The Black Warrior Review*, P.O. Box 2936, University of Alabama, Tuscaloosa, AL 35487. A balance of fiction, poetry, art, interviews, and reviews; two issues a year.
- *Field*, Rice Hall, Oberlin College, Oberlin, OH 44074. Devoted to poetry (including long poems) and essays on poetry; two issues a year.
- *The Georgia Review*, University of Georgia, Athens, GA 30602. A balance of fiction, poetry, interviews, criticism, reviews. Highly competitive.
- *The Gettysburg Review*, Gettysburg College, Gettysburg, PA 17325. Fiction, poetry, articles, satire.
- *Grand Street*, 50 Riverside Dr., New York, NY 10024. Fiction, poetry, articles. Highly competitive.
- *The Kenyon Review*, Kenyon College, Gambier, OH 43002. Fiction, poetry, articles, reviews.
- *The Missouri Review*, 1507 Hillcrest Hall, University of Missouri–Columbia, Columbia, MO 65211. Fiction, poetry, articles, interviews, reviews. Three issues a year.
- *New England Review*, Middlebury College, Middlebury, VT 05753. Fiction, poetry, articles, longer poems and parts of novels.
- *The North American Review*, University of Northern Iowa, Cedar Falls, IA 50614. Mostly fiction (including short-shorts); some poetry; nonfiction with an environmental focus.
- *Paris Review*, 541 E. 72nd St., New York, NY 10021. Fiction, poetry, articles; famous for its interviews with authors and poets. Larger circulation than most little magazines.
- *Ploughshares*, Emerson College, 100 Beacon St., Boston, MA 02116. Poetry and fiction primarily; revolving editorship with special issues often limited to one genre.
- *Poetry*, 60 West Walton St., Chicago, IL 60610. Poetry and reviews; informally known as "Poetry Chicago"; 12 issues a year; copyright does not revert to the author.
- *Poetry East*, Department of English, DePaul University, 802 W. Belden Ave., Chicago, IL 60614. Mainly poetry; also fiction, articles, interviews, criticism; some issues limited to a particular topic.
- *The Poetry Miscellany*, English Department, University of Tennessee, Chattanooga, TN 37403. Mostly poetry with some interviews, criticism, reviews; a very impressive list of contributors.
- *Prairie Schooner*, 201 Andrews Hall, University of Nebraska, Lincoln, NE 68588-0334. Fiction, poetry, articles, interviews.

- *Sewanee Review*, University of the South, Sewanee, TN 37375. Articles, fiction, poetry, about in that order.
- *Stories*, P.O. Box 1467, Arlington, MA 02174-0022. Exclusively short stories; send s.a.s.e. (self-addressed, stamped envelope) for guidelines before submitting.
- *Story*, 1507 Dana Ave., Cincinnati, OH 45207. Strictly fiction; becoming one of the foremost fiction magazines; two of the stories in this volume originally appeared in *Story*.
- *Story Quarterly*, P.O. Box 1416, Northbrook, IL 60065. Fiction primarily; also interviews, art, satire; two issues a year.
- *TriQuarterly*, Northwestern University, 2020 Ridge, Evanston, IL 60208. Fiction, poetry, criticism; write for contributors' guidelines.
- *The Virginia Quarterly Review*, One West Range, Charlottesville, VA 22903. Articles, poetry, fiction, reviews, about in that order.

Poetry Anthologies and Collections

The following anthologies will serve to introduce you to a wide variety of contemporary poets.

- *Contemporary American Poetry*, A. Poulin Jr., ed., Houghton Mifflin (paperback). This extensive paperback collection offers a good variety of poets. Women and black poets are well represented. It is frequently adopted for college courses.
- *The Har. ard Book of Contemporary American Poetry*, Helen Vendler, ed., Harvard University Press. This is a solid collection compiled by a distinguished critic, but it is not available in paperback.
- *No More Masks! An Anthology of Poems by Women*, F. Howe and E. Bass, eds., Anchor/Doubleday. From Amy Lowell to Nikki Giovanni—a full spectrum of women poets in this century. Unfortunately it is no longer in print, but is available in most libraries.
- *Strong Measures: Contemporary American Poetry in Traditional Forms*, Dacey and Jauss, eds., Harper & Row. This 492-page paperback is devoted to poetry in a great variety of metrical forms; there is no free verse. It includes a useful appendix with definitions of metrical terms.

Anthologies like those above should not be read like novels. If you own your own copy, you can come to know many different poets over a period of months. Browse and explore. Then consider collections. Collections are volumes devoted to the work of a single poet. When you have identified a number of poets whose work you like, see if they have collections in print by using the "Authors" section of the *Books in Print* catalogue in any library or bookstore. You can order copies through your bookstore or directly from the publisher (addresses in *LMP*). Collections are often available at poetry readings as well. Owning your own copy will allow you to study the poet's work at leisure.

Poets Writing About Their Craft

Although the best way to learn from poets is to read their poetry, it is also helpful to read what they have written in prose about their craft. Here is a brief sampling:

- *Letters to a Young Poet*, Rainer Maria Rilke; paperback editions of this classic still available from both Norton and Random House.
- *On the Poet and His Craft: Selected Prose of Theodore Roethke*, Ralph J. Mills, ed., University of Washington Press.
- *Poetry and the Age*, Randall Jarrell, Echo Press.
- *The Triggering Town: Lectures and Essays on Poetry and Writing*, Richard Hugo, Norton.
- *Twentieth Century Pleasures: Prose on Poetry*, Robert Hass, Echo Press.

Listening to Poetry

There are two ways to hear poets read their own work. First, attend poetry readings. Almost every college and university offers a series of poetry readings that are open to the public. Often colleges will place you on a mailing list if you are not a student. In addition, larger libraries and organizations like the Y.M.C.A., Y.W.C.A., and Y.M.H.A. invite poets to read their works. Attending writers' conferences in the summer (listings in *LMP*) is also a good way to hear poets read their own work.

The second approach is through recordings. Many libraries have good cassette and video cassette collections. Compact discs and tapes may also be ordered through any music store.

For Fiction Writers: The Big Three

In addition to the little magazines listed earlier, these three large-circulation magazines are of special interest to writers of fiction:

- *The Atlantic* (one or two stories each issue)
- *Esquire* (usually one story; published fortnightly)
- *The New Yorker* (normally one serious and occasionally one light story each week)

Fiction Anthologies and Collections

There are two widely read annual anthologies of short stories published in magazines during the previous year. While no two editors will agree on the "best" stories published in any year, these volumes provide a fine overview of good contemporary fiction.

- *The Best American Short Stories,* Houghton Mifflin. This volume has been published annually since 1915. Edited for 36 years by Martha Foley, the collection is still referred to informally as "the Foley collection." The editorship is now changed each year.
- *Prize Stories: The O. Henry Awards,* William Abrahams, ed., Doubleday. Better known as "the O. Henry collection," this is another view of the best fiction published during the previous year. It serves as an excellent companion work to *The Best American Short Stories.*

In addition to these two annuals, there are many short-story anthologies designed mainly for college use. They offer an opportunity to discover authors you may not have read. Here is a listing:

- *Classic Short Fiction,* Charles H. Bohner, ed., Prentice-Hall. This large paperback gives a sampling of nineteenth-century fiction but focuses primarily on the major writers of our own period.
- *Editors' Choice: New American Stories,* George E. Murphy, Jr., ed., Bantam. There are several volumes under this title, all paperback. The selections were made by magazine editors.
- *Look Who's Talking,* Bruce Webber, ed., Pocket Books. An inexpensive collection of American stories from the 1930s to the present.
- *Modern Short Stories,* A. Mizener, ed., Norton. A good, comprehensive collection of twentieth-century work.
- *Modern Short Stories: The Fiction of Experience,* Lesser and Morris, eds., McGraw-Hill. An anthology stressing the relationship between personal experience and fiction.
- *Necessary Fictions: Selected Stories From the Georgia Review,* Lindberg and Corey, eds. An anthology of recent work from a distinguished quarterly.
- *New American Short Stories: The Writers Select Their Own Favorites,* Gloria Norris, ed., New American Library. There is also a second anthology with the same title followed by "2." Both volumes consist of contemporary short stories, each selected by the individual author and accompanied with a brief commentary by him or her. These commentaries are of particular interest to those who write fiction.

As with poetry anthologies, these volumes will introduce you to a variety of work. But when you find an author you admire, see if he or she has published a collection of stories. In many cases you can find such volumes in your local library. But if you wish to order your own copy, turn to the "Author" section of *Books in Print* in your library or bookstore.

A number of university presses publish collections of short stories by a single author in paperback. Among the first to do this was the University of

Illinois Press (Urbana, IL 61801). They have been publishing four paperback collections a year since 1975. This admirable policy has been adopted in modified forms by The Johns Hopkins University Press (Baltimore, MD 21218), the University of Pittsburgh Press (Pittsburgh, PA 15260), and a few others. Write to these publishers if you wish a list of their short-story collections and prices.

Books About the Craft of Fiction

As in the case of poetry, there is no substitute for reading extensively in the genre itself, but as a supplement here are four works on fiction writing that will be useful:

- *The Art of Fiction: Notes on Craft for Young Writers*, John Gardner, Random House.
- *Becoming a Writer*, Dorothea Brande, Tarcher.
- *Writing Down the Bones: Freeing the Writer Within*, Natalie Goldberg.
- *Writing Fiction: A Guide to Narrative Craft*, Janet Burroway.

Magazines for Playwrights

- *Drama Review*, 55 Hayward, Cambridge, MA 02142. This quarterly focuses on contemporary avant-garde drama. Articles are often in depth and cover a wide range of generally innovative drama: women's theater, European trends, mixed-media productions, and so on.
- *Poets and Writers Magazine*, 72 Spring St., New York, NY 10012. Listed earlier as a resource for poets and fiction writers, this bimonthly is occasionally valuable for dramatists.
- *Theater*, 222 York St., New Haven, CT 06520. Calling itself "a critical journal of contemporary theater," this publication appears three times a year. In addition to articles, it has interviews, reviews, and some plays.

Books for Playwrights

- *Best Short Plays*, Chilton Book Co. (paperback edition, Applause Theater Book Publishers). This annual has been published for decades. Back issues can be found in many libraries.
- *Dramatists Sourcebook*, Theater Communications Group, 355 Lexington Ave., New York, NY 10017. This annual is fully revised each August. It contains a wealth of current information including submission policies of many theaters, contests, and the like. It is *the* basic source of information for any playwright.
- *One Act: 11 Short Plays of the Modern Theatre*, Samuel Moon, ed., Grove Weidenfeld.

A good collection of twentieth-century short plays, but none more recent than the 1970s.

- *Twenty-Four Favorite One-Act Plays*, Catmell and Cerf, Doubleday. This paperback collection contains a variety of fairly traditional plays, from serious to light.

Publishers of Play Scripts

These publishers buy, print, and sell play scripts—both one-act and full-length. Since they deal largely with schools and regional companies, their selections tend to be conservative and easily playable. Each publisher puts out a catalogue describing its plays briefly.

- *Baker's Plays*, 100 Chauncy St., Boston, MA 02111. In business since 1845, Baker's Plays offers not only a great many rather light comedies and mysteries, but also a number of serious dramas that have had Broadway success. Their scripts are relatively inexpensive and offer a good way to study plays not found in drama anthologies.
- *The Dramatic Publishing Co.*, 4150 N. Milwaukee Ave., Chicago, IL 60641. Established in 1885, this company prints from 40 to 60 titles a year.
- *Samuel French, Inc.*, 25 W. 45th St., New York, NY 10036. The oldest (1830) of these three venerable publishing houses, Samuel French, Inc. has branches in England and Canada and publishes about 50 titles a year.

In addition to these publishers specializing in drama, many other houses print paperback editions of plays. Copies may be difficult to find, however, because few bookstores stock more than a sampling. The best solution is the same as it is for poetry and fiction: Start with the card or computer file in your library. If you want to order a copy, turn to the "Authors" section of *Books in Print* and order through your bookstore or directly from the publisher (addresses in *LMP*).

Remember, finally, that if your interest is in play writing, it is essential that you see as many productions as you can. Whenever possible, combine your study of the script with the experience of seeing the work performed. Each approach will provide insights the other cannot.

GLOSSARY-INDEX

This section can be used both for a quick review of literary terms and as an index. The definitions are limited to the aspects discussed in the text. Numbers refer to pages and *ff.* means the discussion continues on following page(s). Words in small capitals indicate cross-reference either in the same or a closely related form; e.g., METERED may be found under **meter,** RHYMING under **rhyme.**

Abstraction, 28, 34. A word or phrase that refers to a concept or state of being. It is at the opposite end of a scale from *concrete* words, which refer to objects we can see and touch. *Peace* is an abstraction; *dove* is a concrete word.

Absurdist, 314. See THEATER OF THE ABSURD.

Alliteration, 48. See SOUND DEVICES.

Ambivalence, 15, 85. Conflicting or contrasting emotions which are held at the same time. Lack of ambivalence sometimes results in SIMPLE WRITING.

Anapestic foot, 64. See METER.

Anecdote, 225. A clever, sometimes humorous account usually told in conversation rather than written. Anecdotal FICTION tends to be SIMPLE, depending more on a twist of events (PLOT) than on CHARACTERIZATION.

Archaic diction, 29. Words that are primarily associated with an earlier period and are no longer in general use.

Arena stage, 319. See STAGE DESIGNS.

Assonance, 48. See SOUND DEVICES.

Automatic writing, 145. See STREAM OF CONSCIOUSNESS.

Ballad, 95. A NARRATIVE POEM often written in quatrains (see STANZA) of alternating iambic tetrameter and trimeter, RHYMING *abcb. Folk ballads* are often intended to be sung and are relatively SIMPLE. *Literary ballads* are a SOPHISTICATED use of the old form.

Base time, 179. See PLOT.

Black theater, 335ff. Plays written by African-Americans. Although playwrights like Langston Hughes and Ossie Davis wrote hundreds of works in the 1930s and 1940s, the term is most frequently used to refer to those who have come into prominence since the 1960s, such as Amiri Baraka, Paul Carter Harrison, Lonne Elder III, Adrienne Kennedy, August Wilson, and Athol Fugard.

Black verse, 83. VERSE written by African-Americans such as Lucy Smith, David Henderson, Conrad Kent Rivers, Lucille Clifton (p. 126), Maya Angelou (p. 124), Gwendolyn Brooks (p. 124), and Nikki Giovanni (p. 123).

Blank verse, 65. Unrhyming iambic pentameter (see VERSE and METER).

Breath units, 77. See RHYTHM.

Caesura, 60. A pause or complete break in the RHYTHM of a LINE of VERSE frequently occurring in the middle. It is particularly noticeable in Old English alliterative verse (see SOUND DEVICES) such as *Beowulf.* It is also found in METERED VERSE.

Catalyst, 294. A minor, often undeveloped ("flat") character (or an apparently minor event) in drama or fiction that nonetheless advances the plot in some significant way or reveals some important piece of information.

Catastrophe, 278. See PLOT.

Central concern, 232ff. See THEME.

Characterization, 207ff., 288ff., 310. The illusion in FICTION or DRAMA of having actually met someone. The illusion depends on consistency of details, complexity of insight, and individuality. SIMPLE characterization stresses consistency at the expense of complexity and often results in a STOCK CHARACTER, a form of SIMPLE WRITING.

Cinquain, 94. A five-line STANZA, also called QUINTET.

Cliché, 25ff. A METAPHOR or simile which has become so familiar from overuse that the vehicle (see METAPHOR) no longer contributes any meaning whatever to the tenor. It provides neither the vividness of a good metaphor nor the strength of a single, unmodified word. "Good as gold" and "crystal clear" are clichés in this specific sense. The word is also used to describe overused but nonmetaphorical expressions such as "tried and true" and "each and every."

Comedy, 338ff. DRAMA which is light in TONE and ends happily. Such plays are usually characterized by humor, wit, and occasionally satire. When comedy is used to lighten the TONE of a play, it is called *comic relief.*

Comic relief, 341. See COMEDY.

Commercial fiction, 139. FICTION which is SIMPLE and conforms to certain rigid CONVENTIONS of PLOT and CHARACTER, usually for the sake of publication and profit. Forms include the "pulps" (confessionals such as *True Romance*) and the "slicks" (*McCalls, Redbook,* and the like). The so-called slick magazines, however, have also published some sophisticated fiction.

Concept, 256. A brief, factual description of a play (or film script) that describes the basic situation, some type of conflict or struggle, and the outcome. It is not to be confused with THEME, which describes in abstract terms that portion of a work that comments on the human condition generally.

Concrete poetry, 73. VERSE in which TYPOGRAPHY is employed in an extreme fashion to make the words and word fragments suggest a shape or picture which becomes of greater importance than RHYTHM or sound. Also called *shaped poetry.*

Concrete words, 33. See ABSTRACTION.

Conflict, 192ff., 281ff. See TENSION.

Connotation, 80. The unstated suggestion implied by a word, phrase, passage, or any other unit in a literary work. This term includes everything from the emotional overtones or associations of a word or phrase to the symbolic significance of a character, setting, or sequence of actions. It is contrasted with *denotation,* the literal meaning.

Consonance, 48. See SOUND DEVICES.

Convention, 10, 141ff. Any pattern or device in literature that is repeated in a number of different works by a number of different writers. It is a broad term which includes basic devices like PLOT, DIALOGUE, the division of a play into acts and SCENES, and the FIXED FORMS of POETRY like the SONNET and BALLAD. It also refers to recurring patterns in subject matter. Such conventions can be subtle or HACKNEYED. The term includes everything that is not unique in a work of literature.

Cosmic irony, 85. See IRONY.

Couplet, 51, 93. See STANZA.

Creative writing, 133. Generally used to describe college courses in the writing of FICTION, poetry (see VERSE), and DRAMA, or any combination of these. It excludes courses in expository writing, assertive writing, and (usually) COMMERCIAL WRITING. Although all forms of writing require creativity in the broad sense, *creative writing* normally applies to the three more imaginative GENRES.

Dactylic foot, 65. See METER.

Denotation, 80. See CONNOTATION.

Density, 5ff., 240. The degree of compression in a poem or story. High density means that a great deal is implied about character and/or theme. The PACE may necessarily be slower. Low density reveals less but usually increases the pace.

Dialogue, 213ff., 283. Any word, phrase, or passage which quotes a character's speech directly. It normally appears in quotation marks to distinguish it from thoughts. *Monologue* is reserved for relatively lengthy and uninterrupted speeches. *Soliloquy* refers to monologues spoken in plays. *Indirect dialogue* is the same as *indirect discourse;* it echoes the phrasing of dialogue without actually quoting. Dialogue and thoughts constitute two of the five NARRATIVE MODES.

Diction, 238. The choice of words in any piece of writing. Diction is a major factor in determining STYLE.

Dimeter, 65. See LINE.

Distance, 83. That aspect of TONE which describes how closely identified an author (or narrator) appears to be with his or her fictional character. Highly autobiographical and subjective works tend to have very little distance. METAMORPHOSING the PROTAGONIST or adding an IRONIC or humorous TONE increases the distance.

Double rhyme, 50. See RHYME.

Drama, 254ff. Writing intended primarily for presentation by performers speaking and acting on a stage. Drama is characterized, generally speaking, by the following: it is a "dramatic art" in the sense that it has an emotional impact or force; it is a visual art; it is an auditory art; it is physically produced on a stage; it moves continuously; and it is intended for spectators.

Dramatic conflict, 192ff. See TENSION.

Dramatic irony, 85. See IRONY.

Dramatic question, 196ff. The emotional element in a play or work of FICTION which holds the attention of an audience or readers. An initial dramatic question is sometimes called a *hook*. Dramatic questions are usually SIMPLE emotional appeals based on curiosity or SUSPENSE. When dramatic questions are stressed at the expense of THEME or CHARACTERIZATION, the result is usually MELODRAMA.

Elizabethan sonnet, 95. See SONNET.

End-stopped line, 67. See ENJAMBMENT.

Enjambment, 52, 67. LINES in VERSE in which either the grammatical construction or the meaning or both are continued from the end of one line to the next. One function of this technique is to mute the rhythmical effect of METER and/or RHYME. It is contrasted with *end-stopped lines*, which are usually terminated with a period or a semicolon.

Epiphany, 183. A moment of awakening or discovery on the part of a FICTIONAL character, the reader, or both. Originally suggested by James Joyce, this term is generally limited to FICTION.

Exposition, 137. Generally, factual writing. In fiction: passages that give background information or commentary directly, not through action or dialogue. It is one of the five NARRATIVE MODES.

Expressionism, 313ff. See REALISTIC DRAMA.

Eye rhyme, 50 See RHYME.

Falling action, 278. See PILOT.

Falling meter, 66. See METER.

Feminine rhyme, 50ff. See RHYME.

Fiction, 134ff. Writing which tells an untrue story in PROSE. It may be SIMPLE like most COMMERCIAL WRITING or SOPHISTICATED. Fiction is also classified loosely by length: Short-short stories tend to be from three to eight pages of typed, double-space manuscript; short stories range upward to 24 or 30 pages; novellas are often in the 100-to-150-page range, after which the work is considered a novel. Complexity of PLOT tends to increase with length.

Figurative language, 36ff. See IMAGE.

Figure of speech,   36, 229ff. See IMAGE.

First-person narration,   161ff. See PERSON.

Fixed forms,   94. Traditional VERSE forms that follow certain CONVENTIONS in METER, RHYME scheme, or syllabics (see RHYTHM). Examples: the BALLAD, SONNET, and HAIKU.

Flashback,   179ff. See PLOT.

Focus,   165ff. The character or characters who are the primary concern of a story. When it is a single individual, he or she is also referred to as the PROTAGONIST. If the protagonist has an opponent (especially in drama), this character may be referred to as the *antagonist.*

Foil,   283. A secondary character in FICTION or DRAMA who sets off a primary character by contrast in attitude, appearance, or in other ways.

Foot,   64. See METER.

Forewarning,   244. The technique in FICTION of preparing the reader for a shift in tone or for some turn of PLOT. Also referred to as a *pre-echo.*

Formula,   141. Popular CONVENTIONS that characterize SIMPLE FICTION and DRAMA. These conventions are usually patterns of PLOT combined with STOCK CHARACTERS. Sample: The-sincere-brunette who competes with The-scheming-blonde for the attentions of The-rising-young-executive who at first is "blind to the truth" but who finally "sees the light."

Frame story,   180. See PLOT.

Free verse,   97ff. VERSE which is written without METER, depending instead on RHYTHMICAL patterns derived from TYPOGRAPHY, syntactical elements, the repetition of words and phrases, syllabics (see RHYTHM), or breath units (see RHYTHM). Free verse contains no regular RHYME, depending instead on SOUND DEVICES such as assonance, consonance, and alliteration.

Genre,   1ff., 254ff. Any of several types of imaginative writing. In common usage, genres refer to FICTION, POETRY, and DRAMA. Classifications like "mysteries," "Westerns," and "science fiction" are often referred to as *sub-genres* or *genre writing.*

Gimmick,   143. An unusual twist of PLOT or CHARACTERIZATION. This somewhat colloquial term is generally used in a pejorative sense to describe contrived, attention-getting details.

Hackneyed language,   26ff. A broad term which includes CLICHÉS as well as non-metaphorical phrases and words which have been weakened by overuse. Such language is closely associated with SENTIMENTALITY and with STOCK CHARACTERS.

Haiku,   44, 94. Originally a Japanese VERSE form. In English it is usually written as a three-line poem containing five syllables in the first LINE, seven in the second, and five in the third.

Heptameter,   65. See LINE.

Hexameter,   65. See LINE.

Hook,   277. See DRAMATIC QUESTION.

Horizontal rhythm,   72. See RHYTHM.

Hyperbole, 38. A figure of speech (see IMAGE) employing extreme exaggeration, usually in the form of a simile or METAPHOR.

Iambic foot, 64. The most popular type of METER (ta-*tum*).

Image,16, 33ff. Any significant piece of sense data in a poem or story. It may be used in a literal statement, as a SYMBOL, or in a figure of speech. A figure of speech (also called *figurative language*) uses an image in a stated or implied comparison. METAPHORS are the most common figures of speech. When several contain images which are closely related, the result is an *image cluster* (p. 36). Other figures of speech include similes, PUNS, HYPERBOLE, and SYNECDOCHE.

Image cluster, 100. See IMAGE.

Indirect discourse, 214. See DIALOGUE.

Irony, 85ff., 197ff. A reversal in which the literal statement or actual event is contrasted with the intended meaning or expected outcome. Irony can take three forms. The first is *verbal irony*, in which a statement by the author or a character is knowingly the opposite of the actual meaning (like saying, "Great day for a sail" during a hurricane). The second is *dramatic irony*, in which events, not words, are reversed (like the messenger in *Oedipus Rex* who says "Good news" when unknowingly he brings disastrous information). The third is *cosmic irony*, which is usually thought of as a reversal on the part of fate or chance (like the firefighter who dies from smoking in bed).

Italian sonnet, 95. See SONNET.

Legitimate theater, 253. Plays performed by actors on a stage as contrasted with television DRAMA, cinema, and the like.

Line, 1ff., 64ff. A unit of VERSE which when printed usually appears without being broken, the length of which is determined by the poet alone. The inclusion of the line as a part of the art form rather than merely a printer's concern is one of the fundamental distinctions between VERSE and PROSE. In METERED VERSE, lines usually contain the same number of feet (see METER); in *sprung rhythm* and *alliterative* VERSE, lines are linked by having the same number of stressed syllables; and in FREE VERSE, the length of lines is more of a visual concern (see TYPOGRAPHY). The following represent eight types of lines used in metered verse: (1) monometer (one foot), (2) dimeter (two feet), (3) trimeter (three feet), (4) tetrameter (four feet), (5) pentameter (five feet), (6) hexameter (six feet), (7) heptameter (seven feet), (8) octometer (eight feet).

Lyric, 59. Originally a Greek term referring to VERSE to be accompanied by a lyre. Today, it generally refers to a short poem which presents a single speaker expressing a strongly felt emotion. Thus, poems of love, observation, and contemplation are "lyrics" in contrast with BALLADS and other types of NARRATIVE POETRY. *Lyrical* is often used loosely to describe poetry which sounds musical because of its SOUND DEVICES and RHYTHM.

Means of perception, 158ff. The agent through whose eyes a piece of FICTION appears to be presented. This character is also the one whose thoughts are revealed directly. The term is synonymous with *point of view* and *viewpoint*. It is generally limited to a single character in short fiction.

Melodrama, 89, 142. SIMPLE WRITING (usually DRAMA or FICTION) which is dominated by SUSPENSE and exaggerated forms of dramatic TENSION. SOPHISTICATED LITERA-

TURE also uses conflict, but melodrama does it blatantly and at the expense of other literary concerns. It usually makes use of STOCK CHARACTERS as well.

Metamorphosis, 148ff. Radical transformation of an experience or of an existing draft of a story or play in order to create fresh literary work. This process can be either conscious or unconscious. It is usually employed either to clarify existing patterns or to break up patterns that appear to be too neat or contrived. It may also help a writer to regain control over an experience that is still too personal to develop in literary form.

Metaphor and **simile,** 36ff. A *simile* is a figure of speech (see IMAGE) in which one item (usually an abstraction) is compared with another (usually concrete) which is different in all but a few significant respects. The comparison uses *like* or *as.* Thus, "She fought like a lion" suggests courage but not the use of claws and teeth. The item being described is called the TENOR (the true subject) and the one utilized is the VEHICLE. A metaphor implies rather than states this same sort of comparison and so becomes a statement which is literally untrue, but when successful, figuratively stronger than a simile. It does not use *like* or *as.* "She was a lion when fighting for civil rights" is not taken literally because the reader recognizes it as a literary CONVENTION. In both cases, the base or starting point is the tenor. The reverse of this—using the vehicle as base and merely implying the tenor—is a SYMBOL ("It was the lion, not the lamb that ruled England in those years").

Meter, 62ff. See table on p. 65. A system of STRESSED and unstressed syllables which creates RHYTHM in certain types of verse. The CONVENTIONALIZED units of stressed and unstressed syllables are known as *feet.* Metered verse normally contains the same number of feet in each LINE and the same type of foot throughout the poem. The effect is usually muted by occasionally substituting other types of feet. If the pattern ends on a stressed syllable, it is called *rising meter;* if the pattern ends on an unstressed syllable, it is called *falling meter.*

Mixed metaphor, 37. A METAPHOR that is internally confusing or illogical because the two vehicles (see METAPHOR) are contradictory. Example: "The *bitter aftertaste* of rejection *rang in my ears.*"

Modes, 137, 240ff. See NARRATIVE MODES.

Monologue, 283. See DIALOGUE.

Multiple flashback, 180. See PLOT.

Narrative modes, 137, 240ff. The five methods by which FICTION can be presented: DIALOGUE, thoughts, action, description, and exposition. Most writers use all five in varying proportions.

Narrative poetry, 98. VERSE that tells a story. This may take the form of the BALLAD, the epic, or a tale in verse such as Hecht's "Lizards and Snakes" (p. 111).

Neutral style, 236. See STYLE.

New Formalism, 68. A recent poetic movement (1980s and 1990s) based on a renewed interest in metrical forms and, often, innovative use of such forms.

Nonrealistic drama, 308. See REALISTIC DRAMA.

Nonrecurrent stanzas, 93. STANZAS of unequal length. They are usually found in FREE VERSE and serve some of the same functions as paragraphs in PROSE.

Novel, 138. See FICTION.

Novella, 138. See FICTION.

Octave, 94, 95. An eight-lined STANZA in METERED VERSE. Also, the first eight lines of a SONNET.

Octometer, 65. See LINE.

Off rhyme, 53. See RHYME.

Omniscient point of view, 161. The MEANS OF PERCEPTION in which the author enters the mind of all major characters. *Limited omniscience* restricts the means of perception to certain characters. Most short FICTION and a majority of novels limit the means of perception to a single character.

Onomatopoeia, 48. See SOUND DEVICES.

Orientation, 226ff. The sense in FICTION, DRAMA, or NARRATIVE POETRY of being somewhere specific. This includes awareness of geography, historical period, season, and time.

Overtone, 56. See CONNOTATION.

Pace, 276ff. The reader's sense that a story or play either "moves rapidly" or "drags." This is determined by the RATE OF REVELATION and by the STYLE.

Paradox, 86. A statement that on one level is logically absurd yet on another level implies a reasonable assertion. Example from Heller's *Catch 22*: "The Texan turned out to be good-natured, generous, and likable. In three days no one could stand him."

Pentameter, 64. See LINE.

Person, 161ff. Any of several methods of presentation by which fiction is given the illusion of being told *by* a character, *about* a character, about the *reader* and the like. The third person ("he") is the most common; the first person ("I") can be written either in a neutral STYLE or an "as-if-told" style. The second person singular ("you") and the third person plural ("they") are seldom used. *Person* is *how* a story is presented; the MEANS OF PERCEPTION is *who* appears to present it.

Persona, 24, 83ff. Broadly, a character in a poem, story, or play. The term is more frequently used to identify a fictitious narrator (implied or identified) in poetry.

Plot, 178ff., 183ff., 309ff. The sequence of events, often divided into SCENES, in FICTION, DRAMA, or NARRATIVE POETRY. This may be chronological, or it may be non-chronological in any of three ways: By *flashback* (inserting an earlier scene), or by *multiple flashbacks* (as in Vonnegut's *Slaughterhouse Five* and Conrad's *Lord Jim*), or by using a frame (beginning and ending with the same scene). *Base time* refers to the primary plot from which flashbacks and, less often, flash forwards depart. In traditional drama the increasing complications are called *rising action*, the turning point is the *climax*, which is followed by *falling action*, which in turn leads to the final *catastrophe*, often the death of the protagonist. Contemporary drama often follows modified versions of this structure.

Poetic, 1ff. In addition to being an adjective for "poetry" (*see* VERSE), this term is used to describe fiction or drama which makes special use of RHYTHM, SOUND DEVICES, figurative language (see IMAGE), SYMBOL, and compression of meaning and implication.

Poetry, 1ff. See VERSE.

Point of view, 158ff. See MEANS OF PERCEPTION.

Private symbols, 40. See SYMBOL.

Prose, 3. Writing in which the length of the LINES is not determined by the author and so has nothing to do with statement or form. Prose also tends to be less concerned with RHYTHM, SOUND DEVICES, and compression of statement than is VERSE.

Prose poetry, 77. Short LINES written so as to resemble poetry but usually lacking in RHYTHM, SOUND DEVICES, and figurative language (see IMAGE).

Protagonist, 166. The main character in a piece of FICTION, a play, or a NARRATIVE POEM. This character is often opposed by an *antagonist*. The term is broader than *hero*, which suggests greatness. Protagonists who are perpetual victims are sometimes referred to as *anti-heroes*.

Public symbols, 40. See SYMBOL.

Pun, 38. A figure of speech (see IMAGE) in which two different but significantly related meanings are attached to a single word. Most SOPHISTICATED uses of the pun are a form of METAPHOR with a vehicle (see METAPHOR) which has two meanings, as in Dylan Thomas' "some grave truth."

Pyrrhic foot, 65. See METER.

Quatrain, 51. See STANZA.

Quintet, 94. See STANZA.

Rate of revelation, 181. The rate at which new information or insights are given to the reader regarding CHARACTER, THEME, or PLOT. It is one of the primary factors which determine PACE.

Realistic drama, 308ff. DRAMA which creates the illusion of the world about us. Costume, set, and PLOT appear to be borrowed from what we see or might expect to see in life. This is opposed to *nonrealistic drama*, which creates its own world in somewhat the same manner as a dream. *Expressionism* is sometimes used as a synonym for nonrealistic drama, but more strictly it refers to a dramatic school culminating in the 1920s and 1930s with the works of O'Neill, Rice, and others.

Refrain, 96, 330. A phrase, LINE, or STANZA which is repeated periodically in a poem.

Resonance, 99. That aspect of TONE in SOPHISTICATED WRITING which is created by the use of SYMBOLIC and suggestive details. It is a layering of meaning and implication not found in SIMPLE WRITING. Resonance adds to the DENSITY of a work.

Rhyme, 49ff. A device found exclusively in VERSE and consisting of two or more words linked by an identity in sound which begins with an accented vowel and continues to the end of each word. The sounds preceding the accented vowel in each word must be unlike. This is *true rhyme*. *Slant rhyme* and *off rhyme* use similar rather than identical vowel sounds. *Double rhyme*, also called *feminine rhyme*, is a two-syllable rhyme as in "running" and "sunning." In an *eye rhyme*, the words look alike but sound different. *Rhyme scheme* is a pattern of rhymed endings which is repeated regularly in each STANZA of METERED VERSE.

Rhyme schemes, 46. See RHYME.

Rhythm, 4, 59ff. A systematic variation in the flow of sound. Traditional rhythms include established patterns such as METER, *alliterative verse*, and *syllabic verse*. Unique rhythms are those created uniquely for a particular poem as in FREE VERSE. In METERED VERSE rhythm is achieved through a repeated pattern of stressed and unstressed syllables. In *alliterative* VERSE the pattern is determined by the number of stresses in each line without regard for the unstressed syllables. In *syllabic verse*, the number of syllables in any one line matches the number in the corresponding line of each of the other STANZAS. In FREE VERSE, rhythms are achieved by TYPOGRAPHY, repeated syntactical patterns, and *breath units*. Rhythms in PROSE are achieved by repeating key words, phrases, and SYNTACTICAL patterns. Variations in line length (both left and right margins) and extra spacing within the line create what are called *horizontal rhythms*. Space between lines creates *vertical rhythms*.

Rising action, 278. See PLOT.

Rising meter, 66. See METER.

Run-on line, 52. See ENJAMBMENT.

Satire, 87ff., 198ff. A form of wit in which a distorted view of characters, places, or institutions is used for the purpose of criticism or ridicule. At least some measure of exaggeration (if only through a biased selection of details) is necessary for satire to be effective.

Scanning, 65. The analysis of METER in metered VERSE, identifying the various feet (see METER) and the type of LINE used.

Scansion, 65. The noun which refers to SCANNING.

Scene, 178ff., 273ff. In DRAMA, a formal subdivision of an act marked in the script and indicated to the audience by lowering the curtain or dimming the lights, or a more subtle subdivision of the PLOT marked only by the exit or the entrance of a character. The former are here called *primary scenes* and the latter *secondary scenes*. In FICTION, the scene is a unit of action marked either by a shift in the number of characters or, more often, a shift in time or place.

Sentimentality, 89, 143. A form of SIMPLE WRITING that is dominated by a blunt appeal to the emotions of pity and love. It does so at the expense of subtlety and literary SOPHISTICATION. Popular subjects are puppies, grandparents, and young lovers.

Septet, 94. A seven-line STANZA.

Sestet, sextet, 94, 95. A six-line STANZA in METERED VERSE. Also the last six lines of the SONNET.

Set, 318ff. See SETTING.

Setting, 219ff., 312ff. Strictly, the geographic area in which a PLOT takes place; but more generally, the time of day, the season, and the social environment as well. In DRAMA the setting is usually specified at the beginning of the script. What the audience sees on the stage (excluding the actors) is the *set*. Set design of *The Collection* appears on p. 301 ff.

Short-short story, 138. See FICTION.

Short story, 138. See FICTION.

Simile, 36ff. See METAPHOR.

Simple writing, 6ff., 134ff. Writing in which the intent is made blatant, the STYLE is limited to a single effect, or the TONE is limited to a single emotion. It includes the adventure and horror story (MELODRAMA), many love stories, most greeting-card verse (SENTIMENTALITY), most patriotic VERSE and politically partisan FICTION and DRAMA (propaganda), and that which is single-mindedly sexual or sadistic (pornography). It also includes work which is so personal or so obscure that its intent fails to reach even a conscientious reader. The antonym for *simple* is SOPHISTICATED.

Slant rhyme, 53. See RHYME.

Sonnet, 95. A METERED and RHYMED FIXED FORM poem of fourteen LINES usually in iambic pentameter (see LINE). The first eight lines are known as the OCTAVE and the last six as the SESTET. The Italian or Petrarchan sonnet is often rhymed *abba, abba; cde, cde.* The Elizabethan sonnet is often thought of as three quatrains and a final rhyming couplet: *abab, cdcd, efef, gg.*

Sophisticated writing, 6ff, 134ff. Writing in which the intent is complex, having implications and ramifications, the STYLE makes rich use of the techniques available, and the TONE has a range of suggestion. It is the opposite of SIMPLE WRITING. Not to be confused with the popular use of *sophisticated.*

Sound devices, 3, 48ff. The technique of linking two or more words by *alliteration* (similar initial sounds), *assonance* (similar vowel sounds), *consonance* (similar consonantal sounds), *onomatopoeia* (similarity between the sound of the word and the object or action it describes), or RHYME. In addition, *sound clusters* link groups of words with related vowel sounds which are too disparate to be called true samples of assonance.

Spondaic foot, 65. See METER.

Stage designs, 319ff. The *conventional stage* has a raised playing area which is set behind a *proscenium arch* from which a curtain is lowered between acts and SCENES. The effect is like seeing a performance in an elaborate picture frame. *Theater in the round, theater in the square,* and *arena theater* place the action in a central arena with the audience seated on all sides. Compromise designs include a variety of *apron stages* with the audience on three sides.

Stanza, 51ff., 93ff. Normally, a regularly recurring group of lines in a poem which are separated by spaces and frequently (though not necessarily) unified by a metrical system and by rhyme. Common forms include the *couplet* (two lines); *tercet* or *triplet* (three lines); *quatrain* (four lines); *quintet* or *cinquain* (five lines); SESTET or *sextet* (six lines); *septet* (seven lines); OCTAVE (eight lines). The term is occasionally applied to irregular divisions in FREE VERSE which are used more like paragraphs in PROSE.

Stock character, 141ff. Characters in FICTION or DRAMA that are SIMPLE and that also conform to one of a number of types that have appeared over such a long period and in so many different works that they are familiar to readers and audiences. Their DIALOGUE is often HACKNEYED and their presence can reduce a work to the level of SIMPLE FICTION or DRAMA.

Stream of consciousness, 145. FICTION in the form of a character's thoughts quoted directly without exposition. Although wandering and disjointed, the technique is designed to reveal character. This is in sharp contrast with *automatic writing,* in which the writer's goal is not CHARACTERIZATION (or even FICTION), but self-exploration.

Stress, 59, 63. In metered VERSE, the relative force or emphasis placed on a particular syllable. In "awake," for example, the second syllable is stressed. See METER.

Style, 236ff. The manner in which a work is written. It is determined by the author's decisions, both conscious and unconscious, regarding DICTION (the type of words used), syntax (the type of sentences), NARRATIVE MODE (relative importance of DIALOGUE, thoughts, action, description, and exposition), and PACE (the reader's sense of progress). It is closely connected with TONE. *Neutral style* is that which is not pronounced and so is barely noticed by the reader.

Subplot, 279, 270. A secondary PLOT in a work of FICTION (usually a novel), or a play which echoes or amplifies the main plot or provides comic relief.

Substitution, 67. The technique in METERED VERSE of occasionally replacing a foot (see METER) which has become the standard in a particular poem with some other type of foot. A common form of substitution is the use of a trochee for emphasis in a poem which is generally iambic.

Suspense, 196. A heightened form of curiosity that creates excitement and a sense of drama. Too much suspense can result in MELODRAMA.

Syllabics, 61ff. See RHYTHM.

Symbol, 39ff., 230ff. Any verbal detail such as an object, action, or state, which has a range of meaning beyond and usually larger than itself. *Public symbols* are those which have become a part of the general consciousness—the flag, the cross, and the like. *Private symbols* are those created by individual writers and made public through a literary work or a series of works such as in the case of Dylan Thomas' use of the color green. Usually the reader is first introduced to the vehicle (see METAPHOR) and then perceives the tenor as an additional or expanded meaning. This is in contrast with similes and METAPHORS, wherein the vehicle is brought into the work merely to serve as a comparison and has no other function.

Synecdoche, 38. A FIGURE OF SPEECH in which a part is used for the whole. "Many hands," for example, suggests many people; "bread for the poor" suggests food generally.

Syntactical rhythm, 74ff. See RHYTHM.

Syntax, 74, 239. Sentence structure; the arrangement of words in the sentence. It is used to create RHYTHM in FREE VERSE and a distinctive STYLE in FICTION.

Tenor, 37, 230. See VEHICLE.

Tense, 241. The verb form used. The past tense ("She was a lawyer.") is traditional in fiction, but the present tense ("She is a lawyer.") is increasingly popular. The past perfect ("She had been a lawyer until her retirement.") is often used to introduce a flashback (see PLOT).

Tension, 84, 192ff. A force and a counterforce within a work of literature. In VERSE this can take the form of thematic conflict, IRONY, or SATIRE. In NARRATIVE POETRY, FICTION, and DRAMA it may also be created through a sense of curiosity, SUSPENSE, and shock. *Conflict* is that form of tension which is generated when one character opposes another character or some other force such as society or nature.

Tercet, 51. See STANZA.

Tetrameter, 64. See LINE.

Theater in the round, 319. See STAGE DESIGNS.

Theater of the absurd, 313. A somewhat loosely defined dramatic "school" in the *expressionistic* (see REALISTIC DRAMA) tradition beginning in the 1950s. Shared convictions are that life is "absurd" in the sense of lacking ultimate meaning and that the intellect cannot determine truth. Shared techniques include the use of nonrealistic situations, SATIRE, and a tendency to develop a static quality rather than a DRAMATIC PLOT. Examples include works by Ionesco, Beckett, Pinter, and some by Albee, Genet, and Adamov.

Theme, 99, 232ff., 329ff. The primary statement, suggestion, or implication of a literary work. It describes that portion of a work which comments on the human condition. The term is used here interchangeably with *central concern*. It does not have the moral implications of *message* nor the didactic element of *thesis*. A thesis states or clearly implies a particular conviction or recommends a specific course of action. Theses are often propagandistic. Most SOPHISTICATED WRITING is unified by a theme rather than a thesis.

Thesis, 329. See THEME.

Third-person narration, 164ff. See PERSON.

Tone, 80ff., 99ff., 243ff. The emotional quality of a literary work itself and of the author's implicit attitude toward the work as well. Some critics prefer to separate the two aspects of this definition, but most writers tend to think of them as two forms of the same quality. Tone is described with adjectives like "exciting," "sad," "merry," "eerie," or "depressing" as well as with terms like "satiric," "sardonic," "ironic," and "dramatic."

Traditional Rhythm, 59ff. See RHYTHM.

Trimeter, 65. See LINE.

Triplet, 51, 93. See STANZA.

Trochaic foot, 64. See METER.

True rhyme, 49. See RHYME.

Truism, 8. A statement which reiterates a well-known truth; a platitude.

Typography, 71ff. The technique in VERSE (and particularly FREE VERSE) of arranging words, phrases, and lines on the printed page to create a RHYTHMICAL effect.

Unique rhythm, 70. See RHYTHM.

Vanity press, 354. A publisher who charges the author a part or all of the printing costs. Regular publishers assume all costs themselves and pay the author an advance and a percentage (generally between 10% and 15%) of the sales. Cooperative presses share the expense with the author or poet.

Vehicle, 37, 230. A word or phrase used to convey the TENOR or true meaning in a figure of speech (see IMAGE) or SYMBOL.

Verbal irony, 85, 197. See IRONY.

Verse, 1ff. The form of literary writing that uses line length as an aspect of the art form and is typically concerned with SOUND, RHYTHM, and compression of language. *Verse* is occasionally used as a synonym for LINE, STANZA, or REFRAIN. Although *verse* is often a general synonym for *poetry*, some prefer that *poetry* refer only to SOPHISTICATED verse.

Vertical rhythm, 72. See RHYTHM.

Viewpoint, 156. See MEANS OF PERCEPTION.

Villanelle, 96ff. A French verse form of nineteen lines divided into five tercets (see

STANZA) and a final four-line STANZA with only two rhymes, in this pattern: *aba aba aba aba aba abaa*. Line 1 is a REFRAIN which is repeated entirely as lines 6, 12, and 18; line 3 is repeated to form lines 9, 5, and 19. One of the challenges of this form (other than the mechanics) is to give subtly different meanings to the repeated lines.

Visual rhythm, 71. See TYPOGRAPHY.

Voice, 162. A writer's implied relationship with his or her narrator. In first-person works, the range varies from autobiographical or confessional to works that appear to be presented through a PERSONA. Voice determines the DISTANCE between narrator and poet and is a major factor in determining the TONE of the work.

INDEX OF AUTHORS AND TITLES

"After Spring" (Chora), 120
Angelou, Maya, 124
Baker, David, 131
"Balances" (Giovanni), 123
"The Bay at West Falmouth"
(Howes), 120
"Bedtime" (Levertov), 116
Bishop, Elizabeth, 130
Brooks, Gwendolyn, 124
"Buffalo Bill's" (Cummings), 117
Chora, 120
Clifton, Lucille, 126
"Comparatives" (Momaday), 129
Cory, Deborah Joy, 185
Cummings, E. E., 117
"The Dalliance of the Eagles"
(Whitman), 115
Endrezze, Anita, 116
"Even with Insects" (Issa), 121
"Fern Hill" (Thomas), 125
Giovanni, Nikki, 123
Goin' West (Phillips), 295
"The Guild" (Olds), 121
"Haiku" (Knight), 128
Hall, Donald, 112

Hayden, Robert, 113
Hecht, Anthony, 111
Hello Out There (Saroyan), 259
Howes, Barbara, 120
Hummer, T. R., 114
"Ice River" (Baker), 131
"In a Station of the Metro"
(Pound), 118
"In the Attic" (Justice), 128
Issa, 121
Justice, Donald, 128
Knight, Etheridge, 128
Kumen, Maxine, 113
Leventhal, Ann Z., 127
Levertov, Denise, 116, 119
"Lizards and Snakes" (Hecht), 111
"Man and Daughter in the Cold"
(Updike), 201
"Merrit Parkway" (Levertov), 119
Merwin, W. S., 129
"Milk the Mouse" (Ryan), 115
Minot, Stephen, 169
Momaday, N. Scott, 129
"Morning Swim" (Kumin), 113
Mueller, Lisel, 120

"Names of Horses" (Hall), 112
"Night Song" (Mueller), 120
Olds, Sharon, 121
"On a Main Beach" (Wilson), 118
"One Art" (Bishop), 130
"The Pardon" (Wilbur), 122
Phillips, Louis, 295
"Phoenix" (Pritchard), 151
"Pilot Error" (Leventhal), 127
Pound, Ezra, 118
Pritchard, Melissa, 151
"Rhymes for Old Age" (Twitchell), 122
"River Sound Remembered"
   (Merwin), 129
Roethke, Theodore, 117
"The Rural Carrier Stops to Kill a
   Nine-Foot Cottonmouth"
   (Hummer), 114

Ryan, Michael, 115
Saroyan, William, 259
"Sausage and Beer" (Minot), 169
"Song Maker" (Endrezze), 116
"This Winter Day" (Angelou), 124
Thomas, Dylan, 125
"Those Winter Sundays" (Hayden), 113
"Three Hearts" (Cory), 185
Twitchell, Chase, 122
Updike, John, 201
"The Waking" (Roethke), 117
"We Real Cool" (Brooks), 124
"What the Mirror Said" (Clifton), 126
Whitman, Walt, 115
Wilbur, Richard, 122
Wilson, Robley, 118